DREAMS IN
LATE ANTIQUITY

DREAMS IN
LATE ANTIQUITY

STUDIES IN THE IMAGINATION
OF A CULTURE

Patricia Cox Miller

PRINCETON UNIVERSITY PRESS   PRINCETON, NEW JERSEY

Library of Congress Cataloging-in-Publication Data

Miller, Patricia Cox, 1947–
Dreams in late antiquity : studies in the imagination of a culture /
Patricia Cox Miller.
p.   cm.
Includes bibliographical references and index.
ISBN 0-691-07422-4
ISBN 0-691-05835-0 (pbk.)
1. Classical literature—History and criticism.   2. Dreams in literature.   3.
Christian literature, Early—History and criticism.   4. Civilization, Greco-
Roman.   5. Philosophy, Ancient.   I. Title.
PA3015.D73M55   1994
880.9'353—dc20   93-40363

This book has been composed in Galliard

Princeton University Press books are printed on acid-free paper and meet
the guidelines for permanence and durability of the Committee on
Production Guidelines for Book Longevity of the Council
on Library Resources

Second printing, and first paperback printing, 1998

http://pup.princeton.edu

Printed in the United States of America

3 5 7 9 10 8 6 4 2

for David

Contents

Acknowledgments

THE COURSE OF research that resulted in the writing of this book began in wonderment at the statement of a late-second-century African theologian that most people derive their knowledge of God from dreams. Since that initial moment of curiosity many years ago, my studies have expanded considerably beyond Tertullian's Carthage into Graeco-Roman culture at large and, as I have explored various angles of the oneiric imagination of late antiquity, I have been supported by many colleagues whose willingness to entertain these ideas I now gratefully acknowledge.

I thank in particular the members of the North American Patristics Society, whose meetings have provided a stimulating and refreshingly critical forum for the presentation of scholarly research. Robert Gregg, Dennis Groh, and especially Frederick Norris have been generous with their encouragement. Elizabeth Clark, whose twenty-five years of friendship I acknowledge with pleasure, has been a constant source of support in the work. I also thank members of the Graeco-Roman Religions Group of the Society of Biblical Literature as well as the organizers of the International Conferences on Patristics at Oxford University.

Thanks are also due to Professors Emeriti A. H. Armstrong and Gilles Quispel for their early support of a younger colleague; to the Theological Faculty of the Université de Strasbourg, for allowing me to use then-unpublished portions of *Biblia Patristica;* to Princeton University, Duke University, Kyoto University, the University of Rochester, and Haverford College, and my respective hosts there, Professors John Gager, Elizabeth Clark, Hayao Kawai, William Green, and Anne McGuire, for their invitations and hospitality; to the Department of Religion at Syracuse University; to the Interlibrary Loan staff at Syracuse University's Bird Library, without whose help this project would have taken even longer to complete; to the editorial staff at Princeton University Press; and to Jessie and Morgan, for their companionship. A fellowship from the National Endowment for the Humanities and two Faculty Summer Research Grants from Syracuse University enabled me to pursue various aspects of this project, and I thank them both for generous financial assistance.

Earlier, briefer versions of some chapters have been printed in *Church History; Vigiliae Christianae; Continuum: A Journal of History, Hermeneutics, and Social Concern; Dreaming;* and *The Journal of Early Christian Studies.* I thank the editors of these journals for their permission to incorporate material from these articles into the book. I also thank the following publishers for permission to reprint from the following resources: the

Theogony by Hesiod and translated by Norman O. Brown. Copyright ©1953 by Macmillan Publishing Company; poem by Morimoto Norio in *One Hundred Frogs* by Hiroaki Sato. Copyright ©1983 by Weatherhill Publishers; *Ovid's Metamorphoses* translated by Charles Boer. Dallas: Spring Publications, 1989. Copyright ©1989 by Charles Boer; *Saint Gregory of Nazianzus: Three Poems,* translated by Denis Molaise Meehan. Copyright ©1987 by Catholic University of America Press; *The Apostolic Fathers,* translated by Joseph M.-F. Marique. Copyright ©1947 by Catholic University of America Press; *Metamorphoses* by Ovid and translated by Rolphe Humphries. Copyright ©1955 by Indiana University Press; *The Odyssey* by Homer and translated by Robert Fitzgerald. Copyright 1963 by Random House; *P. Aelius Aristides: The Complete Works,* translated by Charles A. Behr. Copyright ©1986 by E. J. Brill Publishers; *The Iliad* by Homer and translated by Richmond Lattimore. Copyright ©1951 by The University of Chicago Press; "The Meeting" from *A Part* by Wendell Berry. Copyright ©1980 by Wendell Berry. Reprinted by permission of North Point Press, a division of Farrar, Straus & Giroux, Inc.; *Iphigeneia in Tauris* by Euripides and translated by Witter Bynner. Copyright ©1959 by The University of Chicago Press; *Metamorphoses* by Ovid and translated by Frederick Ahl in *Metaformations.* Copyright ©1985 by Cornell University Press; *The Aeneid* by Virgil and translated by C. Day Lewis. Copyright ©1953 by C. Day Lewis. Reprinted by permission of Sterling Lord Literistic, Inc.; *The Interpretation of Dreams* by Artemidorus and translated by Robert J. White. Copyright ©1975 by Noyes Publications. Reprinted by permission of Original Books, Inc.; *Hecuba* by Euripides and translated by William Arrowsmith. Copyright ©1959 by The University of Chicago Press; *The Greek Magical Papyri in Translation,* edited by Hans Dieter Betz. Copyright ©1986 by The University of Chicago Press; *Passio Perpetuae et Felicitatis* 3–10, translated by Peter Dronke in *Women Writers of the Middle Ages.* Copyright ©1984 by Cambridge University Press.

Most of all, I thank David L. Miller, husband and colleague, friend and fellow scholar, for the wonderfully generous lending of his astute judgment and sense of disciplined imagination to a reading of these pages when they were in process, and for teaching me about the Cheshire Cat and its smile. I dedicate this book to David with gratitude and love.

Abbreviations

(Note: Complete documentation of the primary sources can be found in the Bibliography.)

ACW	*Ancient Christian Writers* (New York: Newman Press, 1946–)
ANF	*Ante-Nicene Fathers* (New York: Christian Literature Company, etc., 1867–97)
CCL	*Corpus Christianorum*, Series Latina (Turnhout, Belgium: Brepols, 1953–)
Comm.	*Commentarius, Commentarii*
C. Ruf	*Apologia contra Rufinum* (Jerome)
CSEL	*Corpus Scriptorum Ecclesiasticorum Latinorum* (Vienna: C. Gerodi et al., 1866–)
De an. et res.	*De anima et resurrectione* (Gregory of Nyssa)
De div.	*De divinatione* (Aristotle, Cicero)
De hom. op.	*De hominis opificio* (Gregory of Nyssa)
De ins.	*De insomniis* (Aristotle, Synesius)
De som.	*De somno, De somniis* (Aristotle, Philo)
Ep.	*Epistula*
GCS	*Die Griechischen Christlichen Schriftsteller der ersten drei Jahrhunderte* (Leipzig: J. C. Hinrichs, 1899–)
Haer.	Irenaeus, *Adversus haereses*
Hom.	*Homilia, Homiliae*
In Dan.	*Commentarius in Danielem* (Jerome)
Mand.	*Mandates, Shepherd of Hermas*
NPNF	*A Select Library of Nicene and Post-Nicene Fathers.* 2nd series (New York: Christian Literature Company, 1887–1902)
Onir.	*Oneirocritica* (Artemidorus)
Or.	*Oratio/Orationes*
Pass. Perp.	*Passio Sanctarum Perpetuae et Felicitatis*
PDM	*Papyri Demoticae Magicae*, in Betz, q.v.
PG	*Patrologia Graeca*, ed. J. P. Migne (Paris: Migne, 1857–66)
PGM	*Papyri Graecae Magicae*, ed. K. Preisendanz, rev. ed. Albert Hinrichs (Stuttgart: B. G. Teubner, 1973–74)
PL	*Patrologia Latina*, ed. J. P. Migne (Paris: Migne, 1844–65)
Praes. haer.	*De praescriptione haereticorum* (Tertullian)

Rep.	*Republic* (Plato)
RSV	Revised Standard Version, *The Holy Bible* (New York: Thomas Nelson and Sons, 1952)
Sim.	*Similitudes, Shepherd of Hermas*
T.	Testimony (in Edelstein, q.v.)
TDNT	*Theological Dictionary of the New Testament,* ed. Gerhard Friedrich, tr. Geoffrey Bromiley (Grand Rapids: Eerdmans, 1964–76)
Vis.	*Visions, Shepherd of Hermas*

Part I

IMAGES AND CONCEPTS OF DREAMING

Introduction

TRADITION has it that Socrates dreamed on the night before he met Plato that a young swan settled in his lap and, developing at once into a full-fledged bird, it flew forth into the open sky uttering a song that charmed all hearers.[1] A Hellenistic parody of this dream plays tradition another way: Socrates dreamed that Plato became a crow, jumped onto his head, and began to peck at his bald spot and to croak.[2] Historians of philosophy may want to decide between the heroic Plato who transformed his master's words into charming songs, on the one hand, and the comic Plato who croaked as he pecked on the teacher's bald head, on the other. What interests me, however, is the use of dreams as a way of portraying a philosophical relationship. With their vivid concatenation of images, these dreams lend tangibility and concreteness to the intangible, abstract idea of philosophical influence. This, I will argue, was one of the major functions of dreams in late antiquity: as one of the modes of the production of meaning, dreams formed a distinctive pattern of imagination which brought visual presence and tangibility to such abstract concepts as time, cosmic history, the soul, and the identity of one's self. Dreams were tropes that allowed the world—including the world of human character and relationship—to be represented.

It seems strange to suggest that dreams bestowed tangibility. Is it not paradoxical to say that the material is conveyed by the ephemeral? Perhaps, but Graeco-Roman dream literature shows that there was a late-antique predilection to confound apparently discrete categories, and it was in this predilection that dreams found their proper signifying ground. It is important to note immediately the difficulty of speaking about the relation between such categories as "dream" and "reality" or the "tangible" and the "intangible" without reifying or essentializing them and so missing a striking feature of the late-antique imagination. In another cultural context, Wendy Doniger O'Flaherty has explored the conceptual twists and turns

---

[1] Alice Swift Riginos, *Platonica*, pp. 21–24. This story was popular in late antiquity, as the numerous extant testimonia show. It was used to demonstrate Plato's philosophical skills (e.g., Apuleius, *De Platone* 1.1; Origen, *Contra Celsum* 6.8) and one author, Tertullian, used it as an example of the soul's activity during sleep, when the mind is at rest (*De anima* 46.9).

[2] Riginos, *Platonica*, pp. 54–55. As Riginos notes, this anecdote is preserved only in Athenaeus' *The Learned Banquet* 11.507C–D (second century C.E.), although, as Riginos has shown, Athenaeus took the anecdote from the *Memoirs* of Hegesander of Delphi (second century B.C.E.), thus demonstrating the lengthy history that this and the preceding anecdote had in Greek and Roman tradition.

that talk of dreams provokes, and because her observations are pertinent to this discussion, I turn briefly to her recent book, *Dreams, Illusion, and Other Realities*.

One of the intriguing observations in O'Flaherty's book shows that it is possible to falsify the hypothesis that one is dreaming—by waking up; but it is not possible to verify that one is awake by falling asleep. The thought that one cannot verify the fact that one is awake but can only falsify the fact the one is asleep (by waking up) delivers something of a jolt to Western "common sense," which typically takes for granted the distinctness of such categories as "real" and "unreal," "conscious" and "unconscious," "dream" and "waking life." Yet, as O'Flaherty points out, we know that we cannot see ourselves seeing an illusion, just as we cannot verify the "reality" of ourselves in the moment when we are engaged in testing our reality.[3]

Although the kinds of dichotomous structures just mentioned (real and unreal, and so forth) may be epistemologically useful, they are ontologically suspect, and when the lines of demarcation that support such structures are probed deeply enough, they tend to wobble, if not to disappear altogether. This is especially the case when one is considering the relationship between dreams and waking life, where, as Socrates says in the *Theaetetus*, "there is plenty of room for doubt."[4] Indeed, across the centuries there has been so much room for doubt that, as O'Flaherty shows so well, people have insisted on tantalizing themselves with the thought that dreams are real and the "real" world is a dream: the line not only wobbles, the categories change places.

In the company of such thoughts, we are in a kind of twilight zone where, to borrow a phrase from Marianne Moore, there are imaginary gardens—with real toads in them.[5] We cannot escape this twilight zone by dismissing it as the product of O'Flaherty's exotic Hindus immersed in *māyā;* the Western tradition has its own frogs, and nowhere are they livelier than in late antiquity. Perpetua, after all, awoke from her dream of eating paradisal cheese with the taste of something sweet in her mouth, and Macrobius thought that a vision of the entire cosmos lay encoded in a dream: monotheist and polytheist, martyr and philosopher alike subscribed to the figurative world of dreams.[6]

Socrates can help again in exploring the particular kind of "imaginary

[3] Wendy Doniger O'Flaherty, *Dreams, Illusion, and Other Realities*, pp. 198–99.

[4] Plato, *Theaetetus* 158d, in *Collected Dialogues*, p. 863. See the discussion by Steven S. Tigner, "Plato's Philosophical Uses of the Dream Metaphor," pp. 204–12. Tigner argues that Plato "recognized in certain familiar features of dream-consciousness a conceptually potent model for man's epistemological situation" (211).

[5] Marianne Moore, "Poetry," in *A College Book of Modern Verse*, p. 325.

[6] For Perpetua, see *Passio Sanctarum Perpetuae et Felicitatis* 4.10 (ed. Van Beek, p. 14); for Macrobius, see *Commentarii in somnium Scipionis*.

garden" that was the ancient dream world. As though echoing what he had said in the *Theaetetus* about our perceptual uncertainty when pressed to say whether we are awake or dreaming that we are awake, Socrates remarks in the *Symposium* that his "understanding is a shadowy thing at best, as equivocal as a dream."[7] This is a statement of the kind of wisdom that belongs to dreams. It involves a mode of discourse that is shadowed and equivocal, speaking with more than one voice, as in the following poem:

> In a dream I meet
> my dead friend. He has,
> I know, gone long and far,
> and yet he is the same
> for the dead are changeless.
> They grow no older.
> It is I who have changed,
> grown strange to what I was.
> Yet I, the changed one,
> ask: "How you been?"
> He grins and looks at me.
> "I been eating peaches
> off some mighty fine trees."[8]

In this poem, the "I" in the dream meets a dream figure, a friend, who is dead, "gone long and far." The friend in the dream is dead (even though he grins, looks, and speaks), while the dream "I" is convinced of his own status as not-dead because he is conscious (although he is dreaming) that he has changed. Yet it is the dreamer who feels that he has "grown strange" to himself, while the dead man is the one who calls up the sensuous imagery of a world that is alive, "eating peaches off some mighty fine trees." Who is "really" alive, and who is dead?

I think that ancient readers would have liked this poem, because it gives expression to a dimension of dream-reality that runs fairly consistently through the classical and late-antique traditions: that is, that the dream is the site where apparently unquestioned, and unquestionable, realities like life and death meet, qualify each other, even change places. A particularly striking representation of the equivocal qualities of the dreamworld forms part of Ovid's *Metamorphoses*. It will take us more squarely into the imagistic world of the late-antique oneiric imagination.

---

[7] Plato, *Symposium* 175c, in *Collected Dialogues*, p. 530. For a discussion of the equivocal status of dreams in Plato's thinking, see Tigner, "Plato's Philosophical Uses of the Dream Metaphor," pp. 206–11, and David Gallop, "Dreaming and Waking in Plato," pp. 187–94.

[8] Wendell Berry, "The Meeting," in *A Part*, p. 18.

Part of Book 11 of the *Metamorphoses* tells the story of King Ceyx, who dies in a torrential storm at sea.[9] Meanwhile, his wife Alcyone, knowing nothing of her husband's death, continues to burn incense at the altar of Juno as petition for his safe return. Juno, irked by the touch of Alcyone's unconsciously mourning hands, summons Iris to go to "the drowsy house of Sleep," "to tell that god to send Alcyone a dream of Ceyx, to tell the truth about him." So Iris goes to the kingdom of Sleep, a place of "dusky twilight shadows" where she delivers her plea to Sleep: "O mildest of the gods, most gentle Sleep, Rest of all things, the spirit's comforter, Router of care, O soother and restorer, Juno sends orders: counterfeit a dream to go in the image of King Ceyx to Trachis, to make Alcyone see her ship-wrecked husband." Sleep wakes up Morpheus, who is the best of all his sons at imitating humans, "their garb, their gait, their speech, rhythm, and gesture."

Morpheus flies to Alcyone's bedside and stands there with the face, form, pallor, and nakedness of the dead Ceyx: "His beard was wet, and water streamed from his sodden hair, and tears ran down as he bent over her: 'O wretched wife, do you recognize your husband? Have I changed too much in death? Look at me! You will know me, your husband's ghost, no more your living husband. I am dead, Alcyone.'" Still asleep, Alcyone knows that "the voice of Morpheus was that of Ceyx; how could she help but know it? The tears were real, and even the hands went moving the way his used to." She weeps and tries to touch this dream figure, crying for him to wait for her. But her own voice wakes her, and she screams: "'The queen Alcyone is nothing, nothing, dead with Ceyx.'"

Ovid's portrait of the dreamworld insists on its equivocality. In a twilight realm, Sleep, called the "mildest of gods" and "the spirit's comforter," sends as his soothing message a counterfeit, his shape-shifting son, living phantasm of the dead Ceyx. Morpheus, unsubstantial yet somehow alive as the drenched ghost of the king, speaks, as Alcyone's dream, what no living person could ever say literally: "I am dead." Yet Alcyone knows in her sleep, conscious as she lies unconscious, that the tears are real, though the dream cannot be seen in the lamplight when she opens her eyes. What is unreal is real—the unsubstantial figment of the imagination (the "phantasm") conveys the essential message. What is counterfeit is true, what is alive is dead, what is divine is human—and also the reverse. There is no final resting point, no end to the paradoxical turns in this story. Certainly in Ovid's presentation, the dream does not dissolve reality but rather crystallizes it.

The idea that a figurative language or, in contemporary terminology, a discourse of tropes (a "tropical discourse," as Hayden White would have

---

[9] Ovid, *Metamorphoses* 11.400–750 (trans. Humphries, pp. 272–82).

it[10]) might make one's sense of the real more rather than less crisp is directly related to antiquity's association of dreams and their interpretation with divination. Classically defined, divination, derived from the Latin *divinare,* "to predict," has been called an "occult science" that assembles as a group such practices as "foretelling the future, interpreting the past, and, in general, discovering hidden truth (by way of clairvoyance, precognition, telepathy, and other such phenomena)."[11] The basic assumption upon which divination is usually said to be founded is that of "cosmic sympathy," which views the universe as an immense living organism whose parts are intricately interconnected with one another, such that observation of one part could lead to insight about other parts.[12]

This definition is fine as far as it goes, but it leaves out what is for my purposes a crucial aspect of divinatory practice, namely, its function as a technique for reading the intersection of the human condition and the natural world. Rather than highlighting the connection between divination and prediction, as is the standard scholarly practice, I prefer to understand divination as an imaginal and poetic appropriation of aspects of the natural world (including human relationships and activities) toward the construction of a language of signs. As forms of what could be called an ancient semiotics, these sign languages, because they are visually articulate, give shape and form and so a way to explore those hopes, fears, anxieties, and other feelings that simmer under the surface of ordinary consciousness and might, except for the imagistic patterning provided by divinatory techniques, remain inchoate and so "hidden."

The *Alexander Romance,* one of the most popular novels from late antiquity, offers a list of some of these sign languages. Early on in the text, one of the main characters, Queen Olympias, asks the prophet Nektanebos about methods for arriving at true predictions. He replies: "'There is a wide choice of method, O Queen. There are horoscope casters, sign solvers, dream specialists, oracular ventriloquists, bird observers, birth-date examiners, and those called *magoi,* who have the gift of prophecy.'"[13] Diviners found their signs in animal bodies—the patterns made by flights of birds, for example, or the sheen of an animal's liver; they found their signs in cosmic space—the configurations made by stars and planets; and they found their signs in the images of people's dreams.[14]

[10] See Hayden White, *Tropics of Discourse* and *Metahistory* for discussions of the tropological character of historical thought.

[11] Georg Luck, *Arcana Mundi,* pp. 231, 229.

[12] Ibid., pp. 230–31. Earlier classic studies of divination are W. R. Halliday, *Greek Divination;* André-Jean Festugière, *La Révélation d'Hermès Trismégiste,* vol. 1; and Martin Nilsson, *Geschichte der griechischen Religion,* vol. 2.

[13] Pseudo-Callisthenes, *The Alexander Romance* 4 (ed. Reardon, p. 657).

[14] A convenient summary of the various kinds of Hellenistic divination, from theriomancy to astrology to oneiromancy, is given by Luther Martin, *Hellenistic Religions,* pp. 40–53.

The questions that people brought to the practitioners of these sign languages tended largely to focus on such down-to-earth matters as love and marriage, health, and economic fortune.[15] Given the earthiness of such concerns, it is not surprising that people turned to "earthy" images of their everyday surroundings—birds, stars, dreams—to gain insight into their own situations. Divination was solidly rooted in the ordinary; yet it was an ordinariness charged with a sense of the extraordinary. Robin Lane Fox includes as part of his delightfully detailed chapter on divinatory practices the following story from Pausanias, which exemplifies divination's connection with the ordinary.

> The market-place of Pharai [in Achaea] is an old-fashioned, big enclosure, with a stone statue of Hermes in the middle that has a beard: it stands on the mere earth, block-shaped, of no great size. . . . They call it Market Hermes and it has a traditional oracle. In front of the statue is a stone hearthstone, with bronze lamps stuck onto it with lead. You come in the evening to consult the god, burn incense on the hearthstone, and fill up the lamps with oil; then you light them all and put a local coin on the altar to the right of the god; and then you whisper in the god's ear whatever your question is. Then you stop up your ears and go out of the market-place, and when you get out, take your hands away from your ears and whatever phrase you hear next is the oracle.[16]

Insight into life's situations can be gleaned from the chance phrase of a passerby! In divination, almost anything—even so common a thing as an overheard remark—can be used to construct meaning. Insight floats on the surface of everyday life—but it does so enigmatically and so needs a disciplined language to interpret it.

From the philosophical—"Does the soul survive death?"—to the economic—"Will I be sold into slavery?"—to the poignantly personal—"Does she love me?"—the questions that people brought to diviners involved pressing concerns.[17] "It was normal," as Lane Fox has observed, "to prefer divination to indecision."[18] Yet, however "normal" the recourse to divination and its techniques may have been, divinatory practice has typ-

---

Useful collections of samples from a wide variety of divinatory practices may be found in Frederick C. Grant, *Hellenistic Religions,* pp. 33–63, and in Luck, *Arcana Mundi,* chs. 4–6.

[15] See the examples given in Robin Lane Fox, *Pagans and Christians,* p. 211, and the remark by Grant, *Hellenistic Religions,* p. 33: "People in all walks of life consulted them [oracles] for help with every type of problem. Many of the questions asked reflect the wistful, utterly human character of the problems submitted."

[16] Pausanias, *Guide to Greece* 7.22.2 (trans. Lane Fox, *Pagans and Christians,* p. 209).

[17] For texts and discussion, see Ramsay MacMullen, *Paganism in the Roman Empire,* p. 56; Lane Fox, *Pagans and Christians,* p. 211; and John J. Winkler, *The Constraints of Desire,* pp. 71–98.

[18] Lane Fox, *Pagans and Christians,* p. 211.

ically been shadowed by the charge of irrationality in scholarly discussion. Conceptualized as the weak sister of such enterprises as medicine, astronomy, and mathematics, divination has been seen as a parasite feeding on legitimate, "rational" sciences.[19] Interesting in light of this modern predisposition is the fact that the question of divination's rationality did not seem to most late-antique thinkers to be a question worthy of debate.[20] Cicero was the major exception to this rule—but his skepticism about the viability of divinatory signs to convey meaning was not characteristic of the age at large.[21] Much more characteristic was the Stoic belief that the universe was a vast and varied sign system whose decoding could be revelatory of the human condition.[22]

In the face of ancient testimony to the value of divination's ability to provide techniques for meditating on human problems, it is curious that many modern scholars have insisted that the nature of divinatory practice was dubious, even deceptive. As one of the mantic arts, dreams and their interpretation in late antiquity have not escaped the judgmental onus placed upon divination as a whole. A classic example of this perspective on divination by dreams is the standard lexical essay on the topic in the *Theological Dictionary of the New Testament*.[23] Albrecht Oepke, the author of this survey, has no doubt that with regard to the dreamworld, late-ancient people had "gone primitive." He argues that a mark of one's distance from "rational explanation" is the degree to which one invests dreams with meaningful intelligibility.[24] For Oepke, the picture presented by the dreams of late antiquity is "in the main one of wild and riotous fantasy" in which "disgusting themes are all to the fore."[25] While he notes that dreams were thought to address such everyday concerns as health, financial well-being, love, and sexual fulfillment, these are for him "trivi-

---

[19] The classic statement of this perspective is Festugière's extended discussion of "le déclin du rationalisme" in *La Révélation d'Hermès Trismégiste*, 1:1–18, which can be paired with Nilsson's view that "religion made science its underling. . . . The analogies with which Greek rationalism worked shot up like weeds in the hothouse of mysticism. There was no longer any difference between religion and science, for both rested upon divine revelation; religion had swallowed science up" (*Greek Piety*, pp. 140–41). See also Naphtali Lewis's references to "the grip of the irrational" and "a massive flight from reality" (*The Interpretation of Dreams and Portents*, ix) and Lane Fox's comment on the "dubious attendants" that "found a home in the company of rational astronomy, mathematics, and medicine" (*Pagans and Christians*, p. 211).

[20] Lane Fox, *Pagans and Christians*, p. 211. See also Luck, *Arcana Mundi*, p. 257.

[21] Cicero's *De divinatione* was a major statement—and critique—of divinatory practice and theory in late antiquity. It will be discussed in Chapter Two.

[22] On the doctrine of *sympatheia* that underlay this cosmic sign system, see the detailed discussion in Festugière, *La Révélation d'Hermès Trismégiste*, 1:89–101.

[23] *Theological Dictionary of the New Testament*, vol. 5, s.v. *onar*, by Albrecht Oepke, pp. 220–38.

[24] *TDNT*, 5:225.

[25] Ibid., p. 228.

alities" of a "bourgeois" mindset "in the worst sense."[26] In their dreams, ancient people are in Oepke's view "unmasked": they show little philosophical, and even less theological, sophistication. As Oepke says, *"in somnio veritas,"* and this is what he means: "For all its scientific aspirations, the ancient interpretation of dreams is little more than a mixture of fatalism, superstition, and filth."[27]

It seems that scholarship such as Oepke's has suffered from an overly Cartesian frame of reference wherein reason and unreason are the only two categories available for judging perceptions of world and self.[28] This kind of binary framework, which uses only the oppositional categories of logic and illogic, cannot recognize or account for a "third," imaginal category of perception and judgment. From a Cartesian perspective, a phenomenon like divination can only be metaphysical tomfoolery or bad empirical science. Hampered by this limiting framework, scholarship on divination has been in something of the same position as that of the friends who were with Socrates on his last day: "While they were preparing the hemlock, Socrates was learning a tune on the flute. 'What good will it do you,' they asked, 'to know this tune before you die?'"[29]

Perhaps, as Harold Bloom has suggested, "we all suffer from an impoverished notion of poetic allusion."[30] What scholarship on divination needs is a reading of such practice as a poetics that allowed late-ancient people to handle ordinary problems in an imaginal way.[31] If, for example, one views dream-divination as a *discourse,* as a method that allows for an articulate construction of meaning, one can avoid the debilitating Cartesianism of an interpreter like Oepke, which produces an ancient populace that is credulous, foolish, intellectually inferior. When divination is granted its proper status as a genuine epistemology, its terms need no longer be essentialized and ridiculed.

A good example of the difference between a dualistic reading such as Oepke's and the kind of reading that I am proposing involves the term *fatalism.* From a perspective like that of Oepke, the divinatory language about fate is not a construal or construction of the world in imaginal terms; in fact, it is not a "language" at all. Rather, "fate" is taken to be a

26 Ibid.

27 Ibid.

28 For a succinct discussion of the limits of binarism, see Jonathan Culler, *Structuralist Poetics,* pp. 14–16.

29 Italo Calvino, *The Uses of Literature,* p. 134 (quoting E. M. Cioran).

30 Harold Bloom, "The Breaking of Form," p. 15.

31 Luck takes a step in this direction when he remarks, "In a universe where supernatural powers were thought to influence every act and thought, ancient divination was essentially a form of psychotherapy. It helped people cope with their worries about the future, and it forced them to reach decisions after all the rational angles had been explored" (*Arcana Mundi,* p. 257).

transparent window upon a conceptual world of dogmatic belief in the rule of deterministic forces that calls forth fetishistic practices. I argue, on the other hand, that when one understands language—including the language of fate—as one of the modes of the production of meaning, that is, as a set of mediatorial figures that allow the world to be represented, then a reading of divinatory terms emerges that avoids Oepke's primitivizing view. Consider the following statement by Achilles Tatius about dreams:

> It is a favorite device of the powers above to whisper at night what the future holds—not that we may contrive a defense to forestall it (for no one can rise above fate) but that we may bear it more lightly when it comes. The swift descent of unforeseen events, coming on us all at once and suddenly, startles the soul and overwhelms it; but when the disaster is expected, that very anticipation, by small increments of concern, dulls the sharp edge of suffering.[32]

In this passage, fate is not "fatalistic," nor is it personified as a cosmic power that is relentlessly deterministic of particularities of the future. Rather, fate serves as a cipher for the future, which is itself a temporal metaphor for what is unknown. In the face of an understandable dread at the thought of life's disastrous possibilities, dreams—one of the languages of fate—"dull the sharp edge of suffering" by articulating the possible shapes of that very suffering. When fear is named, it loses some of its terrifying power. This passage from Achilles Tatius suggests that, as a divinatory practice, dream-divination was situated not in superstitious attempts to control the course of events but rather in formulations of a language of self-understanding. At least in this case, the use of divination leads to emotional stability—"that we may bear it more lightly when it comes"—and not to the "wild and riotous fantasy" that Oepke's perspective would lead one to believe.

To ask questions out of binarism, then, is to literalize and so to misconstrue one of the major languages with which late-ancient people attempted to interpret themselves to themselves. The wager of this book depends upon an argument for "the value of recognizing the equivocal richness of apparently obvious or univocal language."[33] The oneiric discourses of late antiquity are only "obvious" and "univocal" when the interpretive model within which they are allowed to speak is characterized

[32] Achilles Tatius, *Leucippe and Clitophon* 1.3 (trans. Winkler, p. 178). See the similar comment by Ptolemy, *Tetrabiblos* 1.3.11, "We should consider that even with events that will necessarily take place their unexpectedness is very apt to cause excessive panic and delirious joy, while foreknowledge accustoms and calms the soul by experience of distant events as though they were present, and prepares it to greet with calm and steadiness whatever comes" (text and trans. in Robbins, p. 23).
[33] J. Hillis Miller, "The Critic as Host," p. 223.

by what Peter Brown has called a "cramping dualism."[34] One feature of this dualistic model of historical interpretation that has produced misleading stereotypes regarding dream-literature is its division of thought and practice into two opposing categories: "high" literate culture and "low" vulgar practice.[35] This model consigns late-antique interest in dreams to the latter category as something that only disreputable figures like magicians and other "commoners" meddled in. The fact that such privileged representatives of "high" culture as Augustine, Gregory of Nyssa, and Jerome were vitally interested in dreams is dismissed by this model as unimportant, if their interest is mentioned at all.

When the distinction between elite and vulgar is abandoned, a shift in perspective occurs which allows the interpreter to focus on the thoughts and practices that highlight the shared human concerns of theologians like Augustine and users of magical spells, concerns that cut across lines of social status and intellectual attainment. This book focuses on a type of imagination that was deeply embedded in the culture at large; from my perspective, all of the people who tapped the resources of the imaginal forms of dreams can be viewed as ordinary people going about the ordinary business of trying to understand themselves and their world.

I emphasize the ordinariness of this widespread use of oneiric discourses because it is so easy to privilege as exotic what seems to us, so distant in time and space, to be an alien practice. Furthermore, once a phenomenon has been designated as exotic, it becomes fair game for either idealization or denigration, as early anthropological writing about "the primitive" demonstrates.[36] Jonathan Z. Smith has argued that when religion is imagined as an ordinary rather than an exotic category of human expression and activity, that choice is "more productive for the development of history of religions as an academic enterprise."[37] In his view, "there is no primordium—it is all history."[38] I agree with this view and have attempted in the discussions that follow to view the dream-literature of late antiquity in the ways in which Smith suggests viewing religious texts—"as texts in context, specific acts of communication between specified individuals, at specific points in time and space, about specifiable subjects."[39]

The book is divided into two parts. Part I deals with images and concepts of dreaming. It focuses particularly on how a culture imagines for itself one of its own processes of imagining, as well as on the various

---

[34] Peter Brown, *Society and the Holy in Late Antiquity,* p. 13.
[35] See the discussion by Brown, *Society and the Holy in Late Antiquity,* pp. 8–13.
[36] For a thorough exploration of this phenomenon, see Marianna Torgovnick, *Gone Primitive: Savage Intellects, Modern Lives,* especially pp. 3–41.
[37] Jonathan Z. Smith, *Imagining Religion,* xiii.
[38] Ibid.
[39] Ibid.

theoretical and classificatory systems that were used to decipher and manage oneiric phenomena. Attention is given to the role of dreams as a technology for managing hopes, fears, and anxieties, and to their role as a discourse that provided occasion for articulations of ethical and philosophical ideas. Part II is composed of a series of essays on Graeco-Roman dreamers. These essays are detailed explorations of the ways in which specific individuals used dreams to construct worlds of personal meaning.

CHAPTER ONE

Figurations of Dreams

W.J.T. MITCHELL has pointed to the "recursive problem" that arises when one gives one's attention "to the way in which images (and ideas) double themselves: the way we depict the act of picturing, imagine the activity of imagination, figure the practice of figuration."[1] Problematic though it may be, a consideration of how dreams, as an activity of imagination, were imaged is an important step toward demonstrating the semiotic character of the literature of dreams as well as the practices of dream interpretation. Because many of the images that were used in late antiquity to picture the imaginal world of dreams were borrowings or refinements of yet more ancient depictions, the discussion will begin with classical and preclassical texts.

In Homer's *Odyssey*, dreams were located spatially in an imaginal land-scape that was in close proximity to the dwelling place of the dead. Book 24 of this Homeric text opens with a description of the journey taken by Penelope's slain suitors, a journey that takes them from the concrete space of empirical reality through a fantastic geography.

> [Hermes] led them down dank ways,
> over grey Ocean tides, the Snowy Rock,
> past shores of Dream [*dēmos oneirōn*] and narrows of the sunset,
> in swift flight to where the Dead inhabit
> wastes of asphodel at the world's end.[2]

Also translated as "village of dreams" and "people of dreams," the *dēmos oneirōn* is located beyond Okeanos, the mythological river that encircled the "real" world.[3] Described as "the land where reality ends and everything is fabulous," the regions of Okeanos inscribe a boundary in cosmic space.[4] Beyond that boundary is a realm of images and ghosts, a space that one

---

[1] W.J.T. Mitchell, *Iconology*, p. 5.

[2] Homer, *Odyssey* 24.10–14 (ed. Stanford, p. 177; trans. Fitzgerald, p. 445). Fitzgerald's translation of *dēmos oneirōn* as "shores of dream" seems odd, given the usual connotations of *dēmos* as a term denoting a human, rather than a geographical, phenomenon. I prefer the translation of *dēmos* as either "village" or "people."

[3] Respectively, these are the translations of Angelo Brelich, "The Place of Dreams in the Religious World Concept of the Greeks," p. 298, and Robert Lamberton, *Homer the Theologian*, p. 70.

[4] *Oxford Classical Dictionary*, s.v. *Oceanus*, p. 744.

interpreter has characterized as an "anticosmos," "the reverse side of the cosmic order" that mirrors its other in fantastic, phantasmal ways.[5] This, then, is the spatial location of dreams in the Homeric cosmos.

The fact that the word *dēmos* has been translated as "village," an architectural construct, and as "people," a race of living beings, provides an interesting (if unintentional) clue to two further features of the Homeric view of dreams that were to persist in late-antique characterizations of dreams.

Architecturally speaking, the dream-village of Homer had gates. In *Odyssey* 4.809, Penelope is pictured as "slumbering sweetly in the gates of dream."[6] Later on, again in connection with one of Penelope's dreams, these gates are further specified.

> Truly dreams are by nature perplexing and full of messages which are hard to interpret; nor by any means will everything [in them] come true for mortals. For there are two gates of insubstantial dreams; one [pair] is wrought of horn and one of ivory. Of these, [the dreams] which come through [the gate of] sawn ivory are dangerous to believe, for they bring messages which will not issue in deeds; but [the dreams] which come forth through [the gate of] polished horn, these have power in reality, whenever any mortal sees them.[7]

This passage has occasioned a good deal of scholarly debate, particularly regarding the meaning of Homer's choice of ivory and horn to characterize the materials out of which the two gates are constructed.[8] As a general statement about the quality of dreams, the meaning is clear: all dreams are *amēchanoi*, things that are "intractable" or "hard to cope with either physically or emotionally."[9] Dreams are further specified as *akritomūthos*, a kind of speech that is *akritos*, "indiscriminate" or "numberless" and so hard to interpret.[10]

[5] Brelich, "The Place of Dreams in the Religious World Concept of the Greeks," p. 298.

[6] *Od.* 4.809 (ed. Stanford, p. 71; trans. Fitzgerald, p. 77). For a discussion of this image, see A.H.M. Kessels, *Studies on the Dream in Greek Literature,* p. 108.

[7] *Od.* 19.560–67 (ed. Stanford, p. 119; trans. Anne Amory, "The Gates of Horn and Ivory," p. 31).

[8] The best recent discussions are Amory, "The Gates of Horn and Ivory," pp. 3–57, and Kessels, *Studies on the Dream in Greek Literature,* pp. 100–103. The book by E. L. Highbarger, *The Gates of Dreams,* argues that "the gate of 'ivory' was probably a pure Greek concept . . . originally picturing the gate of clouds which Homer describes as the way of entrance to Mount Olympus," while "the gate of 'horn(s)' was traced to ancient Egyptian and Babylonian religious beliefs" (quotation from Highbarger's summary of his book in *Proceedings of the American Philological Association* 76 [1945]:xxxiii). While Highbarger's ideas are interesting, they have been convincingly refuted by both Amory and Kessels in the literature cited above.

[9] Amory, "The Gates of Horn and Ivory, pp. 16–17; Kessels, *Studies on the Dream in Greek Literature,* p. 103.

[10] Amory, "The Gates of Horn and Ivory," pp. 17–18; Kessels, *Studies on the Dream in Greek Literature,* p. 104.

As for the two gates, Amory has pointed out that the dreams that issue through them "are not described adjectivally as 'true' and 'false.' Instead the dreams are distinguished by verbal phrases, pertaining to what they do after they have come through their contrasted gates."[11] All dreams are equivocal, but some, associated with ivory, are "dangerous," while others, associated with horn, "have power in reality." Why horn and ivory? I follow Amory's argument that the three most probable explanations for Homer's choice of these materials were already being discussed in antiquity. As presented in the vast compilation of commentaries on Homer written by Eustathius in the twelfth century, they are as follows:[12]

(1) The reason that the poet makes a horn gate the source of dreams which are true and accomplish true things is that there is a certain resemblance in sound between the words *krainein* [to accomplish] and *kerasi* [horns], as if from the word *keras* were derived *keraino*, that is, *kraino*. [Similarly the poet makes] an ivory gate the source of dreams which are false and deceptive, that is, which mislead, cheat, and only arouse expectations [the verb *elephairo*, "deceive" or, in Amory's translation, "dangerous to believe," being hypothetically derived from *elephas*, ivory].

(2) Some, understanding the speech differently, more symbolically, interpret the horn gate as the eyes, taking the part for the whole, in that the outermost covering of the eye is horny. And they say that the mouth is the ivory [gate] because of the ivory-colored teeth, so that the wise Penelope is saying symbolically that the things which are seen as actual events are more trustworthy than things which are simply said to be so. Therefore, obviously [she means that] she will believe the things that are said about Odysseus as dream interpretations [only] when she sees them.

(3) Some say that the true [gate] is of horn, that is, transparent, whereas the false [gate] is of ivory, that is, blurred or opaque, because it is possible to see through horn . . . but not through ivory.

Amory petitions these passages from Eustathius as part of her argument that the association of dreams with the substances of ivory and horn was a popular tradition that Homer appropriated rather than merely a poetic fiction of his.[13] She shows further that, while the passages from Eustathius

---

[11] Amory, "The Gates of Horn and Ivory," p. 22; see also Kessels, *Studies on the Dream in Greek Literature*, p. 104.

[12] The following passages from Eustathius, *Commentaria ad* "Iliadem" *et* "Odysseam" 1877.26–39, are quoted from the translation of Amory in "The Gates of Horn and Ivory," pp. 4–6.

[13] Amory, "The Gates of Horn and Ivory," pp. 32–33. Kessels, *Studies on the Dream in Greek Literature*, argues on the contrary that the image of the gates of dreams was one of Homer's poetic inventions and bases his argument on the fact that this image "did not find further application in Homer's dream episodes" (107).

are important in that they preserve an ancient connection of speech with the ivory gate and sight with the gate of horn, nonetheless Eustathius has made a distinction between true and false dreams which Homer did not make.[14] The issue of the transparency of the two materials, as in Eustathius' third explanation, is the one that Amory finds to be the likeliest basis for the contrast between them and the dreams that they usher forth—but not, as Eustathius has it, because ivory is opaque and horn transparent. Rather, it is a case of contrasting kinds of transparency: "*xestos*, applied to the smooth polished substance of horn, and *pristos*, used of the intricately carved and decorated substance of ivory, both reinforce the contrast in transparency between the two materials."[15] She concludes with an affirmation of the Homeric view of the ambiguity of dreams: "For the fact that neither substance is completely transparent corresponds to the fact that all dreams are by nature obscure, as Penelope says at the beginning of her speech."[16]

Whereas Amory prefers the third of Eustathius' explanations of the two gates, I find his second explanation equally suggestive because it brings forward the association of dreams with ivory, teeth, and language on the one and, and horn, eyes, and vision on the other. For Homer, dreams were both linguistic and visual events, and they were linked spatially with villa ,e gates whose elaborately overdetermined meaning, growing out of etyr ological puns and imagistic associations, certainly makes them fitting arc itectural monuments of the *dēmos oneirōn*.

′ /hen the *dēmos oneirōn* is understood not as a *village* of dreams but rat ier as the *people* of dreams, another important feature of Homer's way of figuring the figurative phenomenon of dreams comes to the fore. The w ird that is usually used in Homeric texts to denote a dream is *oneiros*, w ich designates a dream-*figure* (and not the more generalized idea of dream-*experience*).[17] As Dodds notes, "this dream-figure can be a god, or a ghost, or a pre-existing dream-messenger, or an 'image' (*eidōlon*) created specially for the occasion; but whichever it is, it exists objectively in space and is independent of the dreamer."[18] As "people," then, dreams were autonomous; they were not conceptualized as products of a personal sub- or unconscious but rather as visual images that present themselves to the dreamer. Thus Homeric dreamers spoke of *seeing* a dream, not of *having* one as modern dreamers do.[19]

[14] Amory, "The Gates of Horn and Ivory," p. 22n.26.

[15] Ibid., p. 34.

[16] Ibid.

[17] E. R. Dodds, *The Greeks and the Irrational*, p. 104; Kessels, *Studies on the Dream in Greek Literature*, pp. 178–79.

[18] Dodds, *The Greeks and the Irrational*, p. 104.

[19] Ibid., p. 105; Kessels, *Studies on the Dream in Greek Literature*, pp. 156–57, 194.

One of the most striking instances of a dream presenting itself to a dreamer in Homer involves Penelope. In the *Odyssey* 4, Penelope is sick with worry over the fate of her son Telemachus, who has left Ithaca to seek out news of his father Odysseus. "Sweet sleep" overtakes her, and the following scene ensues:

> Now it occurred to the grey-eyed goddess Athena
> to make a figure [eidōlon] of dream in a woman's form—
> Iphthime, great Ikarios' other daughter,
> whom Eumelos of Pherai took as bride.
> The goddess sent this dream to Odysseus' house
> to quiet Penelope and end her grieving.
> So, passing by the strap-slit through the door,
> the image came a-gliding down the room
> to stand at her bedside and murmur to her:
> "Sleepest thou, sorrowing Penelope?
> The gods whose life is ease no longer suffer thee
> to pine and weep, then; he returns unharmed,
> thy little one; no way hath he offended."[20]

As this scene continues, the dream is described as a "dim phantom," a "wavering form" that "withdrew along the doorbolt into a draft of wind." Penelope awakes "in better heart for that clear dream in the twilight of the night."[21]

Several features of this scene can be used to typify the Homeric "people of dreams." First, they are connected with divine beings, who either send an image or appear as the dream-figure themselves, though always in disguised form.[22] Certainly the connection with the gods serves to underscore the dream's autonomy and the authoritative quality of its message. Yet this is a strange kind of authority, embodied by a dim and wavering phantom that glides in and out of keyholes on drafts of wind. For Homer, the dream appears to be a kind of technique for overcoming epistemological uncertainty that nevertheless participates in that very dynamic. Thus the second feature to note about the people of dreams is the equivocal status of their airy substance.[23] This quality of dreams has already been alluded to in Penelope's statement in *Odyssey* 19.562, where she says that there are two gates of *insubstantial* (*amenēnōn*) dreams. As an adjective, the term *amenēnos* is generally taken to mean either a lack of strength, hence "feeble" or "insubstantial," or a lack of staying power, hence "fleeting."

[20] *Od.* 4.795–807 (ed. Stanford, p. 71; trans. Fitzgerald, pp. 76–77).

[21] Ibid. 4.824, 838–41 (ed. Stanford, p. 72; trans. Fitzgerald, p. 78).

[22] Kessels, *Studies on the Dream in Greek Literature,* pp. 86–87, 115n.10.

[23] On the issue of "airy substance," see Kessels, *Studies on the Dream in Greek Literature,* pp. 155–56.

Amory shows, however, that "all the other usages in Homer make it certain that the first meaning, 'lacking physical strength' and therefore 'incorporeal' is the correct one."[24] Although these figures lack physical strength, they do not lack imaginal power. Penelope, indeed, awakes from her dream "in better heart"; however dim, the *eidōlon* of her twilight experience has given her a perceptual clarity.

The Homeric people of dreams lack bodies; but they give a *sense of* body and substance to experience. As images, they give emotion a tangible clarity.[25] A final Homeric dream portrays this dynamic, this "order" of ambiguity, in a striking way, and it will also take us back to the beginning of our discussion of Homer by the way in which it situates the people of dreams spatially in the land of dreams. In Book 23 of the *Iliad,* the Greek warrior Achilles refuses to be cleansed of the bloodstains of war until his friend Patroclus is properly buried. Having made preparations for the burial the next day, Achilles, deep in grief, falls asleep.

> There appeared to him the ghost [*psūche*] of unhappy
> Patroklos all in his likeness for stature, and the
> lovely eyes, and voice, and wore such clothing as
> Patroklos had worn on his body. The ghost came
> and stood over his head and spoke a word to him:
> "You sleep, Achilleus; you have forgotten me; but
> you were not careless of me when I lived, but only
> in death. Bury me as quickly as may be, let me pass
> through the gates of Hades. The souls, the images
> of dead men [*psūchai, eidōla kamontōn*] hold me at a
> distance, and will not let me cross the river and
> mingle among them, but I wander as I am by Hades'
> house of the wide gates."

Achilles answers this apparition of Patroclus:

> and with his own arms reached for him, but could not
> take him, but the spirit went underground [*psūche de kata chthonos*],
> like vapour, with a thin cry, and Achilleus started
> awake, staring, and drove his hands together, and spoke,
> and his words were sorrowful: "Oh, wonder! Even in
> the house of Hades there is left something, a soul and
> an image [*psūche kai eidōlon*], but there is no real

[24] Amory, "The Gates of Horn and Ivory," pp. 19–20.
[25] See the essay by David L. Miller, "Theologia Imaginalis," pp. 1–18, for an in-depth discussion of the importance of image and metaphor as ways to "sense" experience. As he writes, the issue of insubstantial images "has to do with the mystery of a sense of 'body' coming precisely with the letting-go of notions of literalness with regard to body" (4–5).

heart of life in it. For all night long the
phantom [*psüche*] of unhappy Patroclus stood over
me in lamentation and mourning, and the likeness
to him was wonderful, and it told me each thing
I should do."[26]

As with Penelope, so here with Achilles, the dream galvanizes emotion and
makes it palpable by giving it articulate, imagistic expression. This is an
unusual Homeric dream in that the dream-figure is neither a god in disguise nor an image fabricated by a god. Instead it is the soul of a dead man
whose likeness to life is "wonderful." However, it is like Penelope's dream
in its airy substantiality, and it too is described as an *eidōlon,* which in this
case "ghosts" the life of the dreamer and crystallizes his experience of grief.

As Kessels has pointed out, this dream may be evidence of an ancient
Greek belief that the unburied dead haunted the living in (or as) dreams.[27]
My interest, however, is in the placement of Patroclus' *eidōlon* as a dream.
The dream-figure is not *in* Hades but *by* Hades' house, in the fabulous land
beyond the frontier of the real with which this description of Homeric
texts began. The village of dreams and the people of dreams have been
united in this text. The further specification of the location of this dream-
figure, that it is not only by Hades' house but also *kata chthonos,* "under-
ground," makes contact with a genealogical view of dreams as found in
other ancient Greek texts, and to those I now turn.

When ancient Greek literature presents a figuration of dreams from a
genealogical standpoint, they assume a more fearful, baneful aspect than
they do in Homeric texts. A striking example of the genealogy of dreams is
presented in Euripides' play *Hecuba,* which derives the lineage of dreams
from earth. Early in this drama, the fallen Trojan queen Hecuba has seen a
dream that portends the deaths of two of her children. Frantic with terror,
she says,

> What apparition rose,
> what shape of terror stalking the darkness?
>
> O goddess Earth [*potnia Chthōn*]
> womb of dreams [*mēter oneirōn*]
> whose dusky wings
> trouble, like bats, the flickering air!
>
> Beat back that dream I dreamed,
> that horror that rose in the night, those phantoms of children,
> my son Polydorus in Thrace, Polyxena, my daughter!
> Call back that vision of horror![28]

[26] *Il.* 23.65–107 (ed. Allen, pp. 295–98; trans. Lattimore, pp. 452–53).
[27] Kessels, *Studies on the Dream in Greek Literature,* pp. 53, 155.
[28] Euripides, *Hecuba* 69–76 (text in Way, p. 252; trans. Arrowsmith, p. 497).

Here dreams are pictured as children of earth. This is not the nourishing earth of agricultural productivity but a darker, more primordial earth, the majestic goddess Chthōn.[29] As black-winged apparitions issuing from the womb of Chthōn, these dreams do not have the almost playful aspect of the many Homeric dreams that bend over the head of the dreamer to engage in conversation.

Elsewhere Euripides describes dreams as "truth's shadows upfloating from Earth's dark womb" and specifies the reason for their birth.[30] Originally, the oracle at Delphi had belonged to Chthōn.[31] When Apollo killed her sacred serpent and took the site of the oracle for himself, Chthōn retaliated.

> But Earth had wished to save the oracle
> For Themis, Her own daughter,
> And so in anger bred a band of dreams
> Which in the night should be oracular
> To men, foretelling truth.[32]

A reason for the frightful aspect of dreams when imaged genealogically is their birth in anger, and it was this angry, doom-saying speech of dreams that predominated in classical drama.[33]

The terrible vengefulness of dreams as powers of earthy darkness is carried in the alternative genealogy of dreams reported by Hesiod. In the *Theogony*, dreams are figured as children not of earth but of night: "Night gave birth to hateful Destruction and the Black Specter and Death; she also bore Sleep and the race of Dreams."[34] As Brelich has remarked, this passage does not turn on a banal association of sleep, dreams, and ordinary nighttime: "the Nyx [Night] in the *Theogony* is not the night of our daily rest." Rather, she is "one of the most serious and formidable powers the Hellenic imagination was capable of creating."[35] A daughter of chaos, Nyx gives birth, in Brelich's translation, to "Moros (odious destiny), to ominous Ker (archaic demon associated with inexorable doom), to Thanatos (death), to Hypnos (sleep), and to the people of dreams."[36] Linked through their mother Night with chaos, the people of dreams are part of that vast gulf of possibility that is the condition and foundation of all life

[29] For a discussion of *Chthōn*, see Walter Burkert, *Greek Religion*, pp. 199–200.

[30] Euripides, *Iphigeneia in Tauris* 1278 (text and trans. in Way, pp. 392–93).

[31] See the discussion of Euripides, *Iph. Taur.* 1244–51, in Dodds, *The Greeks and the Irrational*, p. 110.

[32] Euripides, *Iph. Taur.* 1259–65 (text in Way, pp. 390, 392; trans. Bynner, p. 400).

[33] See especially Aeschylus, *The Persians* 215–25 (trans. Benardete, p. 227) and *The Libation-Bearers* 523–50 (trans. Lattimore, p. 112).

[34] Hesiod, *Theogony* 212 (trans. Brown, p. 59).

[35] Brelich, "The Place of Dreams in the Religious World Concept of the Greeks," p. 299.

[36] Ibid.

in Hesiod's cosmogonic vision.[37] And that they are a necessary condition of life is what is implied by the company of siblings in which they find themselves, the inexorable, inescapable forces of the imaginal darkness of night.

As the foregoing figurations show, dreams belonged, in Brelich's words, "to the spatial and temporal peripheries of the cosmos, to the antiworld that surrounds the world, to the antireality that is found outside real time and real space."[38] These configurations functioned like a mirror held up to the ancient Greek imagination as it gave image to its own dynamic. Picturing the act of picturing was an art that required an imaginal vocabulary "outside the real" so that the real could be presented to itself in meaningful terms. This strategy of using dreams to present the world in articulate and nuanced ways had a lasting impact. The spatial and temporal metaphors that ancient Greeks used to picture this world of pictures helped to shape late-antique imaginings in significant, and sometimes surprising, ways.

FIGURATIONS OF A FIGURATIVE WORLD: LATE ANTIQUITY

Two Latin poets at the beginning of the Graeco-Roman era continued the Homeric idea that dreams were a world situated in a cosmic space that was closely connected with the realm of the dead. However, both Ovid and Virgil painted their pictures of this dream-world with an intensity of description that surpassed that of their precursor.

Like Homer, Ovid located dreams spatially in close proximity to the land of the dead, in a cavern under a Cimmerian mountain.[39] This is a place of "dusky twilight shadows" where the ground is dark with mist and fog.[40] Total silence reigns, save for the whispering of a branch of the river Lethe, "murmuring over mumbling stones inviting sleep."[41] Inside the cave's doorway, which is festooned with poppies and other narcotic plants, lies the god Somnus, Sleep, in langorous repose. Around him lie his children, "as numerous as the wheat-ears of the harvest," and so dense that anyone entering has to brush them aside as though clearing a path through thick cobwebs.[42] These children are "the empty dream-shapes, mimicking many forms" (*varias imitantia formas somnia vana*).[43]

[37] Hesiod, *Theog.* 116 (trans. Brown, p. 56).
[38] Brelich, "The Place of Dreams in the Religious World Concept of the Greeks," p. 300.
[39] Ovid, *Meta.* 11.592 (text and trans. in Miller, pp. 162–63).
[40] Ibid. 11.594–95 (text and trans. in Miller, pp. 162–63). Humphries' mistranslation of *dubiaeque crepuscula lucis* ("dusky twilight shadows") as "a dubious twilight" (277) is a telling if unintentional commentary on the character of the dreamworld.
[41] Ovid, *Meta.* 11.602–4 (text in Miller, p. 162; trans. Boer, p. 243).
[42] Ibid., 11.605–17 (text in Miller, pp. 162, 164; trans. Humphries, p. 278).
[43] Ibid., 11.613–14 (text and trans. in Miller, pp. 162–63).

There is something undecidable about the choice of the adjective *vanus* as a modifier for dreams. Are they merely "empty," "unsubstantial," and "vain"? The unsubstantiality of dreams is certainly underscored by their placement in a fabled geography, but Ovid's construction of this landscape as a lavish setting, lush even in its gloom, suggests that there is something substantial, full, and significant about these airy beings. It may be that the word *vanus,* if taken only at face value, is misleading.

As Frederick Ahl has argued, Ovid was a master of the "multiple entendre"; the Ovidian world is one of "radical multiple realities" in which "the strife of opposites and everchanging shapes" rules—and bewilders—one's perceptual sense.[44] This is particularly true of the world of dreams—so much so, in fact, that one interpreter has argued that the dream may be a cipher for the process of metamorphosis itself. According to Charles Boer, "while metamorphosis is the one almost constant feature of the poem that we observe, it is like the observance of a dream, where images keep shifting, the tone keeps changing, and where we are never sure of motives or morals."[45]

In his discussion of the way in which Ovid based the structure of his long poem on wordplays and soundplays, Ahl reinforces Boer's view of the constant inconstancy of the Ovidian world, again in reference to dreams. The context for Ahl's observations is the story of Alcyone and her dream of her dead husband Ceyx, which is itself the pretext for Ovid's spatial description of the dreamworld. When asked to send a dream to Alcyone to convey the truth about her husband, Somnus chooses his son Morpheus who is "an artist and simulator of appearance" (*artificem similatoremque figurae*).[46] As Ahl points out, the Latin word *MORPHEus* contains a cross-linguistic play on the Greek word *MORPHĒ,* "shape," and hence on the title of Ovid's work, *MetaMORPHoses.*[47] In the same passage, the play on the ideas of shape, change, and dream is continued in the statement that "dreams, in imitation, equal true forms" (*somnia, quae veras aequant imitamine FORMas*), where *FORMas* is a cross-language anagram of *MORPHē.*[48] The shifting shapes of language itself match the qualities of the Ovidian oneiric landscape.

Thus dreams are empty *and* full, vain *and* significant, insubstantial *and* substantial. They are part of what Ahl has called the savage reality of the Ovidian world, where one dimension of the savagery is an acceptance of the "notion of simultaneous and contradictory realities."[49] A striking example of this Ovidian paradox—and an example as well of how the geographical

---

44 Frederick Ahl, *Metaformations,* pp. 58, 101, 273.
45 Charles Boer, *Ovid's Metamorphoses,* xix.
46 Ahl, *Metaformations,* p. 60, quoting *Meta.* 11.634.
47 Ibid., pp. 59–60.
48 Ibid., quoting *Meta.* 11.626.
49 Ahl, *Metaformations,* p. 101.

landscape of the dreamworld is simultaneously a psychological landscape—
is the story of the dreamer Byblis, a young woman delirious with love for her
brother. In the beginning of her story she did not recognize her passion:
"she was long deceived by the semblance [*umbra*] of sisterly affection."[50]
However, repressed desire found its outlet—in dreams of sexual love.
Caught between the dictates of sexual mores, on the one hand, and passionate desire, on the other, Byblis longs for the dream of physical union to
return again and again: "'A dream lacks a witness, but does not lack a
substitute joy [*imitata voluptas*],'" she says.[51]

Ovid is playing here with the notion of the shifting status of what might
be considered real. The *umbra*—shade, shadow, uninvited guest—is invited
in; as a dream, the guest becomes host to a sensuous pleasure that is all the
more real for being an imitation, and all the more an artifice for being
imaginal, "only" a dream. Byblis asks herself, "'But what weight have
dreams? or have dreams weight?'"[52] In the Ovidian world, dreams do have
"weight" by virtue of their ability to shift the grounds of perception and to
give shape to emotion. Indeed, they *are* the shifting of the ground, mimicking the many forms of a pluralized reality.

Ovid maintained the Homeric connection between dreams and death not
only in his placement of the dreamworld in an under- or otherworldly cavern
but also by means of a further wordplay carried in the name of the god
Morpheus. The Latin word for death, *Mors*, sounds in the name of the
dream as master artificer, *Mor*pheus. Further, as Ahl says, "Sleep, in Latin, is
proverbially the brother of death, MORs," and as one of Ovid's characters
suggests, "metaMORphosis lies somewhere between life and death."[53]
Ovid thus does not place the deathly dimension of dreams in a world apart
but rather places it squarely in the context of life's turmoil. Because they
carry change, they are deadly, yet they embody the ongoing rhythms of
living.

If, for Ovid, dreams were one aspect of "the unbearable lightness of
being," to borrow a recent phrase, this was not the case for his older contemporary Virgil.[54] Virgil's presentation of Homer's spatial metaphor was unrelievedly dark and more rigid than that of the younger poet. It would
appear that Virgil's reworking of the Homeric trope has been colored by the
horrific face of dreams as presented in tragic drama.

Early in Book Six of the *Aeneid*, the hero Aeneas is being led by the Sibyl
to visit the *imago*, the phantom or imaginal residue, of his dead father. The
way to the world of the dead lies through the mouth of a deep cave; before

---

50 Ovid, *Meta.* 9.459–60 (text and trans. in Miller, pp. 34–37).
51 Ibid., 9.480–81 (text and trans. in Miller, pp. 36–37).
52 Ibid., 9.496 (text and trans. in Miller, pp. 38–39).
53 Ahl, *Metaformations*, p. 60.
54 This phrase is the title of a recent novel by Milan Kundera.

entering, Aeneas says a prayer to Earth, *terra,* a sign that Virgil has, like the dramatists, adopted a chthonic view of this underworldly region rather than the Homeric view of a fabled land.[55] Nonetheless, like Homer and especially like Hesiod, Virgil peoples with fearful presences the territory just outside the entryway to the land of the dead.

The terror of the place, which is implicit in Homer, is specified by Virgil in painful detail. First one encounters personified emotions and afflictions: grief, anxiety, fear, hunger, agony, and death.[56] This is the company in which Sleep finds its place, and Virgil, following the tradition noted by Ahl, describes Sleep as death's blood relative (*consanguineus Leti Sopor*).[57] Life's emotional afflictions are accompanied by monsters:

> Besides, many varieties of monsters can be found
> Stabled here at the doors—Centaurs and freakish Scyllas,
> Briareus with his hundred hands, the Lernaean Hydra
> That hisses terribly and the flame-throwing Chimaera,
> Gorgons and harpies, and the ghost of three-bodied Geryon.[58]

In the midst of all this monstrousness there is a tree, a huge, shadowy elm that "spreads wide its branches like arms." Here "the unsolid dreams [*somnia vana*] roost, clinging everywhere under its foliage."[59] Like Ovid, Virgil characterized dreams as insubstantial, but he has changed the metaphorical shape of these vain beings: instead of the cobwebby, langorous creatures of Ovid's imagination, now dreams roost like bats beneath the leaves of a tree, an organic metaphor in keeping, perhaps, with Virgil's chthonic, earthy placement of this realm. Aeneas, terrified at the sight of all this, takes out his sword, but the Sibyl assures him that the lives of these beings are "thin and bodiless; they flutter about in an empty semblance of form" [*volitare cava sub imagine formae*].[60]

Like Ovid, Virgil has amplified the imaginal significance of Homer's spatial metaphor for the place of dreams, though in a more ponderous way. He has, however, made explicit the psychological contours of this realm by placing personified emotions there. The monsters of the underworld are creatures of the human imagination, unsolid yet fearfully alive. Again, it is the semblance of form that makes the perception of form possible.

Virgil continued the play on the idea of semblance in his appropriation of the Homeric gates of dream.

[55] Virgil, *Aeneid* 6.264–67 (ed. Ribbeck, p. 487).
[56] *Aen.* 6.274–77 (ed. Ribbeck, p. 488).
[57] Ibid. 6.278 (ed. Ribbeck, p. 488).
[58] Ibid. 6.285–89 (ed. Ribbeck, p. 489; trans. Lewis, p. 138).
[59] Ibid. 6.282–84 (ed. Ribbeck, p. 489; trans. Lewis, p. 138).
[60] Ibid. 6.292–93 (ed. Ribbeck, p. 489).

> There are two gates of Sleep, one of which is said to be
> of horn, and through it true shades [*veris umbris*] are
> given a ready outlet; the other shines with the gleam of
> polished ivory, but false are the dreams [*falsa insomnia*]
> which the shades send upward by it.[61]

Although he continues the notion that there is truth in shadows, Virgil gives a twist to the Homeric passage on the gates that was to have a lasting impact on Graeco-Roman dream theory. Homer had maintained the equivocality of *all* dreams; the two gates do not preside over separate realms of truth and falsity. Virgil has rigidified or systematized what in Homer remains finally undecidable, namely, the quicksilver intractability of oneiric phenomena as a whole. Virgil's appropriation of the Homeric metaphor of the gates as a way of characterizing dreams is thus really a misappropriation, but the distinction he made between true and false dreams became the basis of an oneiric hermeneutic that touched the imaginal lives of Graeco-Roman people from Artemidorus to Synesius. The Virgilian mistake fathered *oneirokritica*, the judgment of dreams.

The final twist that Virgil gives to the Homeric trope of the gates will take us to the remaining, extended exploration of Homer's visual presentation of the land of dreams. Immediately following the passage about the two gates, Aeneas and his father Anchises part, their conversation concluded. "Anchises escorted his son and the Sibyl as far as the ivory gate, and sent them through it."[62] This passage has occasioned debate: why did Anchises send his son back to the "real" world through the gate of false dreams? Is Virgil suggesting that Aeneas is a legendary figure, not "true"? Is he implying that the world that is usually thought to be real is a figment, while the realm of shades and shadows is the substantive world?[63] There is no determinable answer to these questions—a tribute, perhaps, to the shadowy landscape of the dreamworld.

Answerable or not, the idea that people, as well as dreams, might travel through the gates appealed to Lucian of Samosata; his comic use of a trip through the ivory gate forms part of his picture of the land of dreams, the final Graeco-Roman trope on Homer's land of dreams that will be considered here. Lucian's *A True Story,* a "tall-tale travelogue" modeled on the adventures of Odysseus in Homer's *Odyssey,* contains an extended description of Homer's spatial metaphor for dreams.[64] The passage is an amusing parody—a testimony to the fact that, by the mid-second century C.E.,

[61] Ibid. 6.893–96 (ed. Ribbeck, p. 529; trans. Grant, p. 214).
[62] Ibid. 6.897–98 (ed. Ribbeck, p. 529; trans. Lewis, p. 155).
[63] See the discussions by Robert J. Getty, "Insomnia in the Lexica," pp. 13–14, and W. F. Jackson Knight, *Elysion,* p. 135.
[64] The description of Lucian's travelogue as a tall tale is by Lionel Casson, trans., *Selected Satires of Lucian,* p. 13.

Homer's picture of the dreamworld had become a convention so well known that it could be subjected to the spoofing that it receives in Lucian's hands. Caricatures, after all, depend on familiarity for their satiric punch.

Lucian's narrator passes into the land of dreams through the ivory gate, reversing the direction of Aeneas and perhaps emphasizing the statement in the preface of the work, that "the one and only truth you'll hear from me is that I am lying."[65] Lying or not, Lucian begins his parody of the heroic dream-figures of Homer with a down-to-earth observation: the Isle of Dreams, "dim and hard to make out," behaves "very much the way dreams do; as we approached, it receded, moving further away and eluding us."[66] Her then gives the following description of the "city" of dreams:

> It's completely surrounded by a forest of lofty poppy and mandrake trees where hordes of bats, the only species of bird on the island, roost. Alongside flows Nightway River, as it's named, and by the gates are two springs called Sleepy-time and Allnight. The city wall is high and gaily painted the colors of the rainbow. There are four gates, not two as Homer says. One of iron and one of ceramic lead to Drowsy Meadow; we were told that nightmares and dreams of murder and violence leave by these. Then two others lead to the water front and the sea, one of horn and the one we came through, of ivory.[67]

Lucian continues on in this way, as though he were writing a tourist's guide, pointing out such notable local monuments as "the twin temples of trick and truth" and so on.[68]

Into this comic cityscape Lucian introduces his version of the *dēmos oneirōn*, the people of dreams. His evocation of this Homeric trope will provide a good transition into late-antique figurations of dreams as "people." Lucian's narrator says:

> As for the dreams, no two are alike in either character or appearance. Some are tall, with good features and good looks, others short and ugly; some are golden, others plain and cheap. There were dreams with wings, freakish dreams, and dreams which, dressed up like kings, queens, gods, and the like, looked as if they were going to a carnival. Many we recognized because we had seen them long ago. These actually came up and greeted us like old friends, then invited us to their homes and, putting us to sleep, extended us the warmest and most generous hospitality. . . .[69]

The dreams of Lucian's imagination look as though they were going to a carnival, just as his discourse is itself "carnivalesque" insofar as its irreverent

65 Lucian, *A True Story [Verae historiae]*, 1.4 (trans. Casson, p. 15).
66 Ibid., 2.32 (trans. Casson, p. 47).
67 Ibid., 2.33–34 (trans. Casson, p. 47).
68 Ibid., 2.34 (trans. Casson, p. 47).
69 Ibid., 2.34–35 (trans. Casson, pp. 47–48).

humor pokes fun at epic tradition.[70] Yet Lucian's topsy-turvy version of Homer's people of dreams instantiates that view even as it parodies it—but with a twist. His description of the physical appearance of dreams in this passage is reminiscent of a section of his satire entitled *Zeus the Opera Star*, in which the gods are described in terms of their statues. Some are made of gold, others of cheap materials, bronze and stone; some are comely and beautifully sculpted, others crudely made and ugly.[71] The dream-figures are described in similar terms—golden and cheap, handsome and unattractive. Although Lucian has not made explicit the statuary quality of his dream-people, the implicit connection is a telling one, because one of the ways in which the ancient idea that dreams are autonomous figures lived on in the late-antique imagination was as statues of the gods.[72]

Like painting, dreams were a form of iconization. This is particularly clear in the many instances in which the gods appear in dreams in the form of their statues. In these cases the exactitude of the oneiric imagination is especially evident, as is the dependence of this kind of thinking on visual articulation for its construction of meaning.[73] While Plato may have worried about the epistemological status of copies of copies, dreamers knew that appearances were a source of knowledge.

These late-antique appearances differed from their Homeric predecessors in an essential respect, related to the quality and precision of their mimetic effect. In Homer, when the gods appear as dreams, they do so in disguise, fabricated so as to look like people familiar to the dreamer. As Lane Fox has pointed out, "It is particularly significant that the dreams and visions in Homer show none of art's effects, for Homer had composed the epics before portrait statues had been widely available. . . . As Greek sculpture developed, it fixed mortals' ideas of their gods as individuals; the distinct 'personality' of the Greek gods has been questioned, but art was an enduring mould which helped to form it."[74] Implicit in Lane Fox's observation is the thesis

---

[70] For a discussion of the term *carnivalesque* as it is used in some forms of contemporary literary criticism, see Julia Kristeva, "Word, Dialogue, and Novel," pp. 78–80.

[71] Lucian, *Zeus the Opera Star [Iuppiter Tragoedus]*, 7–11 (trans. Casson, pp. 140–42).

[72] See the discussion by Lane Fox, *Pagans and Christians*, pp. 153–63.

[73] Commenting on Apuleius' use of the word *signum* to denote a statue of Diana (*Metamorphoses* 2.4), Françoise Meltzer makes the following observation that is pertinent to my point here:

Signum is a marvelous word-play for what we have been discussing here, for the word *signum* has as its first meaning "a sign, mark, token." It is only secondarily "a figure, image, statue." A statue, then, in a culture of an imaged religion, is also a *sign:* a mark or token of divine presence. . . . We might formulate all of this thus: in an imaged religion, mimetic art or representation is the mark of presence, the inscription (or trace) of divinity. (*Salome and the Dance of Writing*, p. 102)

[74] Lane Fox, *Pagans and Christians*, p. 153.

of E. R. Dodds about culture-patterns of dreaming, namely, that social milieu and cultural expectation have an influence on the forms in which dreams present themselves and are remembered.[75] It would indeed seem to be the case that the ubiquity of artistic representations of the gods had an influence on the late-antique appropriation of the people of dreams.

A deep familiarity with the dream-images of his fellow Mediterraneans assured Artemidorus of the iconistic verity of these gods-as-dreams. A large section of the second book of his hefty compendium of dream-images and their significations, the *Oneirocritica*, reports on the appearances of gods in dreams. His rule of thumb for the interpretation of these dreams is that "statues of the gods have the same meaning as the gods themselves."[76] Furthermore, each of the gods and goddesses has characteristic signs, so that it is important to notice the age, attributes, activities, material of composition, and clothing of these oneiric statues to determine the identity and meaning of the dream.[77] That these images can be identified with exactitude Artemidorus has no doubt; they are inclusive visual images whose depth of meaning lies on their aesthetic surface.

It is noteworthy that when Artemidorus says that the gods, as statues (and the statues, as gods) have "characteristic signs," he uses the word *parasēma*.[78] *Parasēmon* is a word that denotes a mark that can either be distinguishing or marginal; as a sign, it can either be indicative or it can be counterfeit; it is an emblem or password that can be misleading, as in one of the verbal forms from which it stems, "to betray by one's expression."[79] J. Hillis Miller has observed about what he calls "words in *para*" that they call up their apparent opposites and have no meaning without those counterparts. He goes on to say that *para*- is a double antithetical prefix signifying at once proximity and distance, similarity and difference, interiority and exteriority, . . . something simultaneously this side of a boundary line . . . and also beyond it, equivalent in status and also secondary or subsidiary. . . ." He continues:

A thing in 'para,' moreover, is not only simultaneously on both sides of the boundary line between inside and out. It is also the boundary line itself, the screen which is a permeable membrane connecting inside and outside. It confuses them with one another, allowing the outside in, making the inside out, dividing them and joining them. It also forms an ambiguous transition between one and the other. Though a given word in 'para' may seem to choose

---

[75] Dodds, *The Greeks and the Irrational*, ch. 4: "Dream-Pattern and Culture-Pattern," esp. pp. 102–4.

[76] Artemidorus, *Onir.* 2.39 (ed. Pack, p. 176; trans. White, p. 123).

[77] Ibid. 2.35, 2.44, 4.72 (ed. Pack, pp. 159–60, 178–79, 293–94).

[78] Ibid. 2.44 (ed. Pack, p. 179): *hoi theoi echousi parasēma*.

[79] Liddell, Scott, Jones, *A Greek-English Lexicon*, s.v. *parasēmon*.

univocally one of these possibilities, the other meanings are always there as a shimmering in the word which makes it refuse to stay still in a sentence.[80]

In the light of this perspective, Artemidorus has, by his choice of word, pointed to the equivocal richness of these aesthetic appearances of the gods as people of dreams.

The oneiric imagination confounds the conventional distinction between (real) thing and (false) copy. Emphasis is placed instead on aesthetic scrutiny of the image: appearance is all.[81] Yet in the mimetic world of dreaming, images are uncanny, as Artemidorus knew. Immediately following his statement that equates statues of the gods with the gods themselves, he moves into a discussion of the materials out of which these imaginal statues are composed.

Statues that are fashioned from a substance that is hard and incorruptible as, for example, those that are made of gold, silver, bronze, ivory, stone, amber, or ebony, are auspicious. Statues fashioned from any other material as, for example, those that are made from terra cotta, clay, plaster, or wax, those that are painted, and the like, are less auspicious and often even inauspicious. We must also bear in mind that it is auspicious to see the statues of gods who signify something good in themselves or through their statues, if the statues are not smashed to bits or broken. But if the gods themselves or their statues indicate something bad, it is auspicious to see their statues disappear.[82]

Clearly, it is not enough simply to dream of a statue of a god. Attention must also be given to the substance, the material out of which the statue is formed, because imaginal substances "matter" more, carry more signifying weight, than do the objects themselves. Furthermore, these imaginal substances carry what Gaston Bachelard called the "individualizing power" of matter: they are finely wrought, and every detail counts.[83] Again, Artemidorus:

Whenever the gods are not wearing their customary attire, whenever they are not in their proper place, and whenever they are not conducting themselves as they should, everything that they say is nothing but a lie and a deception. Therefore one must take everything into consideration at the same time: the

[80] Miller, "The Critic as Host," p. 219.

[81] The following comments of Lane Fox are pertinent: "Were the gods also seen openly without a formal invocation? Here, too, we touch on patterns of psychology which our own modern case histories may not do much to illuminate: in antiquity, unlike our own age, 'appearances' were part of an accepted culture pattern which was passed down in myth and the experiences of the past, in art, ritual, and the bewitching poetry of Homer" (*Pagans and Christians*, p. 117).

[82] *Onir.* 2.39 (ed. Pack, p. 176; trans. White, pp. 123–24).

[83] Gaston Bachelard, *L'Eau et les Rêves*, p. 3.

speaker, what is being said, the place, the conduct, and the clothing of the speaker.[84]

This statement makes clear the difference between Homer and the tradition that followed him concerning the people of dreams. These Graeco-Roman figures are not in disguise; rather they are truly *parasēma*, capable of signifying *both* similarity *and* difference at once. The deciphering of meaning lies with the aesthetic astuteness of the observer.

Artemidorus says that these dream-statues speak, move, wear clothing, and so on. This kind of mobile iconization draws on a widespread understanding among Graeco-Roman polytheists about the relationship between statues and deities. Ramsay MacMullen has written that these people "thought first to touch the gods through images, because that was where the gods lived, or at least to images they could be brought by entreaty, there to listen and to act."[85] Indeed, the many reports from this era of statues moving, trembling, winking, and so on suggest that these objects had been conceptualized in such a way as to endow the aesthetic with life.[86] In his third century C.E. work on statues, Callistratus wrote of a statue of Asclepius that "the god infused his own powers" into it; within the statue "the power of the indwelling god is clearly manifest . . . in a marvelous way, it fathers proof that it has a soul; the face, as you look at it, entrances the senses."[87] Similarly, the character Lucius in Apuleius' novel *Metamorphoses* characterizes statues of the gods as "breathing images" (*simulacra spirantia*), as did the author of the Hermetic treatise *Asclepius*, who thought them to be "pleines de souffle vital," to quote the French translator's pungent phrase.[88]

Theorists of the role of images in religion knew that what was involved in this view of statues was not mere magic. The Neoplatonic philosopher Plotinus, writing like Callistratus in the third century C.E., had this to say about statues:

> I think that the wise men of old, who made temples and statues in the wish that the gods should be present to them, looking to the nature of the All, had in mind that the nature of soul is everywhere easy to attract, but that if someone were to construct something sympathetic to it and able to receive part of it, it would of all things receive soul most easily. That which is sympathetic to it is

---

[84] *Onir.* 4.72 (ed. Pack, p. 293; trans. White, p. 214).

[85] MacMullen, *Paganism in the Roman Empire,* pp. 59–60.

[86] Ibid. p. 175n.42 for examples.

[87] Callistratus, *Ekphraseis* 10 (text in Fairbanks, p. 411; trans. Lane Fox, *Pagans and Christians,* p. 160). In the same passage, Callistratus goes on to describe the statue as not merely a replica or outline (*tūpos*) but as a "figure of truth" (*tēs alētheias plasma*).

[88] Apuleius, *Meta.* 11.17 (ed. Griffiths, p. 90); *Corpus Hermeticum, Asclepius* 24.11 (ed. Nock, trans. Festugière, 2:326).

what imitates it in some way, like a mirror able to catch [the reflection of] a form.[89]

In this view, the statue as mimetic object provides a sympathetic space for the presencing of the gods. The animate world of soul can be reflected in the inanimate world of matter when the latter is formed aesthetically.

As Françoise Meltzer has aptly observed, in an imaged religious sensibility such as this, "the representational, or highly mimetic *simulacra* will . . . cause the sensory to mirror meaning, and celebrate the *techne* and lifelike quality of sacred art."[90] The blunt statement of the author of the *Corpus Hermeticum* underscores this view: "Statues are adored because they contain in them the forms [*ideas*] of the intelligible world [*tou noetou kosmou*]."[91] The sensuous image can "contain" such forms because that which is bodiless (*asomata*) is reflected in bodies (*somata*) and the reverse is also true: the world of the senses (*ton aistheton*) is reflected in the noetic world (*ton noeton kosmon*).[92] The reflecting process between what is intangible and what is tangible is a two-way dynamic; as the nexus or connecting point between the two, the image is the message.

I argued earlier that divination at large was a poetizing process. So too was this way of conceptualizing the role of statues in that it involved an imaginal appropriation of the natural and the supernatural worlds. Furthermore, as a semiotic construction, this "language" of statues had a decided tendency toward enabling people to situate themselves more comfortably and securely in the everyday world around them. By "entrancing the senses," as Callistratus said, statues could provide emotional comfort. An Epicurean of the second century C.E. wrote, "Some gods are angry with fortunate men, as the goddess Nemesis seems to be to most people. But the statues of gods should be made cheerful and smiling so that we may smile back at them rather than fear them."[93] When the statue smiles, we smile back; this is a poetry of the invisible that lifts the weight of the world with an aesthetic touch. Italo Calvino has called this dynamic "a lightness of thoughtfulness," a perspective echoed by Porphyry's sense that making an image of a friend or a statue of a god has as its aim to honor, respect, and remember.[94] Thus these "breathing images" could also work to instill life

[89] Plotinus, *Enn.* 4.3.11.1–8 (text and trans. in Armstrong, 4:71).

[90] Meltzer, *Salome and the Dance of Writing*, p. 101.

[91] *Corpus Hermeticum* 17.11–12 (ed. Nock, trans. Festugière, 2:244).

[92] Ibid. 17.8–11 (ed. Nock, trans. Festugière, 2:244).

[93] M. F. Smith, "Diogenes of Oenoanda: New Fragments 115–121," p. 193; text trans. by Lane Fox, *Pagans and Christians*, p. 159.

[94] Italo Calvino, *Six Memos for the Next Millenium*. p. 10; Porphyry, *Contra Christianos*, fr. 76 (ed. Harnack); for a discussion of the authenticity of this and other fragments, see T. D. Barnes, "Porphyry Against the Christians: Date and the Attribution of the Fragments,"

with a sense of virtuous filiation and a sense of thoughtfulness toward one's relationships.

In this world of statues, then, it was the sensuous image that carried meaning. When these *simulacra* appeared in dreams, they were not derided as mere copies of copies; on the contrary, their emotional and epistemological charge was heightened by virtue of their doubly imaginal character. Nowhere was this more obvious than in the cult of Asclepius, where the influence of statues on dreams was perhaps most pronounced among the dream-traditions of late antiquity. Asclepius was the god of health, and suppliants at his many shrines and temples regularly saw dreams of this healer in the form of his statues. The cult of this god was a kind of oneiric therapy, and the healing was aesthetically induced.[95] It would appear that most, if not all, of the sites sacred to Asclepius had a statue of the god as their central point of attraction. Pausanias, inveterate traveler and recorder of tourist attractions, wrote in his second-century C.E. *Guide to Greece* about the Asclepian shrines that he visited. All of them had statues of Asclepius. Sometimes made of stone, sometimes of gold and ivory, sometimes accompanied by his animal companions the dog and the serpent, sometimes holding the medicinal pinecone, this god was thoroughly iconized, and he was a remarkably "live" artistic presence in the dreams of his constituents.[96]

It is tempting to call this dream-Asclepius "statuesque," for as Lane Fox notes, many of his statues were "colossal" and "combined awe with a friendly quality," certainly a desirable trait in a doctor.[97] To those in need of medical help, Asclepius as statue would appear as a dream, either giving prescriptive advice or performing surgery. The following dream reported by Artemidorus was typical:

> A man with a stomach disorder implored Asclepius for a medical prescription. He dreamed that he went into the temple of the god and that the god stretched out his right hand and offered the man his fingers to eat. The man ate five dates and was cured. For the fruits of the date palm, whenever they are in excellent condition, are called "fingers."[98]

---

pp. 424–42; on the issue of the relation between statues and gods, see Patricia Cox, *Biography in Late Antiquity*, pp. 107–10.

[95] For discussion of the cult of Asclepius, see Howard C. Kee, "Self-Definition in the Asclepius Cult," pp. 118–36; C. A. Behr, *Aelius Aristides and the Sacred Tales*, pp. 23–40; the collection of ancient testimonies in Emma J. and Ludwig Edelstein, *Asclepius: A Collection and Interpretation of the Testimonies;* and Ch. 4 *infra*.

[96] Pausanias, *Guide to Greece* 2.4.6; 2.10.2–3; 2.11.6; 2.27.1; 7.20.5; 7.23.5; 10.32.8 (trans. Levi, 1:141, 153–54; 157; 193–94; 280; 289; 492).

[97] Lane Fox, *Pagans and Christians*, p. 160.

[98] *Onir.* 5.89 (ed. Pack, p. 323; trans. White, p. 242).

As one of the people of dreams, this statue is not only mobile but edible, at least in terms of the substitutionary code that brings the imagery of the dream into the sensuous world of the everyday, where dates can cure a stomach ache. This dream is a good example of the way in which Graeco-Roman dream-figures can function as *parasēma*, as equivocal signs. A statue's fingers are not dates; yet in the imaginally charged constructions of the dream, stone takes on sensory qualities that have real consequences for the health of the dreamer.

The best-known instances of the appearance of Asclepius as a dream-statue were recorded by his most famous devotee, Aelius Aristides. Rhetorician and dreamer extraordinaire, Aristides was an aristocrat from Smyrna who studied in Athens and won fame in Rome for his ability to declaim. Yet despite his fame and wealth, Aristides was not a happy man. Plagued by a string of illnesses, he sought relief, in the mid-second century c.e., in the temple of Asclepius at Pergamum. By submitting himself to the process of dream incubation, he hoped to receive curative prescriptions from the divine doctor.[99]

His hopes were richly fulfilled; not only did he receive prescriptions, Asclepius became his nighttime familiar. In *The Sacred Tales* that record his dream-visits, Aristides described the god. Here is one of the most striking of these descriptions of an oneiric appearance of Asclepius:

> [In the temple] first the statue was seen, which had three heads, and shone about with fire, except for the heads. Next we worshippers stood by it, just as when the paean is sung, I almost among the first. At this point, the God, now in the posture in which he is represented in statues, signaled our departure. Therefore all the others went out, and I turned to go out, and the God, with his hand, indicated for me to stay. And I was delighted by the honor and the extent to which I was preferred to the others, and I shouted out, "The One," meaning the God. But he said, "It is you."[100]

Aristides commented about this dream, "For me this remark, Lord Asclepius, was greater than human life, and every disease was less than this, every grace was less than this. This made me able and willing to live."[101]

Unlike the statues of Asclepius described by Pausanias, this one has three heads and shines with a fiery light. As an image, the dream-statue is not merely mimetic to "real" statues but takes on a life of its own. This dream is a good example of the way in which the oneiric imagination infuses its matter with an emotional intensity that both reflects and shapes the sensibility of the dreamer. The surreal statue of the dream singles out Aristides in a gesture of honor; echoing that gesture, Aristides says, "The One," in an effort to praise the divinity of the god. But the statue says, "It is you." An identification of dreamer and dream-god has occurred. The oneiric Aristides has merged with the dream-statue of the god Asclepius and so has assumed the form of an aesthetic ideal of himself. The dream "translates" Aristides into another idiom, reformulating his identity in terms of the imaginal figure of his dream. Further, the reformulation takes him not out of the world but more deeply into it, as he himself said, "This made me able and willing to live." Curiously, when the extraordinary happens, when stone speaks, ordinary life seems more livable.

Lane Fox has observed that Aristides' dreams "reinforced his sense of a special relationship" with the god—and I would add, with himself.[102] The forging of bonds through the aesthetic medium of an oneiric image was an important characteristic of these late-antique people of dreams—not only when dreams took the artistic form of statues, but also when they appeared along the lines of the older Homeric model. Perpetua, a young woman from Carthage who died in defense of her Christian belief in the early third century, was visited twice by a dream in the figure of her dead brother. Appearing first with the facial cancer that killed him, and then cured, happily at play, this image appears to have enabled Perpetua to establish a therapeutic relationship with a haunting memory.[103] As in the literary portrayal of Achilles encountering the ghostly dream of his dead friend Patroclus, the oneiric image sharpens and clarifies relationships by giving them visual articulation. A similar case is that of a late-first or early-second-century Roman, the author of a book entitled the *Shepherd of Hermas*. This dreamer, Hermas, was visited repeatedly by a dream in the form of an old woman, who presented him with allegorical visions of proper Christian ethical behavior. Having once been tormented by adulterous longings, Hermas is instructed by his oneiric visitor and forges new relationships with his religious identity. His dream-woman is, like the older Homeric gods, a figure in disguise; she is an allegory of the church, and her visits reorient the dreamer's moral sensibility.[104]

The reconciling function of these Graeco-Roman "people of dreams" is testimony to the representative power of these figurations of a figurative world. The psychic *liveliness* of these mobile icons is by now clear, but what of their *psychic* liveliness? Among some of the Platonists of late antiquity there was an appropriation of the Homeric people of dreams that connected them specifically with constructions of the soul. Insofar as it touches on

[102] Lane Fox, *Pagans and Christians,* p. 162.
[103] *Pass. Perp.* 7–8 (ed. Van Beek, pp. 18–23).
[104] For a detailed discussion, see Ch. 5 *infra.*

discussions of the theoretical underpinnings of the practices of dream interpretation, this Platonic convention will provide a transition to an exploration of the oneiric theory of late antiquity in which views of the imaginative
functions of the psyche were fundamental to understanding the discourses
of dreams.

The writings of a second-century Pythagorean, Numenius of Apamea,
are the probable source of a leitmotif that occurs in Neoplatonic discussions
of the cosmic travels of the soul, whereby Homer's image of the *dēmos
oneirōn* was placed in the context of Plato's construction of cosmic space in
the tale that ends the *Republic,* the myth of Er. Numenius' speculations were
adopted by Neoplatonists who were attempting to explicate their view of
the cosmos in terms of Platonic and Homeric imagery.[105] In his essay on the
Homeric image of the cave of the nymphs (*Od.* 13.110–12), Porphyry made
the following observations.

> He [Homer] somewhere talks of "gates of the sun" [*Od.* 24.12] by which he
> means Cancer and Capricorn, for these are the limits of its [the sun's] travel as it
> descends from the home of the North Wind into the South and then returns
> back up to the North. Capricorn and Cancer mark the extremities of the Milky
> Way and lie near it, Cancer in the North and Capricorn in the South. According
> to Pythagoras, the souls are the "people of dreams" [*Od.* 24.12] who, as he
> says, are assembled in the Milky Way [*galaxia*] which derives its name from
> "milk" [*gala*] because they are nourished with milk when they first fall into
> *genesis.*[106]

Working with a much more complicated, astronomical view of the cosmos
than Homer had, Porphyry here directs his attention to the spatial position
of disembodied souls, that is, souls as they exist before they enter the earthy
plane of life in a body. Such souls are the people of dreams, living a purely
imaginal existence.

This intricate astronomical fantasy concerning the soul's oneiric identity
was still alive a century after Porphyry wrote, and in an even more complicated form. Proclus, the last of the major Neoplatonic thinkers of late
antiquity, presented a more extensive version of Numenius' thoughts than
Porphyry had. The portions relevant to this discussion are related by Proclus
as he attempts to decide how to locate the place of the judgment of souls as it
is described in the myth of Er (*Rep.* 10.614c–d).

> Numenius says that this place is the center of the entire cosmos, and likewise of
> earth, because it is at once in the middle of heaven and in the middle of the
> earth. . . . By "heaven" he means the sphere of the fixed stars, and he says there
> are two holes in this, Capricorn and Cancer, the one a path down into *genesis,*

105 Lamberton, *Homer the Theologian,* pp. 66–77.
106 Porphyry, *De antro nympharum* 28 (trans. Lamberton, p. 36).

the other a path of ascent. . . . He invokes the poem of Homer as a witness to
the two chasms . . . when it sings of "the gates of the sun and the people of
dreams" [Od. 24.12], calling the two tropical signs the "gates of the sun" and
the Milky Way the "people of dreams," as he claims. For he also says that
Pythagoras in his obscure language called the Milky Way "Hades" and "a place
of souls," for souls are crowded together there. . . . Furthermore, he claims
that Plato, as mentioned, is describing the gates in speaking of the two
"chasms" and that in describing the light that he calls the "bond of heaven" he is
really referring to the Milky Way. . . . He claims the signs of the Tropics, the
double chasms and the two gates are different only in name, and again that the
Milky Way, the "light like a rainbow" and the "people of dreams" are all one—
for the poet elsewhere compares disembodied souls to dreams. . . .[107]

In his wonderfully lucid discussion of this passage, Robert Lamberton has
pointed out the two sets of identifications that have been assembled here.
One set identifies the Homeric "gates of the sun" with the Platonic image of
two cosmic chasms through which souls travel; these have been further
identified with the astrological signs of Capricorn, the passage taken by
souls traveling out of this world, and of Cancer, the passage taken by souls as
they enter this world. The other set identifies the Homeric "people of
dreams" with the Platonic image of the rainbow, "the light that binds
heaven" (Rep. 10.616c); the people of dreams are then further identified
with the Milky Way and with disembodied souls.[108]

The idea that the soul is a dream was not developed further in Neoplatonic writings. It sits enigmatically in a corpus of Homeric exegesis that
was more interested in establishing than in exploring the teasingly suggestive metaphoric connections that it spun out. Yet there is in this same
exegetical tradition a hint that might help toward understanding how a
transfer of meaning between soul and dream might have been possible. At
one point in his treatise on the river Styx, Porphyry is commenting on the
passage in the Odyssey that describes Odysseus' meeting with the ghost of his
mother Anticleia. In this passage, ghost, dream, and soul appear to be
metaphors for each other.

> I [Odysseus] bit my lip,
> rising perplexed, with longing to embrace her [Anticleia],
> and tried three times, putting my arms around her,
> but she went sifting through my hands, impalpable
> as shadows are, and wavering like a dream.[109]

[107] Proclus, In rem publicam 2.128.26–130.14; 2.130.15–16; 2.131.8–14 (text and trans. in
Lamberton, Homer the Theologian, pp. 66–67).
[108] Lamberton, Homer the Theologian, p. 70.
[109] Od. 11.204–8 (ed. Stanford, p. 174; trans. Fitzgerald, p. 191).

Anticleia answers:

> All mortals meet this judgment when they die.
> No flesh and bone are here, none bound by sinew,
> since the bright-hearted pyre consumed them down—
> the white bones long exanimate—to ash;
> dreamlike the soul flies, insubstantial.[110]

Porphyry had this to say about these "images of dead men" (*brotōn eidōla kamōntōn; Od.* 11.476).

> The idea is that souls are like the images [*tois eidōlois*] appearing in mirrors and on the surface of water that resemble us in every detail and mimic [*mimeitai*] our movements but have no solid substance that can be grasped or touched. This is why he calls them "images of dead men."[111]

In this passage, Porphyry has described the soul with many of the same terms and ideas that were used to describe dreams. The soul is a ghostly image, insubstantial yet nonetheless in movement, and it works by means of mimesis, reflecting us to ourselves "in every detail." Apparently it was these shared characteristics that made possible a metaphoric resonance between the soul and the image of the "people of dreams."

Although the exegetical context of this Neoplatonic juxtaposition of soul with Homer's "people of dreams" did not allow for an exploration of the connection between the two, the fact of the coming together of these two phenomena is telling. In the dream theory of late antiquity, soul and dream were intimately connected. The next chapter explores the ways in which dreams were conceptualized as one of the major imaginative languages of the soul.

---

[110] Ibid., 11.218–22 (ed. Stanford, p. 175; trans. Fitzgerald, p. 192).

[111] Porphyry, *Peri Stygos [The Styx]*, in Stobaeus, *Eclogae* 1.41.50 (text and trans. in Lamberton, *Homer the Theologian*, p. 114 and n.100).

CHAPTER TWO

Theories of Dreams

LATE ANTIQUITY at large was a culture that invested much energy in theoretical explorations of the intangible presences that presided over everyday life. Gods, angels, daemons, souls—all were subjected to scrutiny, the mechanics of their movements diagramed, their composition dissected, the principles governing how their messages were to be understood intricately set forth. Dreams, too, gave rise to an extensive theoretical literature. This literature was embedded both in psychology, that is, in theories that explored the soul's capacity to govern thought and emotion and to produce images of its activities, and in theology, in cases where dreams were seen as appurtenances of a divine sensibility. Oneiric theory also drew on what would today be called literary criticism because, in order to be subject to interpretation, a dream had to be told or written. In the most immediate sense, dreams were phenomena of language as well as of psychic imagination and divine intention.

Two vignettes drawn from ancient theories about dreaming will help to situate the discussion in some of the theoretical issues that seemed most pressing to late-antique thinkers. In each case, a theoretical position on dreams from the period prior to late antiquity will serve as a foil for a late-antique position in order to highlight the latter's distinctiveness.

The first vignette concerns the relation between the soul and dreams. The foil is Plato. Unlike Aristotle, Plato did not write a sustained essay on dreams, but comments on them, often contradictory, are scattered throughout his works. In the *Timaeus* he turns his attention to prophetic dreams as one feature of the art of divination given to human beings by the gods:

> No man achieves true and inspired divination when in his rational mind, but only when the power of his intelligence is fettered in sleep or when it is distraught by disease or by reason of some divine inspiration. But it belongs to a man when in his right mind to recollect and ponder both the things spoken in dream or waking vision by the divining and inspired nature, and all the visionary forms that were seen, and by means of reasoning to discern about them all wherein they are significant.[1]

[1] Plato, *Timaeus* 71E (trans. Bury, p. 187).

Plato does not deny that dreams can signify truly; however, their meaning can only be discerned when the dreamer wakes from the mantic frenzy of sleep. Dreaming is portrayed here as a phenomenon of the irrational part of the soul, which is the medium for the perception of *phantasmata*, the "visionary forms" of inspired sleep.[2]

Eight centuries later, a Christian bishop in Alexandria, Egypt, was still engaged in theorizing about connections between the soul and dreams. However, Athanasius used the experience of dreams as proof that the soul is rational and immortal!

> When the body is still, at rest and sleeping, a man is in inner movement—he contemplates [*theōrei*] what is outside himself, he traverses foreign lands, he meets friends, and often through them [the dreams] he divines (*man-teuomenos*] and learns in advance his daily actions. What else could this be but a rational soul [*psūchē logikē*]?[3]

Dreams break the barrier between the soul and a much larger (normally unseen but very "real") world "outside"—a world of foreign lands, friends, and true beholding (*theōreō*). Further, in sleep the soul imagines, it sees phantasmal sights (*phantazetai*), and those phantoms of the night embody the basic, because immortal, logic of the psyche. For Athanasius, it would seem that, *pace* Plato, one sees most clearly only in the dark.

Athanasius shared with his predecessor a vocabulary that designated oneiric phenomena as mantic and phantasmal, and a conviction that dreams are properly situated in theories about psychic experience, particularly in terms of the soul's connection with the world of the gods (whether through divine inspiration, as with Plato, or through ontological status, as with Athanasius' comment about immortality). What is astonishing is the complete reversal of opinion concerning rationality. For Athanasius, dreams were not products of our wild-eyed, irrational selves; on the contrary, they were evidence and guarantee of our powers of understanding. Across the gap of this difference of opinion lies the late-antique preoccupation with theories about the mechanics of the production of dreams as well as about the status of dreams with regard to issues of epistemology and ontology.

The second vignette concerns the autonomy of dreams as well as their connection with visual articulation of meaning. The foil from early antiquity comes from the Presocratic philosopher Heraclitus of Ephesus. Two of his statements are pertinent:

> The waking have one world in common, whereas each sleeper turns away into a private world of his own.[4]

---

[2] See Gallop, "Dreaming and Waking in Plato," pp. 188–89.

[3] Athanasius, *Contra Gentes* 31.38–44 (ed. and trans. Thomson, p. 87).

[4] Heraclitus, fr. 15 (Diels-Kranz 89) (trans. Wheelwright, p. 70).

Man in the night kindles a light for himself, Though his vision is extinguished. . . .[5]

As both these fragments show, for Heraclitus sleep and the dreaming state attendant upon it were intensely private experiences. The dreamworld turns the dreamer away from community, away from the "one world in common," and directs the vision inward. One commentary on the second of these fragments intensifies its sense of inwardness. About the image of kindling a light in a world of one's own, Kessels suggested that Heraclitus may have meant that during sleep the eyes, made of fiery material, "turned round and directed their beams towards the human interior."[6] The dreamworld is here envisaged as one of private illumination.

Quite different from the cocoon-like sense of Heraclitus' dreamworld was that of St. Augustine. For Augustine, dreams could take the dreamer *into* communal conversation and shared experience, as the following passage from *The City of God* shows:

> I believe that a person has a phantom which, in his imagination or in his dreams, takes on various forms through the influence of circumstances of innumerable kinds. This phantom is not a material body; and yet with amazing speed it takes on shapes like material bodies; and it is this phantom, I hold, that can in some inexplicable fashion be presented in bodily form to the apprehension of other people when their physical senses are asleep or in abeyance.[7]

An example of this phenomenon, which, Augustine assures his readers, he has gotten on good authority from someone who would never lie, concerns a man who reported that

> in his own house, at nighttime, before he went to bed, he saw a philosopher coming to him, a man he knew very well; and this man explained to him a number of points in Plato, which he had formerly [that is, in person] refused to explain when asked. Now this philosopher was asked why he had done something in the other's house which he had refused to do when requested in his own home, and he said in reply, "I did not do it, I merely dreamed that I did."[8]

"This shows," says Augustine, "that what one man saw in his sleep was displayed to the other while awake by means of a phantom appearance."[9] Augustine had no doubt that the dreams we see in sleep have an independent existence (and are even capable of philosophical erudition!). This

[5] Heraclitus, fr. 48 (Diels-Kranz 26) (trans. Marcovich, p. 244).
[6] Kessels, *Studies on the Dream in Greek Literature*, p. 195.
[7] Augustine, *De civitate Dei* 18.18 (trans. Bettenson, pp. 782–83).
[8] Ibid. (trans. Bettenson, pp. 783–84).
[9] Ibid. (trans. Bettenson, p. 784).

particular kind of dream may be a phantom, but it is a phantom with a public persona that functions to put people in touch with each other, to make their one world more common. Heraclitus and Augustine agreed that in sleep a world is constructed, but there has been a stunning reversal from the isolated privacy of Heraclitus' image to the public intelligibility and autonomous movement of Augustine's oneiric figures. Across *this* gap arose the issues of decipherment and classification of dream images, issues that were based in part on theorists' view that, in dreaming, people had a world in common. This chapter focuses on theories that pertain to the etiology of dreams, while Chapter Three deals with strategies for oneiric interpretation and classification.

DREAMS AND THE SOUL: PSYCHOBIOLOGICAL THEORY

As the first vignette suggested, dream theorists in antiquity usually connected the phenomenon of dreaming with a psychic dynamic, whether the soul was viewed as receptive of the visions of dreams, or productive of them, or both. In a very real sense, dreams were not distinguishable, in theory, from the movements by which they were traced. Basically, there were two ways of conceptualizing the "mechanics" of the production of dreams. One was psychobiological and attempted to naturalize the phenomena of sleep and its attendant phantasms; the other was theological and connected the dreaming soul with an invisible but very real realm of spiritual beings—angels, daemons, gods. Although these views were opposed to each other, both were haunted by a persistent question regarding the status of the human imagination and its ability to construct distinctive patterns of meaning.

The naturalist position was neatly summarized in a brief comment by Pliny the Elder, who wrote his *Naturalis Historia* containing "20,000 important facts" in the first century c.e.[10] One of those "facts" was a definition of sleep: "Sleep is nothing but the retreating of the soul into its own midst" (*Est autem somnus nihil aliud quam animi in medium sese recessus*).[11] The soul retires into itself as into a nook or secret recess. Pliny continues his brief statement by adding that it is obvious that "besides human beings, horses, dogs, oxen, sheep, and goats dream."[12] This catalogue of animals that dream shows that Pliny had read his Aristotle, for in *Historia animalium* (536b27–30) Aristotle cites the same list as examples of quadrupeds that dream. Pliny was one of a handful of Graeco-Roman authors who carried on Aristotle's psychobiological views of dreams,

---

[10] Pliny, *Naturalis historia*, praef. 17 (text in Rackham, 1:12).
[11] Ibid. 10.98.211 (text in Rackham, 3:426.).
[12] Ibid. (text in Rackham, 3:428).

which persisted as a minor leitmotif in late-antique dream theory well into the fourth century C.E. A brief recounting of Aristotle's theories will help provide context for the perspectives of his successors.

Aristotle did not accept the Homeric view that dreams are messages from the gods or in any way connected with divine presence.[13] He viewed them instead as images produced by interconnecting physiological and psychic processes. For Aristotle, sleep and the dreams that occur during it are essentially products of the digestive process, during which heat rises and falls though the body. Once asleep, the primary perceptual capacities of the soul, having been "cooled," cease to function; the eyelids droop, yet some sort of perception continues to occur nonetheless.[14] As he explains it, "sense-objects corresponding to each sense-organ provide us with perception. And the affection produced by them persists in the sense-organs, not only while the perceptions are being actualized, but also after they have gone."[15] What the soul sees during sleep are the "appearances" (*phantasmata*) and "residual movements deriving from sense-impressions" perceived previously when the soul—and the body—were awake.[16] Thus Aristotle defines a dream as "an appearance [*phantasma*] that arises from the movement of the sense-impressions, while one is in the sleeping state."[17] Body and soul work together to produce simulacra that mimic ordinary perceptual images.

Dreams, then, are traces of waking perception and, as David Gallop has explained it, they are "a sort of replay of previous waking experience, sometimes bizarrely scrambled as a result of physiological experience."[18] Further, they are products of the imagination (*to phantastikon*).[19] It is this activity of the soul that weaves together its perceptual traces to produce

[13] Aristotle, *De divinatione per somnum* 462b12–26 (text and trans. in Gallop, pp. 102, 107).

[14] Aristotle, *De somno* 456a30–b11; 456b17; 457a33–b26; *De insomniis* 459a1–22 (text and trans. in Gallop, pp. 69–71, 75–77, 85).

[15] Aristotle, *De insom.* 459a24–28 (text and trans. in Gallop, p. 87).

[16] Ibid. 461a18–20 (text and trans. in Gallop, p. 85).

[17] Ibid. 462a29–31 (text and trans. in Gallop, p. 101).

[18] Gallop, *Aristotle on Sleep and Dreams,* p. 19.

[19] Aristotle, *De insom.* 459a15–17 (text and trans. in Gallop, p. 85). See Gallop's extensive discussion of the complicated role that *phantasia,* imagination, plays in Aristotle's thought (18–25). Gallop suggests that Aristotle's conception of imagination should be interpreted "not simply as a capacity for mental imagery, but as one whereby something 'appears to,' or is interpreted by, an observer in a certain way. At its broadest, it will be a capacity that enters into all of a creature's perceptual and cognitive engagement with the world around it" (21). With regard to dreams in particular, Gallop notes, "Aristotle distinguishes 'imagination' (*phantasia*) from 'judgment' (*doxa*), which may either endorse or oppose imagination's deliverances, or which may do neither. In dreaming it simply fails to oppose them, so that the appearances presented to the subject gain acceptance by default (*De insom.* 461b29–462a8, cf. 459a6–8, 461b3–7)" (Gallop, p. 21).

phantasmata, the appearances that are dreams. Aristotle does not doubt that *to phantastikon* can produce true dreams; for example, direct visions of one friend by another arise from their mutual engagement with and receptivity to each other.[20] Overall, however, he felt that dreams that are fulfilled happen only by coincidence, luck, and good guessing.[21] Thus Aristotle's view of dreams had two major tendencies. One was to root the phenomenon of dreams solidly in the soul's participation in the biological process; the other was to undercut the role of dreams in divinatory practice.

Early in the Graeco-Roman era, the most outspoken proponent of the kind of oneiric theory proposed by Aristotle was Cicero. In his long treatise on divination, he uses Aristotelian psychobiological arguments to explain the dream as a naturalistic phenomenon; from this standpoint he exposes divination by dreams as an inexact pseudo-science that trades on human credulity and on an erroneous set of assumptions about the gods. Basically, Cicero's argument was as follows:

> By nature I mean that essential activity of the soul [*animus*] owing to which it never stands still, and is never free from some agitation or motion or other. When in consequence of the languor of the body it is able to use neither the limbs nor the senses, it falls into varied and uncertain visions that arise, as Aristotle says, from the clinging remnants of the things the soul did and thought while awake. Strange kinds of dreams sometimes arise from the confusion [caused by the remnants].[22]

Like Aristotle, Cicero argues that dreams occur when interconnecting psychic and physiological processes are set in motion. The ever-active soul produces confused relics of its daytime activities when the body is weary, no longer able to support active sense-perception.[23] Cicero even uses the same kinds of examples—tricks of vision—to show that the *visiones,* the "apparitions" of sleep, are illusory and so untrustworthy as sources of meaning.[24] "Why need I mention," says Cicero, "how many false things are seen by drunks and crazy men?"[25]

His explanation of dreams according to the tenets of scientific empiricism is the basis upon which Cicero proceeds to lampoon divinatory practices based on dreams. Having demonstrated, at least to his own satisfaction, that dreams are psychobiological phenomena, he can then assert

---

[20] Aristotle, *De div.* 464a27–b5 (text and trans. in Gallop, p. 111).

[21] Ibid. 463a31–463b22 (text and trans. in Gallop, pp. 107–9).

[22] Cicero, *De divinatione* 2.128 (ed. Pease, pp. 554–55).

[23] Ibid. 2.139–40 (ed. Pease, pp. 569–70); cf. Aristotle, *De insom.* 461a18–23 and Aristotle, *De div.* 463a21–30 (text and trans. in Gallop, pp. 95, 105).

[24] *De div.* 2.120 (ed. Pease, pp. 544–46); Aristotle, *De insom.* 461b31–462a5 (text and trans. Gallop, p. 99).

[25] Ibid. 2.120 (ed. Pease, p. 545).

with confidence that "there is no divine power that creates dreams."[26] In fact, it is demeaning to suppose that the gods communicate with human beings through such phenomena, and for several reasons. Are we really to imagine, asks Cicero sarcastically, that immortal gods spend their time flitting about the beds and pallets of mortals and that, "when they find someone snoring, they cast before him tortuous and obscure visions which awaken him out of sleep in terror so that he has to consult a diviner?"[27] The truth of the matter, says Cicero, is that most people don't even remember their dreams; do the gods then care for people by sending them crucial information in vain packages?[28] Furthermore, if the gods really wanted to communicate with us in this way, why wouldn't they send messages in ordinary, everyday speech instead of in obscure and enigmatic images? According to Cicero, the proponents of dream-divination put the gods in the position of a doctor who prescribes for a patient "an earthborn, grass-crawling, bloodless creature that carries its house on its back" instead of simply saying, "a snail."[29]

Having shown that dreams are ill-suited to a respectful characterization of the gods, Cicero then turns his scathingly critical remarks against the diviners themselves. His strong suspicion is that the interpretation of dreams is geared more toward displaying the sagacity of the interpreter than it is toward demonstrating the connections between dreams and natural law.[30] In fact, he says, interpretations and reality only coincide by virtue of a hit-or-miss procedure based on chance and luck, just as Aristotle had argued.[31] Cases of opposing interpretations of the same dream clinch his argument. One example is that of a runner who dreamed that he was carried in a chariot drawn by four horses. One interpreter said he would win his race, because winning was implied by the strength and speed of the horses; another interpreter, however, said he would lose, because the four horses indicated that four ran ahead of him. A similar case involved a woman who wanted to conceive a child. When she dreamed that her womb had been sealed, she wondered whether she were pregnant and so consulted two interpreters. The first told her that she was not pregnant, because conception is impossible when the womb is sealed; but the second told her that she was indeed pregnant, because it is against custom to seal something that is empty.[32] On the basis of such evidence,

---

[26] Ibid. 2.124 (ed. Pease, p. 551).

[27] Ibid. 2.129 (ed. Pease, p. 556).

[28] Ibid. 2.125 (ed. Pease, pp. 551–52).

[29] Ibid. 2.133 (ed. Pease, pp. 560–61).

[30] Ibid. 2.144 (ed. Pease, p. 574).

[31] Ibid. 2.108; 2.121 (ed. Pease, pp. 525, 546–47).

[32] Ibid. 2.144–45 (ed. Pease, pp. 574–76). For the long tradition of the dream of the sealed womb, see Pease, ed., *M. Tulli Ciceronis De Divinatione*, pp. 575–76n.6.

Cicero concludes that the art of dream-interpretation consists in using one's talent to defraud.[33]

The only area in which Cicero was willing to allow dreams a useful function was in medicine:

> They say that from some kinds of dreams the physicians even can gather indications concerning a patient's health, as whether the internal humors of the body are excessive or deficient.[34]

In allowing a role for dreams in medical evaluations of a patient's health, Cicero appears to be relying on a Hippocratic tradition that viewed dreams as indicators given by the soul that reflect the state of the body.[35] Since the Hippocratic corpus was the foundation for all medicine in antiquity, it is not surprising that Cicero might appeal to this well-known literature, especially because it underscored his own view of dreams as products of a psychobiological dynamic.

Cicero's view of dreams as scrambled figments of the soul's perceptual apparatus did not achieve widespread acceptance in late antiquity. Even in the medical establishment, one could find a view of dreams that did not follow the Hippocratic view of them as only diagnostic pictures of the body's condition. The eminent second-century physician Galen accepted the diagnostic usefulness of dreams but found that they could also be useful in other ways. Indeed, on the basis of a dream from a god, Galen wrote his treatise on the use of the parts of the body.[36] He found dreams enlightening in another way as well:

> Some people scorn dreams, omens, and portents. But I know that I have often made a diagnosis from dreams and, guided by two very clear dreams, I once made an incision into the artery between the thumb and the index finger of the right hand, and allowed the blood to flow until it ceased flowing on its own, as the dream had instructed. I have saved many people by applying a cure prescribed in a dream.[37]

Clearly for Galen, and other ancient doctors as well, dreams were not always tied to physiology but could operate as autonomous signifiers in a way very different from their diagnostic use.[38]

Among interpreters of dreams, the idea that dreams are the result of

[33] *De div.* 2.145 (ed. Pease, p. 576).
[34] Ibid. 2.142 (ed. Pease, p. 572).
[35] See Pease, ed., *M. Tulli Ciceronis De Divinatione*, p. 572n.1; for a discussion of the connection between Hippocratic medicine and dreams in the Graeco-Roman period, see Owsei Temkin, *Hippocrates in a World of Pagans and Christians*, pp. 184–89.
[36] Galen, *De usu partium* 10.14 (ed. Helmreich, 2:110); for discussion and further sources, see S.R.F. Price, "The Future of Dreams: From Freud to Artemidorus," p. 23.
[37] Galen, *Comm. in Hippocr. de humor.* 2.2 (ed. Kuhn, 16:222–23).
[38] Price, "The Future of Dreams," p. 23.

cooperation between mind and body continued, but only to be dismissed. Exemplary of this position was Artemidorus's view. One of the main kinds of dreams in his system of classification is the *enūpnion*, a dream that is connected with physical disturbances that arise in conjunction with, or as a result of, waking preoccupations.[39] Such dreams are remnants of present states of body and mind, though some pertain only to the mind's emotional entanglements, and others pertain only to bodily processes, particularly in cases of illness and of overindulgence in food and drink.[40] These dreams have no meaning and, because they are visions signifying nothing, Artemidorus dismisses them.[41] Thus the psychobiological view of dreams persisted, but only as a branch of oneirology that was of no interest to interpreters.

Judging on the basis of extant literature, the psychobiological theory of dreams did not receive extensive discussion again until the fourth century, when Gregory of Nyssa wrote his treatise *De hominis opificio*. Gregory begins his remarks on the phenomenon of dreaming with a Heraclitean image that he applies to sleep. Alternating states of sleeping and wakefulness form a harmony of opposites that are necessary to the health of the body, and particularly of the body's organs of sense-perception.[42] As Gregory explains it, to be awake is to be "strained tight" (*sūntonos*); sleep provides a necessary respite from this intensity for the perceptual senses (*tas aisthētikas*), loosing them "like horses from their chariots after a race."[43] Like Aristotle long before him, Gregory links sleep with digestion and the accompanying movements of vapors upward and downward through the body."[44]

While the sleeping body is being thus nourished, its perceptual "horses" at rest, there is nonetheless activity in the soul. According to Gregory, dreams are the "fantastic nonsense" (*phantasiōdeis phluarias*) that occur during sleep when "certain appearances of the activities of the mind are by chance formed in the less rational part of the soul."[45] In Gregory's anthropology, the human being is united or "mixed up" with intellect (*nous*) through the operations of sense-perception; when the latter are at rest, the

[39] Artemidorus, *Onir.* 1.1 (ed. Pack, p. 3). The word for "physical disturbances" is *oneirōgmos*, a disturbance usually of an unhealthy kind and often, in dreamers, pertaining to the emission of sexual fluids (by both men and women). See Winkler, *Constraints of Desire*, p. 92.

[40] Artemidorus, *Onir.* 1.1 (ed. Pack, pp. 3–4).

[41] Ibid. 1.1; 4, praef. (ed. Pack, pp. 4, 238–39).

[42] Gregory of Nyssa, *De hominis opificio* 13.1–2 (*PG* 44.165B–C). Cf. the fragments of Heraclitus grouped together by Marcovich, *Heraclitus*, pp. 158–255, as examples of Heraclitus' view of *coincidentia oppositorum*. It is the Heraclitean idea of alternating rhythms that Gregory is petitioning in this passage.

[43] *De hom. op.* 13.2 (*PG* 44.165B–C).

[44] Ibid. 13.2–4 (*PG* 44.165C–D); see Aristotle, *De som.* 456a30–458a32 (text and trans. in Gallop, pp. 69–79).

[45] *De hom. op.* 13.5 (*PG* 44.168B–C).

mind is inactive. Thus released from the rational, guiding activity of the mind, the nutritive part of the soul is set free, and it gives "echoes and shadows" of perceptual activities that occurred when mind and body were awake.[46] Thus, in sleep, the dreamer is lost in imagination (*phantasioutai*), wandering among confused hallucinations.[47]

Gregory softens somewhat this hallucinatory view of dreams when he appropriates Plotinus' metaphor of the musician playing a lyre to explain how mind, soul, and sense-perception interact during sleep. Plotinus had used this metaphor to explain how the mind, the musician, uses and cares for the body, the lyre.[48] Gregory has transformed the metaphor so that it refers to internal relations of the human faculties during sleep.

> Just as a musician, when he strikes the plectrum against the loosened strings of a lyre, produces no rhythmic melody, for that which is not drawn tight will not sound; but his hand often moves skillfully, bringing the plectrum to the proper position of the notes, but no sound occurs, except only so far as it produces an indistinct and irregular humming in the movement of the strings—so in sleep, when the condition of the perceptual organs is relaxed, either the musician is completely at rest since the instrument is totally loosened due to satiety or torpor, or [the results of his actions will be] weak and faint, the perceptual organ not allowing for skillful precision.[49]

In this extended metaphor, and in the explanatory passage that precedes it, Gregory has qualified his earlier statement that intellect is inactive during sleep. Because, as he explains, the mind is never severed from that with which it has once been joined, including even the less rational, nutritive part of the soul, it can continue to operate during sleep, though less attentively than during waking periods.[50] This is an important qualification, because it is here that Gregory diverges from the psychobiological tradition that he has been following to this point. It is precisely the mind's ability to remain active, however faintly, that leads Gregory to accept the possibility that dreams may contain foreknowledge (*prognōsis*) of things to come.[51] The kind of oneiric signification that Gregory is talking about is not the kind of coincidental fulfillment of dreams by luck or repetition as expressed in the theories of Aristotle and Cicero; rather, these are the type of enigmatic dreams familiar to dream-interpreters skilled in the decipherment of ambiguous oneiric images.[52]

[46] Ibid. 13.5–6 (*PG* 44.168B–D). On Gregory's anthropology, see Jean Daniélou, *L'Être et le Temps chez Grégoire de Nysse.*

[47] *De hom. op.* 13.7 (*PG* 44.168D).

[48] Plotinus, *Enn.* 1.4.16.23–24 (text and trans. in Armstrong, 1:210–11).

[49] *De hom. op.* 13.9 (*PG* 44.169C–D).

[50] Ibid. 13.7 (*PG* 44.169A–B).

[51] Ibid. 13.10 (*PG* 44.169D).

[52] Ibid. (*PG* 44.172A). Gregory refers in this passage to "those who interpret such things," a reference to authors like Artemidorus who classified dreams according to their types. For a

In the space of a few paragraphs, Gregory has moved from a view of dreams as "fantastic nonsense" to a view that allows for the occurrence of meaningful dreams, however enigmatic their imagistic constructions may be. His next move, even more surprising given the psychobiological base from which he started, shows Gregory acting as a Christian theologian protective of Scriptural tradition. Immediately following his remark about enigmatic dreams, which shows his knowledge of the classificatory schemas of oneirocritical literature, Gregory recites briefly the dreams of the butler and the baker familiar from the Biblical story of Joseph (Gen. 40.1–9). Both butler and baker had dreams, each seeing himself performing his usual duties; Gregory explains that these "images were imprinted on the part of the soul that has foresight" (*ta eidōla tō prognōstikō tēs psūchēs entūpōthenta*) and enabled the dreamers to have prophetic power for a time.[53] What Gregory does not say directly is that both of these dreamers were baffled by their dreams; in their case, the prophetic power lay in the dreams but was not evident to the dreamers themselves. Discerning the meaning of these dreams was the province of Joseph, to whom Gregory turns next.

It becomes clear that the existence of such heroic biblical dreamers and dream-interpreters as Daniel and Joseph has presented something of a problem for Gregory's view of dreams. Would Scripture hallow "fantastic nonsense"? No, says Gregory, and he saves the biblical text from hallucination by appealing to yet another kind of dream, one that is neither biologically induced nor enigmatically obscure. Gregory says that Daniel, Joseph, and other Biblical dreamers were "taught by divine power" (*theia dūnamei . . . proepaideuonto*) about things to come, with no "turbidity" clouding their sense-perception.[54] This kind of insightfulness cannot arise from a spontaneous natural process, Gregory reasons, for if it did, one would have to say that divine visions seen during wakefulness were not miracles but simply natural occurrences.[55] Hence Gregory is led to the following view:

> While all people are governed by their own minds, there are a few who are judged worthy of direct divine communication (*tēs theias homilias ek tou emphanous*); thus, although the imagination [which is active] in sleep [*tēs en hūpnois phantasias*] occurs according to nature to all equally and in common, there are some, not all, who participate by means of their dreams in some diviner manifestation (*theioteras tinos dia tōn oneirōn tēs emphaneias*). But for all the others, even if foreknowledge of something does come out of dreams, it occurs in the way that has already been spoken of.[56]

---

discussion of the *oneiros*, the enigmatic dream, see Artemidorus, *Onir.* 1.2 (ed. Pack, pp. 4–11).

[53] *De hom. op.* 13.11 (*PG* 44.172A).
[54] Ibid. 13.12 (*PG* 44.172B).
[55] Ibid. (*PG* 44.172B).
[56] Ibid. (*PG* 44.172B).

This view contains a curious reversion to the old Homeric model of dreams as divine presentations, and it is in accord, also, with the oneirocritical view that there are "classes" of dreamers, some more important than others.[57] Artemidorus, for example, remarked that moral people do not have meaningless dreams and irrational fancies.[58] Gregory has adopted this division between ordinary and extraordinary dreamers, but his view of the latter category is much more narrow than that of Artemidorus. Only dreamers who have been favored by God have dreams that are untouched by the fancies of ordinary dreams.

Gregory ends his remarks on oneiric phenomena with a return to the psychobiological explanation of dreams with which he began. Now it is the medical literature that claims his attention, and he discusses it by using an anecdote from his own experience. While attending a relative who was ill, Gregory witnessed the man crying out descriptions, in the imagistic language of dreams, that matched his actual physical condition. This Gregory explains on the basis of a sympathetic relationship between the body and the soul, a view common to medical literature.[59]

Gregory's use of the term *sympatheia* in this context may provide a clue toward understanding the oddness of his remarks on dreams as they jump back and forth between opposed theories of psychobiological causation and divine inspiration. *Sympatheia* was the term used by Stoics to defend the truth of divination, including divination by dreams. According to this concept, the world of human life, especially the life of the soul, was interrelated as microcosm to macrocosm to universal soul and so to the gods as well. In principle, *any* soul could divine; in principle, *any* person could dream a meaningful dream.[60] This way of conceptualizing the metaphysical basis of dreams would not allow for the kind of divine intervention that Gregory wanted to preserve for biblical dreamers. Thus Gregory accepted the concept of *sympatheia* when it suited his need to describe a class of ordinary dreamers whose fantasies arose from a sympathetic connection between the irrational soul and the body; he appears, in other words, to have geared the Stoic idea of sympathy toward psychobiological theory. But he rejected the idea of sympathy, and psychobiological theory as well, when he sought to account for a class of extraordinary dreamers, replacing *sympatheia* with a theory of divine election. Theological necessity resulted in uneven dream theory.

Gregory's predicament was an interesting one, particularly with regard to

---

[57] Artemidorus, *Onir.* 1.2 (ed. Pack, pp. 9–10), for his view that unimportant people do not dream of "great affairs" beyond their capacity for reflection. Such dreams are reserved for powerful public figures like kings or magistrates.

[58] Artemidorus, *Onir.* 4, praef. (ed. Pack, p. 239).

[59] *De hom. op.* 13.15–16 (PG 44.172D–173B).

[60] See the discussion by Brown, *The Making of Late Antiquity*, p. 65, on the ease of access to the divine world offered by dreams.

imagination and its possible influence on human life. He seems at once enticed by and wary of the dreamy *eidōla* that haunt the soul. He was not alone in his bemused fascination with such imagistic constructions; but others in late antiquity, among polytheists as well as in his own monotheistic tradition, were more willing to give such constructs a place in processes of ordinary human understanding.

DREAMS AND THE SOUL: THEOLOGICAL THEORY

Investigating the mechanics of the production of dreams from the perspective of theology takes one into a late-antique thought-world whose atmosphere is dense with spiritual powers. As E. R. Dodds observed, by the second century C.E. "virtually every one, pagan, Jewish, Christian, or Gnostic, believed in the existence of these beings and in their function as mediators, whether he called them daemons or angels or aions or simply 'spirits' (*pneumata*)."[61] Similarly, Peter Brown, in his memorable portrait of the late-antique "friends of god" who were able to establish contact with these powers, describes the situation in the early centuries of the era as one in which "the boundaries between the human and the divine had remained exceptionally fluid. The religious language of the age is the language of an open frontier."[62] Agreeing with Dodds's view that dreams were the most widespread means of establishing contact with the powers, Brown designates the dream as "the paradigm of the open frontier: when a man was asleep and his bodily senses were stilled, the frontier lay wide open between himself and the gods."[63] Lane Fox has joined company with Dodds and Brown, referring to late-antique dream-experience as a "nightly screening of the gods": it was "epiphany's most open level" that people did their best to encourage.[64]

I agree with these evaluations. In a world so thickly populated with invisible powers, the dream was a fitting technology for making contact with them—a daemonic fabrication to match daemonic being that functioned to make the invisible visible. Even though opinion varied as to whether dreams were daemonic or god-sent, and whether dreams presented themselves to the sleeping soul, or whether the soul, like a vagabond, traveled during sleep to meet these spirits of the air, still the tendency to cultivate the dream as a vehicle of meaning was so strong in this era as to make Cicero's naturalist views seem marginal to the temper of the times.[65]

[61] Dodds, *Pagan and Christian in an Age of Anxiety,* p. 38.
[62] Brown, *The Making of Late Antiquity,* p. 65.
[63] Ibid. p. 65.; Dodds, *Pagan and Christian in an Age of Anxiety,* p. 38.
[64] Lane Fox, *Pagans and Christians,* pp. 165, 149, 151.
[65] Ibid., p. 150.

DREAMS AND FATE

Ironically, it was Cicero himself who preserved one of the major arguments in favor of a view of dreams as a meaningful language of signs. The first book of *De divinatione* uses Cicero's brother Quintus as spokesman for the case in favor of divination, a case that stems mainly from the thought of the Stoic Posidonius; it is this lengthy statement that Cicero refutes in his own voice in the treatise's second book.[66] The Stoic view of divination as preserved by Cicero derived the name of this practice from the Latin *divi*, "gods"; by its means, people are able to come near divine power.[67] In the particular instance of divination by dreams, divine power is within human reach because the soul, the locus of dreaming, is derived from the gods. One part of the soul—the part that presides over the senses—cannot be separated from the actions of the body; but the part that has reason and discernment is strongest when it is most distant from the body.[68] The soul can only "divine" by dreams when sleep has distanced it from the contagion of physical processes: "for although the sleeping body lies as if dead, the soul is alive and flourishing."[69] Unlike psychobiological theory, in which the body was implicated in the dreaming process, Stoic theory saw the body as an impediment; only when that part of the soul that possesses understanding is disjunct from the body can it be receptive of the "approach of the gods" (*adpulsu deorum*).[70]

Stoic theory explained divine dreams in three ways:

> First, the soul by its very nature has foresight because of its connections with the reasoning power of the gods; second, the air is full of immortal souls in whom the clear marks of truth are visible; and third, the gods themselves hold conversations with people when they are asleep.[71]

This is a very generous view of human subjectivity. Yet its touching optimism regarding the soul's powers of discernment was grounded not in a boastful inflation of the human intellect but rather in a hope that human beings might be able to sense an orderly structure in an otherwise inscrutable and chancy world.

The Stoic idea was that, in dreams, the individual human soul could make contact with, and learn from, a pervasive governing principle within whose

---

[66] See Pease, ed., *M. Tulli Ciceronis De Divinatione,* pp. 20–24, for a discussion of the Stoic sources of Cicero's synopsis.
[67] *De div.* 1.1 (ed. Pease, p. 40).
[68] Ibid. 1.70 (ed. Pease, pp. 215–16).
[69] Ibid. 1.63 (ed. Pease, p. 205).
[70] Ibid. 1.64 (ed. Pease, p. 208).
[71] Ibid. (ed. Pease, pp. 207–8).

purview all life unfolds.[72] One of the names by which this cosmic principle was discussed among Stoics was fate.[73] In their understanding of this term, fate did not designate a hostile structure that imprisoned human lives in a relentlessly deterministic world; it was used instead to give assurance that life has meaning, that it is not simply a collection of random, accidental events. Cicero's Quintus, for example, defines divination, of which dream interpretation was a branch, as "the foreseeing and foretelling of events considered as happening by chance" (*id est de divinatione, quae est earum rerum, quae fortuitatae putantur, praedictio atque praesensio*).[74] The verb *putantur* is important in this definition: events may be *supposed* to happen by chance, but their fortuitous appearance is misleading. In fact, Quintus argues, things happen by fate, which is defined as "an orderly series of causes in which cause is linked to cause and from each cause an effect is produced."[75] If there were a person insightful enough to perceive the connections that join cause to cause, that person would know what the future will be because the passage of time is "like the uncoiling of a rope: it creates nothing new but produces each event in its order."[76] There is, however, no such person. Only gods have direct knowledge of these causal links. What *is* available for human beings to read are the signs (*signa*) that indicate these connections.[77]

The terms that are repeatedly used in this discussion to refer to predicting or foreseeing the future are *praesensio* and *praesentio*.[78] Neither of these words carries the notion of magical crystal-ball gazing that the word *prediction* has come to have in contemporary parlance. *Praesensio* is defined as a "foreboding" or a "presentiment"; *praesentio*, as "to feel or perceive beforehand, to have a presentiment of."[79] What a divinatory reading of signs yields is a sense or feeling for the shape of things to come. As a temporal metaphor, the "future" designates that which is not yet "uncoiled," not yet disclosed in the present. In the particular case of oneiromancy, Stoics understood dreams as signs of a reality into which the present would flow. Thus dreams were predictive of the future—not merely predictive but deeply revelatory of the flow in time of configurations embedded in the present.

[72] Ibid. 1.125 (ed. Pease, pp. 320–22). For a discussion of the interchangeability of the Stoic concepts of god, nature, and fate, see Luther H. Martin, "Artemidorus: Dream Theory in Late Antiquity," pp. 103–4).

[73] *De div.* 1.125 (ed. Pease, p. 321 and n.9 for sources dealing with the definition of fate as a series of causes and effects.

[74] Ibid. 1.9 (ed. Pease, p. 67; cf. p. 68n.2 on *putantur*).

[75] Ibid. 1.127 (ed. Pease, pp. 322–23).

[76] Ibid. 1.127 (ed. Pease, pp. 323–24).

[77] Ibid. 1.9, 34, 63, 127, etc. (ed. Pease, pp. 67, 150, 204, 324); cf. ibid. 1.65–66 (ed. Pease, pp. 209–12) for a discussion of *praesagire*.

[78] See Lewis and Short, ed., *A Latin Dictionary*, s.v. *praesensio* and *praesentio*.

[79] Ibid.

To yield a foreboding of the future is not the same as to deliver a logical proposition concerning it. Thus George Steiner has coined the striking phrase "hieroglyphics of futurity" to characterize antiquity's understanding of dreams as an imagistic language.[80] However, continued emphasis on the future as a temporal construct skews the Stoic understanding of dreams as divinatory signs. In fact, the language of the future that ancient dreamers used to characterize their understanding of what dreams were speaking about is not properly situated in a metaphysics of time. Basing his discussion both on Stoic thought and on Artemidorus' views, Luther Martin has argued that "oneiromancy did not predict the 'future' in any temporal sense. The Stoic-divinatory notion of the future was a cosmic or spatial metaphor for an inevitability which unfolds. . . . "[81] He concludes that divination by dreams was "a literate reading of the objective signs of the world as ordered by the syntax of fate."[82]

Martin's observations are an important correction to misreadings of the Stoic understanding of the future, and his characterization of fate as a syntax is an appropriate description of the lexicon of signs that structure communication between the soul and the ordering principle of the cosmos. However, his insistence on the objectivity of divinatory practice, particularly in light of the contrast he draws between ancient interpretation of dreams and Freud's understanding of dream interpretation as "the translation of a temporally concealed subjective reality into consciousness," does not account for the feeling tone of ancient understanding.[83]

It is true that, in the Stoic schema, oneiric signs put the human soul in touch with a cosmic structure to which it is akin, but those signs had meaning in the concrete, existential experience of those who received them. If the future was a coded term for the unknown space into which an actual human life was being lived, the signs of dreams gave presentiments and forebodings about the actual shape that life might take. As a language, dreams gave dreamers a way to imagine and to interpret their lives as they were in the midst of living them, offering a reconciling power in the face of cruelty and loss.[84] Quintus the Stoic, in fact, remarks that most of the stories of divinatory dreams that he has presented have come from tragedy, which seems to me to be an appropriate reflection of the entanglement of divinatory practice with life's real emotions.[85] In Stoic theory, dreams allow the soul to stand outside its immersion in the everyday and to reflect on its course in a broader context, conceived theologically as a cosmic structure

---

[80] George Steiner, "The Historicity of Dreams (Two Questions to Freud)," p. 13.
[81] Martin, "Artemidorus: Dream Theory in Late Antiquity," p. 104.
[82] Ibid., p. 108.
[83] Ibid.
[84] Patricia Cox Miller, "Re-imagining the Self in Dreams," pp. 38–39.
[85] Cicero, De div. 1.68 (ed. Pease, p. 213).

undergirded by the gods. Divination by dreams was geared toward such imaginative shaping of individuals' subjectivity. Without this recognition, it can only be seen as a mechanical technique, and not as the lived practice that it was.

DREAMS AND DAEMONS

The view that dreams could shape human subjectivity by enlarging its sphere of reference was shared by Platonic theorists, although for them the sphere was populated not by gods but by daemons. The major spokesmen for a daemonic provenance for dreams were the Middle Platonists Plutarch and Apuleius, whose placement of dreams in a daemonic context served to underscore their mediatorial and transformative function. When speaking of "daemon" as a term that designates the character of those presences pulsating in the aerial spaces around us, it is important to remember that "the daemonic" is less a substantive than it is a situational category.[86] I follow Jonathan Z. Smith's persuasive argument that "the demonic is a relational or labeling term . . . and is part of a complex system of boundaries and limits. In certain situations, the breaking of limits is creative; in others, it is perceived as leading to chaos. In some situations the fixing of boundaries is positive; in others, it leads to repression."[87]

In Middle Platonist theorizing about daemons, the boundary that separates human life from the region of the gods is recognized, but its importance lies, at least in part, in its "brokenness," in its permeability by the daemons whose function is to relate the human with the divine. Paraphrasing Apuleius, John Dillon has observed that in Middle Platonist theory, "the world does not tolerate a gap."[88] Filling the gap with daemons, then, the Middle Platonists constructed a cosmic map whose "middle zone" embodied the dialogical dynamic that activated the whole system. The fixing of boundaries on this map was not repressive but rather creative of a space within which "an interpretive and ministering nature" (tēn hermeneutikēn kai diakonikēn phūsin), as Plutarch called it, came to expression.[89]

For Plutarch, the daemon functions as the capacity of every person to construct a framework within which to interpret experience. "Floating on the surface in contact with the person's head," the daemon-as-hermeneut saves human beings from the "shipwreck" of the unreflected life: "When we

[86] See Jonathan Z. Smith, "Towards Interpreting Demonic Powers in Hellenistic and Roman Antiquity," pp. 425–439.

[87] Ibid., p. 429.

[88] John Dillon, The Middle Platonists, p. 317; cf. Apuleius, De deo Socratis 6 (ed. and trans. Beaujeu, p. 26).

[89] Plutarch, De defectu oraculorum 416F (text and trans. in Babbitt, p. 388).

are head over ears in the welter of worldly affairs . . . [daemons] allow us to fight our way out and persevere unaided, as we endeavor by our own prowess to come through safe and reach a haven."[90] Susceptible to the turmoil of human emotion and suffering (*pathē thnēta*), daemons also possess divine power (*theou dūnamin*)—which is to say that daemons figure a particular kind of sensibility that avoids being overwhelmed by circumstance and looks instead for patterns of meaning, however somber their figurations might be.[91]

Dreams are one of the expressions of the daemonic imagination. On his cosmic map, Plutarch located all daemonic phenomena, including dreams, in the region of the moon. Subject to waxing and waning, the moon was a fitting locale for the transformative negotiation of boundaries signified by the daemonic.[92] In his work *The Divine Vengeance*, Plutarch provided a striking description of this locale, a description that forms part of a sightseeing journey of a disembodied soul in the middle region of the cosmos.

> He saw in the distance what he took to be a large crater [mixing bowl] with streams pouring into it, one whiter than sea-foam or snow, another like the violet of the rainbow, and others of different tints, each having from afar a luster of its own. On their approach the crater turned out to be a deep chasm in the ambient, and as the colors faded, the brightness, except for the white, disappeared. He beheld three daemons seated together in the form of a triangle, combining the streams in certain proportions. . . . "This [says the soul-guide] is an oracle shared by Night and the Moon; it has no outlet anywhere on earth nor any single seat, but roves everywhere throughout humankind in dreams and visions; for this is the source from which dreams derive and disseminate the unadorned and true, commingled, as you see, with the colorful and deceptive."[93]

Pictured here as products of a cosmic mixing bowl in which the true and the deceptive are mingled, dreams partake of the necessary ambiguity of the daemonic sensibility in which only close examination can distinguish between the deceptive colorations of the surface and unadorned insightfulness.[94] If daemons represent for Plutarch the potential for living a life

---

[90] Plutarch, *De genio Socratis* 591D–E, 593F (text and trans. in De Lacy and Einarson, pp. 471, 483).

[91] Plutarch, *Def. or.* 416C–D (text and trans. Babbitt, pp. 384, 386); the phrase "sombre figuration" is the title of a poem by Wallace Stevens (in *Opus Posthumous*, ed. Morse, p. 66). For a contemporary discussion of somber figuration as it pertains to an imaginal realm that mediates between mind and experience, see David L. Miller, *Christs*, xxii–xxiv.

[92] Plutarch, *Def. or.* 416C–F (text and trans. in Babbitt, pp. 384–88); see the discussion by Dillon, *Middle Platonists*, pp. 216–17.

[93] Plutarch, *De invidia et odio* 566B–C (text and trans. in De Lacy and Einarson, pp. 286–88).

[94] On the colors of the daemonic streams that mingle to form dreams, De Lacy and Einarson remark that "the white corresponds to the truth in dreams, the varied colors to their

well-examined in the midst of its alternating rhythms, then the means of examination must themselves also be closely examined; only then will the "flower and radiance" of the soul's power of discernment be disclosed.[95]

Writing in the mid-second century, some fifty years after Plutarch, Apuleius used his predecessor's ideas in the development of his own demonological theory, although he was more systematic in his attempt to define the nature and activities of the daemons.[96] A Latin writer, Apuleius nonetheless adopted the Greek term *daemon* as the most appropriate designation for these aerial beings in his major work devoted to them, *De deo Socratis*.[97] Elsewhere, however, he experimented with Latin names—*genius, numen, deus, lemur, manes, larva, lar*.[98] This is an intriguing list, because it shows Apuleius' tendency, more explicit than Plutarch's, to understand daemons as deeply embedded in human affairs. Several of these terms—*lemur, larva,* and *manes*—refer to ghosts of the dead, ancestral shades, while *lar* refers to domestic deities and *genius* to an individual's tutelary spirit. In light of this list, daemons appear to be those factors that enlarge the sphere of the merely personal by putting it in touch—"ghosting" it—with the collective wisdom of the human community.

Apuleius' generic name for the daemons in *De deo Socratis*—*potestates*—has been characterized as "a personalization of power," but I think that Apuleius' conceptualization of these "powers" can be more adequately conveyed if they are understood as psychic "abilities."[99] This is so because Apuleius describes the guardian daemons, in whom he is most interested, as "lodged like an intimate guest deeply in the mind," where they "inspect all and know all, like the conscience" (*omnia visitet, omnia intellegat, in ipsis penitissimis mentibus vice conscientiae deversetur*).[100] It is this superior class of

---

deceptiveness; at a distance, (that is, when one does not examine closely), the deceptive and many-colored is more prominent; close at hand the white predominates" (*Plutarch's Moralia,* 7:289, note e). For a discussion of the term *poikilos,* "many-colored," as a description of the world of movement, multiplicity, and ambiguity, see Marcel Detienne and Jean-Pierre Vernant, *Cunning Intelligence in Greek Culture and Society,* pp. 18–20.

[95] Plutarch, *Def. or.* 432C (text and trans. in Babbitt, p. 466).

[96] For a comparison of Plutarch's and Apuleius' theories of the daemon, particularly as they apply to the daemon of Socrates, see P. G. Walsh, "Apuleius and Plutarch," pp. 20–32. For a detailed discussion of Graeco-Roman thought on daemons, including the theories of Plutarch and Apuleius, see Frederick E. Brenk, S. J., "In the Light of the Moon: Demonology in the Early Imperial Period," pp. 2068–2145.

[97] Apuleius, *De deo Socratis* 6.133 (ed. and trans. Beaujeu, p. 26).

[98] See the discussion by Brenk, "In the Light of the Moon: Demonology in the Early Imperial Period," p. 2134, and by Jacqueline Amat, *Songes et Visions,* pp. 161–63.

[99] Brenk, "In the Light of the Moon: Demonology in the Early Imperial Period," p. 2134. The word in question, *potestates* (*De deo Soc.* 6.133), "powers," can also mean "abilities." See Lewis and Short, *A Latin Dictionary,* s.v. *potestas.*

[100] Apuleius, *De deo Soc.* 16.156 (ed. Beaujeu, p. 36; my translation). The verb *deversor* carries the sense of "tarrying" or "lodging anywhere as a guest." See Lewis and Short, *A Latin Dictionary,* s.v. *deversor.*

daemons, says Apuleius, that "furnish each person with witnesses and guardians of everyday life, continually present as watchers of our acts and thoughts."[101] Apuleius mentions by name only two of these mental guests—*Amor*, "love," and *Somnus*, "sleep."[102] Sleep is important in this context because, as Apuleius had noted earlier in his discussion, one of the important offices of the daemons as interpreters is the fashioning or skillful shaping of dreams.[103] Sleep, then, is as important an activity as love, because it provides the occasion for the "intervention" of oneiric signs, particularly in situations of distress, obscurity, and danger.[104]

Thus for Apuleius as for Plutarch, the placement of oneiric phenomena in a daemonic context was not a demotion of dreams to irrationality. Instead, his daemonizing of dreams was based on his view of such "sign languages" as an important psychic apparatus with distinctive ethical overtones, "promoting the good," as Apuleius says, by encouraging an interpretive, selective, meditative style of perception.[105] Dreams retained their connection with the future, but, as with the Stoics, it was a future conceived in the mode of *praesagia*—of the presentiments and forebodings that stem from insightful engagement with experiences in the present.[106]

As a daemonic language—that is, as a medium of exchange between an ideal world (of the gods) and a flawed world (of human beings)—the dream can provide a discourse for articulating the need for finer tuning of the sensibilities. Nowhere is this use of dream-discourse clearer than in Apuleius' novel *Metamorphoses*. The protagonist of the novel, Lucius, is presented at the outset as a young man with a serious flaw of character that might best be described as thoughtlessness: in his curiosity about magic, he is disregardful of the laws of nature, and in his confusion of love with lust, he is manipulative with regard to other human beings.[107] Turned into an ass, a literal reflection of his flawed perspectives, Lucius is made to suffer the human condition deeply as he is subjected to a variety of cruel and perverted behaviors.[108] His recognition of his own need for reflective engagement with the world, which in his case involves giving up his pretentious willful-

---

[101] *De deo Soc.* 16.155 (ed. and trans. Beaujeu, p. 36).

[102] Ibid. (ed. and trans. Beaujeu, pp. 35–36).

[103] Ibid. 6.134 (ed. and trans. Beaujeu, p. 27): *somnis conformandis*.

[104] Ibid. 16.156 (ed. and trans. Beaujeu, pp. 36–37).

[105] Ibid. (ed. and trans. Beaujeu, p. 37).

[106] Ibid. 6.134 (ed. and trans. Beaujeu, p. 27).

[107] In *Metamorphoses* 11.15, a priest of Isis observes that Lucius' woe stems from lust and curiosity. See the discussion by J. Gwyn Griffiths, *Apuleius of Madauros: The Isis-Book (Metamorphoses, Book XI)*, pp. 47–49 (text of *Meta.* 11.15 in Griffiths, p. 86).

[108] Most of the novel (Books 4–10) deals with the various torments endured by Lucius as ass; see Martin's discussion of Lucius' experiences from the perspective of Hellenistic cosmology and soteriology in *Hellenistic Religions*, ch. 1: "The Golden Ass in a Labyrinthine World," pp. 16–34.

ness, is presented as a dream of the goddess Isis. Apuleius presents this oneiric exchange between the divine and the human as a rebirth "from the depth of trouble" to a renewed humanity.[109] Dream-language and the negotiation of psychological change form a pair. Thus when dreams were seen as a daemonic production, they took on an epistemological function as sources of self-awareness and ethical reflection.

DREAMS AND ANGELS

Graeco-Roman thinkers populated the intermediary regions of the cosmos with a wide variety of message-bearers that could appear in or as dreams. Along with the daemons were the angels, whose oneiric agency is noted in a variety of religious texts that span the spectrum of polytheist, Jewish, and Christian thought and practice. In the context of the fabrication, sending, and interpretation of dreams, the angels, like the daemons, formed part of what Michel Foucault has called a "technology" of the self, a hermeneutics of self-knowledge that enabled the dreamer to express a sense of "an upward extension of the individual," as Peter Brown has phrased it.[110]

In the Greek magical papyri, oneiric angels "extended the individual upward" by functioning as "detectives of the heart's secrets."[111] Appearing both in rituals to induce a dream in oneself or to send a dream to someone else, these angels were part of a late-antique cultural practice of exploring psychic terrain by petitioning and manipulating imaginal figures conceived of as existing outside of and usually "higher" than oneself. As John Winkler has astutely observed, in magical ritual the psyche is a place of performance for the staging of self-dramatizations that "provide an unusually intimate picture of private and heart-felt anxieties."[112]

Although angels are not the only figures associated in the magical papyri with the inducing and sending of dreams, they are among the most prominent.[113] In one text (*PGM* VII.862–918), which appears to stem from the same thought-world that produced Plutarch's lunar daemons who weave dreams, the moon-goddess Selene sends forth twelve angels, each of whom

[109] See Griffiths, *Apuleius of Madauros: The Isis-Book (Metamorphoses, Book XI)*, pp. 51–52, for a discussion of Apuleius' use of the term *renatus*, "reborn."

[110] Brown, *The Making of Late Antiquity*, p. 68.

[111] The latter phrase comes from Winkler, *The Constraints of Desire*, p. 71. Winkler uses the phrase to describe the physiognomist Polemo's practice of plumbing the depths of human character by reading signs of the body's surface; I have appropriated the "detecting" trope to describe the action of dream-angels in magic because, as I will argue, they too specialized in discerning "the heart's secrets."

[112] Winkler, *The Constraints of Desire*, p. 73.

[113] See the discussion by Samson Eitrem, "Dreams and Divination in Magical Ritual," p. 176.

presides over one hour of the night.[114] Doing the bidding of Selene, here called "gracious daimon, lady of the night," these "nocturnal hour-angels," as Eitrem called them, are effective in the sending of dreams.[115] Although this spell will "send dreams until you accomplish what you want" (1.918), its stated form of accomplishment is erotic. Prior to the naming of the hour-angels, the spell directs the practitioner to ask Selene to "give a sacred angel or a holy assistant who serves this very night, in this very hour . . . and order the angel to go off to her, NN ("so-and-so"), to draw her by her hair, by her feet; may she, in fear, seeing phantoms [*phantazomenē*], sleepless because of her passion for me and her love for me, NN, come to my conse-crated bedroom" (11.884–890). Here it would appear that the angel does not simply send a dream; it is itself the dream, because the object of desire is made to see something from the realm of the phantasmal that is so often the locus of dreams. Although the therapeutic role of dreams in magic will be explored more thoroughly in a later chapter, it is important to note that this dream is dramatizing, and so negotiating, a difficult psychic terrain, that of erotic attraction and desire. An "angelized" consciousness can use dreams to express the depths of human longing and need.

Message-bearing figures in the magical dream oracles are often repre-sented along Homeric lines as shapes that appear to the dreamer rather than as part of narrative tableaux. This is true of angels as well. *PGM* VII.478–90 begins by petitioning Eros to "send me my personal [angel] tonight to give me information about whatever the concern is."[116] Similarly, in "Pythag-oras' request for a dream oracle and Demokritos' dream divination" (*PGM* VII.795–845), "the entering angel" enters "in the form of your friend whom you recognize" and reveals the matters of concern "through dreams with accuracy."[117] The *Sepher ha-Razim,* a Jewish magical text, lists forty-four angelic names and then observes that "these are the names of the angels in charge of dreaming, to make anyone who approaches them in purity know what the dream (was) and what its interpretation is."[118] In the context of angels, the character of the dream as a scene of recognition and a trope for accurate personal information is clear.

In texts from philosophical and apocalyptic Judaisms of the early centu-ries of the Graeco-Roman period, the oneiric angel again functions as a kind of *agent provocateur* that opens the mind of the dreamer to unexamined dimensions of what might seem at first sight to be a very mundane world. As the American poet Wallace Stevens wrote, the "Angel of Reality" is a "Nec-

---

[114] *Papyri Graecae Magicae* VII.900–910 (ed. Preisendanz, 2:39–40).

[115] Eitrem, "Dreams and Divination in Magical Ritual," p. 180; for the titles of Selene in this text, see *PGM* VII.881 (ed. Preisendanz, 2:38).

[116] *PGM* VII.478 (ed. Preisendanz, 2:22; trans. Betz, p. 131).

[117] Ibid. VII.796–99 (ed. Preisendanz, 2:35; trans. Betz, p. 140).

[118] *Sepher Ha-Razim,* "The First Firmament," lines 210–17 (trans. Morgan, pp. 40–41).

essary Angel" because in its sight "you see the earth again."[119] This sort of poeticized "seeing again," but as though for the first time, was given a theological foundation in the work of Philo of Alexandria. For Philo, the angels were "divine words" (*logoi theioi*) that effected the manifestation, in human life, of the *logos*, the hypostatized intelligence of God.[120] As he says in his essay *On Dreams*, angels are the "ears and eyes" of God:

> These are called daemons by the other philosophers, but the sacred record [Scripture] habitually calls them angels, using an apter title, for they both convey the biddings of the father to his children and report the children's need to their father. In accordance with this they are represented by the law-giver as ascending and descending: not that God, who is already present in all directions, needs informants, but that it was a boon to us in our sad case to avail ourselves of the services of words (*logois*) acting on our behalf as mediators.[121]

Philo here uses an image from Jacob's dream in Genesis 28:12–16, in which angels are ascending and descending on a ladder that connects heaven with earth, to describe the cosmic movement of angels as they mediate between the divine and the human. Elsewhere in this essay, however, Philo uses the figure of the stairway as a psychological trope: in human beings, the stairway is the soul, which connects the mind with sense-perception. Up and down the "stairway" of everyone's soul, angels are in constant motion, infusing us with what Philo calls a "healing breath."[122] Angels heal; they provide a therapy of consciousness whereby "seeing the earth again" means to reconceive human experience as the arena for a heavenly journey.[123]

In Philo's terms, angels conduct the soul on its heavenly journey. One of the forms that this journey takes is the dream. In fact, dream, divine word, and angels are so closely associated in Philo's dream-theory that it is difficult to distinguish between them in a categorical sense.[124] Philo's account of

---

[119] Wallace Stevens, "Angel Surrounded by Paysans," in *The Collected Poems of Wallace Stevens*, p. 496. I am indebted to Miller, "Theologia Imaginalis," pp. 2–3, for his discussion of Stevens's angel as a trope of the imagination.

[120] Philo, *De somniis* 1.148 (text and trans. in Colson and Whitaker, p. 375). For discussions of Philo's conception of the *logos* in connection with angels and daemons, see Alan F. Segal, *Two Powers in Heaven*, pp. 162–75, and Brenk, "In the Light of the Moon: Demonology in the Early Imperial Period," pp. 2104–5. Also useful are Dillon, *Middle Platonists*, pp. 158–66, 171–74, and Robert M. Berchman, *From Philo to Origen*, pp. 27–53.

[121] *De som*. I.140-42 (text and trans. in Colson and Whitaker, p. 373).

[122] Ibid. I.146–48 (text and trans. in Colson and Whitaker, p. 375); cf. ibid. I.69 (p. 333), where Philo says that God's *logoi* "act as physicians of the soul and completely heal its infirmities" by giving "holy instructions" (*paraineseis hieras*).

[123] On the heavenly journey as a major thematic in Philo's thinking, see Segal, *Two Powers in Heaven*, pp. 171–72.

[124] *De som*. I.1–2 and 190 (text and trans. in Colson and Whitaker, pp. 295, 399).

Jacob's dream of the angelic ladder, to which much of *On Dreams* is devoted, presents the dream as a "divine word" that "offers itself as a fellow-traveller to a lonely soul."[125] In this overdetermined image, the angel is the speech of the dream, the form of the dream, as well as the ability to conceptualize experience with a poetic, "angelic" eye. As Philo says, interpreters of dreams are able to "track the scent through symbols."[126] Thus, as angel, the dream is a journey through a vast array of theological signs that signal the wellspring of meaning in human life.

Like Philo, many apocalyptic writers saw the angel, the dream, and the heavenly journey as interconnected phenomena. However, unlike Philo, who presented his views in the form of allegorical interpretation of Scripture, apocalyptists presented their views of what is ultimately real as dreams and visions that they had themselves experienced. Following the Graeco-Roman cultural convention that dreams were not the personal property of dreamers but were rather sent from a divine source, many of these texts begin with a visionary blow to the author's mundane consciousness. Thus the *Ethiopic Book of Enoch* recounts that its author's "eyes were opened by the Lord, and he saw a holy vision in the heavens which the angels showed to me." Later, the same author says, "And behold, a dream came to me, and visions fell upon me. . . ."[127] Different from the ascending and descending dream-angels of Philo's imagination, these dreams seem to be invasive, and they open the eyes, usually to elaborately detailed secrets about the composition and intentions of the heavenly spheres.[128]

Usually these apocalyptic dream-visions are not presented as though they were themselves angels. Instead, angels are said to preside over true visions, or the dream consists of a conversation between an angel and the person receiving the revelation.[129] In a sense, the dreamer is himself given angelic mobility as he ascends through the ranks of the heavenly spheres. The point of recounting these heavenly journeys is not simply to dazzle the reader with fantastic descriptions of the divine dwelling places; rather, angelic instruc-

---

125 Ibid. I.71 (text and trans. in Colson and Whitaker, p. 333).

126 Philo, *De Iosepho* 7 and 104 (text in Colson, pp. 145, 191; my translation). In both these passages, Philo uses the verb *ichnēlatēsai*, which carries the sense of tracking an animal by scent or other signs, such as footprints. For a discussion of the word *ichnos* in Graeco-Roman hermeneutical contexts, see Patricia Cox, "'Adam Ate from the Animal Tree': A Bestial Poetry of Soul," pp. 179–80.

127 *1 Enoch* 1.2; 13.8 (ed. and trans. Knibb, 2:57, 94). For examples of other apocalyptic dream-angels, see D. S. Russell, *The Method and Message of Jewish Apocalyptic*, p. 163.

128 On the phenomenon of the invasive dream, see Patricia Cox Miller, "'All The Words Were Frightful': Salvation By Dreams in the Shepherd of Hermas," p. 329. A thorough discussion of the motif of the heavenly journey in late-antique texts, including especially apocalyptic texts, can be found in James D. Tabor, *Things Unutterable*, pp. 57–111.

129 A good example is *The Testament of Levi* 2.5–8.19, which is a lengthy conversation between Levi and a dream-angel (ed. and trans. Hollander and De Jonge, pp. 132–55). An interesting early Christian example of a dialogue between a dreamer and angels is *The Vision of Dorotheus* (ed. and trans. Kessels and Van Der Horst, in *VC* 41 [1987]:313–59.

tion aims at teaching both the standards and the rewards for ethical behavior.[130] The conversational quality of many of these angelic dream-journeys, as well as the mobile view of the mind that they seem to imply, appear to me to be important indicators of how the human being is conceptualized in an oneiric context. Driven by a dialogical dynamic, consciousness is permeable (even if it has to be invaded!) to reflection on the constituents of a qualitative life, one not enslaved to the vagaries of the everyday.

The use of angels as a way of picturing interior conversations of the self with its own, "higher," ideas was current among Christian writers as well. Hermas, a Roman Christian of the late first century, wrote about his "angel of repentance," a permanently indwelling figure that instructed him in dreams about moral issues.[131] In the third century another Roman, Natalius, had been misled into theological error, embracing a heretical view of the Christ as merely human. Often warned in visions about the danger of this erroneous stance, as the church historian Eusebius reports, Natalius "was at last scourged all night long by holy angels" and, displaying his dream-inflicted bruises, he went to the bishop to repent.[132] In the next century, the distinguished exegete Jerome reported a dream in which he, too, was whipped by a "judge" as punishment for his enjoyment of pagan literature.[133] Apparently this kind of interaction with a dream-angel was a technique for confronting a bad conscience, a re-viewing of one's intentions with the goal of redirecting them and so minimizing inner turmoil. As in the magical papyri, dream and angel function together as tropes for an interior dialogue in which heartfelt anxieties are explored.

Despite all of the foregoing testimony to the conviction that dream-speech is angelic, some in late antiquity did not share this perspective. As Lane Fox has observed, "To the Jews, demons were not the ambiguous intermediaries whom pagans placed between gods and men; they were outright agents of evil, the troupe of Satan himself."[134] The splitting of the daemons into unambiguous bands of good and evil forces—already evident, it would seem, in Philo's preference for the Biblical term *angel*—is clear in the following statement from the Talmudic tractate *Berakoth:*

When Samuel had a bad dream, he used to say, "The dreams speak falsely."
When he had a good dream, he used to say, "Do the dreams speak falsely, seeing

[130] See, for example, the many passages of judgment and exhortations to righteousness in *1 Enoch* and *The Testament of Levi*, as well as the discussion by Tabor, *Things Unutterable*, pp. 75–76, and his bibliographical notes 1 and 33 on pp. 98, 102.
[131] *Shepherd of Hermas, Vision* 5.7 (text and trans. in Lake, p. 71). See the discussion by Lane Fox, *Pagans and Christians*, pp. 381–87, especially pp. 386–87, where the angelic instructions in virtue, morality, and social responsibility are treated.
[132] Eusebius, *Ecclesiastical History* 5.28.10–12 (text and trans. in Lake, p. 521). For Natalius' historical context, see Robert M. Grant, *Eusebius as Church Historian*, pp. 91–93.
[133] Jerome, *Ep.* 22.30 (*CSEL* 54:190–91).
[134] Lane Fox, *Pagans and Christians*, p. 327.

that it is written, 'I [God] do speak with him in a dream.'?" Raba pointed out a contradiction. It is written, "I do speak with him in a dream" [Num. 12:6], and it is written, "the dreams speak falsely" [Zech. 10:2].—There is no contradiction; in the one case it is through an angel, in the other through a demon.[135]

In this passage, an apparent contradiction in Scripture is resolved by recourse to the dichotomy between angelic and demonic inspiration. In the early Christian community, some appealed to the same dichotomy, but the context in which it was used was not Biblical exegesis but theological polemic.

Among the apologists of the second century whose aim was to prove to the Roman world that Christianity was a rational religion worthy of legitimate status, the attack on dreams took the form of an attempt to show that Christians have no truck with demons. Thus Justin Martyr warned the readers of his first apology that they should be on their guard against demons who would try to cloud their apprehension of the truth of Christianity through appearances in dreams and in magic.[136] Similarly, Athenagoras in his plea on behalf of Christianity warned that a "tender and susceptible soul which is ignorant of sound teaching" is prey to the irrational fantasies of demons who bedevil the soul in dreams.[137] In the third century, Clement of Alexandria took another line of attack: for him, proving the superior qualities of the Christian religion entailed a demonstration of the fantastic foolishness of the polytheist traditions. Among those ruled by the "tyranny of demons" are practitioners of divination, including specifically those who interpret dreams (*tous oneirōn kritas*). Such structures of religious knowledge are impious sophistry, "gambling games of pure illusion."[138]

Theological polemic within the Christian community itself also provided a basis for linking dreams and demons. In this context, concern was focused on Simon the Magician, a Samaritan Christian who became infamous, in heresiological speculation, as one of the founders of Gnosticism.[139] According to heresiologists Irenaeus and Hippolytus, Simon and his followers were addicted not only to oddities of theological belief but also to magic: "The disciples of this [magus] celebrate magical rites, and resort to incantations. And [they profess to] transmit both love-spells and charms, and the demons said to be senders of dreams, for the purpose of distracting whom-

[135] *Berakoth* 55b (trans. Simon, p. 341).

[136] Justin, *Apology* 1.14 (trans. Richardson, p. 249).

[137] Athenagoras, *Legatio* 27 (trans. Richardson, p. 330).

[138] Clement of Alexandria, *Protrepticus* 1.3.2 and 2.11.2–3 (ed. and trans. Mondésert, pp. 55, 67–68). For a discussion of early Christian associations of dreams, demons and magic, see Amat, *Songes et Visions*, pp. 159–96.

[139] Simon first appears in the New Testament, in Acts 8:9. See the detailed discussions of Simon in Simone Pétrement, *A Separate God*, pp. 233–46, and Robert M. Grant, *Gnosticism and Early Christianity*, pp. 70–96.

ever they please.”[140] This “Simonian fantasy” persisted well into the fourth century, when the author of the *Clementine Homilies* staged a literary debate between the apostle Peter and Simon. Representing orthodoxy, Peter firmly links dreams with demons and with insecure knowledge and tellingly contrasts phantasmal appearances—“apparitions”—with revelation, conceived as a face-to-face encounter with Christ.[141] When heresy was the issue, dream, demon, and magic formed a convenient unholy triad for use in distinguishing types of imaginal knowledge: my angel is your demon, just as my (true) revelation is your (false) dream.[142]

This astonishing array of opinion regarding the placement of dreams in the context of angelic (or demonic) figures surely underscores the mediatorial function of dreams in Graeco-Roman culture at large. But it also shows how important the ideological context and conviction of individual interpretations were in the assigning of value to the oneiric imagination. In situations of social and theological conflict, as in the Christian apologetic and heresiological battles just considered, the phenomenon of dreaming could be used negatively as a polemical weapon against those who threatened a community's self-definition, whether from within or without. However, in situations of personal crisis—whether of conscience or erotic desire—as well as in contexts of the formulation of communal and theological ideals, dreaming provided an ideational ground for the negotiation and expression of emotion and idea. Overall, when dreams appear under the trope of the angel, they can be considered as ancient anticipations of what David Miller has called *theologia imaginalis*, a way of figural thinking in which images give tangibility to our sense of what really matters. Addressing the angel in particular, Miller observes that “if Angels as images are the differentiations of being, then the goings and comings, ascendings and descendings, the ups and downs on whatever ladders there may be—all these give slant, inclination, leaning, climate, atmosphere, perspective.”[143] The same could be said for the late-antique sense of angels as dreams.

DREAMS AND THEOLOGICAL PSYCHOLOGY

Most of the late-antique theorists of dreams agreed that dream-speech was divine speech. Apart from nightmares and nocturnal visions inspired by

---

[140] Hippolytus, *Refutation of All Heresies* 6.15 (*ANF* 5: 80–81); cf. Irenaeus, *Against Heresies* 1.23.4 (*ANF* 1:348).

[141] Pseudo-Clement, *Homilies* 14–19 (*GCS* 42:236–40).

[142] On magic as a polemical category, see Alan F. Segal, “Hellenistic Magic: Some Questions of Definition,” pp. 349–75.

[143] Miller, “Theologia Imaginalis,” pp. 12–13. See especially the discussion on p. 12 of the etymology of the word *ladder* and its association with matters of “slant, inclination, and leaning.”

demons or anxiety, dreams were thought to be somehow significant and divinely appointed, although the mechanics of their relation to the gods was subject to debate.[144] As Lane Fox has observed, the debate was this: "Were dreams sent by the gods themselves, or did the soul reach upwards while the senses were sleeping and somehow make contact with higher reality?"[145] On the one side of the debate—the position that dreams were sent by the gods themselves—was the influential Homeric picture in which a god or goddess sends a dream to a sleeper. In the *Odyssey*, for example, Athena makes a figure of dream in a woman's form to send to the grieving Penelope.[146] Later authors carried on and elaborated this view. In the *Metamorphoses*, Ovid pictured the god Hypnos counterfeiting a dream by sending Morpheus to a human dreamer as a phantasm of her husband.[147] Aelius Aristides, the second-century rhetorician, saw innumerable dreams in the very form of their sender, the healing god Asclepius.[148] Emblematic of the other side of the issue—the position that the soul reached upward in dreams to the sphere of divinity—were the views of the fourth-century Christian theologian Athanasius, who imagined the dreaming soul as a rational and immortal traveler.[149]

These two positions regarding the source of dreams were not in serious contention with each other as exclusive explanatory perspectives. In fact, most dream theorists viewed them as two intertwined dispositions regarding the production of dreams. Among those who gave sustained theoretical attention to the joint involvement of god and soul in dreaming—that is to say, among those who situated dreaming in theological psychology—were Tertullian of Carthage, in the early third century, and Synesius of Cyrene, in the early fifth. Because they offered particularly elegant statements of the intertwining of the two positions, their theories merit exploration in some detail.

As Jacqueline Amat has noted, "the dream that represents subconscious remorse by means of visions of punishment is a constant thematic feature of Greco-Latin literature."[150] Judging by the few actual dreams that Tertullian recorded, this was the kind of dream that interested him most, particularly when the content of the dream matched his concerns about female modesty and about the contaminating threat of polytheist ritual practices. An example is the dream he recounts in *On the Veiling of Virgins:* a young woman in the church in Carthage was wearing a veil that was too short, thus immod-

---

[144] Miller, "Re-Imagining the Self in Dreams," p. 39.

[145] Lane Fox, *Pagans and Christians,* p. 150.

[146] *Od.* 4.795–807 (ed. Stanford, p. 71; trans. Fitzgerald, p. 78).

[147] *Meta.* 11.400–750 (trans. Humphries, pp. 272–82).

[148] See pp. 33–35 above.

[149] *Contra Gentes* 31.38–44 (ed. and trans. Thomson, pp. 86–87).

[150] Amat, *Songes et Visions,* p. 100.

estly exposing her neck to public view, an act that, in Tertullian's view, was tantamount to advertising her sexual availability. This improperly veiled woman dreamed that an angel struck her on the nape of her neck while making sarcastic remarks about the elegance of her "nudity."[151] For Tertullian, the importance of this dream went beyond its function of chastizing the questionable behavior of a fellow parishioner; rather, the dream of an individual provided a theological charter of social demeanor for all women.[152] In this regard, Tertullian's biographer Timothy Barnes has aptly observed that, "as was his constant practice, [Tertullian] related his apparently abstruse reasonings to the familiar context of life in Carthage.[153]

Tertullian did have "abstruse reasonings" about dreams. He was, in fact, the first late-antique Latin author to compose a sustained oneiric theory, which occupies several chapters of his work *On the Soul*.[154] Tertullian's pronouncement that "just about the majority of people get their knowledge of God from dreams" surely puts the dream on solid theological ground.[155] Relying heavily on Stoic ideas about the salutary nature of sleep and the perpetual mobility of the soul, Tertullian argues that sleep is a natural state, part of the rational work of God (*rationale aliquod opus dei esse*).[156] No further proof of sleep as a natural state is needed than the biblical prototype of Adam, who slept as well as ate and drank. But there is more to this scriptural proof: Adam's sleep was the type of the death of Christ: "For as Adam was a figure of Christ, so Adam's sleep was a figure of the death of Christ."[157] Sleep is "so salutary and so rational" because sleep is an image (*exemplar*) of the divine dispensation.[158] As Waszink has observed, for Tertullian "the activity of the soul during sleep is an image of its survival after death, and its reanimating of the body after sleep a symbol of resurrection."[159]

Part of what makes sleep so salutary is that during sleep the soul dreams. "During sleep the soul behaves itself in such a way that it seems to be elsewhere because it conceals its presence . . . and yet during all that time it dreams. If you ask me whence these dreams proceed, I shall refer to the

---

[151] Tertullian, *De virginibus velandis* 17.3 (*CCL* 2:1226). See also Amat, *Songes et Visions*, pp. 99–101, for analysis of similar admonitory dreams in Tertullian's *De spectaculis* and *De idolatria*.

[152] Martine Dulaey, *Le Rêve dans la Vie et la Pensée de Saint Augustin*, p. 41.

[153] Timothy Barnes, *Tertullian*, p. 124.

[154] Tertullian's dream theory occupies chs. 42–57 of his *De anima* (ed. Waszink, pp. 58–78).

[155] *De an.* 47.2 (ed. Waszink, p. 65).

[156] Ibid. 43.7 (ed. Waszink, p. 59). For analyses of Tertullian's reliance on Stoic theory, see Amat, *Songes et Visions*, pp. 93–94, and Dulaey, *Le Rêve*, pp. 55–56.

[157] *De an.* 43.10 (ed. Waszink, p. 60).

[158] Ibid.

[159] Waszink, *Tertulliani De Anima*, p. 461.

special activity of the never-resting soul."[160] Always in movement because of its immortality and divinity, the soul during sleep is not able to use the parts of the body to aid in its activity, so it uses its own "parts." Tertullian offers the following image to illustrate the process of dreaming:

> Imagine a gladiator without his weapons or a charioteer without his team, miming all of the habits and efforts of his occupation: he fights, he contends, but the agitation is in vain.[161]

In this description of dreaming, the soul enacts a silent mime. As Tertullian explains, the dynamic at work here is *ecstasis*, "a withdrawing of sense-perception and an image of insanity" (*excessum sensus et amentiae instar*).[162] This view of the illusory ravings of the dreaming soul would appear to be in conflict with Tertullian's view of the rational quality of sleep, but, as Waszink has noted, "this peculiar form of ecstasy is not a real insanity, but only an image of it; it has the task to take the mind out of itself, not to shatter it."[163] Further, Tertullian continues to affirm the ability of dreams to convey truth, divine truth not the least.[164]

Nonetheless, Tertullian's theory that dreams are fueled by an ecstatic force that obscures the reason introduces an ambiguity into his view of dreaming as an activity of the soul, particularly because he argues earlier in *On the Soul* that *ecstasis* is an invasive force that the soul suffers rather than a power that it exercises.[165] This ambiguity about the dynamics of dreaming is reflected in his fourfold classification of types of dreams, in which the types of dreams are distinguished by their source.

The first category is also the largest: these are the dreams that are inflicted on us by demons, whom Tertullian characterizes as continually flying around in the air, "afflicting human beings with imaginings (*imaginibus*) not only in temples but also in their bedrooms."[166] As in the discussion above of the connection that some Christians made between dreams and demons, this idea that demons can counterfeit divine power by producing dreams was standard apologetic fare. The second category consists of dreams that come from God. These are the dreams that edify, and Tertullian links them with the scriptural promise in Joel 2:28 that God will pour out

[160] *De an.* 43.12 (ed. Waszink, p. 60; trans. on p. 472).
[161] Ibid. 45.2 (ed. Waszink, p. 62).
[162] Ibid. 45.3 (ed. Waszink, p. 62).
[163] Waszink, *Tertulliani De Anima*, p. 480; see ibid., p. 481, and Amat, *Songes et Visions*, p. 94, for positions arguing that Tertullian's view of the ecstatic inspiration of dreams was due to Montanist influence on his thinking.
[164] *De an.* 46 (ed. Waszink, pp. 62–65).
[165] See Amat, *Songes et Visions*, pp. 94–95, for an analysis of Tertullian's theory in the context of prophetic revelation, and Waszink, *Tertulliani De Anima*, pp. 481–82, for Tertullian's understanding of ecstasy as a *stupor mentis*.
[166] *De an.* 46.12–47.1 (ed. Waszink, p. 65).

his spirit in prophecies, dreams, and visions.[167] Although he does not say so, the examples of admonitory dreams that Tertullian narrates in other treatises belong in this category. In both of these two categories the soul is a passive recipient of dreams, but in the third category it is an actor. This class contains dreams that "the soul is said to show to itself by means of an intent contemplation of the coherence of all things."[168] This kind of dream appears to stem from the natural, image-forming power of the soul—perhaps like the tropes of gladiator and charioteer offered earlier.[169] As oneiric theories go, the fourth category was peculiar to Tertullian: these dreams, made by the soul in connection with ecstasy and its own perpetual movement, are beyond the reach of interpretation and even of narration.[170]

Tertullian is a good example of a theorist whose categorization of dreams managed to affirm both sides of the theological debate about the source of dreams. On the one hand, they are God-sent and, as one of God's gifts to humankind, they show God's gracious disposition toward people in revealing everything in images, "thus stretching out the hand to facilitate our faith through images and parables" (*per imagines et parabolas.*).[171] Thus dreams are conceptualized as God's intervention in human life by way of a divine imagination that presents itself to the dreamer as parables of divine intention. On the other hand, dreams are ecstatic activities of the soul itself, and, however illusory their movements, they nonetheless give the world a sense of "coherence," as Tertullian says, that it would presumably not otherwise have.

Amat has argued that Tertullian situated the dream "on a middle road between the biblical and prophetic gift conferred by the Holy Spirit, and divination, a natural faculty of the soul."[172] I think she is right to explain the strains in Tertullian's oneiric theory as the product of a sometimes uneasy

[167] Ibid. 47.2 (ed. Waszink, p. 65).

[168] Ibid. 47.3 (ed. Waszink, p. 65; trans. on p. 500).

[169] Amat, *Songes et Visions*, p. 96.

[170] *De an.* 47.4 (ed. Waszink, p. 66). Waszink, *Tertulliani De Anima*, pp. 500–502, gives a detailed account of the threefold classification of types of dreams prior to and following Tertullian. Both Amat, *Songes et Visions*, pp. 97, 104–16, and Dulaey, *Le Rêve*, pp. 57–65, discuss the influence of Tertullian's oneiric theory on later Latin Christian authors. Lactantius, for example, adopted the idea of the perpetual movement of the soul, but he abandoned Tertullian's Stoic-inspired material psychology that granted the soul its own "limbs," favoring instead a view that emphasized the soul's delight in images. As Lactantius explains in his *De opificio dei* 18, when the body is asleep the soul's own perceptual sensibility flares up like a flame and engages in what Amat calls "un vagabondage imagé" (201). In the sixth hymn of his *Cathemerinon*, Prudentius presents a theory of dreams that relies on both Tertullian and Lactantius and capitalizes especially on the idea of the vagabond soul flitting about in the ethereal element that is natural to it (see Amat, *Songes et Visions*, pp. 222–24 and Dulaey, *Le Rêve*, pp. 63–65, for discussions and texts).

[171] *De an.* 43.11 (ed. Waszink, p. 60).

[172] Amat, *Songes et Visions*, p. 96.

alliance between Stoic and Christian ideas. However, given the evident preference of Tertullian for the kind of God-sent, punitive dreams suffered by the Carthaginian woman whose veil was too short, I would suggest further that he used ideas about God-sent dreams as a control on the dreaming activity of the soul itself. He seems to have been wary of the soul's own imagination, perhaps fearing that it might range beyond the theological and social confines that he thought to be appropriate.

Synesius, by contrast, was more positive about the connection between dreams and imagination. In his hands, the self as an abstract concept springs to life in a shimmering world of reflected images, where dreaming brings the soul into contact with a process of imagining that does not dissolve or obscure the real but rather gives it edge and focus.[173] For Synesius, the entire cosmos is a heterogeneous unity of "signs that appear [sēmainei] through all things."[174] With the cosmos thus completely metaphorized, dreaming functions as a semiotic code, or, perhaps better, as a therapy of the sign that allows the dreamer to negotiate experience with more confidence and also with a more reflective temper. Indeed, in Synesian theory, dreams can be a legitimization of experience insofar as they give self-awareness.[175] An example of this comes from Synesius' own experience as a writer: he reports in his treatise On Dreams that dreams had helped him write books, not only "preparing the mind and making the diction appropriate to the thought" but also criticizing his inflated style when he attempted to emulate an archaic rhetoric that was, as he says, foreign to him.[176] Thus dreaming forced Synesius to be honest with himself about his own "style"; as a therapy, the dream helped the dreamer to become more familiar with, less "foreign" to, himself.

Although he became a Christian bishop, Synesius was essentially a Neoplatonic thinker who had been schooled in this tradition in the philosophical circle of the Alexandrian teacher Hypatia.[177] His essay On Dreams, written in 405–6, was a contribution to Neoplatonic speculation on the nature of the soul, particularly regarding the soul's situatedness in phantasia, in imagination. It was in the context of the imaginative nature of the soul that Synesius elaborated his theory of dreams. Like Tertullian, Synesius believed that dreams were divine: "The god comes to one's side when one is asleep—this is the whole system of the initiation."[178] He underscores this

---

[173] Synesius, De insomniis [Peri enūpnion logos] (PG 66:1281–1320).
[174] Ibid. 2 (PG 66.1285B), for heterogeneity; ibid. 2 (PG 66.1284D), for signs.
[175] Ibid. 1–2 (PG 66.1281A–1285D).
[176] Ibid. 9 (PG 66.1308C–D; trans. Fitzgerald, p. 348).
[177] See the biography by Jay Bregman, Synesius of Cyrene, pp. 22–25 on Hypatia, and pp. 36–39 on Synesius' "conversion to philosophy" under her tutelage. Bregman argues persuasively that Synesius "wanted Christianity to be a new form of expression for Hellenism" (59). De insomniis was written in 405–6, prior to Synesius' ordination as bishop, and is thoroughly infused with late-Neoplatonic Hellenism. See Bregman, pp. 145–54.
[178] De ins. 8 (PG 66.1301C; trans. Fitzgerald, p. 343).

point with a striking, even hyperbolic, metaphor: one should consult one's bed as one would the Delphic Pythia's tripod![179] When we dream, there is an oracle in each of us. Indeed, Synesius insists upon the innate ability of everyone to imagine in this way. Furthermore, "this accessibility to all makes divination [by dreams] very humane; for its simple and artless character is worthy of a philosopher, and its freedom from violence gives it sanctity."[180] As Synesius humorously remarks, only by banishing sleep from his kingdom could a tyrant prevent people from consulting their sacred inner oracles.[181]

Open to all in principle, just as the Stoics had argued, this oracular knowledge was situated by Synesius in *phantasia*, in imagination.[182] This, the creation of dreams in fantasy, is the soul's contribution to the dreaming process. Whereas Tertullian's theology led him to emphasize the action of God in the production of dreams, Synesius' Neoplatonic psychology led him to emphasize the activity of the soul in the staging of oneiric visions. The relevant feature of Neoplatonic psychological theory concerns the *ochēma-pneuma*, the "vehicle of the soul" that functioned as an escort to the soul when it entered this world, joined it to the body, and later accompanied it on its return journey.[183] As Jay Bregman has explained, "This soul-envelope makes union with body possible, and, in the condition of union with body it becomes the faculty of imagination (*phantasia*), which functions as a connecting link between the spiritual realm and the coarser realm of sense. As such, it is the basis of sense perception and consciousness. . . ."[184] Synesius' contribution to this doctrine was "the identification of the *eidōlon* or image with the thinking subject."[185] Just as the cosmos as a whole is metaphorized, so too is the human psyche. There is an essential poet at the center of things that enables imaginal thinking.

For Synesius, *phantasia* is not something implanted in human beings as though it were a possession. Rather, *phantasia* is a realm, "the hollow gulf of the universe" in which the soul has its proper place.[186] This hollow gulf is no-thing, nothing, not a substance but a dynamic whereby body and spirit, sense and intellect, are connected. As Synesius says, body and the bodiless are like separate territories until brought together in imagination. There,

---

[179] Ibid. 7 (*PG* 66.1301A).

[180] Ibid. 8 (*PG* 66.1304A; trans. Fitzgerald, pp. 343–44). For the argument about the dream-oracle as a feature of everyone's psychic constitution, see Ibid. 8 (*PG* 66.1304C).

[181] Ibid. 8 (*PG* 66.1304D).

[182] Ibid. 5 (*PG* 66.1292D–1293C).

[183] For a history of the development of the Neoplatonic doctrine of the *ochēma-pneuma*, see E. R. Dodds, *Proclus*, Appendix II: "The Astral Body in Neoplatonism," pp. 313–21; Bregman, *Synesius*, p. 145; and Dulaey, *Le Rêve*, p. 77, on the Porphyrian doctrine that influenced Synesius.

[184] Bregman, *Synesius*, pp. 147–48.

[185] Ibid., pp. 148–50.

[186] *De ins.* 6 (*PG* 66.1297A; trans. Fitzgerald, p. 340).

however, they move from the static to the dynamic and are put in motion.[187] Imagination creates the world, and there is no perception apart from it. As the "borderland" between unreason and reason, the body and the bodiless, *phantasia* is an uncanny dynamic, "taking from both extremes as from neighbors and so imagining in one nature things that dwell far apart."[188] As uncanny, imagination is "difficult to comprehend" because "it borrows anything suitable to its purposes."[189]

In the human realm, imagination is the basis of consciousness; it is a "halfway house between spirit and matter, which makes communication between the two possible."[190] As the proper activity of the soul, *phantasia* is, according to Synesius, "a sort of life in itself," and he explains further that the imagining that happens in dreams is the most valuable, for whereas daytime knowledge comes from teachers, the knowledge in dreams comes from god.[191] Neither sense-perceptive nor intellective—that is, neither sheerly empirical nor sheerly metaphysical—dream-knowledge provides the path for ascent to what is most hidden in things. And what is most hidden is not abstruse ideas or buried gold, but new ways of coping with everyday problems and situations—not only how to tone down one's own inflamed rhetoric but also how to devise stratagems for hunting and for dealing with one's political enemies.[192] Thus, once again, the dream functions as a technique for imagining the world well, so as not to be ensnared by its literalisms.

Reinforcing his view of dreaming as part of the soul's imaginative activity, Synesius says, "If to look upon a god with one's own eye is a happy thing [here he refers to the sun as a visible god], the approach to god by imagination is the more magnificent."[193] That is to say, fantasy provides the only access to divine speech, at least from the perspective of dreams. The Synesian view that imagination is the basis of human consciousness was part of a widespread disposition in late antiquity concerning the construction of meaning. The idea of the imaginal basis of consciousness came to expression particularly when the issue concerned human knowledge of a divine or spiritual register of the real, that is, in the context of a desire to probe the depths of the visible. To offer just a few examples: Plutarch remarked that the gods speak in poetic circumlocutions, in image and metaphor; Philo spoke of tracking the scent of the divine through symbols and dreams; Plotinus said, "Everywhere we must read 'so to speak,'" suggesting that

---

[187] Ibid. 4–5 (*PG* 66.1292B–1293B).
[188] Ibid. 4 (*PG* 66.1292C; trans. Fitzgerald, pp. 334–35).
[189] Ibid. 4 (*PG* 66.1292C; trans. Fitzgerald, p. 334).
[190] Bregman, *Synesius*, p. 148.
[191] *De ins.* 3 (*PG* 66.1288B–1289A; trans. Fitzgerald, pp. 331–32).
[192] Ibid. 9 (*PG* 66.1308D–1309A).
[193] Ibid. 4 (*PG* 66.1289C; trans. Fitzgerald, p. 333).

human speech about its access to the invisible world must always carry within it a metaphoric caution; Porphyry wrote that what is dark, obscure, and resistant to shaping comes to expression as a "shadowing forth in form"; Synesius, indeed, thought that the riddling unclarity of dreams constituted their wisdom, forcing us to do the hard work of interpretation without which no life is well-lived.[194] Many in late antiquity seem to have been devoted to such a rhetoric of indirection.

This imaginal language of the hollow gulf, to borrow Synesius' phrase, was the context within which many theories and practices of dreaming assumed their importance in the construction and construal of meaning. Knowledge was constructed on principles of imagination, but these did not constitute an ephemeral world in our sense of "flights of fancy" but rather the very world in which one lived. As Synesius said, a dreamer does not return to earth upon awakening; he is already there![195] Thus when late-antique dreamers engaged in what Lane Fox called "a nightly screening of the gods," they were not fleeing from themselves or the world but delving more deeply into both.

The theories of dreams explored in this chapter were all aimed at discerning the function of dreaming in human life. Whether dreams were seen as symbolic representations of desire, or of conscience, of social etiquette, of medical diagnosis, or as descriptive of the operations of human psychology as a whole, the fact that dreams hold out the possibility of meaning was largely unquestioned. Yet the issue of *how* the dream as semiotic code was to be decoded was not addressed. Late antiquity did produce a variety of principles for the interpretation of dreams. The next chapter explores the "decoders" of dreams by focusing on those who developed taxonomic and allegorical methods for exposing the meanings lodged in oneiric images.

---

[194] Plutarch, *De Pythiae oraculis* 26.407E (text and trans. in Babbitt, pp. 333–35); Philo *De Iosepho* 7 (ed. and trans. Colson, p. 145); Plotinus, *Enn.* 6.8.13 (trans. MacKenna and Page, p. 607); Porphyry, *De antro nympharum* 4–5 (ed. Nauck, p. 58); Synesius, *De ins.* 1 (*PG* 66.1281C–1284A).

[195] *De ins.* 12 (*PG* 66.1317B).

CHAPTER THREE

Interpretation of Dreams

WHEN THE Talmud quoted R. Ḥisda as saying that "a dream which is not interpreted is like a letter which is not read," it was expressing a widely shared expectation that a message of significance lay encoded in the dream.[1] Like the words of a letter, the images of a dream were thought to offer a message and, like words, they required a hermeneutic to make them readable. Just as a letter has to be unfolded to be read, so a dream must be "unfolded" by an interpretive deciphering of its images.[2] Again, like the words in a folded letter, the images of a dream are secretively concealed until an interpretation makes them legible.

One of the interesting features of Graeco-Roman dream interpretation is its view of the dream as a text in disguise. Another rabbinic anecdote exemplifies the importance that was attached to giving verbal expression to a dream by interpretation:

> There were twenty-four interpreters of dreams in Jerusalem. Once I dreamt a dream and I went round to all of them and they all gave different interpretations, and all were fulfilled, thus confirming that which is said: All dreams follow the mouth.[3]

In this story, a single dream produces twenty-four texts—all of them true—and so confirms the view that a dream has sense only in the context of its interpretation. The supposition underlying this stance on the relationship between a dream and its interpretation appears to be that the dream itself is imagistic babble concealing sense; thus for the purposes of intelligibility, a move from the oneiric register of the visual image to the linguistic register of the textual word is necessary.

This rabbinic anecdote can itself bear another interpretation, however. If a single dream can produce twenty-four true interpretations, its images have an astounding plasticity, that is, an astounding signifying potential. Thus while the oneiric image cannot be "seen" apart from an interpretive system that ushers it into consciousness by situating it in a textual code, the polysemous quality of the image also frustrates the interpretive im-

---

[1] *Berakoth* 55a (trans. Simon, p. 337).

[2] See the discussion of the folding tablets used for letter-writing in Greek antiquity by Anne Carson, *Eros, The Bittersweet*, pp. 100–101.

[3] *Berakoth* 55b (trans. Simon, p. 341).

pulse to systematize and so limit the image's impulse to multiple signification. As exemplified by Artemidorus of Daldis in the second century C.E.,
the classifiers of dream-images operated out of one side of this equation,
namely, the position that a dream cannot be understood apart from the
conceptual apparatus that gives it status. On the other side of the equation
were allegorizers of dream-texts like Philo, Origen, and Augustine, who
operated out of an expectation of textual polysemy and thus reveled in the
convergence of infinite relationships that oneiric images set in motion.

In late antiquity, the interpreters of dreams, whether classifiers or allegorists, directed their attention less to theories of the source of dreams than
to schemas for translating dream-images into useful bodies of knowledge.
In their view, worlds were constructed in dreams—worlds of social, ethical, and exegetical import. Given their perspective that the oneiric image
was bound up with the structure of reality, interpreters recognized the
public intelligibility of their material, as in the case of Augustine's phantom with a public persona discussed earlier.[4] In the hands of such classifiers as Artemidorus and rabbinic onirologists, the dream-image functioned as a pivot upon which the dramatic plot of everyday social life
turned, while in the work of an allegorizer like Macrobius, the very public,
because all-encompassing, details of the scientific makeup of the cosmos
lay encoded in a literary dream.[5] Exposing the availability of the dream for
use as an epistemological technique was thus part of the art of the interpreters of dreams.

As Peter Brown and Luther Martin have both argued, these oneiric
strategies were firmly rooted in ordinary experiences (as Artemidorus himself insisted), which were then conceptualized in terms of relational
networks linking the self with social and cosmological arenas.[6] Similarly,
Jean-Pierre Vernant has argued that "divinatory rationality," of which the
interpretation of dreams is a part, "does not form a separate sector, an

[4] See the discussion above in Ch. 2, pp. 41–42.

[5] Artemidorus' *Oneirocritica* consists in the main of lists of dream-images together with
their largely social and economic meanings. Similar lists are included in a lengthy section of
the Talmudic tractate *Berakoth* 55a–57b (trans. Simon, pp. 337–58). Macrobius' *Commentary on the Dream of Scipio* is a lengthy allegorization of the final portion of the sixth book of
Cicero's *De re publica;* Macrobius used "Scipio's dream" as the pretext for compiling what one
commentator has called "an encyclopedia of general information and an exposition of the
basic doctrines of Neoplatonism" (Stahl, tr., *Macrobius: Commentary on the Dream of Scipio*, p.
13).

[6] Brown, *The Making of Late Antiquity,* pp. 40–41; Martin, "Artemidorus: Dream Theory
in Late Antiquity," p. 105; In *Onir.* 4, praef., Artemidorus reiterates what he says throughout
his work: "I did not rely on any simple theory of probabilities but rather on experience and
the testimony of actual dream-fulfillments" (ed. Pack, p. 236; trans. White, p. 183; in this
chapter, I will cite the page number of White's translation only when his translation is
quoted).

isolated mentality, contrasted with modes of reasoning that regulate the practice of law, administration, politics, medicine, or daily life; it is coherently included in the entire body of social thought. . . ."[7] These are intriguing statements if one draws from them what I think is their logical conclusion: if divinatory intelligence was integrated with ordinary mentality, then ordinary mentality had as one of its components a highly symbolic disposition. Synesius and others had argued that dreaming, as a mode of divinatory intelligence, was constitutive of an important dimension of the human imagination. The real issue for late-antique thinkers was not whether the mind was at home with symbol and metaphor; rather, the issue concerned how to tap that imagistic resource, how to "decode" its enigmas for the purpose of finding meaning and order in everyday life.[8]

Among interpreters of dreams, Synesius was perhaps the most optimistic with regard to the meaning-function of oneiric images. For him there was a *mantikē technē*, a "divinatory technology" within whose parameters all dreams signify.[9] Offering an unusual gloss on the Homeric gates of dreams, Synesius wrote that "the Penelope of Homer assumes that there are two gates of dreams, and makes half of them deceptive dreams, only because she was not instructed in the matter. For if she had been versed in their science [*technēn*], she would have made them all pass out through the gate of horn."[10] Synesius concludes that "we should not confuse the weakness of the interpreter with the nature of the visions themselves."[11] In marked contrast to this Synesian view of the revelatory potential of all oneiric images was the position of the master-classifier of dreams in late antiquity, Artemidorus. More circumspect with regard to the image-world, he put greater trust in the interpreter than in the dreams, thus reversing Synesius' formula. An investigation of his decoding activity, amounting to a virtual recoding of oneiric images, will open to view one way in which the semiotic explosiveness of dreaming was managed in the Graeco-Roman world.

---

[7] Jean-Pierre Vernant, *Mortals and Immortals*, p. 304.

[8] In a commentary on Jean-François Lyotard's *The Post-Modern Condition: A Report on Knowledge,* Fredric Jameson has pointed out that a metaphorizing or "storytelling" consciousness appears as problematic in the context of a scientific or positivistic framework that values "abstract, denotative, or logical and cognitive procedures" and ignores its own status as a constructed, symbolic discourse. Thus what appears as problematic to a late-twentieth-century Western reader conditioned by a scientific and technological value-perspective does not seem so to late-antique thinkers. See his Foreword in Jean-François Lyotard, *The Post-Modern Condition: A Report on Knowledge*, xi.

[9] *De ins.* 8 (*PG* 66.1305D).

[10] Ibid. 8 (*PG* 66.1305D; trans. Fitzgerald, p. 347). See Ch. 1, pp. 15–17 above for a discussion of the Homeric picture of the gates of horn and ivory.

[11] Ibid. 8 (*PG* 66.1308A; trans. Fitzgerald, p. 347).

ARTEMIDORUS AND THE CLASSIFICATION
OF DREAMS

Ramsay MacMullen has observed that in antiquity "dreams as such constitute a very large subject, studied for centuries by learned men—their handbooks published, passed on to the next generation, and so fattened into miracles of sound scholarship under the names of Artemidorus, and others."[12] The "miracle" of his own "sound scholarship," according to Artemidorus, was its empiricism. In his sometimes negative references to his predecessors, Artemidorus criticizes their books as "didactic and speculative"; their work was based on offhanded and intuitive interpretations rather than on the kind of note-taking fieldwork in which Artemidorus says he engaged.[13] In keeping with his own fastidious attention to detail, Artemidorus cites as authoritative those of his precursors who evidenced a similar regard for specialization: thus the onirological work of Antiphon of Athens is trustworthy for dreams about octopuses and squids, as is the work of Aristander of Telmessus on tooth dreams, and that of Panyassis of Halicarnassus on dreams about swimming.[14] Whether admiring or critical, Artemidorus' references to earlier onirological literature—all of which, as he explains, he had "taken special pains to procure" and read—attests to a long and popular tradition of this genre of interpretation.

Born in Ephesus, one of the intellectual centers of Asia Minor, Artemidorus lived during the Antonine Age of the second century C.E.[15] This era witnessed a remarkable renaissance of learning, and one of the distinctive features of the work produced by the savants of the era was its encyclopedic quality. Among Artemidorus' contemporaries, Philostratus wrote a comprehensive series of biographies of the sophists; the physician Galen

---

[12] MacMullen, *Paganism in the Roman Empire*, p. 60.

[13] *Onir.* 1, praef. (ed. Pack, p. 2); for a discussion of those predecessors whom Artemidorus names, see White, tr., *Artemidorus*, p. 67n.4. The dream book of Artemidorus is the only such work from late antiquity that is extant; for fragments of other onirologies, see the collection by D. del Corno, ed., *Graecorum de re onirocritica reliquiae*.

[14] *Onir.* 2.14; 1.31; 1.64 (ed. Pack, pp. 131, 37, 70).

[15] On Ephesus, see G. W. Bowersock, *Greek Sophists in the Roman Empire*, pp. 17–18. For a discussion of famous contemporaries mentioned by Artemidorus—men such as Fronto (teacher of Marcus Aurelius), Maximus of Tyre (to whom the first three books of the *Oneirocritica* are dedicated), Plutarch, and Aristides—see Roger Pack, "Artemidorus and His Waking World," p. 285. As noted by Price, the *Oneirocritica* can be dated to the mid to late second century: "The *termini post quos* are the games founded in memory of Hadrian in A.D. 138 [*Onir.* 1.26] and the gout of Fronto, born c. A.D. 95 [*Onir.* 4.22], and a rough *terminus ante quem* a reference to Artemidorus in Galen: *Corpus medicorum Graecorum*, v.9.1, p. 129, which dates to A.D. 176–9" ("The Future of Dreams: From Freud to Artemidorus," p. 10n.18).

wrote compendious volumes on medicine; Ptolemy wrote detailed astronomical and astrological treatises; and Pausanias composed his minutiae-filled traveler's guide to Greece. This interest among Antonine literati in comprehensiveness and variety characterizes the work of Artemidorus as well, and in several ways. His fieldwork, his delineation of the types of dreams, his attention to the relevance of context to oneiric meaning, and his methodology for the "translation" of dream image to experiential situation: all these bear the mark of the systematizing intellectual curiosity of his age.

Regarding Artemidorus' method for gathering information, contemporary scholars tend to characterize it in anthropological terms: he was a "participant-observer," a "field worker with theories which badly needed proof."[16] He says of himself that he had not only consulted onirological literature but also personally conversed with other professionals, including the "diviners of the marketplace" (whom some dismissed as low-class charlatans, but Artemidorus was eager for data, whatever the source).[17] Traveling in Asia Minor, Italy, Greece and its larger islands, to religious festivals and games, Artemidorus traversed a geographical range that was matched by the diversity of people from whom he collected dreams. In Lane Fox's pithy description, "his conversation and notes embraced all classes, a well-to-do woman in Italy who dreamed she was riding an elephant, members of the upper classes in the Greek cities, orators, Roman knights, a tax collector, convicts and criminals, the poor, the sick and the slaves," as well as numerous athletes, rhetors, and sophists.[18] Thus "patiently listening to old dreams and their consequences," Artemidorus founded his system of classification on an insistence that significant connections between a dream and its meaning for the dreamer are only knowable after the fact, from experience and observation, though, as Winkler noted, "a practiced inter-

---

[16] Winkler, "Unnatural Acts: Erotic Protocols in Artemidorus' *Dream Analysis*," in his *The Constraints of Desire*, pp. 23, 31; Lane Fox, *Pagans and Christians*, p. 155.

[17] *Onir.* 1, praef. (ed. Pack, p. 2). Not only was dream-divination a craft riven by professional rivalries, but also the onirologists had to compete in a market crowded with other forms of prognostic arts; see ibid. 2.69 (ed. Pack, p. 195; trans. White, p. 134), where Artemidorus says rather heatedly that everything said by

> physiognomists, the prophets who divine from dice, from cheese, from sieves, from forms or figures, from palms, from dishes, and the necromancers must be regarded as false and misleading. For the arts of these men are totally specious and they themselves do not have even the slightest knowledge of divination. Rather, they cheat, deceive and strip those that they come upon. The only things left that are true are the utterances of sacrificers, bird augurs, astrologers, observers of strange phenomena, dream interpreters, and soothsayers who examine livers.

[18] For a catalogue of the cities that Artemidorus mentions by name as places where he collected dreams, see Pack, "Artemidorus and His Waking World," pp. 284–85; see also Lane Fox, *Pagans and Christians*, p. 155.

preter will accumulate a fund of observed cases that will enable him to make shrewd diagnoses of the likely meaning of people's dreams."[19] Indeed, the development of a fund of usable prognostic material was the point of the whole enterprise.

There has been a revival of interest in Artemidorus' *Oneirocritica* among contemporary scholars because of the light it sheds on the social mores and practices of Graeco-Roman antiquity. Typical of this approach is the following statement by Winkler: "Artemidorus is therefore in the business of translating people's messages to themselves, not of influencing the content of those messages, let alone 'correcting' that content. In most cases, apart from unique and individual dreams, he naturally finds himself dealing with the whole range of common, public associations and evaluations, which makes him an excellent source for information about daily life in the ancient world."[20] Winkler and Foucault have been particularly engaged in showing how Artemidorus' material reveals the social construction of sexuality in late antiquity in terms of an "economics" of dominance and submission.[21] These are very valuable studies of the public meanings attached to sexual acts and mores, but for my purposes they distract attention from the fact that such valuations were *carried by dreams*. What is needed is a reversal of perspective that enables an exploration of late-antique conceptualizations of the dream as a hermeneutical "space" within which the personal experience of the dreamer could assume sharp focus and a sense of concrete engagement with the social world that would presumably be lacking otherwise.

The following observation by S.R.F. Price is a step in the direction of this altered perspective: "A web of metaphor connects dream imagery and the real world. The interpretation of dreams was based on normative assumptions widespread in Artemidorus' day, and dreams thus belonged not to a baffling private universe but to the public sphere."[22] This statement points to two important features of Artemidorus' view of dreams. One is that dreams do not lead inward toward repressed wishes of the psyche but outward toward matters of actual consequence for the dreamer's life.[23] Thus, for example, Artemidorus writes in his section on

---

[19] *Onir.* 1, praef. (ed. Pack, p. 2); Winkler, *The Constraints of Desire*, p. 25.

[20] Winkler, *The Constraints of Desire*, p. 30. Other socio-historical treatments of Artemidorus are Michel Foucault, *The History of Sexuality*, 3:4–36; Lane Fox, *Pagans and Christians*, pp. 155–58; Brown, *The Making of Late Antiquity*, pp. 38–41.

[21] Foucault, *The History of Sexuality*, 3:29–35; Winkler, *The Constraints of Desire*, pp. 36–41.

[22] Price, "The Future of Dreams: From Freud to Artemidorus," p. 13.

[23] On the differences in interpretive perspective between Freud and Artemidorus, see Winkler, *The Constraints of Desire*, p. 26; Price, "The Future of Dreams: From Freud to Artemidorus," pp. 18, 20–21; Martin, "Artemidorus: Dream Theory in Late Antiquity," pp. 107–8.

dreams of fire that "dreams in which rooms burn with a clear fire without falling down or being destroyed indicate riches for the poor and magisterial positions for the wealthy. But if they smolder in an impure fire, are burnt to ashes, fall to the ground, or are completely destroyed by the fire, they are inauspicious for all men and portend the death of those who are symbolized by the rooms."[24] The other important feature of Artemidorus' view toward which Price's observation points is the "web of metaphor" that he constructs in order to negotiate the ground between oneiric image and existential outcome. This is a complicated matter that merits exploration in some detail because, as in the example above, it is not immediately clear what a burning room and a governmental office have to do with each other.

Nonetheless, the conviction that there is a logic to oneiric imagery was foundational to Artemidorus' enterprise. This conviction is evident already in the word that he used to characterize his work. *Oneirokritica*, as Martin has pointed out, is properly translated not as "*interpretation* of dreams" but rather as "*taxonomy* of dreams." Derived from the verb *krino*, "to distinguish" or "to separate," *oneirokritica* "signifies an ordering or arrangement of or by dreams."[25] Actually, Artemidorus' book is a classification both *of* dreams, according to types of dreams, and *by* dreams, according to oneiric images. Systematization of the dream according to type was one of the ways in which the interpreter could "manage" oneiric phenomena by imposing a semantic structure, while systematization of the dream by the kinds of images that appear in them was another managerial technique for controlling meaning by imposing a semiotic code.

I have used the terms *semantic* and *semiotic* to designate the two kinds of taxonomic operations in the *Oneirocritica* because Artemidorus' own metaphor for his method was linguistic: "I have set down everything in an orderly fashion and as methodically and instructively as possible. . . . School teachers, once they have taught their students the values of the letters, then show them how they are to use the letters together."[26] Artemidorus attends first to "the values of the letters," that is, to the semantic register of dreams whereby they are distinguished according to type. The most basic division separates meaningful from nonmeaningful dreams. The *enúpnion*, the nonmeaningful dream, is meaningless because it simply reproduces, in sleep, the daytime preoccupations of the dreamer. In Artemidorus' succinct definition, an *enúpnion* (literally, "something in one's sleep") is "a dream that has no meaning and predicts nothing, one that is active only while one sleeps and that has arisen from an irrational desire, an

---

[24] *Onir.* 2.10 (ed. Pack, p. 115; trans. White, p. 91).
[25] Martin, "Artemidorus: Dream Theory in Late Antiquity," p. 107.
[26] *Onir.* 3.66 (ed. Pack, p. 234; trans. White, p. 175).

extraordinary fear, or from a surfeit or lack of food."[27] Artemidorus here establishes a first control over the dream-world by declaring some dreams to be, in effect, passive; they are non-significative because they are merely mimetic to the dreamer's emotional and physical excesses and sufferings.

Having thus given theoretical status to Virgil's poetic (mis)understanding of the Homeric gates of horn and ivory as productive of two types of dreams, the true and the false, or, in his terms, those that signify and those that do not, Artemidorus goes on to discuss the *oneiros*, the meaningful dream.[28] The *oneiros* functions by "calling to the dreamer's attention a prediction of future events; but after sleep, it is the nature of the *oneiros* to awaken and excite the soul [*egeirein te kai oreinein tēn psūchēn*] by inducing active undertakings. This is how it originally got its name, if it does not come from 'telling' [*eirein*] 'what is real' [*to on*]."[29] Using the kind of etymological punning that he will often employ as a means of weaving the "web of metaphor" between dream-image and actual event, Artemidorus characterizes signifying dreams with verbs of action: these dreams awaken, excite and tell. Artemidorus formally defines *oneiros* as "a movement or fiction [*kinēsis ē plasis*] of the soul that takes many shapes and signifies good or bad things that will be . . . by means of its own natural images [*di' eikonōn idiōn phūsikōn*] which are called *stoicheia* [elements or letters]."[30]

Artemidorus thought that the soul is by nature prophetic, that is, that it is naturally insightful about the ways in which actions and decisions made in the present will have consequences for the future.[31] The soul presents its

[27] *Onir.* 4, praef. (ed. Pack, p. 238; trans. White, p. 184). In *Onir.* 1.1 (ed. Pack, p. 3; trans. White, p. 14), Artemidorus specifies the *enūpnion* as follows: The *enūpnion*

indicates a present state of affairs. To put it more plainly, it is the nature of certain experiences to run their course in proximity to the mind and to subordinate themselves to its dictates, and so to cause manifestations that occur in sleep, i.e., *enūpnion*. For example, it is natural for a lover to seem to be with his beloved in a dream and for a frightened man to see what he fears, or for a hungry man to eat and a thirsty man to drink. . . . It is possible, therefore, to view these cases in which those types of experiences occur as containing not a prediction of the future state but rather a reminder of a present state.

For commentary, see Behr, *Aelius Aristides and the Sacred Tales*, pp. 184–85; Price, "The Future of Dreams: From Freud to Artemidorus," pp. 10–11; Winkler, *The Constraints of Desire*, p. 24.

[28] For Virgil, see Ch. 1, pp. 24–26 above.

[29] *Onir.* 1.1 (ed. Pack, p. 4; trans. White, pp. 14–15).

[30] Ibid. 1.2 (ed. Pack, p. 5).

[31] Ibid. 4.2 (ed. Pack, p. 246; trans. White, p. 189). Commenting on the difference between Freud and Artemidorus regarding the temporal referentiality of dreams, Winkler remarks that "Artemidorus' soul is looking to the immediate future, Freud's to the distant past," and he observes further that "at times one may wonder which is the stranger supposition—that the unconscious mind is aware of momentous changes in the offing or that it is obsessed with the remote events of one's childhood; Plutarch argues from the strangeness

insights in the form of iconized "letters," a kinetic alphabet that is not less meaningful for being fictive or invented. Thus Artemidorus virtually identifies the soul with a symbolic process whose tropes and metaphors—the oneiric images themselves—bridge the distance between the present and the future.[32] As a symbolic process, this language of the soul is not abstract but *phūsikon*, "natural" or "physical"; thus body parts (ears, eyebrows, penises, knees, and so on); activities like dancing, singing, and taking a shower; foods; flowers; garments; animals; and more provide the material that the soul uses to alert us to the things that really matter, for instance, whether death or money are in the offing, whether a friend will become an enemy, or a spouse will become unfaithful. Meaningful dreams, then, do not merely *re*-present the world; rather, they *present* it in a tangible way and awaken the dreamer to the materiality of his or her own condition.[33]

Continuing in his classification of dreams according to type, Artemidorus distinguishes between two types of the *oneiros*, the meaningful dream. One type consists of dreams that predict the future clearly and unambiguously. These are the *theōrēmatikoi*, which "come true just as they are seen," as in the example of a man at sea who dreamed of a shipwreck and barely escaped drowning when the ship actually sank the next day.[34] Because image and event correspond exactly in such dreams, they do not need interpretation, and Artemidorus devotes little space to them. It is the other type of *oneiros* that interests him. This type consists of the *allēgorikoi oneiroi*, dreams whose images are allusive; they signify through riddles (*di' ainigmatōn*) and so need interpretive intervention.[35] Allegorical dreams operate enigmatically by "signifying one thing by means of another"; for example, "if a man dreams that he sings poorly and off key, it symbolizes unemployment and poverty."[36] Negotiating the terrain between such disparate phenomena as the oneiric off-key song and actual unemployment occupies most of Artemidorus' interpretive activity in the *Oneirocritica*. The allusive quality of allegorical dreams is their most compelling quality; because they do not

---

of our powers of memory to the reasonableness of precognition, *defect. orac.* 432B" (*The Constraints of Desire*, p. 26 and n.).

[32] On the question of the source of dreams, Artemidorus' opinion wavers. See *Onir.* 1.6 (ed. Pack, p. 16; trans. White, pp. 20–21): "I do not, like Aristotle, inquire as to whether the cause of our dreaming is outside of us and comes from the gods or whether it is motivated by something within, which disposes the soul in a certain way and causes a natural event to happen to it." Despite this disclaimer, he says at one point that dreams are creations of the soul alone, but on the other hand, as Price has noticed, he also believes "that the gods are in some way involved and that their appearances in dreams are absolutely authoritative" ("The Future of Dreams: From Freud to Artemidorus," p. 16).

[33] See the discussion by Winkler, *The Constraints of Desire*, pp. 26–27.

[34] *Onir.* 4.1 and 1.2 (ed. Pack, pp. 241 and 4–5; trans. White, pp. 185 and 15).

[35] Ibid. 4.1 (ed. Pack, p. 241).

[36] Ibid. 1.2 (ed. Pack, p. 5; trans. White, p. 15); 1.76 (ed. Pack, p. 83; trans. White, p. 56).

"come true" immediately but only after a lapse of time, they give us the opportunity to develop skills of reasoning and examination.[37]

Following the distinction between theorematic and allegorical dreams, the system of classification presented by Artemidorus becomes almost dizzyingly complex. As Behr observed, "Artemidorus, in theory at least, offers a classification of allegorical dreams, which if carried to its extreme, represents eighty possible permutations."[38] The first of these subclassifications of allegorical dreams sorts them into five types according to whom or what they refer: there are dreams that concern the dreamer, dreams that pertain to a person other than the dreamer, "common" dreams that concern both the dreamer and others, dreams of civic or national import, and dreams that predict occurrences in nature like eclipses and earthquakes.[39] Two further subdivisions of allegorical dreams, each with four categories, deal with the number of images and predictions in a single dream (thus, some dreams foretell many things through many images, while others predict a few things through many images, and so on), as well as with the match between the positive or negative demeanor of a dream and its outcome (thus some dreams seem to predict a negative event but actually signify something good, while others do the reverse).[40] Interestingly, despite the care taken to detail all of these taxonomic distinctions, Artemidorus rarely refers to them when he turns to specifying the meanings of the dream-images that he had so patiently collected.[41] Useful, perhaps, for giving his project the appearance of a *technē*, a scientific art, the semantic register—that is, the classification *of* dreams—was not as compelling as the semiotic register, the classification *by* dreams.

When Artemidorus turns to explaining the methods he uses to determine the link between an oneiric enigma and what it portends, he is insistent on two points. The personal and cultural context of the dreamer must be thoroughly investigated, and attention must be given to the arrangement and interrelationships of all of a dream's images. Just as the particularities of the dreamer—identity, occupation, birth, financial status, health, age, and

---

[37] See ibid. 4.71 (ed. Pack, p. 292; trans. White, p. 214), where Artemidorus remarks that "whenever [the gods] speak in riddles [in dreams] and do not speak plainly, you must attempt to solve the riddles. For it is quite understandable that the gods veil much of what they say in mystery, since they are wiser than we and do not wish us to accept anything without a thorough examination." On the lapse of time between an *oneiros* and its fulfillment, see *Onir.* 1.2 (ed. Pack, p. 5; trans. White, p. 15): "the soul predicts everything that will happen in the future, whether the lapse of time in between is great or small. . . . It does this because it assumes that, in the interim, we can be taught to learn the future through reasoning."

[38] Behr, *Aelius Aristides and the Sacred Tales*, p. 186.

[39] *Onir.* 1.2–4 (ed. Pack, pp. 7–14). For discussion, see Behr, *Aelius Aristides and the Sacred Tales*, p. 186.

[40] *Onir.* 1.5 (ed. Pack, pp. 14–15); see Behr, *Aelius Aristides and the Sacred Tales*, p. 187.

[41] Behr, *Aelius Aristides and the Sacred Tales*, p. 187.

mood—require specification, so also the particulars of the dream need careful perusal so that each sign can be fitted properly to the whole.[42] An example of the importance of the relation between a dreamer's character and the dream's meaning is the collection of dreams by seven pregnant women, all of whom dreamed of a serpent. The serpent signified something different in each case, depending on the woman's character and position in life: the woman who was a prostitute had a child who became an adulterer, "for the serpent slips through the most narrow holes and attempts to escape detection by observers"; the slave-woman had a child who became a runaway slave, "for the serpent does not follow a straight path"; the woman who was a priest's wife had a child who became a hierophant, "for the serpent is a sacred animal and plays a part in secret rites"; and so on through all seven dreams.[43] The following is an example of the importance of attending to the entire image-complex of a dream:

> A cavalryman who had requested a military appointment from the king dreamed that he was summoned by someone, that he left the house where he was staying, descended two flights of stairs, and received from the person who had summoned him a garland of olive branches similar to those that Roman cavalrymen wear in processions. He was overjoyed and those around him were encouraged by the dream. But he failed to obtain his request. For he received the garland after he had descended rather than ascended two flights of stairs. And we say that ascents signify promotions whereas descents mean just the opposite. But the garland signified that he would marry a virgin both because a garland is bound together and because the olive tree is a symbol of a virgin, since it is sacred to the virgin-goddess.[44]

Artemidorus remarks that he has recorded this dream so that the reader will learn "that you must not devote your attention solely to the first images that appear in a dream but rather that you must consider the systematized totality of the dream images. For all those who based their interpretations upon the garland alone and did not take the descent into account misinterpreted the dream."[45]

[42] *Onir.* 1.8–9 (ed. Pack, pp. 17–19); on the importance of the arrangement of images in dreams, see 1.11, 3.66, and 4.28 (ed. Pack, pp. 20, 233, 263).

[43] *Onir.* 4.67 (ed. Pack, pp. 289–90; trans. White, pp. 212–13).

[44] Ibid. 4.28 (ed. Pack, p. 263; trans. White, p. 198). The rabbinic onirological literature, which in many ways resembles the work of Artemidorus, is similarly insistent on the importance of exact specification of the dream images. See, for example, *Berakoth* 56b (trans. Simon, p. 356): "All kinds of beasts are a good sign in a dream, except the elephant, the monkey and the long-tailed ape. But a Master has said: If one sees an elephant in a dream, a miracle will be wrought for him?—There is no contradiction; in the latter case it is saddled, in the former case it is not saddled."

[45] *Onir.* 4.28 (ed. Pack, p. 263; trans. White, p. 198).

Artemidorus clearly thought of himself as an empiricist of fantasy,[46] and contemporary scholars like Winkler have defended his use of social and cultural context to crack the code of oneiric images.[47] However, this emphasis on the contextual dimensions of Artemidorus' interpretive theory obscures his treatment of the dream as a semiotext. It is this dimension of his work that needs further exploration. For Artemidorus, the visual images of a dream function as floating signifiers, as "letters" that need a "grammar" to anchor them in a meaningful system of communication.

It is true that Artemidorus frequently used the social class of the dreamer as a control on the meaning of the dreamer's oneiric signs, and it is also true that he cautioned his reader not to ascribe "excessively difficult enigmas" to dreams, because that would be to misapprehend the "imagination of the dream" (*oneirou phantasias*).[48] Despite this awareness of the need for a managerial technique for controlling the signifying potential of oneiric images, however, Artemidorus did not suffer from an impoverished notion of poetic allusion. He was well aware of the multiple signification of images. The following lengthy extract is a stunning example of this awareness:

> The penis [in a dream] corresponds to one's parents, on the one hand, because it has a relationship with the seed. It resembles children, on the other hand, in that it is itself the cause of children. It signifies a wife or a mistress, since it is made for sexual intercourse. It indicates brothers and all blood relatives, since the relationship of the entire house depends upon the penis. It is a symbol of strength and physical vigor, because it is itself the cause of these qualities. That is why some people call the penis "one's manhood" (*andreia*). It corresponds to speech and education because the penis [like speech] is very fertile. Furthermore, the penis is also a sign of wealth and possessions because it alternately expands and contracts and because it is able to produce and to eliminate. It signifies secret plans in that the word *mēdea* is used to designate both plans and a penis. It indicates poverty, servitude, and bonds, because it is also called "the essential thing" (*anagkaion*) and is a symbol of necessity (*anagkē*).[49]

[46] See ibid. 4.28 (ed. Pack, p. 263), where Artemidorus refers to dream images as *phantasiai*.

[47] See Winkler, *The Constraints of Desire*, p. 28: "The most important feature of Artemidoros' interpretive system is his working principle that the symbols and associations of a coded dream are drawn by the soul from the individual dreamer's own cultural experience, not from a universal Book of Meanings or from the language of the gods." See also Foucault, *The History of Sexuality*, 3:29.

[48] *Onir.* 4.63 (ed. Pack, p. 286). Several modern commentators note that Artemidorus' caution with regard to hidden meaning is a major distinguishing factor between the oneiric approaches of antiquity and Freud. See Price, "The Future of Dreams: From Freud to Artemidorus," pp. 18, 36–37; Martin, "Artemidorus: Dream Theory in Late Antiquity," pp. 106–7; Winkler, *The Constraints of Desire*, pp. 26–29.

[49] *Onir.* 1.45 (ed. Pack, pp. 51–52; trans. White, pp. 38–39).

And the passage goes on, for another paragraph! There are similar extended catalogues for stars, the tongue, serpents, and flying, among others.[50] Artemidorus seems to have had a passion for the storytelling quality of such oneiric images.

There was, however, a limit to the number of "stories" such images could tell. That limit was imposed by the (deceptively simple) formula that Artemidorus used to decode the imaginative structure of the dream. The principle that undergirded all of his interpretive work was that "the interpretation of dreams is nothing other than the juxtaposition of similarities (*homoiou parathesis*)."[51] As Martin has observed, Artemidorus "classified these juxtapositions according to the formula: 'if someone dreams x, this signifies y.'"[52] Thus, for example, "thorns and prickles [in a dream] signify griefs because they are sharp, hindrances because they are capable of holding on to objects, and anxieties and sorrows because they are rough."[53] Martin concludes that "Artemidorus' dream theory was based upon a system of correspondences between dream content and dream significance established by a principle of similitude." Further, he notes, such a "systemic play of resemblance" contributed to "the circle of late antique epistemological possibility."[54]

There is no doubt that Artemidorus' interpretive rule of thumb, the "juxtaposition of similarities," was an epistemological tool designed to overcome uncertainty regarding the signification of an oneiric image. However, as an epistemological tool, it participated in the very uncertainty it was trying to overcome. In other words, Artemidorus' attempt to write the rules for the oneiric imagination fell prey to the dynamic he was trying to control. The reason was that his strategies for arriving at his juxtapositions themselves depended on the semiotic play of language. As he wove the "web of metaphor" that allowed dream-imagery to be juxtaposed with real-life events, Artemidorus relied on such devices as analogy, puns and wordplays, mythic associations, and numerological equivalents of alphabetic letters. The sense of aesthetic appropriateness that is conveyed as Artemidorus uses one or another of these strategies for establishing the intelligibility of his juxtapositions only serves to cloak the figurative ingenuity at work here.

Many of Artemidorus' juxtapositions depend for their coherence on the use of conventional metaphor, in which one thing can be compared with another because they share a particular quality or attribute. For example, "bugs [in dreams] are symbols of cares and anxieties. For bugs, like anxi-

[50] See ibid. 2.36, 1.32, 2.13, 2.68 (ed. Pack, pp. 164–65, 40–41, 126–27, 191–94).
[51] Ibid. 2.25 (ed. Pack, p. 145).
[52] Martin, "Artemidorus: Dream Theory in Late Antiquity," p. 102.
[53] *Onir.* 3.33 (ed. Pack, p. 218; trans. White, p. 166).
[54] Martin, "Artemidorus: Dream Theory in Late Antiquity," p. 102.

eties, also keep people awake at night."[55] Here the oneiric bug, the signifier, and anxiety, its signified, are comparable and so similar because they share the attribute of disturbing sleep. Long sections of the five books of Artemidorus' *Oneirocritica* consist essentially of repeated instances of these conventional metaphorical comparisons as the discussion painstakingly moves from one oneiric image to another, from apples to lobsters to walnuts. The numbing repetitiveness of this interpretive strategy led one contemporary commentator to remark that reading Artemidorus is "a somewhat penitential exercise."[56] There is some truth in this observation, but it misses the excitement of Artemidorus' enterprise as a concrete poetics of unexpected possibilities. Dream-image and lived experience are brought together in a round dance of metaphor. Furthermore, in these catalogues the oneiric image functions as what Italo Calvino has called a "magic object," "an outward and visible sign that reveals the connection between people or between events." Such objects are "charged with a special force" and become "like the pole of a magnetic field, a knot in the network of invisible relationships."[57] Most importantly, they have a narrative function, ingeniously supplied by the filaments of Artemidorus' web of connective meaning; presumably, it was for just such stories that people went to practitioners like Artemidorus.

Artemidorus' habit of supplying the connection that allowed the two terms of his comparisons to resonate as similars has the effect of making his method of decipherment seem obvious and straightforward. However, the relationships between signifying dream-images and their signified outcomes are not always so innocent. This is especially the case when he uses etymological plays on words and linguistic puns in order to establish the sense of his juxtapositions. The etymological wordplays are fairly straightforward. Dreams about watermelons (*pepones*), for example, are "auspicious for friendships and unions, for poets address what is most loved as 'my little watermelon' [*pepon*]"; because of their name (*pison*), peas are a symbol of good luck, because they are a symbol of persuasion (*peithos*); "a ram [*krios*] represents the master of the house, a magistrate, or a king. For early writers used the word *kreiein* in the sense of 'to rule,' and the ram is the ruler of the

[55] *Onir.* 3.8 (ed. Pack, pp. 207–8; trans. White, p. 161). Like Artemidorus, the rabbinic dream-corpus also depends for its meaning on a juxtapositional play of images. However, it differs in that it draws its "web of metaphor" largely from Scripture, not from conventional associations. For example, *Berakoth* 57a (trans. Simon, pp. 351–52): "R. Ḥiyya b. Abba said: If one sees wheat in a dream, he will see peace, as it says: 'He maketh thy borders peace; He giveth thee in the plenty the fat of wheat' [Ps. 147.14]. . . . If one sees in a dream a vine laden with fruit, his wife will not have a miscarriage, since it says 'thy wife shall be as a fruitful vine' [Ps. 128.3]," and so on.

[56] Pack, "Artemidorus and His Waking World," p. 282.

[57] Calvino, *Six Memos for the Next Millenium*, pp. 32–33.

flock"; when an ass (*onos*) appears in a dream, it predicts profit (*onasthai*).[58] Sprinkled throughout the *Oneirocritica*, these etymologies show how visual images are textualized for the purposes of interpretation. Furthermore, such image-texts in effect interpret themselves if one has the wits to follow the linguistic play of their letters.

This linking of quite disparate images—watermelons and friendship, for example—by means of language games is also evident in Artemidorus' use of the numerological equivalents of the Greek alphabet and in his evident delight in linguistic puns. On the topic of numbers, Artemidorus advises that "you should use the principle of equal numerical value whenever dream objects, even apart from their equal numerical values, have the same meaning as other dream objects that are equal in numerical value. For example, if a sick man sees an old woman [in a dream], it is a symbol of death. For both *graus* [old woman] and *hē ekphora* [the carrying out of a corpse for burial] are 704."[59] This is a simple instance of what Artemidorus shows in another passage to be a very complicated procedure, and his use of it suggests both his respect for the polysemous quality of the oneiric image as well as his confidence in the interpreter's ability to tame the image by bridling it with an interpretive technique.[60] Similarly, his handling of puns shows his tendency to "manage" the semiotic play of the dream image. Because puns on words run rampant through the text of the *Oneirocritica*, a single example will have to suffice. It appears to have been one of Artemidorus' favorites.

> It seems to me that Aristander gave a most felicitous interpretation to Alexander of Macedonia when he had blockaded Tyre and was besieging it. Alexander was feeling uneasy and disturbed because of the great loss of time and dreamed that he saw a satyr dancing on his shield. Aristander was in Tyre at the

---

[58] *Onir.* 1.67 (watermelons), 1.68 (peas), 2.12 (ram and ass) (ed. Pack, pp. 74, 119, 120; trans. White, pp. 51, 93–94). It is also the case in rabbinic onirology that the decoding of the similarity between a dream and its outcome by means of scriptural references can be a tricky operation. See *Berakoth* 56b (trans. Simon, p. 348):

> R. Joshua b. Levi said: If one sees a river in his dreams, he should rise early and say: "Behold I will extend peace to her like a river" [Isa. 66.12], before another verse occurs to him, viz., "for distress will come in like a river" [Isa. 59.19]. If one dreams of a bird he should rise early and say: "As birds hovering, so will the Lord of Hosts protect" [Isa. 31.5], before another verse occurs to him, viz., "As a bird that wandereth from her nest, so is a man that wandereth from his place" [Prov. 27.8].

It is clear from these and the many instances that follow that the resonating factor between the dream and its outcome is primary, and one must be quick to choose the proper scriptural verse in order to arrive at a positive valuation. Again, the ingenuity of the interpreter occupies center stage.

[59] *Onir.* 4.24 (ed. Pack, p. 259; trans. White, pp. 196 and 223n.24, for an explanation of the derivation of the number from the letters of the alphabet).

[60] See *Onir.* 2.70 (ed. Pack, pp. 196–99) for an explanation of how to use numbers as a deciphering technique.

time, in attendance on the king while he was waging war against the Tyrians. By dividing the word *satyros* into *sa* and *Tyros* [Tyre is yours], he encouraged the king to wage the war more zealously with the result that he took the city.[61]

In this and other puns, the heterogeneous elements in the juxtaposition—in this case, a satyr and military victory—can be seen as similar if one has a sense for the tricksterish behavior of language.

Thus the "similarities" are "similar" only if the proper decoding device is used. This raises the issue of the deceptive simplicity of Artemidorus' interpretive principle, that "the interpretation of dreams is nothing other than the juxtaposition of similarities." Because the elements in his comparisons are not homogeneous at all, but rather extremely heterogeneous, it is the activity of "juxtaposition" on which the burden of interpretation falls. It is here that an irony in Artemidorus' statement of his principle becomes evident, because the method he uses to harness the semiotic play of the dream-image is itself semiotic. The word used for juxtaposition, *parathesis*, is an indicator of the way in which Artemidorus' text is entangled in, indeed depends on, a semiotic play of difference rather than a mimetic mirroring of likeness.

Parathesis is the opposite of *egkrasis*, "blending." It can be defined not only as "juxtaposition" but also as "neighborhood." In grammar it designates a word composed of two discrete words that have been joined together with no change to either word. For example, *Dioskoroi*, the name of the twin sons of Zeus, is a juxtaposition, in a single word, of *Dios* ("of Zeus") and *koroi* ("young men"), the two words having been placed, as it were, in each other's "neighborhood." A parathetic word differs from words that are synthetic or composite; the latter are also words made up from two words, with the difference that one or both of the words underwent some change when combined and so were "blended."[62] Grammatically, the significant feature of *parathesis* is that both words in the combination retain their own integrity as words, and yet they come together to form a new, third word. This, I would suggest, is the way in which Artemidorus' catalogues of oneiric signifier and its signified are related to each other. The dream image and its outcome both retain their own integrity, and yet they come together through the medium of Artemidorus' decoding devices to form a "third word" in a complex of meaning in which neither would participate by itself. This is in part why it is important to remember that the dreams that Artemidorus collected had already issued in a real-life event—good luck or financial ruin or whatever—so that what he was in fact working with were two disparate but juxtaposed elements whose connection it was his job to decipher. Once he established the interpretive basis for the echoing of these

[61] Ibid. 4.24 (ed. Pack, p. 260; trans. White, p. 196).
[62] See Liddell, Scott, Jones, *A Greek-English Lexicon*, s.v. *parathesis*.

dissimilars, he could then, but only then, justify his method as one of juxtaposing similarities and use his material as a referential guide in the prognosis of new dreams.

The fact that Artemidorus' method was in principle semiotic, open to a potentially infinite play of meaning, is also indicated by the word *parathesis*. Again grammatically speaking, *parathesis* is itself a *parathesis*. *Thesis*, one of the words that form this word, means "setting," "placing," or "position." *Para*, the preposition that forms the prefix to the word, is, as Hillis Miller has noted, "a double antithetical prefix signifying at once proximity and distance, similarity and difference, interiority and exteriority. . . ."[63] Thus the word *parathesis* can mean both "setting toward" and "setting against."

The interpretive method of *parathesis* places or positions two elements next to each other, in each other's neighborhood, but it gives no guarantee whether that placement will result in similitude or difference, or in agreement or conflict, in nearness or distance. And although an interpreter like Artemidorus might choose in a univocal way to fasten on one of the meanings that is unleashed in the course of the juxtaposition, the other possibilities for meaning are still there in an untapped semiotic reservoir. Hillis Miller has described this phenomenon as ungrounded repetition, where meaning "arises out of the interplay of the opaquely similar things, opaque in the sense of riddling."[64] Significance is generated out of the gap between the two terms of the juxtaposition. In Artemidorus' parathetical system, the dream is not an "original" that is mimetically "copied" by its outcome in the dreamer's life. In fact, neither dream nor event signify at all until they are brought together by juxtaposition. One might then say that what Artemidorus handed his clients was not a prediction of a future event but a metaphor to live by, a signifying space within which to understand experience.

Because it is based in the radically metaphorizing dynamic that is set in motion by juxtaposition, Artemidorus' system cannot finally escape polysemy. Despite the best intentions of its complicated techniques for deciding which meaning best suits the juxtaposed elements, his system was vulnerable to the ongoing play of language. Consider, as a final example, the following passage:

A man dreamed that he lost his nose. He was a perfume dealer at the time. Since he did not have a nose in the dream, he lost his store and stopped selling perfumes. For he no longer possessed the means to test his perfumes and it was obvious that he would not continue in the perfume business. When he was no longer a perfume dealer, the same man dreamed that he did not have a nose. He was caught forging a signature and fled his own country. For anything that is

63 Miller, "The Critic as Host," p. 219; see the discussion above in Ch. 1, pp. 29–30.
64 Miller, *Fiction and Repetition*, p. 8.

lacking to a face disfigures and degrades it. And the face is the image of one's respectability and reputation. It is understandable that this man was disgraced. During an illness the same man dreamed that he did not have a nose. He died not long afterwards, for the skull of a dead man has no nose. The first time, when he was a merchant, the dream referred to his perfumes. The second time, when he was a citizen with full rights and franchises, it referred to his reputation. The third time, when he was sick, it referred to his body itself. In this way, then, the same dream came true in three different ways for the same man.[65]

A clearer display of the polyvalence of images would be hard to find, as would a clearer display of Artemidorus' associative genius. It seems obvious that what is primary here is neither the missing nose nor the life event but rather the interpretive play that is effected when they are placed side by side. This is why I noted at the beginning of this discussion of Artemidorus that, unlike Synesius, he put more trust in the interpreter than in the dreams. His concern was to give interpreters an oneiric technology that would make their craft dependable and publicly useful, but his principle of interpretation worked against the achievement of total control of the dreamworld. Artemidorus tried his hand at choreography, but the signifiers continued to dance.

DREAMS AND ALLEGORY

Artemidorus' decoding of dreams amounted in effect to a recoding, a piling up of metaphor upon metaphor. Thus while he attempted to chasten the riddling phantasies of the night by writing rules of order, he was caught in their snare nonetheless. Allegorists also focused on the dream as riddle. For them, however, the figurative play set in motion by oneiric images was not an obstacle to be overcome by an interpretive technique; on the contrary, figurative play was constitutive of the dream's value as a vehicle for the discovery of complex insights about human life. Unlike Artemidorus, those who took dreams as the occasion for allegorical interpretation did not have to travel around the Mediterranean world collecting dreams. Their oneiric material was already "collected"—for Philo, Origen of Alexandria, and Augustine, in the biblical scriptures; for Macrobius, in an antecedent philosophical text. Their material was not only collected, it was also already textualized, and while one might say that their stance toward the polysemy of dream-texts was simply part of their larger allegorical program, it is also true that these authors placed the imagistic language of dreams and the allegorical "word" of scriptural and philosophical texts on a par as two species of the "genus" of figuration.

[65] *Onir.* 4.27 (ed. Pack, p. 262; trans. White, pp. 197–98).

Philo, for example, described the "seeing" in a dream as *amudros,* "dim," "faint," or "obscure," as in a rock dimly seen through water or as in scarcely legible letters.[66] Oneiric images thus have the same status as do the "letters" of the biblical text, which conceal their meanings like shadows.[67] For Augustine, similarly, the soul "wanders through various images" in dreams just as the exegete wanders through the signs of the biblical text.[68] He argues that, in scripture, dreams and allegorical passages are parallel phenomena: "these visions certainly are similar to the descriptions in allegorical passages . . . ; the saints judged their own visions as they would judge if they read or heard such things described by divine inspiration in figurative language."[69] Likewise, Macrobius saw the enigmatic dream as formally analogous to what he called the *narratio fabulosa,* a "fabled narrative" used by philosophers to convey the mysteries of nature by means of allegory.[70]

Origen took this idea of the dream and textual figuration as complementary phenomena one step further by suggesting that the allegorical method of interpretation (as distinguished from allegories in a text[71]) may itself be seen as oneiric. Origen's insistently allegorical approach to scriptural texts is well known. As he says, all of the events in the biblical text have the aspects and likenesses of certain hidden things.[72] The least letter, iota, and dot can be productive of a treasure trove of meaning: "the holy books breathe the spirit of plenitude."[73] In his approach to texts, allegory names an exegetical

---

[66] *De som.* 1.171 (text and trans. in Colson and Whitaker, p. 386). See Liddell, Scott, Jones, *A Greek-English Lexicon,* s.v. *amudros.*

[67] On the relation between literal and allegorical readings in Philo, see Jean Pépin, *La Tradition de l'Allégorie de Philon d'Alexandrie à Dante,* pp. 14–24.

[68] Augustine, *De genesi ad litteram* 10.25.42 (*CSEL* 28.3, p. 329; trans. Taylor, 2:130). For a discussion of dream and allegory as members of the same family of sign languages, see Peter Brown, *Augustine of Hippo, A Biography,* pp. 252–53, 260–63; a thorough treatment of Augustine's allegorical theory is given by Pépin, *La Tradition de l'Allégorie,* pp. 91–104, 137–65.

[69] *De gen. ad litt.* 10.25.43 (*CSEL* 28.3, p. 329; trans. Taylor, 2:130). Augustine placed dreams and epiphanies in the same category of visionary phenomena. The particular vision that he refers to in this passage was Pharaoh's dream of seven ears of corn and seven cows in Gen. 41.26. See Dulaey's detailed discussion of the terms that Augustine used for dreams in *Le Rêve,* pp. 93–96 (*phantasia* and *phantasma*) and 109–13 (*ostensio*).

[70] Macrobius, *Commentarii in Somnium Scipionis* 1.2.9 (ed. Willis, p. 5; trans. Stahl, p. 85).

[71] On the two meanings of allegory as a text's figural language and as an interpretive strategy that amplifies a text's figures by recourse to other sets of images and ideas, see Jean Pépin, *Mythe et Allégorie,* pp. 85–92, esp. p. 91.

[72] *Commentarium in Canticum Canticorum* 3.12 (ed. Baehrens, pp. 208–15). Origen gave a systematic account of his allegorical principles of interpretation in *De principiis* 4: for discussion, see Jean Daniélou, *Origène,* pp. 145–74; R.P.C. Hanson, *Allegory and Event;* Henri de Lubac, "Typologie et allégorisme," pp. 180–226; Henri Crouzel, "La Distinction de la 'typologie' et de l'allégorie,'" pp. 161–74.

[73] *Homiliae in Ieremiam* 50.11.2 (ed. and trans. Nautin and Husson, 2:343). For a discussion of the plenitude of biblical figurations in Origen, see Patricia Cox, "Origen and the Witch of Endor: Toward an Iconoclastic Typology," pp. 137–47.

perspective that affirms what one literary theorist has called "the possibility of an otherness, a polysemy, inherent in the very words on the page; allegory therefore names the fact that language can signify many things at once."[74] It was out of this disposition toward texts that Origen wrote his *Homilies on Genesis*. One of the passages in Genesis that particularly drew his interest was Gen. 25.11: "After Abraham died, the Lord blessed Isaac his son and he dwelt at Beer-la hai-roi," literally, at the "well of vision" (*ad puteum visionis*).[75] What fills this well, "vision," was one of the technical designations for a meaningful dream, and Origen remarks in this passage that he understands *visio* in terms of Jacob's dream of a heavenly ladder (Gen. 28.12–17).[76] He then goes on to consider what the picture of Isaac not only dwelling but also digging wells of vision might mean.

Allegorically, Isaac is the "word of God," a type of the Christ; his digging connotes for Origen the kind of interpretive ability that sees the spirit in the letter, the figurative in the literal.[77] When one can see that the well of scripture is filled with vision, one is, like Isaac, dwelling in dreams. Dream becomes for Origen a figure for scriptural interpretation. And he goes further: "If anyone can know and understand each vision of the things which are in the Law or in the prophets, that man dwells 'at the well of vision.'"[78] Now the term *visio* has been expanded to cover the whole of the scriptural text. Each word has a visionary or dreamlike dimension, which is at the same time its allegorical potential. For Origen, then, "dream" is a figure not only for figural interpretation but also for the biblical words themselves. "Isaac dwelling at the well of vision" is a complicated textual image that expresses both a perspective on the semiotic play of language and a stance concerning the interpretation of that language. Dream has become a figure for figuration, a metaphor for metaphor.

Everyone has the ability to dig and to dwell like Isaac. Using a rhetorical "I," Origen says, "If I shall have been able to perceive some one meaning of the visions of God, I shall appear to have spent one day 'at the well of vision.'

---

[74] Maureen Quilligan, *The Language of Allegory*, p. 26. Typical of Origen's view of linguistic polysemy is the following remark in his *Homiliae in Exodum* 1.1: "I think each word of divine scripture is like a seed whose nature is to multiply diffusely" (trans. Heine, p. 185). For a discussion of this and other passages in which Origen attests to his view of the diffusiveness of words, see Patricia Cox Miller, "Poetic Words, Abysmal Words: Reflections on Origen's Hermeneutics," pp. 165–78.

[75] *Homiliae in Genesim* 11.3 (ed. Doutreleau, p. 286; trans. Heine, p. 172).

[76] In *In somn. Scip.* 1.3.2–4 (ed. Willis, pp. 8–9; trans. Stahl, p. 88), Macrobius gives the Latin equivalents for the Greek terminology for dreams. *Visio*, the equivalent to *horama*, designates a prophetic vision and is one of the types of true dreams. It should be noted that Origen's *Homiliae in Genesim* has survived only in the Latin translation of Rufinus; hence we do not know what word Rufinus translated as *visio*, but the context makes it clear that the referent of the word is an oneiric phenomenon.

[77] *Hom. in Gen.* 12.5 (ed. Doutreleau, p. 302; trans. Heine, p. 181).

[78] Ibid. 11.13 (ed. Doutreleau, p. 288; trans. Heine, p. 173).

But if I shall have been able to touch not only something according to the letter, but also according to the spirit, I shall appear to have spent two days 'at the well of vision.'"[79] To dwell in vision, which is to dwell in scripture, is to experience what Origen calls "the living water" of scriptural meaning.[80] There is such a well of living water in each of us: "Let us attempt to do also that which scripture admonishes: 'Drink the waters of your own springs and wells, and let your spring be your own.' Therefore you also, O hearer, attempt to have your own well and your own spring, so that you too, when you take up a book of the Scriptures, may begin even from your own understanding to bring forth some meaning."[81] Finding such signification constitutes digging wells whose living water is "a kind of heavenly perception and latent image of God."[82]

Latent in each of us is this exegetical ability named by dream. Elsewhere Origen develops this idea further, and with the addition of an important term. In his letter to Julius Africanus, the biblical dreamer Daniel is said to draw his inspiration from visions, dreams, and—concluding this catalogue —angels; in *Against Celsus,* the angelic warning in Joseph's dream (Mt. 2.13) leads Origen to observe that many others have had such "suggestions [*phantasiae*] brought before the soul" by an angel.[83] Such angelic phantasies are "impressions on the mind in dreams" (*to tūpoun to hēgemonikon en oneirō*): they are the marks made in dreams on the authoritative part of the soul.[84] These governing phantasies constitute what Origen calls "a generic divine sense" (*theias aisthēseos*), in effect a scriptural hermeneutic, because the "sense" about which Origen is speaking involves the interpretation of biblical texts. Here again are angels, but now they are inner hermeneuts, and the dreams in which they speak carry the figural mode of interpretation. Both in scriptural text and in the self, angelic speech is dream-language, and the dream functions in formal and material ways as the principle and the substance of interpretation.

Although not so radical as Origen in their conclusions about the relation between dream and allegory, both Augustine and Macrobius placed the riddling dream in the arena of the soul's imagination rather than in the province of the intellect's ratiocination.[85] Also, both took the allegorical

---

[79] Ibid. 11.3 (ed. Doutreleau, p. 290; trans. Heine, pp. 173–74).

[80] Ibid. 13.3 (ed. Doutreleau, pp. 310–26; trans. Heine, pp. 189–95).

[81] Ibid. 12.5 (ed. Doutreleau, p. 306; trans. Heine, p. 183).

[82] Ibid. 13.3 (ed. Doutreleau, p. 324; trans. Heine, p. 191).

[83] *Ep. ad Julium Africanum* 16 (ed. and trans. De Lange, p. 555); *Contra Celsum* 1.66, in *Origène: Contre Celse* (ed. and trans. Borret, 1:263).

[84] *Contra Celsum* 1.48 (ed. and trans. Borret, 1:202).

[85] Augustine gives an extensive theoretical discussion of the creative imagination at work in dreams in *De gen. ad litt.* 12, where he specifically says that spiritual visions—*spiritus* in this case meaning "imagination"—pertain to the powers of the soul, not the mind. See especially *De gen. ad litt.* 12.9.20 (*CSEL* 28.3, p. 391; trans. Taylor, 2:391). On the translation of

language of sacred texts to be pertinent to the soul's semiotic consciousness which, in contrast to the mind's ability to receive direct flashes of awareness, needs such an allusive language of indirection in order to investigate the meaning of things.[86] Such allegorists had, perhaps, a more labyrinthine mindset than did an interpreter like Artemidorus, for they thought that although an allegorical text, like a dream, veils its meaning with obscure images, each such image, if pressed by interpretation, could yield not one but multiple significations.[87] Like Origen's angel, allegorists were vendors of signs. Their method of interpretation was essentially homeopathic: by applying allegorical interpretation to allegorical texts, they produced a proliferation of images, of yet more enigmatic figures whose depths needed to be plumbed.[88]

Macrobius' interpretation of the dream of Scipio is a good example of the way in which the allegorical imagination worked. The text that formed the

---

spiritus as "imagination," see Taylor, *St. Augustine*, p. 301n.13. For a thorough exposition of Augustine's oneiric theory, see Dulaey, *Le Rêve*, pp. 89–107. Macrobius says that philosophers use the *narratio fabulosa*, which includes dreams, when talking about the soul, but not when speaking about intellect (*In somn. Scip.* 1.2.13–17 [ed. Willis, pp. 6–7; trans. Stahl, pp. 85–86]).

[86] See Augustine, *De gen. ad litt.* 12.13.28 (*CSEL* 28.3, p. 397; trans. Taylor, 2:196), where he says that the images in a dream are "signs of other things which it is useful to know." In *De gen. ad litt.* 12.18.39 (*CSEL* 28.3, p. 406; trans. Taylor, 2:204), Augustine remarks about true dreams that their predictions are often given "with dark meanings and, as it were, in figurative expressions" (*obscuris significationibus et quasi figuratis locutionibus praenuntiata*), again bringing allegory and the dream close together, because *significatio* and *figura* were both part of the technical vocabulary of allegorical exegesis. As mediatorial functions of the soul, both dream and allegory were pedagogical. See Pépin, *Mythe et Allégorie*, pp. 90–91 for allegorical terminology, and *La Tradition de l'Allégorie*, pp. 91–104, for the pedagogical functions of allegory. For Macrobius' view of the pedagogical value of the dream and the fabled narrative, especially in terms of an education in virtue, see *In somn. Scip.* 1.2.6–11 (ed. Willis, pp. 5–6; trans. Stahl, pp. 84–85).

[87] Pépin, *La Tradition de l'Allégorie*, p. 30.

[88] Origen, for example, remarked that as soon as the interpreter "has discovered a small fragment of what he is seeking, he again sees other things that must be sought for, and if in turn he comes to know these, he will again see arising out of them many more things that demand investigation." (*De principiis* 4.3.14, trans. Butterworth, p. 311). Brown, *Augustine of Hippo*, p. 260, observes the following about Augustine and allegory:

> The idea of allegory had come to sum up a serious attitude to the limitations of the human mind, and to the nature of the relationship between the philosopher and the objects of his thought. This was a distinctive relationship. The religious philosopher explored a spiritual world that was of its very nature "ever more marvelous, ever more inaccessible" [Augustine, *Confessions* 11.31.41]. It should not be rendered "insipid with veracity" by bald statements; but rather the mind must move from hint to hint, each discovery opening up yet further depths.

Brown quotes from Augustine's *Tract. in Joh.* 14.5: "'If, however, you say: "That's all there is to know," you are lost'" (p. 260n5).

pretext for his polymathic allegorizing, the "Dream of Scipio," originally formed the last part of the final book of Cicero's *De re publica*. Cicero had modeled the closing of his description of the ideal state on the "Myth of Er" with which Plato ended his own construction of a political utopia, the *Republic*. Both of these visionary texts are disquisitions on the immortality of the soul and the ways in which its virtues and vices situate it in regard to cosmic cycles and regions.

Macrobius begins his commentary on the "Dream of Scipio" by placing it in two interpretive frames. First, it is situated in the context of Macrobius' defense of the use of literary fictions such as myth and dream as philosophical expressions that respect the secrets of nature by veiling them in images. As the product of a philosophical technique, the "Dream of Scipio" is a literary artifact that petitions the use of the interpretive tools of allegorical exegesis.[89] Second, Macrobius situates his text in the context of a system for the classification of dreams that is similar to that of Artemidorus.[90] Within this system, the interpretive possibilities of his text are just as expansive as they are in the context of allegory. For Macrobius there were three kinds of reliable dreams: the oracular, in which a parent or other revered figure reveals the future; the prophetic, which comes true as seen; and the enigmatic (of which there are five varieties), whose images are ambiguous and strange.[91] The "Dream of Scipio" fits all three categories. Macrobius' explanation of the signifying reach of his text deserves quotation in full:

> The dream which Scipio reports that he saw embraces the three reliable types mentioned above, and also has to do with all five varieties of the enigmatic dream. It is oracular since the two men who appeared before him and revealed his future, Aemilius Paulus and Scipio the Elder, were both his father [the latter having adopted him], both were pious and revered men, and both were affiliated with the priesthood. It is a prophetic vision since Scipio saw the regions of his abode after death and his future condition. It is an enigmatic dream because the truths revealed to him were couched in words that hid their profound meaning and could not be comprehended without skillful interpretation. It also embraces the five varieties of the last type. It is personal since Scipio himself was conducted to the regions above and learned of his future. It is alien

[89] *In somn. Scip.* 1.2.4–20 (ed. Willis, pp. 4–8; trans. Stahl, pp. 84–87). For a thorough discussion of Macrobius' view of myth, see Pépin, *Mythe et Allégorie,* pp. 210–14.

[90] The systems of the classification of dreams of Artemidorus and Macrobius are similar in that they both devise categories for distinguishing true from false dreams. They differ in that Macrobius' system does not subdivide the enigmatic dream (G. *oneiros;* L. *somnium*) into theorematic and allegorical types, although Macrobius' discussion of the prophetic vision (*visio*) and the oracular dream (*oraculum*) correspond to the features of Artemidorus' theorematic dream. For discussion, see A.H.M. Kessels, "Ancient Systems of Dream-Classification," pp. 395–96.

[91] *In som. Scip.* 1.3.8–11 (ed. Willis, pp. 10–11; trans. Stahl, p. 90).

[*alienum*] since he observed the estates to which the souls of others [*aliorum*] were destined. It is social since he learned that for men with merits similar to his the same places were being prepared as for himself. It is public since he foresaw the victory of Rome and the destruction of Carthage, his triumph on the Capitoline, and the coming civil strife. And it is universal since by gazing up and down he was initiated into the wonders of the heavens, the great celestial circles, and the harmony of the revolving spheres, things strange and unknown to mortals before this; in addition he witnessed the movements of the stars and planets and was able to survey the whole earth.[92]

By so situating the "Dream of Scipio" such that it is both a fictional allegorical text and an actual person's dream subject to several taxonomic categories, Macrobius both underscores the text's semiotic profuseness and creates the space for his own interpretive intervention.

The procedural method that Macrobius used to compose his commentary demonstrates why it was important for him first to establish the massive signifying potential of the Ciceronian text that provided the occasion for the commentary. He begins by excerpting a phrase or a longer passage from the "Dream of Scipio" and positions it at the beginning of a chapter or a group of chapters. His own interpretive uncovering of the meaning(s) of the excerpted passage then follows. Macrobius' work belonged to a genre of commentary, used by other late-fourth- and fifth-century Neoplatonists, which has been described as "a very liberal genre" because it allowed for "the clarification of preliminary explications and the introduction of new perspectives, in order to arrive at a long digression that can take on the appearance of a veritable treatise."[93] The long digression that becomes a treatise in its own right is certainly a feature of Macrobius' commentary. Indeed, as Stahl has observed, the text of the interpretive commentary is sixteen or seventeen times as long as that of the "Dream of Scipio."[94] Macrobius' initial framing of the Ciceronian text in terms of literary-philosophical and oneiric interpretive strategies that ensure the explosive semiotic quality of that text thus provided a necessary rationale for his method of commentary.

As I suggested in the introduction to this chapter, allegorists operated out of an expectation of textual polysemy and so delighted in the convergence of infinite relationships that oneiric images set in motion. However, those relationships are not in fact as infinite as the interpretive strategies that produce them might seem to be. There was a control on the semiotic play of textual images, and that control was provided by the ideational context of

---

[92] Ibid. 1.3.12–13 (ed. Willis, p. 11; trans. Stahl, pp. 90–91).

[93] Jacques Flamant, *Macrobe et le Néo-Platonisme Latin, à la Fin du IVᵉ Siècle*, p. 153; see pp. 148–54 for a discussion of the currency of this genre of commentary in Neoplatonic circles.

[94] Stahl, *Macrobius: Commentary on the Dream of Scipio*, p. 12.

the interpreter. Macrobius was steeped in Neoplatonic learning, and in his hands, Cicero's text expands by means of those treatise-like digressions until it encompasses a synthetic presentation of Neoplatonic philosophy. As a recent interpreter has phrased it, Macrobius' *Commentary on the Dream of Scipio* offers a "harmonious heritage of Roman, Greek, and oriental values, bathed in Neoplatonic light."[95]

According to Macrobius, an entire Neoplatonic encyclopedia lay encoded in this brief dream-text. Because Cicero hinted at "profound truths . . . with amazing brevity, concealing his deep knowledge of things beneath a concise form of expression," Macrobius took as his task the patient unfolding of the depths of knowledge lurking in these alluring hints.[96] He proceeded systematically by following the topics introduced in the "Dream of Scipio" in the order of their appearance. For example, Cicero's mention of the dreamer Scipio's destined age ("seven times eight recurring circuits of the sun") leads Macrobius into a lengthy recitation of Pythagorean arithmetic; mention of the just ruler produces a catalogue of the virtues; a brief description of the celestial spheres issues in a very detailed presentation of astronomical theory; and so on.[97] Macrobius covers three of the four sciences of the *quadrivium,* mathematics, music, and astronomy, and partially covers the fourth (geography being a part of geometry), as well as giving a passionate and lengthy disquisition on Neoplatonic views of the origin, nature, and immortality of the soul.[98]

Possessed of a finely tuned sensibility for the signifying value of Cicero's dream-text, Macrobius exploited that text's cryptic images in order to display the philosophical erudition of the Neoplatonic tradition to which he belonged. Just as a diviner might inspect the spots on an animal's liver, so Macrobius scrutinized the signs of Scipio's dream. Allegorical interpretation might indeed be considered as the linguistic parallel of divination, because it is a procedure that traces the convergence of textual relationships just as divination traces the convergence of relationships in the natural world. As in dream divination, so also in allegorical "divination" of dream-texts, human subjectivity is shaped by the enlargement of its sphere of reference. Artemidorus' divinatory technique enlarged the sphere of reference of his clients by enlightening them about the conundrums of their social situations, but Macrobius' technique was infinitely more expansive, taking his readers outward as far as they could go, to the edges of cosmos itself.

---

[95] Flamant, *Macrobe et le Néo-Platonisme Latin,* p. 686.

[96] *In som. Scip.* 2.12.7 (ed. Willis, p. 131; trans. Stahl, p. 223).

[97] Ibid. 1.5–6 (arithmetic; ed. Willis, pp. 14–34); 1.8 (virtues; ed. Willis, pp. 36–39); 1.17–22 (astronomy; ed. Willis, pp. 66–94). See Flamant, *Macrobe et le Néo-Platonisme Latin,* p. 694 (Appendix), for a convenient chart of the correspondence between Cicero's and Macrobius' texts.

[98] Flamant, *Macrobe et le Néo-Platonisme Latin,* p. 167.

Although a concern for the tight management and ordering of oneiric images does not appear on the "surface" of Macrobius' text as it does on Artemidorus', there is nonetheless in Macrobius' commentary a systematizing of the textual images of Scipio's dream that limits their signifying potential. Despite the encouragement to polysemous play that allegorical and oneiric theory provided, of which Macrobius certainly took advantage, the play of images in his text was confined to a specific playground, bounded by the tenets of Neoplatonic philosophy.

Other allegorists of oneiric texts were also caught in this curious interpretive dynamic whereby the explosive semiosis of textual images was both affirmed and curbed by ideological conviction. One of the most interesting chapters in oneiric allegory concerns the interpretive legacy of Jacob's dream of a heavenly ladder in the biblical book of Genesis. In the allegorical tradition that this dream fostered, the interplay of oneiric trope and religious ideology yielded a very dense sphere of reference, both for the text and for the reader.

The text of Jacob's dream reads as follows:

> Jacob left Beer-sheba, and went toward Haran. And he came to a certain place, and stayed there that night, because the sun had set. Taking one of the stones of the place, he put it under his head and lay down in that place to sleep. And he dreamed that there was a ladder set up on the earth, and the top of it reached to heaven; and behold, the angels of God were ascending and descending on it! And behold, the Lord stood above it and said, "I am the Lord, the God of Abraham your father and the God of Isaac; the land on which you lie I will give to you and to your descendants; and your descendants shall be like the dust of the earth, and you shall spread abroad to the west and to the east and to the north and to the south; and by you and your descendants shall all the families of the earth bless themselves. Behold, I am with you and will keep you wherever you go, and will bring you back to this land; for I will not leave you until I have done that of which I have spoken to you." Then Jacob awoke from his sleep and said, "Surely the Lord is in this place; and I did not know it." And he was afraid, and said, "How awesome is this place! This is none other than the house of God, and this is the gate of heaven." So Jacob rose early in the morning, and he took the stone which he had put under his head and set it up for a pillar and poured oil on the top of it.[99]

The allegorical, interpretive tradition attached to this dream singled out three of its images as particularly rich tropes: Jacob himself, the stone that he used for a pillow and later anointed with oil, and the ladder with its ascending and descending angels. In the work of the allegorists, each of these images is productive of further images by the process of allegorical association. That is, each of these becomes a figure for yet another figure in a

[99] Gen. 28.10–18 (RSV).

constant displacement of terms that one theorist has called the "lateral dance of interpretation," "an incessant movement from one displaced figural point to another."[100] From their textual ground in Genesis, Jacob, the stone, and the ladder become, allegorically, sites of centrifugal chains of figures as their signifying power is multiplied and disseminated. What follows is an excursus, an allegorical journey through Jacob's dream.

First, Jacob. Philo of Alexandria, who gave this dream of Jacob its lengthiest allegorical treatment, and the rabbinic *Midrash Rabbah* both took Jacob to be a type of the virtuous man, and both associated his character closely with Haran, the place in which the dream occurred. For Philo, "Haran" is a coded term for one of the elements of human knowing, sensory perception (*aisthēsis*). As he explains, the senses are "understanding's messengers" (*angeloi dianoias*) and "bodyguards of the soul" (*doruphoroi psūchēs*); they are a refuge for the person who cannot yet understand directly with the mind alone.[101] Jacob, the "lover of virtue," uses the senses in a disciplined way (Philo calls him an *askētēs*, an "ascetic") in order to find a path to the "city of intellect."[102] Philo's philosophical program of coordinating scripture with the tenets of Middle Platonism is clearly evident here, as he uses Jacob as a figure of the *epistrophē* or turning of the soul from material to metaphysical reality.[103] But there is more to Haran than this. In the Greek text of the dream of Jacob that Philo is quoting, Haran is called a "place" (*topos*), a word charged with religious connotations.[104] Although the word is given three allegorical meanings, the one that defines Jacob's position designates this *topos* as a space filled by the divine words (*logoi*) of God, the healing angels linked with dreams.[105] Thus Jacob, as a figure for this topology, is not really a person but a cipher for an epistemological process whereby the forces of the human mind moving from sensory to divine wisdom are explored.

The *Midrash Rabbah* arrives at its estimation of Jacob by asking a more earthbound set of questions. Exploring the statement "And Jacob went out," the authors of this text wondered,

> Was he then the only one who went out from that place? How many ass-drivers and camel-drivers went out with him! Said R. 'Azariah in the name of R. Judah b. Simon and R. Ḥanan in the name of R. Samuel b. R. Isaac: When the

[100] J. Hillis Miller, *Fiction and Repetition*, p. 127; Vincent Leitch, *Deconstructive Criticism*, p. 191–92.

[101] *De som.* 1.27 and 44 (text and trans. in Colson and Whitaker, pp. 308–9; 318–19).

[102] Ibid. 1.45–46 (text and trans. Colson and Whitaker, p. 318–19); the Greek word *askēsis* means "exercise," "practice," or "training."

[103] See Robert Berchman, *From Philo to Origen*, pp. 172–76, for Philo's dependence on Middle Platonic epistemology.

[104] For Philo's use of the word *place* to designate a space of divine revelation, see Segal, *Two Powers in Heaven*, pp. 161–64.

[105] *De som.* 1.61–70 (text and trans. in Whitaker and Colson, pp. 328–33). See Ch. 2, pp. 61–62 above for Philo's linking of angel, *logos,* and dream.

righteous man is in the town, he is its luster, its majesty, and its glory; when he leaves it, its luster, its majesty, and its glory depart.[106]

As the editors of this text note, the point of this passage is that the statement in question, "And Jacob went out," is superfluous, because the fact that he went elsewhere makes his going out obvious and so leads to misleading questions about camel-drivers. Given the apparent superfluity of the statement, there must be something significant about the fact that it was *Jacob* who went out—hence the meditation on the righteous man, of whom Jacob was a type.[107] "Place" is also important in the rabbinic interpretation. Using a typical strategy of piling up scriptural verses that mention "place" such that each succeeding verse supplants its predecessor in a metonymous chain of signification, Jacob's "place" takes on dense religious overtones as a space of divine revelation and prayer.[108]

Among Christian interpreters, Origen of Alexandria was closest to Philo in his troping of Jacob as a figure for the quest for knowledge. Having moved through moral and natural philosophy, "Jacob practises the inspective science, in that he earned his name of Israel ["the one who sees"] from his contemplation of the things of God, and saw the camps of heaven, and beheld the house of God and the angels' paths—the ladders reaching up from earth to heaven."[109] As for Philo, Jacob signifies the ability to see through the riddling aesthetic surfaces of things to their transcendent import.[110] Other Christians interpreted Jacob by using typological exegesis, in which theological affinities between the two Testaments of the Bible were uncovered by a juxtaposition of images, the earlier images being understood as prefigurations of the later.[111] For example, Justin Martyr took Jacob to be, figuratively, a spiritual father of Christians, both because Christians traced the lineage of the Christ through Jacob and because the dream had promised that Jacob's heirs would bring blessings to all the families of the earth.[112] For Ambrose, Jacob was a type of Christ, because of his obedience, while for Tertullian he prefigured Christians because, in his dream, he had seen "Christ the Lord [where Christ is the visible manifestation of God in the dream], the temple of God, and the gate by which heaven is entered."[113]

While the dreamer Jacob seems to have been unusually productive of

[106] *Midrash Rabbah* 68.6 (ed. and trans. Freedman and Simon, p. 619).

[107] Freedman and Simon, *The Midrash Rabbah*, p. 619n.3.

[108] *Midrash Rabbah* 68.9 (ed. and trans. Freedman and Simon, pp. 620–22).

[109] Origen, *Comm. in Cant.*, prologue 3 (ed. Baehrens, pp. 78–79; trans. Lawson, p. 45).

[110] For a discussion of Origen's understanding of the riddling quality of aesthetic images, see Patricia Cox, "Origen and the Bestial Soul: A Poetics of Nature," pp. 118–20.

[111] There is an immense bibliography on the topic of early Christian typology. For a good introduction, see Jean Daniélou, *Gospel Message and Hellenistic Culture*, pp. 197–300.

[112] Justin, *Dialogue with Trypho* 120.1 (ed. and trans. Archambault, 2:214).

[113] Ambrose, *On Belief in the Resurrection* 100 (*NPNF* 10:190); Tertullian, *Adversus Marcionem* 3.24.9–10 (*CCL* 2:543).

multiple significations, the images of his dream were even more active as a tease to the interpretive imagination. Because the Hebrew text says that Jacob "took of the stones of the place" (*one of* the stones being an addition in translation), the *Midrash Rabbah* assumed that he used several stones. Thus Rabbi Judah thought that he took twelve stones, one each for the twelve tribes of Israel that traced their origin through the sons of Jacob; Rabbi Nehemiah thought he took three, one for each of the patriarchs; while others thought he used only two, one each for Abraham and Isaac. Further, in the rabbinic imagination, the stones also had a utilitarian purpose: Jacob was afraid of wild beasts and so used the stones to construct a shelter for his head! Finally, in a passage that again shows the rabbinic method of using scripture to trope scripture, the *Midrash Rabbah* says that "the stone which the Patriarch Jacob put under his head became under him like a feather-bed and a pillow. What was the cover which Jacob prepared? 'The beams of our houses are cedars' [Song of Songs 1.17]—the righteous men and women, the prophets and prophetesses [who sprung from him]."[114]

Moving from the stone as a sign of religious genealogy and protective comfort, one finds Philo and Clement of Alexandria emphasizing not the featherlike quality of the stone but rather its hardness. Clement commends Jacob's rocky pillow because only austere sleeping conditions will yield such superhuman visions.[115] For Philo as well, Jacob and his stone become emblematic of a rigorous ascetic program. Engaging in a lengthy diatribe against those addicted to material comforts, he takes Jacob's stony recline as an indicator of the ethical benefits of philosophical discipline.[116] As usual for Philo, the stone's signifying potential is not limited to ethical reflection. Recalling that the place where Jacob lay is a "holy land full of incorporeal words," Philo takes the stone to be the best of these words; thus the sleeping Jacob is actually awake, reposing on the divine *logos*.[117] A final turn on the figure of the stone comes from Christian typology, in which the rock was seen as a prefiguration of the Christ. The link here depended on a linguistic pun; Jacob had "anointed" the rock after awakening, just as the Christ was the "anointed one" (messiah) of God. Thus Jacob, by sleeping on the anointed rock, could be seen in another sense as the precursor of Christians.[118]

Finally, the ladder. The *Midrash Rabbah* first allegorizes the ladder and its angels in terms of the temple and its cult. In this sense, the ladder represents the stairway leading to the altar; the fact that this ladder reached to heaven is

114 *Midrash Rabbah* 68.11 (ed. and trans. Freedman and Simon, pp. 623–24).

115 Clement of Alexandria, *Paedagogus* 2.9.78 (ed. and trans. Mondésert, 2:157).

116 *De som.* 1.120–26 (text and trans. in Colson and Whitaker, pp. 360–65).

117 Ibid. 1.127–29 (text and trans. in Colson and Whitaker, pp. 364–67).

118 Justin, *Dial.* 86.2 (ed. and trans. Archambault, p. 62); Cyprian, *Ad Quirinum* 2.16 (CCL 3:52).

taken to designate the upward wafting of sacrificial odors; the angels are the High Priests, ascending and descending the stairs to the altar. Next, the scriptural ladder is taken as a prefiguration of another scriptural scene, the coming of Moses and Aaron to Sinai. Now the ladder is the mountain, and Moses and Aaron are the angels. A final twist makes Jacob himself the ladder upon whom angels move: "Some were exalting him and others degrading him, dancing, leaping, and maligning him"—a curious scene of glorification and punishment in which Jacob is compared positively to a king when he does his proper job of judging and negatively to the king when he sleeps, thus neglecting his duty.[119]

Tertullian also connected the ladder with judgment, but he placed the ladder in a Christian eschatological setting. The ladder itself is God's decisive judgment that some will enter the heavenly resting place and some will not; here the angels are ascending and descending human souls.[120] Most Christians, however, followed the Gospel of John in connecting the ladder with the Christ as a mediating figure between the human and the divine: "You shall see the heavens opened, and the angels of God ascending and descending upon the Son of Man."[121] Following this statement in the New Testament, patristic typologists juxtaposed the ladder (which they imagined was made of wood) with the tree of life and the cross of Jesus in order to show the salvific function of the cross and its prefiguration in earlier sacred texts.[122]

Philo's psychological allegorization of the ladder has already been discussed, wherein the ladder designates the soul as an interior stairway along which the *logoi* of God move, connecting mind with body.[123] But Philo gave this image many other tropological turns. One of the most interesting, apparently drawn from Plato's picture of the winged soul in the *Phaedrus*, takes the ladder to be the air between earth and heaven; this air is filled with souls in constant motion, descending into bodies and then ascending back to the heavenly realm in an angelic flutter.[124] Ultimately, for Philo, the ladder with its ascending and descending angels is a figure for the *agōn* or

[119] *Midrash Rabbah* 68.12 (ed. and trans. Freedman and Simon, pp. 625–26).

[120] *Adversus Marcionem* 3.24.9 (*CCL* 1:543); Tertullian also used the ladder as an image of the function of persecution in the church—those ascending had stood the test of persecution, while those descending had not; see *De Fuga in Persecutione* 1.3–4 (*CCL* 2:1135–36).

[121] Gospel of John 1.51 (RSV). In this verse, Jacob's ladder is equated with Jesus as the messianic Son of Man.

[122] Irenaeus, *Demonstratio* 45 (ed. and trans. Fridevaux, p. 104); Hippolytus, *On the Passover* 51 (ed. and trans. Nautin, p. 176); Ambrose, *On Belief in the Resurrection* 100 (*NPNF* 10:190).

[123] *In som.* 1.46–49 (text and trans. in Colson and Whitaker, pp. 318–21); see Ch. 2, p. 61, above.

[124] *In som.* 1.133–39 (text and trans. in Colson and Whitaker, pp. 368–71); Plato, *Phaedrus* 246C–256E (*Collected Dialogues*, pp. 493–502).

struggle of the mystic experiencing the ups and downs of spiritual aspiration.[125]

Originally part of a narrative in which a legendary forefather is historicized, the dream of Jacob breaks out of its contextual frame when, in allegory, its images become autonomous signifiers available for use in the construction of other systems of meaning. Thus loosened from the signified, Jacob, the stone, and the ladder multiply the interpretive operations of inquiry and response. Like dreams themselves, dream-texts such as the dream of Jacob and the dream of Scipio were discourses that functioned mediatorially to lead the interpreter out into other, more richly nuanced regions of apprehension. The qualities of enigma, secret, and disguise that were attributed to such oneiric texts were enhanced by the fact that such texts were also dreams, riddling by definition. Texts like the dream of Jacob were therefore doubly provocative of the kind of interpretive quests in which allegorists engaged. It was no accident, I think, that the two most sustained allegorical interpretations of dream-texts extant from Graeco-Roman antiquity—Macrobius' commentary on the dream of Scipio and Philo's commentary on Jacob's dream—were prefaced with detailed theoretical and taxonomic discussions of the phenomenon of dreams.[126] Implicitly, at least, these authors recognized the essential compatibility of dream and allegory as functions of the imagination that worked to tease the mind into active thought.

The foregoing explorations of the various interpretive strategies employed by Graeco-Roman onirologists and allegorists to decode the puzzling images of dreams and dream-texts have suggested that the dream was both embedded in and productive of an insistently figurative way of viewing the social, psychic, religious, and philosophical dimensions of life. Whatever else one might say about late-antique habits of mind, it seems clear that the various means of manipulating oneiric phenomena attest to a widespread interest in the development of imaginal languages for use in situating and understanding self and world. In the case both of classifiers and allegorists, the decoding of oneiric images amounted to a recoding, a "translation" from image to image, and the emphasis lay on the interpretive process itself and on the relational dynamic thus set in motion. The observation of the philosopher Gaston Bachelard, that "we understand figures by their

[125] *In som.* 1.153–56 (text and trans. in Colson and Whitaker, p. 379). For a discussion of ladder imagery in Graeco-Roman art as well as in texts, see Goodenough, *Jewish Symbols in the Greco-Roman Period*, vol. 8, pt. 2, pp. 148–57.

[126] Philo's theory of dreams is given in *In som.* 1.1–2 (text and trans. in Colson and Whitaker, p. 295); Philo's statement here, which refers the reader back to the (now lost) first book of his tome on dreams, suggests that this section is only a summary of a lengthier discussion. See the analyses of Philo's oneiric theory in Kessels, "Ancient Systems of Dream-Classification," pp. 406–9 and in Waszink, *Tertullian: De anima*, pp. 500–501.

transfiguration," seems a fitting characterization of the perspective that inspired the late-antique texts considered here.[127] Of course, in Graeco-Roman culture, the province of dreams was not confined to the area of textuality; if techniques for decoding dreams provided a "therapy" for the interpretive imagination by enabling an exploration of dreams' seductive allusiveness, it is also true that dreams themselves could be seen as cures for bodily and emotional ailments. In the following chapter, the therapeutic operations of dreams in the lives of Graeco-Roman people will be explored.

[127] Gaston Bachelard, *L'Air et les songes,* p. 13.

CHAPTER FOUR

Dreams and Therapy

As A DISCOURSE of signs, dreams took ancient dreamers not only more deeply into texts, but also more deeply into the very intimate areas of body and emotion. It would be difficult, indeed, to overestimate the role played by dreams in the curing of human suffering. In crises of physical disease and mental distress, many people in the Graeco-Roman era turned to dreams for the healing of their ailments. The ill could seek oneiric remedies from religious institutions, in the temples and shrines that had special "incubation" chambers for overnight stays where sleepers sought healing dreams; or, in a less official way, they could consult individuals who were adept at the sending or inducing of curative dreams by the use of magical praxes or potions. In either case, however, a therapy of body or mind was the hoped-for result. A brief look at four cases of oneiric healing, two physical and two emotional, will give a sense of the very wide range of conditions that fell under the rubric of dreams and therapy.

The first example of dream-induced physical therapy comes from the cult of the healing god Asclepius, whose major center in both classical and late antiquity was at Epidaurus on the eastern coast of the Argolid in Greece. Additional cultic sites rose to prominence in Athens in the fifth century B.C.E. and in Rome in the third century B.C.E. in response to plagues that swept both cities; Asclepian religion was, in the phrase of A. D. Nock, "a religion of emergencies."[1] The following account, by the physician Galen, reports a cure that took place at the Asclepieium in Pergamum in Asia Minor, a cultic center that flourished during the Antonine Age when Asclepian religion was at the height of its popularity in late antiquity.[2]

> Another wealthy man, this one not a native but from the interior of Thrace, came, because a dream had driven him, to Pergamum. Then a dream appeared to him, the god [Asclepius] prescribing that he should drink every day of the drug produced from the vipers and should anoint the body from the

[1] Arthur Darby Nock, review of E. J. and L. Edelstein, *Asclepius* (1945), p. 48. On the spread of the Asclepius cult from Epidaurus to other cities, see Emma J. and Ludwig Edelstein, *Asclepius: A Collection and Interpretation of the Testimonies*, 2:238–55; Dodds, *The Greeks and the Irrational*, p. 193; Kee, "Self-Definition in the Asclepius Cult," pp. 125–26.

[2] On the role of Asclepian religion in the Antonine age, see Lane Fox, *Pagans and Christians*, pp. 151–52; Bowersock, *Greek Sophists in the Roman Empire*, pp. 70–74; Kee, "Self-Definition in the Asclepius Cult," p. 134.

outside. The disease after a few days turned into leprosy; and this disease, in turn, was cured by the drugs which the god commanded.[3]

In this case the dream is a dispenser of healing drugs—the *pharmaka* in whose use Asclepius was a specialist.[4] Even so eminent a figure as the emperor Marcus Aurelius had thanked Asclepius for the remedies prescribed for him in dreams.[5]

But it was not only the rich and the powerful whose bodies were healed in this way. In the African town over whose church Augustine presided as bishop, a shrine containing relics of the martyr St. Stephen had been built in 424. Stephen, as one of the "stars" of the then-burgeoning cult of saints, left mortal remains that were remarkably therapeutic.[6] One of several cures that Augustine recorded in connection with this shrine concerned the children of an aristocratic widow in Cappadocian Caesarea, who had cursed her offspring and cast them out into poverty. The curse left them all with "a hideous shaking in all their limbs"; shamed by this physical disability, the children avoided settling down and wandered around the Roman world.[7] Paulus and Palladia were two of them, and they arrived in Hippo in response to a dream that directed them to the shrine of St. Stephen.[8]

> Now it was about fifteen days before Easter when they came, and they came daily to church, and specially to the relics of the most glorious Stephen, praying that God might now be appeased, and restore their former health. . . . Easter arrived, and on the Lord's day, in the morning, when there was now a large crowd present, and the young man was holding the bars of the holy place where the relics were, and praying, suddenly he fell down, and lay precisely as if asleep, but not trembling as he was wont to do even in sleep. All present were astonished. . . . And behold! he rose up, and trembled no more, for he was healed, and stood quite well, scanning those who were scanning him.[9]

This appears to be a Christianized version of Asclepian incubation, although the lying-in for the purpose of sleep and attendant dream is, admittedly, briefer, colored as it is by the aura of instantaneous miracle.[10] Nonetheless, the conflation of physical suffering and healing dream attests

[3] Galen, *Subfiguratio empirica* 10=Testimony 436 (hereafter T.) in Edelstein, *Asclepius,* 1:250.

[4] For legends regarding Asclepius' education in the use of drugs, see T. 1–6 in Edelstein, *Asclepius,* 1:1–13.

[5] Marcus Aurelius, *Meditations* 1.17.9 (trans. Staniforth, p. 44).

[6] See Brown, *Augustine of Hippo,* pp. 413–18, and *The Cult of the Saints,* pp. 91–92, 102–5.

[7] Augustine, *Civ. Dei* 22.8.22 (trans. Dods in Oates ed., 2:627).

[8] Augustine, *Sermon* 324 (PL 38:1445).

[9] Augustine, *Civ. Dei* 22.8.22 (trans. Dods in Oates ed., 2:627).

[10] On Christian incubation and Augustine's view of healing dreams, see Dulaey, *Le Rêve,* pp. 181–88.

to the persistence of this oneiric practice, and it was one that cut across lines of religious and social difference.

In the area of the emotions, the role of oneiric daemons as keepers of the conscience and detectives of the heart's secrets has already been noted.[11] There were, however, more explicit references to the part played by dreams in the treatment of emotional imbalances. Again Galen, one of the medical doctors who had a cooperative relationship with the Asclepius cult, provides testimony.[12] Apparently cognizant of the interconnection of psychological with physiological conditions, Galen knew, as Peter Brown has observed, that Asclepius "dealt with his patients at the level of their 'heat.'"[13] In this context, Galen offers the following observation:

> And not a few men, however many years they were ill through the disposition of their souls, we have made healthy by correcting the disproportion of their emotions. No slight witness of the statement is also our ancestral god Asclepius who ordered not a few to have odes written as well as to compose comical mimes and certain songs (for the motions of their passions, having become more vehement, made the temperature of the body warmer than it should be); and for others, these not a few either, he ordered hunting and horse riding and exercising in arms; and at the same time he appointed the kind of hunting for those for whom he prescribed this. . . . For he not only desired to awake the passion of these men because it was weak but also defined the measure by the form of exercises.[14]

Thus whether one was hotheaded or depressive, Asclepius had remedies ready to prescribe in dreams and, interestingly, they connected psychic therapy with physical activity—the quiet sitting of literary authorship for the overly passionate, and the vigorous pursuits of hunting and riding for those lacking in emotional drive.

Some centuries later, overwrought passions were troubling not Antonine gentlemen, but Christian monks in the desert. Obsessional fantasies of sexual desire were causing many of these ascetics considerable emotional distress.[15] For these men, dreams were sometimes part of the problem, awakening them with tormenting visions of fetching women.[16] But they could also be a cure. Thus Abba Elias, desperate for the cessation of

---

[11] See Ch. 2, pp. 55–59, above.

[12] On the relationship between the Asclepius cult and the practice of medicine, see Temkin, *Hippocrates in a World of Pagans and Christians*, pp. 79–85; Kee, "Self-Definition in the Asclepius Cult," pp. 134–36; and Behr, *Aelius Aristides and the Sacred Tales*, pp. 162–70.

[13] Brown, *The Making of Late Antiquity*, p. 43.

[14] Galen, *De sanitate tuenda*, 1.8.19–21=T. 413 in Edelstein, *Asclepius*, 1:208–9.

[15] Good discussions of the desert fathers' battles with sexual temptation are in Aline Rouselle, *Porneia*, pp. 147–51, and Peter Brown, *The Body and Society*, pp. 216–40, 375–78.

[16] The most famous instance was Jerome's dream of bands of dancing girls; for detailed discussion, see below, Ch. 8.

his sexual cravings, dreamed that "three angels . . . took hold of him, one by the hands and one by the feet and the third took a razor and castrated him—not actually, but in the dream."[17] The psychic surgery worked, and he was free of his obsession for the rest of his life. As in the Asclepian instance above, this cure also depended on the positing of a relation between body and emotion, although in the case of Abba Elias it was an oneiric body that provided the locus for the healing of emotional turmoil. Still, it is clear that faith in the therapeutic effect of the dream on unruly feelings was part of a culture pattern that persisted through quite different changes of social and religious landscape.

In the materials that will be discussed in this chapter, dreams were not viewed as symbolic representations of physical or mental disease that doctors could use as diagnostic tools, as they were in the Hippocratic literature. The dream was not mimetic to illness, but rather creative of cure. In the Asclepius cult and in magical praxis, dreaming enabled a refashioning of body and soul through the medium of figuration. In these contexts, the clue to the healing of suffering lay in imagination, because the source of health was located in the visual images of dreams.

THE ASCLEPIUS CULT

When Pausanias visited Epidaurus in the second century C.E. for the purpose of entering the sights of the place in his travelogue, the sacred precinct of Asclepius that he saw, with its many fine buildings, had been flourishing since the mid-fourth century B.C.E.[18] His description is worth quoting in full:

> The sacred grove of Asclepius has boundary-stones around it in every direction. Inside that enclosure, no men die and no women bear children. . . . Everyone, Epidaurian or foreigner, consumes his sacrifice inside the boundaries. . . . The statue of Asclepius is half the size of Olympian Zeus at Athens, and made of ivory and gold. He sits enthroned holding a staff, with one hand over the serpent's head, and a dog lying beside him. The carvings on the throne show the deeds of Argive divine heroes, Bellerophon and the Chimaira, and Perseus taking the head of Medusa. Over from the temple is where the ritual suppliants of the god go to sleep. A round construction of white stone called *tholos* which is worth a visit has been built near by. Inside is a picture by Pausias in which Eros has discarded his bow and arrows, and

[17] Palladius, *Lausiac History* 29.4 (trans. Meyer, pp. 89–90).
[18] For a detailed discussion of Epidaurian archaeology, see Lynn R. LiDonnici, *Tale and Dream: The Text and Compositional History of the Corpus of Epidaurian Miracle Cures*, pp. 15–44.

carries a lyre instead. "Drunkenness" is also there, painted by Pausias drinking from a wine-glass; you can see a wine-glass in the painting and a woman's face through it. In my day there are six left of the stone tablets standing in the enclosure, though there were more in antiquity. The names of men and women healed by Asclepius are engraved on them, with the diseases and how they were healed.[19]

In Graeco-Roman antiquity, this healing center, together with the one in Pergamum, was the most venerable among at least two hundred such Asclepian sites; as Ramsay MacMullen has aptly observed, "divine doctors received many calls."[20] Indeed, Asclepius was not the only divine doctor. Sarapis and Isis also healed through dreams; and incubation, the ritual of lying-in at a temple to receive a dream, was practiced in their temples as well. In the Sarapea on the island of Delos, for example, there were *onei-rokritai*, specialists in the interpretation of dreams; the gifts of thanksgiving found there—votive objects of silver and gold made in the shape of eyes—suggest that the healing of diseases of the eye was a specialty of the Delian Sarapis.[21]

Asclepius, however, seems to have been the Panhellenic benefactor of choice. The paean of praise to this "kindly" and "soothing" god by the fifth-century B.C.E. poet Pindar was still being echoed seven centuries later in the words of the rhetorician Aelius Aristides, who characterized Asclepius as a "cheering" god whose ministrations led "from a great sea of despair" to a "calm harbor."[22] The ancient understanding of this god's benefactions was well symbolized by the snake that formed part of the chryselephantine statue described by Pausanias and was frequently noted by others as an attribute, if not a totem, of the god. Annually renewing itself through the shedding of its skin, the snake became emblematic of Asclepius' ability to renew the human body by causing it to shed its "skin" of ill health.[23] At Epidaurus, in fact, the *abaton*, the incubatory building where suppliants slept, was filled with the sacred snakes of the god (and also with dogs, for in legend the child Asclepius had been nourished by one); as Kee has noted, "the serpent and the god are alternate forms of one kind of epiphany," one in which compassion and awe were mixed. "It takes little imagination," as he goes on to say, "to identify with the pilgrim lying in the pitch-dark dormitory, hearing the slithering of the snakes, the pad-

---

[19] Pausanias, *Guide to Greece* 2.27.1–3 (trans. Levi, 1:193–94).

[20] MacMullen, *Paganism in the Roman Empire,* p. 28; see Behr, *Aelius Aristides and the Sacred Tales,* pp. 27–31, for a detailed description of the Asclepieium in Pergamum.

[21] Tran tam Tinh, "Sarapis and Isis," pp. 111–12; Griffiths, *Apuleius of Madauros: The Isis Book,* pp. 139, 236–37.

[22] Pindar, *Pythian Ode* 3.48–54=T. 1 in Edelstein, *Asclepius,* 1:4, Aristides, *Oration* 42.1 and 5 (trans. Behr, *Complete Works,* 2:247–48).

[23] See T. 688–706 in Edelstein, *Asclepius,* 1:360–69.

ding or panting of the dogs—or in a climax of divine favour, the footsteps of the god himself."[24]

The "footsteps" of the god were, of course, the healing dreams, which often took the form of an epiphany of the god in the form of his statue.[25] The preparations made by suppliants prior to incubation and the hoped-for dream were fairly simple: ritual cleansing with water from sacred springs (a possible function of the round house at Epidaurus described by Pausanias); sacrifices, whether of animals or food; the singing of hymns and recitation of prayers, culminating with the ritual response, "Great is Asclepius"; and the lighting of candles.[26]

After entering the place of incubation, the sufferers were told to be silent and to go to sleep.[27] Aelius Aristides, one of the god's greatest enthusiasts in the second century C.E., gives a lively picture in his *Sacred Tales* of the conversations held the next morning among suppliants and between suppliants and temple wardens concerning the dreams that had occurred during the night.[28] If a healing dream had been given, a thank-offering was due to the god; this took the form of meals shared with the god, sacrificial animals, hymns, money, garlands, or votives in the shape of the part of the body that had been healed.[29] The sanctuary at Epidaurus, for example, was filled with such votive offerings: "free-standing as in sculpture and benches, flat, plaque-shaped, covering every vertical surface in the temenos; and replicas of body-parts either cured or in need of cure, which hung from walls and ceilings in sanctuary buildings."[30]

One of the most important witnesses to the oneiric therapy that took place at Epidaurus was the set of stelae located in the sacred precinct there. According to Pausanias, six of these were still standing; two of them, plus fragments of two others, have survived to the present.[31] In what remains of the stelae, seventy tales of cures by Asclepius are recorded, often along with the name and residence of the person cured. Most of the tales deal with cures effected in dreams during incubation. Because the stelae on which these stories of divine healing were inscribed were available for public inspection within the Asclepian compound, it is likely that they were displayed with the intentions of heartening those who were suffering

[24] Kee, "Self-Definition in the Asclepius Cult," p. 123.

[25] Lane Fox, *Pagans and Christians*, pp. 153–63.

[26] Edelstein, *Asclepius*, 2:184–94; Behr, *Aelius Aristides and the Sacred Tales*, pp. 32–35, for detailed descriptions of rituals for the sick.

[27] Behr, *Aelius Aristides and the Sacred Tales*, pp. 34–35.

[28] See *Sacred Tales* 2.34–35, 47–48, 72–73; 3.14; 4.16–18, 46 (trans. Behr, *Complete Works*, 2:298, 300, 305, 310, 320–21, 327).

[29] See T. 523–545 in Edelstein, *Asclepius*, 1:296–306.

[30] LiDonnici, *Tale and Dream*, p. 2.

[31] See ibid., *Tale and Dream*, pp. 36–44, for philological and archaeological analysis of the stelae.

and of "preconditioning" them to the appropriately Asclepian mode of dreaming.[32]

A recent study has argued persuasively that the Epidaurian stelae contain redactions of earlier "Asclepian experiences" in which oral tradition as well as the influence of pictorial votives played a part in the grouping and narrative expansion of the tales.[33] The tales fall into three major stylistic groups, each of which emphasizes a different aspect of the Asclepian mode of healing, although all three sustain faith in the actuality of the restoration of health in the sacred precinct. One group highlights the instantaneous and miraculous cures of the god, while another pictures Asclepius as operating like a human doctor, and a third is concerned with the curative effect of the sanctuary's animals.[34] Yet, even though this narrative stylization introduces "a real separation between the text as we have it [on a given stele] and the mind and thoughts of the person who [originally] dedicated it," the stelae are valuable as a witness to patterns of expectation that undergirded the experience of Asclepian dreaming, particularly because similar kinds of stories continued to be told and recorded in late antiquity, several centuries after the composition of the Epidaurian tales.[35]

The stelae show that oneiric cure was sought for a wide variety of physical ailments: sterility, blindness, infestation with worms and lice, paralysis, epilepsy, festering sores, headaches, and baldness, among others. The following tales are typical of the way in which Asclepian therapy is presented in the Epidaurian record.

> Euphanes, a boy of Epidauros. Suffering from stones, he slept here. It seemed to him the god stood by him and said, "What will you give me if I should make you healthy?" The boy replied, "Ten dice." The god, laughing, said that he would make it stop. When day came he left healthy.[36]
>
> Once a man came as a suppliant to the god who was so blind in one eye that, while he still had the eyelids of that eye, there was nothing within them and they were completely empty. Some of the people in the sanctuary were laughing at his simple-mindedness in thinking that he could be made to see, having absolutely nothing, not even the beginnings of an eye, but only the socket. Then in his sleep, a vision appeared to him. It seemed that the god boiled some drug, and then drew apart his eyelids and poured it in. When day came he departed with both eyes.[37]

[32] For discussion of psychological preconditioning in connection with the public display of the stelae, see LiDonnici, *Tale and Dream*, pp. 11–13, 43–44; Kee, "Self-Definition in the Asclepius Cult," p. 122; Dodds, *The Greeks and the Irrational*, pp. 112–13.

[33] LiDonnici, *Tale and Dream*, pp. 204–47.

[34] Ibid., pp. 276–78.

[35] Ibid., p. 278.

[36] Stele A.8 (text and translation in LiDonnici, *Tale and Dream*, p. 54).

[37] Stele A.9 (LiDonnici, *Tale and Dream*, p. 55).

A man from Torone, leeches. When he was sleeping, he saw a dream. It seemed to him that the god ripped open his chest with a knife, took out the leeches and gave them to him in his hands, and sewed his breast together. When day came he left having the animals in his hands, and had become healthy. He had drunk them down, after being tricked by his stepmother who had thrown them into a potion that he drank.[38]

Tinged as they are with an aura of the supernatural, these testimonies nonetheless provide witness to a very ancient trust in the therapeutic effects of the somatic imagination, here expressed in the form of dreams. As aspirations toward a new body, a renewed physical self, such tales suggest that, in the context of illness, dreams were viewed as vehicles of a very material kind of metamorphosis. The unusual images in these dreams may be stylized, but to the dreamer they were facts of real ontological significance as witnesses to the powers of vision at work in nature itself.

The status of Asclepian dreams as effective curative devices has been the subject of debate from antiquity to the present. In his *Lives of the Sophists,* Philostratus recorded an anecdote about the early-second-century C.E. sophist Polemo, who had gone to the temple of Asclepius at Pergamum seeking relief from arthritis. "He slept in the temple, and when Asclepius appeared to him and told him to abstain from drinking anything cold, 'My good sir,' said Polemo, 'but what if you were doctoring a cow?'"[39] Contemporary scholarly discussion has not continued Polemo's tone of arrogant sarcasm, but skepticism has tended to be the prevailing attitude. Some have viewed the record of the Epidaurian stelae as an intentional forgery by Asclepian priests aimed at boosting the prestige and the income of the healing center, while others have suggested that the ill were drugged or hypnotized and then treated by very human temple attendants disguised as the god, and it is still standard to compare (irrational) Asclepian religion with (rational) medicine.[40] Even E. R. Dodds, who supports the view that the Asclepian experience was a genuinely religious one, frames the phenomenon in terms of the anthropologist E. B. Tylor's concept of the vicious circle: "what the dreamer believes he therefore sees, and what he sees he therefore believes."[41]

Yet, whether Asclepian centers are imagined to be the equivalent of an out-patient clinic (classical Epidaurus) or a spa for the well-to-do (late-antique Pergamum),[42] it seems to me that continued use of categories of

---

[38] Stele A.13 (LiDonnici, *Tale and Dream,* p. 60).

[39] Philostratus, *Lives of the Sophists* 1.25.4=T. 433 in Edelstein, *Asclepius,* 1:249.

[40] Behr, *Aelius Aristides and the Sacred Tales,* p. 36; Kee, "Self-Definition in the Asclepius Cult," pp. 124–25, 134–36; Edelstein, *Asclepius,* 2:139–80; Temkin, *Hippocrates in a World of Pagans and Christians,* pp. 171–96.

[41] Dodds, *The Greeks and the Irrational,* p. 112.

[42] Kee, "Self-Definition in the Asclepius Cult," pp. 134, 136.

reason and unreason, of empirical science versus religious credulity, as bases for evaluation sidesteps the fact of the centuries-long popularity and vitality of oneiric therapy as one of the ways in which people attempted to cope with the large and small desperations of everyday life. How, for example, to account for Teucris of Cyzicus, who went to the Asclepian temple in Pergamum around 100 C.E. seeking a cure for his epilepsy: Asclepius "appeared to him, and they struck up a conversation, and he developed a quartan fever and through it recovered from epilepsy."[43] As Ramsay MacMullen observes, "They 'struck up a conversation'— extraordinary!"[44] The intimate relationship pictured here between Teucris, his god, and his body is testimony neither to bad science nor to religious credulity; the canons of what constitutes science and faith vary too much from age to age to allow certain judgment. What can be said, however, is that, in the Asclepius cult as elsewhere, the dream continued to function as one of the modes of the production of meaning, deeply embedded in intensely personal feelings of hope and despair.

Although the Epidaurian stelae were still on view in late antiquity, one kind of tale that is typical of them, in which Asclepius performs oneiric surgery, does not play a role in Graeco-Roman descriptions of the cult. One of the god's devotees in the mid-second century, Aelius Aristides, reported that such dream-operations had occurred two generations before, but in his record of his own experiences with Asclepius, *The Sacred Tales,* he gave no indication that he had experienced a surgical dream.[45] Instead, Graeco-Roman suppliants received pharmacological dreams, in which the god directed the dreamer to take various kinds of potions and mixtures, and prescriptive dreams in which the god ordered the dreamer to embark on regimens of exercise, bodily purgations (e.g., vomiting, enemas, fasts), and changes of climate and diet.[46] This shift in the pattern of Asclepian dreaming, from supernatural surgery to more earthy kinds of physical therapy, has been explained as "the significant shift in life-world from Hellenistic times in Epidaurus to the sophisticated ambience of Smyrna [the home of Aristides] and Pergamum in the Antonine period."[47] Thus, as a vehicle of meaning, the dream kept pace with changing cultural circumstances.

However, not all late-antique suppliants were wealthy aristocrats. An inscription from Rome dated to the second century records the healings of four men, presumably ordinary citizens because they are otherwise un-

[43] T. 425 in Edelstein, *Asclepius,* 1:238 (text only; trans. by MacMullen, *Paganism in the Roman Empire,* p. 66).
[44] MacMullen, *Paganism in the Roman Empire,* p. 66.
[45] *Sacred Tales* 4.64 (trans. Behr, *Complete Works,* 2:331).
[46] Behr, *Aelius Aristides and the Sacred Tales,* pp. 36–40.
[47] Kee, "Self-Definition in the Asclepius Cult," p. 129.

known. There was Gaius, a blind man, who was instructed by Asclepius in a dream to touch the base of his statue with his hand and then to touch his eyes; Lucius, suffering from pleurisy, was told to make a poultice of wine and ashes from Asclepius' altar and apply it to his side; to Julian, who was vomiting blood, it was revealed that eating seeds of a pinecone mixed with honey would be curative; and Valerius, a blind soldier, was instructed to make a salve for his eyes out of honey and the blood of a white cock.[48] All of these men were cured—"saved," as the text says—and their stories attest to the persistence, in Graeco-Roman times, of the atmosphere of mysterious wonder that attended the oneiric healing of Asclepius. Despite the shift in cultures, the restoration of good health remained a miraculous gift.

The unusual, even magical aspect of the god's pharmacopeia, as seen in the healings of Lucius and Valerius above, was characteristic of the oneiric prescriptions given to the sophisticated clientele of the temple of Pergamum as well. The orator Hermocrates, for example, was ordered by Asclepius to eat partridge stuffed with frankincense; Aristides exclaimed in an address to Asclepius that "there is very much of the marvelous in the unambiguous dreams of the god, for example one man drinks chalk, another hemlock. . . ."[49] The regimens prescribed in dreams were also strange, "the very opposite of what you would expect," as Aristides remarks.[50] Aristides himself had been "honored [by Asclepius] in this fashion, by stopping catarrhs and colds with baths in rivers and the sea, by curing our difficulty in reclining in bed with long walks, by adding indescribable purges to continual fasting, and by commanding me to speak and write when I found it difficult to breathe. . . ."[51] Not every cure required such heroics. Aristides admitted that some had been "very easy and pleasurable," and Dodds has observed that "in some instances they are quite rational, though not exactly original, as when the Divine Wisdom prescribes gargling for a sore throat and vegetables for constipation."[52] However, even such seemingly "rational" cures were occasions for rejoicing; they were, after all, the oneiric gifts of a god.[53]

Even though their drugs were curious and their regimens paradoxical, Asclepian dreams functioned by making the healing process palpable. To the ill, dreams presented striking visual images, often in the form of a visitation by the god Asclepius himself, and these images redirected the attention of the dreamer away from disease and toward cure. The ability of

[48] T. 438 in Edelstein, *Asclepius,* 1:250–51.

[49] T. 434 (Hermocrates) in Edelstein, *Asclepius,* 1:249; Aristides, *Or.* 42.8 (trans. Behr, *Complete Works,* 2:248).

[50] *Or.* 36.124 (trans. Behr, *Complete Works,* 2:222).

[51] Ibid. 42.8 (trans. Behr, *Complete Works,* 2:248–49).

[52] Ibid., 42.9 (trans. Behr, *Complete Works,* 2:249); Dodds, *The Greeks and the Irrational,* p. 115.

[53] See T.432 in Edelstein, *Asclepius,* 1:248, for a typical expression of gratitude.

dreams to reorient the disposition of the dreamer has already been noted in this study. Indeed, the constantly repeated thematic of reorientation—toward one's conscience, toward one's future, toward one's body—suggests that the various oneiric techniques and perspectives on dreams in late antiquity were not isolated or disconnected phenomena. On the contrary, each was a particular "dialect" of a discrete cultural"language," the discourse of dreams, which was geared toward enabling the articulation of a need for reorientation. Interestingly, the oneiric re-viewing of relationships (to one's god, one's love life, one's health) seems often to have produced the desired change in perspective or life-circumstance simply by giving it expression.

In the special case of Asclepian dreaming, dreamers were reoriented not only with regard to their bodies but also with regard to deity; it too was made more palpable as Asclepius appeared in person showing kindly concern in very individualized ways. No one in antiquity expressed more clearly the sense of well-being conveyed by Asclepius as oneiric friend than did Aristides. Here is his description of one such dream-epiphany of the god:

> For there was a seeming, as it were, to touch him and to perceive that he himself had come, and to be between sleep and waking, and to wish to look up and to be in anguish that he might depart too soon, and to strain the ears and to hear some things as in a dream, some as in a waking state. Hair stood straight, and there were tears of joy, and the pride of one's heart was inoffensive. And what man could describe these things in words? If any man has been initiated, he knows and understands.[54]

How many others had felt the same? Perhaps the graphic eloquence of Asclepian temples filled with votive replicas of healed ears and hands and eyes is similarly expressive of the warmth of presence conveyed by the Asclepian experience.

It may be that Asclepian religion persisted as long as it did in the face of attempts by Christian emperors to extirpate polytheist practice precisely because of the attention paid to the individual and also because the perspective fostered by the cult, that dreams could be therapeutic, gave suppliants the courage to face their sufferings with hope. There is evidence that ritual practice continued at least until the late fifth century, and Asclepius was kept alive theologically by later Neoplatonists like Macrobius and Proclus, who underscored the cosmic significance of this god by equating him with the sustaining force of the sun in a world of change.[55]

It is one of the ironies of history that, despite virulent attacks on Asclepian

---

[54] *Sacred Tales* 2.32 (trans. Behr, *Complete Works*, 2:298).

[55] T.301, 304–314 in Edelstein, *Asclepius*, 1:149–55 and the discussion in 2:106–8 concerning Neoplatonic interpretation of Asclepius; for accounts of Christian persecution of the Asclepius cult, see Pierre Chuvin, *A Chronicle of the Last Pagans*, pp. 33–34, 43–44, and Edelstein, *Asclepius*, 2:255–57.

religion by Christian apologists from Tertullian to Eusebius, who viewed Asclepius as a rival to their own healing god, Asclepius lived on in Christianity in the cult of the saints.[56] The most spectacular instance of the Christian appropriation of Asclepius is found in the mid-fifth century in the cult of St. Thecla in Seleucia, on the Mediterranean coast of what is now Turkey. First renowned in early Christian fiction as the converted follower of St. Paul, Thecla became the patron saint of an incubatory cultic center. She healed by appearing in dreams to the sick who were sleeping in her church. Proficient in the application of miraculous medicine, Thecla wore the mantle of Asclepius, now in the guise of a female saint.[57] The conviction that dreams can heal was too deeply embedded in the cultural imagination for it to succumb to the vagaries of religious rivalry. In the figure of Thecla, oneiric aspirations to health lived on.

HEALING DREAMS AND MAGIC

From antiquity to the present, the term *magic* has often been used as a negative label to discredit religious practices and beliefs that differed from one's own. Practices that were viewed in one tradition as pious and prayerful could be decried by another as nocturnal meddling with spiritual forces properly beyond human control—one person's "divine man" was another's "magician."[58] Magic was particularly a problem in early Christianity, because Jesus' "miracles" were susceptible to charges of magical manipulation.[59] Among polytheists, too, magic was problematic. Apuleius, for example, was brought to trial on a charge of magic because such objects as a mirror, bird feathers, and smoke had been found in his house—an irony because the protagonist of his novel, *Metamorphoses,* had suffered precisely from viewing magic as a manipulative technique devoid of spiritual content.[60]

Among modern interpreters as well, magic has been viewed as compulsive and egotistic, presuming as it does to summon divine presence into the human realm. Establishing a "lien on God" rather than a "means of ap-

[56] For apologists' attacks on Asclepius, see T. 103, 233 (Tertullian); T. 128, 584 (Arnobius); T. 294, 298–99 (Eusebius), in Edelstein, *Asclepius,* 1:52, 109, 62, 324–25, 143, 147–48.

[57] Thecla's activities as oneiric healer are recorded in the *Miracles of Saint Thecla* (ed. and trans. Dagron); see Dagron, pp. 103–8, for a discussion of her incubatory cult.

[58] For an analysis of the categories "divine man" and "magician," see Eugene Gallagher, *Divine Man or Magician?* pp. 33–50.

[59] See Morton Smith, *Jesus the Magician,* passim.

[60] For a discussion of Apuleius' *Apologia,* in which he defends himself against the specific charges brought against him, see Stephen Benko, *Pagan Rome and the Early Christians,* pp. 104–8.

proach to him," magicians have been said to mock the true spiritual life with their mutterings of meaningless sounds and mixings of odd potions.[61] Thus magic has been condemned as a debased form of religion in which conjuration replaced contemplation and arrogance toward the gods replaced humble submission to them. Recently, however, texts designated as "magical" have been shown to be much more sophisticated and complex, and it has been demonstrated that the term *magic* itself had in antiquity a very wide range of applicability from true piety to quackery.[62] As Hans Dieter Betz has observed, the Greek magical papyri, as a collection of texts, reflect "an amazingly broad religious and cultural pluralism" and, I would add, a similarly broad representation of religious practices, from spells and recipes to prayers to detailed techniques for effecting an ascent of the soul to the heavens.[63] In the present discussion of the function of dreams in magic, I will follow Betz in his construction of the magician as a craftsman who took seriously human dependency on "the unfathomable scramble of energies coming out of the universe" and tried to direct those energies to the profit of his clients. According to Betz, the magician was "a religious functionary who operated as a crisis manager" in the lives of ordinary people; his succinct summary of the magician's craft merits quotation in full, because it describes accurately the circumstances in which magical dreams operated.

> Applying his craft, the magician could give people the feeling that he could make things work in a world where nothing seemed to work the way it used to. He had handbooks of magic, which contained the condensed wisdom of the past, wisdom made effective to solve the problems of the present. . . . He knew the code words needed to communicate with the gods, the demons, and the dead. He could tap, regulate, and manipulate the invisible energies. He was a problem solver who had remedies for a thousand petty troubles plaguing mankind: everything from migraine to runny nose to bedbugs to horse races, and, of course, all the troubles of love and money. In short, it was this kind of world in which the magician served as a power and communications expert, crisis manager, miracle healer and inflicter of damages, and all-purpose therapist and agent of worried, troubled, and troublesome souls.[64]

The magical papyri that concern dreams fall into two categories: requests for a dream for oneself, and requests for sending a dream to another person. The magician is thus called upon in the service of communication, in cases where need for personal revelation is expressed, and in the service of the management of crises, particularly crises of erotic desire, in cases where

---

[61] Arthur Darby Nock, "Greek Magical Papyri" (ed. Stewart, 1:176–94, especially p. 190); see also Festugière, *La Révélation d'Hermès Trismégiste*, 1:283–309.

[62] See Segal, "Hellenistic Magic: Some Questions of Definition," pp. 349–75.

[63] Betz, *Greek Magical Papyri*, xlv.

[64] Ibid., xlvii.

dreams are sent to others (usually by love-struck men to women). In these contexts, dreams functioned, on the one hand, as a therapy of ignorance, and on the other, as a therapy of overwrought emotion.

The prescribed procedures for requesting dream-revelations can be quite simple or very complex. Schematically, they involve ritual purification, recitation of petitionary formulas to a lighted lamp, the inscribing of the request on strips of linen or tin, and invocations of the divine figures involved, often in the untranslatable "nonsense" language characteristic of the magical papyri as a whole.[65] Of particular interest is the standard formula with which many of these requests end: "Come, lord, reveal to me concerning the so-and-so matter, without deceit, without treachery, immediately, immediately; quickly, quickly."[66] For "so-and-so," the petitioner fills in his or her own request for a dream tailor-made to the specific matter of pressing concern about which enlightenment is needed. As in Asclepian dreaming, the appeal of such magical spells for dreams lies in their offer of attentiveness to an individual's need, here cast as an urgent need for information that cannot be gotten from a human source. Further, the rhetoric of control—the imperative "come immediately, quickly"—functions not as an assertion of human control over divine agency, but rather as a rhetoric of desire for certainty in a world where there are too many gaps in human knowledge. To fill in those gaps, the seeker turns to the dream-sending "others," the gods, goddesses, angels, and demons of the magical pantheon.

Most of the spells for requesting a dream share the direction to recite a petitionary prayer or formula *to* a lighted lamp(and not simply in a room in which there is a lamp). Some are brief: "Formula to be spoken to the day lamp: 'NAIENCHRE NAIENCHRE, mother of fire and water, you are the one who rises before, ARCHENTECHTHA; reveal to me concerning the NN matter."[67] Others are elaborate, as in the following spell that the would-be dreamer is directed to recite seven times to the lamp.

> Hermes, lord of the world, who're in the heart,
> O circle of Selene, spherical
> And square, the founder of the words of speech,
> Pleader of Justice's cause, garbed in a mantle,

---

[65] Requests for dream oracles are found in *PGM* IV.3172–3208; V.370–446; VII.222–49, 250–54, 255–59, 359–69, 478–90, 664–85, 703–26, 727–39, 740–55, 795–845, 1009–16; VIII.64–110; XII.190–92; XXIIb.27–31, 32–35 (ed. Preisendanz, 1:176–77, 194–96; vol. 2, pp. 10–12, 16–17, 22, 30–31, 32–34, 35–37, 44, 48–50, 71, 149–50).

[66] The example cited here is *PGM* VII.247–49 (ed. Preisendanz, 2:11; trans. W. C. Grese, in Betz, *Greek Magical Papyri*, p. 123. Translators of the *PGM* use the formulaic "NN" for the Greek word *deina*, which means "so and so" or "such and such" and designates the space in which the operator of the spell fills in individualized information.

[67] *PGM* VII.250–53 (ed. Preisendanz, 2:11–12; trans. W. C. Grese in Betz, *Greek Magical Papyri*, p. 123).

With golden sandals, turning airy course
Beneath earth's depths, who hold the spirit's reins,
The sun's and who with lamps of gods immortal
Give joy to those beneath earth's depths, to mortals
Who've finished life. The Moirai's fatal thread
And Dream divine you're said to be, who send
Forth oracles by day and night; you cure
Pains of all mortals with your healing cares.
Hither, O blessed one, O mighty son
Of the goddess who brings full mental powers,
By your own form and gracious mind. And to
An uncorrupted youth reveal a sign
And send him your true skill of prophecy.[68]

These entreaties spoken into the flame of a lamp are striking given the particular divine figures who are summoned in them. Hermes, Osiris, the Egyptian god Besas, and Selene are all divinities connected with the underworld, with deathlike darkness but also with lunar light. One of the formulas makes explicit the fact that to speak into the lamplight is to speak to these "lights" in the depths: "Speak the following to the lamplight, until it is extinguished: 'Be well, O lamp, who light the way to Harsentephtha and to Harsentechtha, and to the great [father] Osiris-Michael.'"[69] The flame of the lamp works as an object of oneiric revery that puts the seeker in touch with an "underworld" where the resources of "full mental powers" can be tapped. As Gaston Bachelard has suggestively written, "Any dreamer of flame knows that the flame is alive. . . . And what a full, what a beautiful moment when the candle burns well! . . . The values of life and dream then reach their full association."[70]

In their presentation of the way in which dreams appear to those in search of oneiric revelation, the magical papyri adhere to the Homeric figuration of dreams as autonomous presences speaking to the dreamer. For example, in a spell to summon the power of a goddess with the magical name AK-TIOPHIS, a spell said to "accomplish dream revelations marvelously," the seeker is instructed to say, "'Stand beside me, Mistress, and reveal to me about the NN matter.' And she will stand beside you and will tell everything without deception."[71] In another case, the revelatory dream stands beside

---

[68] PGM VII.668–81 (ed. Preisendanz, 2:30–31; trans. E. N. O'Neil in Betz, Greek Magical Papyri, p. 137).

[69] PGM XXIIb.28–30 (ed. Preisendanz, 2:149–50; trans. D. E. Aune in Betz, Greek Magical Papyri, p. 261).

[70] Gaston Bachelard, La Flamme d'une Chandelle, p. 58 (trans. Gaudin, p. 107).

[71] PGM IV.2444, 2501–4 (ed. Preisendanz, 1:148, 150; trans. E. N. O'Neil in Betz, Greek Magical Papyri, pp. 82, 84).

the dreamer in the form of a friend.[72] A particularly graphic instance of this practice of manipulating imaginal figures as a technique to induce meditation is found in a magical ritual for obtaining dreams that ends with a spell to Hermes similar to the one quoted above. Here one is instructed to use dough to make a figure of Hermes holding his herald's staff. The spell is written on papyrus or on a goose's windpipe and inserted into the doll "for the purpose of inspiration"—presumably so that the figure can breathe in the necessary message. At bedtime, the seeker is directed to place the doll by his or her head and to go to sleep. Then the god will prophesy.[73] Who is the observer, and who is the observed? It would seem that the "I" of the magical practitioner seeking a dream is an observing "eye" which is actually looking at itself in the fabricated image of the other, the god, who functions as a projection of the dreamer's own inspiration. The insistence on Hermes in his role as herald, that is, as the god well-known to be adept at interpretation, underscores this text's expression of the desire for a hermeneutic that will enable a new sense of understanding.[74]

Finding a language that will light up one's own underworld was also the concern of magical texts that pertain to the sending of dreams from one person to another. Again the Homeric model of the autonomous dream is operative in these texts: one could appear oneself in someone else's dream, or one could write down the dream that the god or daemon would then send, or one could direct a specific oneiric figure to appear to the other person, in some instances "like the god whom she worships."[75] Many of these rituals for sending dreams are spells of attraction, as the following makes clear.

There is also a rite for acquiring an assistant, who is made out of wood from a mulberry tree. He is made as a winged Eros wearing a cloak, with his right foot lifted for a stride and with a hollow back. Into the hollow put a gold leaf after writing . . . "Be my assistant and supporter and sender of dreams." Go late at night to the house [of the woman] you want, knock on her door with the Eros and say, "Lo, she NN resides here; wherefore stand beside her and, after

[72] *PGM* VII.798–99 (ed. Preisendanz, 2:35, trans. J. P. Hershbell in Betz, *Greek Magical Papyri,* p. 140).

[73] *PGM* V.377–422 (ed. Preisendanz, 1:194–96; trans. E. N. O'Neil in Betz, *Greek Magical Papyri,* pp. 108–9).

[74] See, for example, *PGM* VII.670 (ed. Preisendanz, 2:30; trans. E. N. O'Neil in Betz, *Greek Magical Papyri,* p. 137), where Hermes is called "the founder of the words of speech." On Hermes as interpreter, see William G. Doty, "Hermes' Heteronymous Appellations," p. 128, and Burkert, *Greek Religion,* p. 158, who points out that the word *hermeneutic* comes from the allegorical association of Hermes with speech and words.

[75] *PGM* VII.407–10; XII.107–21; IV.2441–2621; IV.1842–69 (ed. Preisendanz, 2:18, 65–66; 1:148–54, 128–30).

assuming the likeness of the god or daimon whom she worships, say what I propose." And go to your home, set the table, spread a pure linen cloth, and seasonal flowers, and set the figure upon it. Then make a burnt offering to it and continuously say the spell of invocation. And send him, and he will act without fail.[76]

As with the manipulation of the Hermes doll, which expresses the desire for greater interpretive acumen, so here the ritual use of a figurine of the god Eros expresses the need to articulate erotic desire. All of the spells to send dreams are situated in the desire to tell, to communicate something that has urgent importance in the mind of the sender.

There is a question, however, about who the recipient of these transmitted dreams really is, especially in regard to what one spell calls a "fetching charm."[77] Geared toward attracting the (usually female) recipient to the bedroom of the (usually male) sender, these oneiric commands typically take the following form: "Bring NN, the daughter of NN, to the house, to the sleeping-place in which is NN, the son of NN!"[78] On the face of it, such spells of erotic attraction are unsavory compulsive techniques, speaking as they do a rhetoric of sexual imperialism. Yet, as John Winkler has argued persuasively, these *agōgai*—spells designed to "lead" or "draw" another person to oneself—can also be read as remedies for *eros*. As he points out, in Mediterranean antiquity intense desire was considered to be a "diseased state affecting the soul and the body"; *eros* was felt as a "powerful involuntary attraction and described in a pathology of physical and mental disturbance."[79] Additionally, in her book on the "bittersweetness" of *eros,* Anne Carson discusses the sense of loss that accompanies this strong emotion: "When I desire you a part of me is gone: my want of you partakes of me. So reasons the lover at the edge of eros. The presence of want awakens in him nostalgia for wholeness. His thoughts turn toward questions of personal identity: he must recover and reincorporate what is gone if he is to be a complete person."[80]

Given such cultural conceptualizations of erotic attraction as psychic disturbance, Winkler dismisses a literalistic reading of these erotic oneiric dispatches. In his view, the rhetoric of domination that characterizes such spells is directed not toward the intended recipient of the dreams, but rather toward the sender himself, with the aim of defusing erotic obsessions and reestablishing emotional stability. The following set of observations states the case clearly:

[76] *PGM* IV.1842–69 (ed. Preisendanz, 1:128–30; trans. E. N. O'Neil in Betz, *Greek Magical Papyri*, p. 71).

[77] *PDM* xiv.1077 (trans. Janet H. Johnson in Betz, *Greek Magical Papyri*, p. 246).

[78] *PDM* xiv.1076–77 (trans. Janet H. Johnson in Betz, *Greek Magical Papyri*, p. 246).

[79] Winkler, *The Constraints of Desire*, pp. 82, 84.

[80] Carson, *Eros The Bittersweet*, pp. 30–31.

Between the agent and the victim, as depicted in these scenarios, there is a curious transference. The rite assigns a role of calm and masterful control to the performer and imagines the victim's scene as one of passionate inner torment. But if we think about the reality of the situation, the intended victim is in all likelihood sleeping peacefully, blissfully ignorant of what some love-struck lunatic is doing on his roof, while the man himself, if he is fixated on this particular woman, is really suffering in that unfortunate and desperate state known as *eros*. The spells direct that the woman's mind be wholly occupied with thoughts of the lover: from the evidence of the ritual we can say rather that the lover himself is already powerfully preoccupied with thoughts of the victim.[81]

Thus the fetching charms are a form of "psychodrama" in which passionately disturbing emotions are treated.[82] Using a vocabulary of voyeurism, the oneiric spells of attraction allow the sender to see himself in the mirror of his victim; such dreams heal by providing a space for reflective engagement with one's own feelings. Thus, in the act of confronting the other, one confronts oneself. The therapeutic value of magical dreams lies in such revealing confrontation. Just as Asclepian dreaming healed the body, so magical dreaming provided a therapy for the mind.

[81] Winkler, *The Constraints of Desire*, p. 87.
[82] Ibid., p. 93.

Part II

DREAMERS

Introduction

"MADMEN and dreamers believe what is false."[1] So Socrates thought, and many in the contemporary world might well agree. To believe in the ephemeral fancies of dreams is a mad enterprise, a slap in the face of logic. If reason and unreason are the only categories available for judging our perceptions of the world and ourselves, then Socrates was undoubtedly right: dream knowledge is false knowledge.

However, across the centuries, a dreamer's "belief in what is false" has been understood otherwise. Rather than placing dreams within a binary framework that opposes logic to illogic, dreamers from Artemidorus to Freud have situated dreams neither in logic nor in illogic, but in imagination. For this tradition of thinkers, dreams can be occasions not for "belief" but rather for reflection on constructions of self-identity. Oneiric literature has been remarkable for its recognition, whether implicit or explicit, that the self *is* an imaginal construct—that we are ourselves ephemeral fancies, continually in the process of further fabrication.

In the current postmodern climate of critical discourse, which has heralded the "death of the author" and the decentering of a once-dominical self, it is probably risky and potentially misleading to use such terms as "self," "self-identity," and even "individual."[2] When I use such terms in the following studies, I do not mean to imply that Graeco-Roman people conceptualized the self as a stable essence beyond the reach of cultural construction, nor do I mean to imply that they were just like contemporary theorists, preoccupied with dismantling a centuries-long construct of a unitary, objectifying ego that blinks its own vulnerability to change. What I do mean to point to by using such terms is that, in their interaction with dreams, late-antique people revealed their understanding of the human person as possessed of an interiority, indeed of a lively interior "space" in which analysis of very particular aspects of the person's life was conducted. Whether one is dealing with such disparate figures as a moody lover staring at the flame of a candle or a monk asleep in his cave, still the function of the dream as a form of *self*-address, as an agent of insight into a life conceived as truly individual, seems clear.

In the essays on particular dreamers that follow, I will argue that,

---

[1] Plato, *Theaetetus* 158b (*Collected Dialogues*, p. 863).

[2] See, for example, Roland Barthes, "The Death of the Author," pp. 12–48; Michel Foucault, "What Is an Author?" pp. 141–60; Michel de Certeau, *Heterologies: Discourse on the Other*, pp. 80–100; M. Sprinker, "Fictions of the Self: The End of Autobiography," pp. 321–42; Jacques Derrida, *The Ear of the Other*, pp. 41–89.

through their metaphors and tropes, dreams extended the consciousness of the dreamers by provoking engagement with matters of intimate signifi-cance: Perpetua's painful memories of her young brother, Hermas' battle with adulterous desires, Jerome's struggle with his elitist literary tastes, the two Gregorys' coming to terms with asceticism, Aristides' ambivalence toward cultural norms of masculinity. As signifying moments in the formation—or deformation—of identity, dreams will be viewed as projec-tions of desire that alter existing frameworks of self-understanding. My interest in this section lies in exploring how the oneiric imagination acted as the spur to a process of reconstructing what an individual experienced as real, as significant.

Dreams will here be read as a lexicon of self-expression that entailed a re-reading of experience in light of the dream, a re-reading in which the dream has the effect of the twist of a kaleidoscope; the pieces of a life's experience throw themselves together in a new pattern, a new way of picturing or visualizing one's self in one's own context. As an interpreter, I have tried to match my method of presentation with the synchronic dy-namic that I see at work in the effect of dreams on these ancient dreamers. Thus the studies that follow are not biographical in the sense of charting the linear unfolding of events in a life. Instead, they are "snapshots" that attempt to represent the moment when a fortuitous event—in these cases, a dream or set of dreams—forces a reconfiguration of the elements that compose a life.

Further, I am interested in the way in which a focus on dreams leads to insights into a person's life and culture that might not have been possible otherwise. Dreams lead not only inward but also outward, opening sur-prising connections to and perspectives on other facets of the dreamer's experience and cultural situation. Following the tracery of dreams has led me to investigations of other topics of significance in the Graeco-Roman world (for example, the body) as well as to the adoption of interpretive strategies that differ from the historical-philological model (for example, French feminist hermeneutics). Dreams have constituted a "semiotic won-derland" not only for the subjects of this discussion, but also for this interpreter.[3]

The dreamers who are the principals of these studies were chosen either because they were prolific dreamers who left written records of their dreams (Hermas, Perpetua, and Aelius Aristides), or because of the strik-

---

[3] The phrase "semiotic wonderland" comes from a discussion of the biographical self as a narrative construct by William H. Epstein, *Recognizing Biography*, p. 36; his statement is worth quoting in full: "It no longer seems possible to treat a biographical 'event' as a 'natural' occurrence in the concrete world; rather, the contemporary theoretical crisis suggests, we must treat a biographical 'event' as an epistemological operation to which ontological status is frequently, if inappropriately, granted, as a transient, discursive moment in a constantly receding and endlessly replicating semiotic wonderland."

ing qualities of individual dreams (Jerome, Gregory of Nyssa, and Gregory of Nazianzus). The religious affiliations of these dreamers did not influence my selection of them, because part of the argument of this book is that dreaming was a cultural discourse that cut across lines of difference in religious belief and practice. Of course the *forms* of dreaming varied: Asclepian dreaming took a different form from magical dreaming, for example. As I have pointed out, dreaming was a "language" with many "dialects." The normative character of dreaming as a cultural phenomenon lies rather in its widespread *practice,* irrespective of the forms it took in specific religious traditions and institutions.

The fact that five of the six dreamers who have been singled out for special attention were Christian should not be construed as an implicit affirmation on my part of the view that Christianity fostered a new or deeper or more comprehensive view of the self. The issue of how "self" and "person" were conceptualized in classical and late antiquity is a thorny one with a large bibliography.[4] I raise the issue here because a perspective advanced at the turn of this century by Wilhelm Dilthey and Georg Misch, which argues that an authentic concept of an inner life, and hence of personality, did not exist before Augustine wrote his *Confessions,* has recently been revived.[5] This argument in its revived form, which continues to focus on Augustine's writing as the locus of clearest expression, credits to Christianity the creation of "a newly reflexive self, that is, a subject turned back upon itself in ways unknown before."[6] Arguing against Foucault's concept of Christian, especially ascetic Christian, self-renunciation, this perspective argues that a new view of the person as a "whole self" was made possible in Christianity in part by its theological affirmation of the body, now seen to be as essential to the concept of the person as the soul.[7]

This argument overstates its case by privileging a particular kind of self-

[4] The *locus classicus* for discussions of concepts of the self in Greek and Roman antiquity is Georg Misch, *A History of Autobiography in Antiquity,* 2 vols.; see also Jean Daniélou, "La Notion de personne chez les Pères grecs," pp. 113–21; Maria Daraki, "La Naissance du sujet singulier dans les Confessions de Saint Augustin"; F. M. Schraeder, "The Self in Ancient Religious Experience," pp. 337–59; for discussions of the corporate identity of religious sects, see *Jewish and Christian Self-Definition,* 3: *Self-Definition in the Greco-Roman World,* ed. Meyer and Sanders; for works that define the person by using socio-historical methodologies, see *A History of Private Life,* vol. 1: *From Pagan Rome to Byzantium* (ed. Veyne, trans. Goldhammer, pp. 5–409); and Foucault, *The History of Sexuality,* 3:37–95.

[5] For Dilthey's theory of narrative self-revelation, see *Gesammelte Schriften,* 7: *Der Aufbau der Geschichtlichen Welt in den Geisteswissenschaften,* pp. 191–251; for Misch's discussion of Augustine, see *History of Autobiography,* 2:625–67. These views appear in contemporary form (although without the appeal to mysticism that is prominent in Misch's study) in Gedaliahu G. Stroumsa, "*Caro Salutis Cardo:* Shaping the Person in Early Christian Thought," pp. 25–50.

[6] Stroumsa, "*Caro Salutis Cardo:* Shaping the Person in Early Christian Thought," p. 26.

[7] Ibid., pp. 30, 33–35, and *passim.*

examination and thus denying concepts of interiority and personhood to the non-Christian "others" of late antiquity, that is, to the polytheist and Jewish traditions.[8] Yet, as Foucault has shown in an extensive study, there were in late antiquity a variety of practices of self-examination, which he examines under the rubric of "the care of the self."[9] Furthermore, Arnaldo Momigliano has shown that Greek and Roman (polytheist) biographers had an acute sense of individual character.[10] The discussion about late-antique concepts of the self needs to be injected with evidence from arenas other than theology and philosophy—arenas like dreams, which would, I suggest, give the discussion a more generous, because more nuanced, range. Thus I see no reason why Augustine's *Confessions* should continue as the standard against which the personhood of others is judged and found wanting. In the present context, the fact of conceptualizing a person as possessed of a soul that either receives or fabricates dreams (or both) certainly suggests the presence of an understanding of inner life, and this was as true of magicians as it was of Augustine. It was Augustine, after all, who thought he had appeared as a phantom in someone else's dream. As a phenomenon, this strikes me as stemming from the same mental climate as that of the magician who sends a dream to another person.[11]

In the following essays, then, the dreamers who have been selected for detailed discussion will be treated, first and foremost, as *dreamers,* and dreaming will be seen as one of the techniques of the care of the self that was a cultural preoccupation not aligned with particular religious persuasions. Presiding over all of these studies is an inquiry into the phenomenon of late-antique dreaming as representative of the construction of new narrative discourses of the self.

[8] See the astute observations by Arnaldo Momigliano, "Marcel Mauss and the Quest for the Person in Greek Biography and Autobiography," pp. 83–92, especially 84–85.

[9] Foucault, *History of Sexuality,* 3:39–68, focuses on the following topics: the era's individualistic attitude, its positive valuation of private life, and the intensity of relations to the self.

[10] Momigliano, "Marcel Mauss and the Quest for the Person in Greek Biography and Autobiography," pp. 89–92; see also his *The Development of Greek Biography.*

[11] Augustine, *De cura pro mortuis gerenda* 11.13 (*CSEL* 41.642, 12–643,4).

CHAPTER FIVE

Hermas and the Shepherd

As I walked along I began to fall asleep, and a spirit seized me and took me away through a certain pathless region through which no one could walk because it was steep and broken up by streams of water.[1]

WITH THIS statement, a Roman dreamer of the late first century C.E. named Hermas introduced his dream-book, a book of considerable length.[2] The title of the work, *The Shepherd,* refers to the central revelatory figure, an "angel of repentance," who appears to Hermas in the last of a series of five oneiric visions and directs him to write down the collection of mandates (commandments) and similitudes (parables) that compose the bulk of the book.[3] Addressed to the community of Christians in Rome, *The Shepherd* deals with issues concerning purity of heart and the necessity for repentance understood broadly as salvation from ethical misbehavior in matters of both attitude and practice.[4] Yet it is also a document of poignant personal testimony to the difficult struggle that the author Hermas suffered with affairs of conscience, with "the tensions of his own heart," as Brown phrases it.[5]

The document that Hermas wrote is the most complete extant testimony to the late-antique conceptualization of self-scrutiny as a series of conversations with a dream-angel. What Plutarch and Apuleius understood philosophically in terms of the transformative effect of oneiric daemons on the psyche is here depicted in autobiographical terms as an angelic therapy of consciousness. In fact, the text appears to be aware of its own angelic trope, because one of the mandates that the oneiric shepherd gives to Hermas explains how to discriminate between trustworthy and untrustworthy angelic revealers. The shepherd says:

[1] *Vis.* 1.1.3. References to the text of *The Shepherd of Hermas* will follow the standard divisions of the text: *Vis.* (*Visions*), *Mand.* (*Mandates*), and *Sim.* (*Similitudes*). References are to the Greek text in Joly, ed. and trans., *Hermas le Pasteur.*

[2] For a thorough discussion of the evidence in support of placing the composition of *The Shepherd* at the end of the first century, see Harry O. Maier, *The Social Setting of the Ministry as Reflected in the Writings of Hermas, Clement, and Ignatius,* pp. 55–58.

[3] The angel of repentance first appears in *Vis.* 5.1–5.

[4] Brown, *The Body and Society,* pp. 69–72; Maier, *The Social Setting of the Ministry,* pp. 72–78.

[5] Brown, *The Body and Society,* p. 69.

There are two angels who accompany the human being, the angel of justice and the angel of wickedness. "But how am I to know their operations," I said, "if both are dwelling within me?" Listen, he said, and you will understand them. The angel of justice is sensitive, modest, gentle, and calm. So, when this angel comes into your heart, he will immediately converse with you about justice, purity, holiness, self-control, every just work and glorious virtue. When all these thoughts enter your heart, you can be sure that the angel of justice is within you. . . . Now, observe the deeds of the angel of wickedness. First of all, he is of a violent temper, bitter, and silly. His deeds are evil, the undoing of the servants of God. So, when he enters your heart, know him from his deeds.[6]

Because the qualities of the angel of justice as described in this passage are precisely those that the shepherd teaches Hermas, this mandate functions as the text's affirmation of its own revelatory strategy. Overall, *The Shepherd* gives a uniquely personalized portrayal of the way in which dream-angels were thought to aid in the fine-tuning of an individual's sensibilities.[7]

As a dream-book, *The Shepherd* is formally parallel to another oneiric journal, *The Sacred Tales,* written half a century later by Aelius Aristides. Both take the form of vividly imaged dreams in which a divine figure appears to the dreamer to convey some kind of essential information, and in both the oneiric revealer becomes a permanent companion; in Hermas' case, the shepherd states that he will live with Hermas in his house for the rest of his life.[8] Also, in both dream-books the information given by the dream-figure gives the dreamer a sense of relief and a conviction that he has been saved from disaster in the midst of life's turmoil. Aristides explicitly named his oneiric companion Asclepius "Savior."[9] And Hermas' question after his first dream, "How shall I be saved?" can be read as the question to which the rest of the book is answer.[10]

In Graeco-Roman religious texts, "salvation" designated the desire for, or experience of, a resting place, a place in which to dwell safely. As a religious concept, *sōtēria,* salvation, carried the general sense of delivery, preservation, safe return.[11] Particular understandings of what might constitute such a "safe return" varied widely, however. Pouring a libation of wine to Zeus *Sōtēr* in thanks for a safe voyage obviously situates the concept of salvation differently than, say, the Pauline vision of the victory of the imperishable over the perishable signified by the cosmic *sōtēr* Christ.

[6] *Mand.* 6.2.1–4 (trans. Marique, pp. 268–69).
[7] See above, Ch. 2, pp. 59–65, for the function of oneiric angels; on Hermas and angels, see Lane Fox, *Pagans and Christians,* pp. 388–89.
[8] See *Vis.* 5.2 and *Sim.* 9.1.3; for a discussion of Aristides' dream-book, see Ch. 7 below.
[9] Aristides, *Oration* 42.4 (trans. Behr, *Complete Works,* 2:247).
[10] *Vis.* 1.2.1.
[11] See *TDNT* 7, s.v. *sōzō,* pp. 965–1003.

In the one case, the "return" is to the earthy reality of everyday life at home, while in the other, "return" is ethereal, out of this world and into some other where the physical threat of death carries no sting.

Between these extremes lies a third understanding of salvation, one in which the "safe return" is understood as a conscious awareness of dwelling in an invisible safe place *in the midst of* everyday earthy reality. This conception of salvation was a psychological one, and in the case of Hermas, the consciousness it provoked was mediated by dreams. First in his dreams, and then in his oneiric conversations with the shepherd, Hermas gradually found a resting place, a haven of "safe return" from various kinds of spiritual and moral malaise.

The first section of *The Shepherd* is composed of a series of five "visions" (*horaseis*) that come to Hermas "when [he gets] sleepy," "while sitting on [his] bed," and so on.[12] The status of these visions as dreams needs some exploration, especially in light of Lane Fox's assertion about Hermas' first visionary experience that Hermas "had not seen a dream; he had gone into a trance," a trance induced by prayer and fasting.[13] The text in question reads as follows: "After some time, while I was going to Cumae, and glorifying the creation of God for its greatness and splendor and might, as I walked along I became sleepy (*aphūpnōsa*). And a spirit seized me and took me away. . . . "[14] While Lane Fox understands this scene to indicate a trance-state, another commentator, J. Reiling, takes *aphūpnōsa* to entail not a trance but "a state of somnambulism."[15] I prefer to take Hermas more nearly at his word: he got sleepy, and began to dream, an experience described as seizure by a spirit. Further, the term used by Hermas to characterize all five visions, *horaseis*, was a metaphor of seeing, like the Latin *visio*, that constituted part of the technical vocabulary of oneiric description in antiquity.[16] Hermas himself refers to "revelations" shown to him at night "while I slept"; those revelatory visions were dreams.[17]

Hermas, then, was a dreamer, and he dreamed elaborate dreams that provoked a profound metamorphosis, leading Hermas to an understanding of himself and his religious context that was considerably deepened as he moved through one dream after another. By the final dream in his text, Hermas has become an enthusiastic and sophisticated interpreter of his dreams, and he receives a dream-figure who will dwell with him permanently and whose task is to show Hermas again all of his dreams, as

---

[12] *Vis.* 1.1.3; 5.1.1.
[13] Lane Fox, *Pagans and Christians,* p. 382; see pp. 386, 389 on fast-induced trances.
[14] *Vis.* 1.1.3 (trans. Lake, pp. 7–9).
[15] J. Reiling, *Hermas and Christian Prophecy,* p. 157 and n.6.
[16] See Dodds, *The Greeks and the Irrational,* p. 105 and Patricia Cox Miller, "'A Dubious Twilight': Reflections on Dreams in Patristic Literature," p. 158.
[17] *Vis.* 2.4.1; 3.1.2.

though they were texts that demand re-readings, for they represent "the main points which are helpful to you."[18] This indwelling dream-figure, the shepherd, is called an "angel of repentance" (*angelos tēs metanoias*), literally a "messenger of a change of mind."[19] Through dreams, Hermas experiences a "safe return" and is given a resting place in the form of a changed consciousness.

In his discussion of the significance of dreams for religion in the first centuries of the Graeco-Roman era, Peter Brown remarks that the dream "was the paradigm of the open frontier: when a man was asleep and his bodily senses were stilled, the frontier lay wide open between himself and the gods."[20] The metaphor of the open frontier serves Brown's point about the ease of access to the gods that the dream afforded the dreamer because, as we have seen, for late-antique dreamers it was preeminently divine figures who spoke in dreams. Yet I would argue that this formula can, in the case of Hermas, be turned around: the dream was also conceptualized such that it afforded to the gods an ease of access to people.

For the circumstances that Brown addresses, "open frontier" is a geographical metaphor that is analogous to Lane Fox's cinematic image of the "nightly screening of the gods" that enabled late-antique dreamers to tap the resources of divine wisdom.[21] Both are positive metaphors used to convey the sense of easily available congress with the gods that dreams bestowed on those who received them. Such optimism concerning oneiric contact is true particularly of such dreamers as Perpetua of Carthage and Aelius Aristides who both, in their separate ways, *asked for* dreams, the one by prayer, the other by the practice of incubation.[22] Whether by simple request, by Asclepian ritual, or by even more elaborate rituals such as those prescribed in the magical papyri, one could ask for and receive direct communication with the divine world.

This cultural construction of the practice of dreaming did not, initially, apply to Hermas. The beginning of his oneiric adventures, as he tells them, was not set in motion by petition, nor by incubation at a shrine, nor by writing in myrrh on linen. Instead, Hermas was invaded by his dreams. For him the open frontier was more sinister than it was for others; he was easy prey for divine incursions across the boundary.[23]

As *The Shepherd* opens, Hermas is on the road: "As I walked along I

---

[18] *Vis.* 5.5.1.

[19] *Vis.* 5.5.7.

[20] Brown, *The Making of Late Antiquity*, p. 65.

[21] Lane Fox, *Pagans and Christians*, p. 164.

[22] *Pass. Perp.* 4.1–2 (ed. Van Beek, pp. 10–12); Aristides, *Sacred Tales* 1.4 (trans. Behr, *Complete Works*, 2:278) and *passim*.

[23] For arguments in favor of the authenticity of Hermas' visionary experiences, see Lane Fox, *Pagans and Christians*, pp. 381–82; Reiling, *Hermas and Christian Prophecy*, p. 174.

began to fall asleep, and a spirit seized me and took me away. . . . " In this outer or framing dream, the spirit leads Hermas through a nightmarish landscape, pathless, precipitous, riven by streams of water. Hermas makes his way to level ground, begins to pray, and with that the heavens open and the first of two feminine dream-figures, both dreams within the framing dream, makes her appearance.[24]

Hermas' seizure and speedy escort into nightmare, which happens while he is "glorifying the creations of god for their greatness and splendor and power," bears a formal resemblance to the opening of the Hermetic tractate *Poimandres*.[25] There the narrator, while "thinking about being," feels his bodily senses "held back as it happens to those overwhelmed by heavy sleep" and is then confronted by a gigantic dream-figure.[26] Also similar, especially in tone, to Hermas' experience is the report of Maximus the decurion, who wrote on the wall of the temple of Mandulis at Talmis in Egypt: "A sleeping nook induced me to descend, even though I was a bit afraid to abandon myself to visions of dream; and sleep, having seized me, transported me rapidly to a country dear to me."[27] Later dreamers as well—a notable example is St. Jerome—found themselves unexpectly (and uncomfortably) confronted with an oneiric revelation whose images were too compelling to ignore.

The image of the "open frontier," then, should not be used to construct a picture of Graeco-Roman dreaming as solely a petitionary practice; invasion by these divine messages, understood by dreamers as autonomous forces, was also a feature of oneiric experience. For Hermas, as for the Hermetic philosopher and the Roman bureaucrat, thinking thoughts about such fundamental issues as Being and God makes them prey to the subjects of their thoughts. Enticed or somehow constrained, asleep and seized, they suddenly find themselves in dream. Unlike Maximus, however, Hermas did not find himself in a "dear country"—at least, the country of dream was not yet dear to him, though it was to be by the time that the dreamworld had had its way with him.

Dreaming, Hermas prays and confesses his sins; suddenly, a dream appears within this outer dream. It is a young woman who personifies one sin that Hermas is not confessing, because he has denied it before being

---

[24] *Vis.* 1.1.3–1.2.2.

[25] *Vis.* 1.1.3.

[26] *Corpus Hermeticum, Poimandres* 1.1 (ed. Nock, trans. Festugière, 2:7). The author of this text remarks later about his dream: "I was in extreme joy. For in me the sleep of the body had become the wakefulness of the soul, the closing of my eyes a true vision (*horasis*)" (*Poimandres* 1.30 [ed. Nock, trans. Festugière, 2:17]); here the *Corpus Hermeticum* employs the same word for *vision* as does Hermas (e.g., *Vis.* 2.1.1, 2.4.2, 3.1.1). In both cases, the vision is a dream.

[27] The text of Maximus' inscription is translated in Festugière, *La Révélation d'Hermès Trismégiste,* 1:48. See also A. D. Nock, "A Vision of Mandulis Aion," pp. 53–104.

seized by the dream. Because this dream introduces elements that will be important in showing how Hermas' text uses dreams to mediate conflicts between the pragmatic concerns of life in the world and the spiritual concerns of the Christian community, it will be quoted in full:

> During my prayer I saw the heavens open and that woman of whom I was enamored saluting me with the words: "Greetings, Hermas!" With my eyes fixed on her, I said: "Lady, what are you doing here?" Her answer was: "I have been taken up to convict you of your sins before the Lord." To this I said: "Are you my accuser at this moment?" "No," she said, "but you must listen to what I am about to tell you. God who dwells in heaven, the creator of beings out of nothing, he, who increases and multiplies them for the sake of his holy church, is angry with you for your offenses against me." For answer I said: "Offenses against you! How so? Have I ever made a coarse remark to you? Have I not always regarded you as a goddess? Did I not always show you the respect due to a sister? Lady, why do you make these false charges of wickedness and uncleanness against me?" With a laugh she said: "In your heart there has arisen the desire of evil. Surely you think it evil that an evil desire arises in the heart of a good man. It is a sin," she said, "yes a great sin. For the good man aims at justice. And in this aim at justice his good name in heaven is secure and he keeps the Lord propitious in every action of his, while those who pursue evil draw death and captivity on themselves, in particular those that reach out for this world and glory in their riches and do not hold fast to the blessings to come. Their souls will be sorry, for they have no hope. Instead, they have abandoned their [true] selves and their [real] life. As for you, pray God and he will heal you of your sins, yours, your whole household's, and those of all the saints.[28]

This oneiric figure is Rhode, a Christian woman ("sister") in whose household Hermas had served as a slave before he was freed. As Hermas tells the reader, Rhode had once asked him, her servant, to help her out of the Tiber after a bath, a gesture whose casual insensitivity toward the slave's sexual feelings "had not been calculated to increase our prophet's peace of mind," as Brown remarks.[29] Entranced by the sight of Rhode's naked loveliness, the married Hermas had felt adulterous longings which he had not repressed altogether successfully.[30] The oneiric Rhode is thus a figura-

---

[28] *Vis.* 1.1.4–9 (trans. Marique, pp. 233–34).

[29] *Vis.* 1.1.1–2; on Rhode, see Brown, *The Body and Society,* p. 70, and Lane Fox, *Pagans and Christians,* p. 382.

[30] See *Vis.* 1.1.1–2: "He who brought me up sold me to a certain Rhode at Rome. After many years I made her acquaintance again, and began to love her as a sister. After some time I saw her bathing in the river Tiber, and gave her my hand and helped her out of the river. When I saw her beauty I reflected in my heart and said: 'I should be happy if I had a wife of such beauty and character.' This was my only thought, and no other, no, not one" (trans. Lake, p. 7).

tion of his erotic desire in dreamlike reality, and she charges Hermas with the sexual sin of lust ("desire of evil in the heart") but counsels that prayer will bring healing.

Although this dream shows Hermas to be an early witness to the concern for self-control in sexual matters that Christians shared with others in the culture at this time, sexual misconduct is not the primary ethical dilemma that Hermas' text addresses.[31] Hermas did not attempt to impose a program of radical sexual austerity and idealized virginity on the Roman Christian community the way that Jerome did three centuries later; he was, after all, married and was addressing a community of married householders.[32] Instead, Hermas was engaged in defining the Christian community in terms of a purity of moral purpose that he constructed as a childlike simplicity not rent by conflicting inner drives.[33] As the above monologue of the dream-within-a-dream suggests, the concern for ethical integrity was expressed in the form of a critique of the behavior of the wealthy, whose secular business interests clashed with the spiritual neighborliness required for the cohesion of the religious community. A second, very important, problematic in the area of ethics was the issue of repentance, later amplified as the doctrine that, after baptism (the first repentance or forgiveness) one could sin and repent only once in order to receive salvation.[34]

It is important to remember that, in these attempts to negotiate the intersection of world and church, of business and the spirit, Hermas' own experience as a dreamer is presented as the paradigm for the resolution of conflict. Hermas' text presents another instance of the function of dreaming in late antiquity as a strategy of rhetorical indirection whereby the dreams of an individual are taken to signify inferentially for a whole community.[35] A return to Hermas as dreamer will demonstrate how this strategy of indirection takes the reader at the same time into the divided heart of the text's protagonist and that of the reader as well.

[31] For Hermas' preaching on continence, see *Mand.* 4.1.1–10 and the discussion in Brown, *The Body and Society,* pp. 70–72; on practices of self-control in the context of sexuality, see Foucault, *The History of Sexuality,* 3:59–60, 124–32.

[32] Brown, *The Body and Society,* p. 70.

[33] *Mand.* 2.1: "He [the shepherd] said to me: 'Have simplicity and be innocent and you shall be as the children who do not know the wickedness that destroys the life of men" (trans. Lake, p. 71). For discussions of the theme of purification in *The Shepherd,* see Maier, *The Social Setting of the Ministry,* pp. 65–72; Brown, *The Body and Society,* pp. 70–71; Lane Fox, *Pagans and Christians,* p. 386.

[34] *Vis.* 1.1.9; 2.2.4–8. On the interconnection of the issues of apostasy, wealth, and repentance, see Maier, *The Social Setting of the Ministry,* pp. 58–65; L. Wm. Countryman, *The Rich Christian in the Church of the Early Empire,* p. 135. Carolyn Osiek, *Rich and Poor in the Shepherd of Hermas,* gives a thorough analysis of the social context of the conflicts in Hermas' community.

[35] See above, Ch. 2, pp. 66–67, for a similar universalizing use of a dream by the Christian theologian Tertullian; on the rhetoric of indirection, see Ch. 2, p. 73.

In Hermas' text, there is a metonymous movement from the literary consciousness of Hermas as author to the oneiric consciousness of Hermas as dreamer and on to the interpretive consciousness of the individual reader and the communal assembly of readers for whom the text operates as a mirror. This complicated structure of writerly and readerly perspectives is reflected, for example, in the way in which Hermas as character in the text is presented as being invaded by dreams, while the author of the text later represents himself as an avid seeker of dreams and, as author, has assembled the dreams in a literary composition that charts a paradigmatic course of moral progress. The unsuspecting Hermas of the text differs from the author Hermas as moral prophet, and this doubled textual voice matches the doubled role of dreams as instruments of personal and social reform.

Interestingly, the complexity of the text is also reflected in the structure of the first dream that visits itself upon our hapless hero: it is a dream within a dream, presented as having a strikingly tactile and autonomous existence. Attributions of independence and sensuous presence to dreams were, of course, as old as Homer; what is unusual here is that a dream-figure like Rhode should appear within the frame of another dream and, further, that such a dream-within-the dream should be doubled by the appearance of a second oneiric revealer.[36] As in the case of this text's implied affirmation of its own angelic trope discussed earlier in this chapter, so also here the text shows itself to be one that demands to be read as a referential structure in which form and content mirror each other.

To return, then, to Hermas as dreamer. When the oneiric Rhode departs, Hermas is back in the nightmarish outer dream, "shuddering and in grief."[37] He begins an interior dialogue: "If this sin is recorded against me, how shall I be saved?" The dream has created in Hermas a new—indeed, a shocking—awareness of his situation. The fact that a dream might provoke enlarged or deepened understanding of one's condition is not surprising to us as beneficiaries of the depth-psychological insights initiated by Freud and his colleagues. Nor would it be a surprise to such late-antique thinkers as Artemidorus, whose catalogue of world-changing dreams is ample testimony. So also, I suggest, for Hermas: the patterns of connections woven by dreams will profoundly alter his understanding of himself and his world.

---

[36] There are parallels to the phenomenon of the dream-within-a-dream in *The Sacred Tales* of Aristides. Behr, *Aelius Aristides and the Sacred Tales,* observes that "the authoritative dream figure, for the ancients the vehicle of the dream oracle . . . , has often become for Aristides an interpreter to explain the significance of the dream action in the same dream sequence" (p. 195). See especially *Sacred Tales* 1.17; 3.37; 5.20; 5.65 (trans. Behr, *Complete Works,* 2:280, 314, 343, 351).

[37] *Vis.* 1.2.1.

At the close of his conversation with himself, Hermas begins to doubt. His doubt introduces what will be another major problematic of the text, an exploration of the emotional and intellectual condition of *dipsúchos*, of being double-minded.[38] As the dreams, and then later the mandates and parables, unfold, it becomes clear that double-mindedness and *metanoia*, repentance, are intertwined issues in this text's view. Meanwhile, in Hermas' moment of doubt, a second dream-within-the-dream makes its appearance:

> While I was considering and doubting these things in my heart I saw before me a white chair of great size made of snow-white wool; and there came a woman, old and clothed in shining garments with a book in her hand, and she sat down alone and greeted me: "Hail, Hermas!" And I, in my grief and weeping, said: "Hail, Lady!"[39]

The old woman, feigning ignorance, asks Hermas why he is so gloomy. He explains about the fears aroused by Rhode, she reveals her knowledge of his sorry state, and then she offers to read to him from the book in her hand. At this point, Hermas' doubt turns to fright.[40]

The dream announces that the words she will read will be "the glory of God." Hermas' response to the glory of God is as follows: "I heard great and awesome things which I cannot remember; for all the words were frightful, such as a man cannot bear."[41] As the old woman reveals, the frightful words are words addressed to "heathen and apostates." Perhaps what Hermas finds so terrifying is his own apostate self, given the devastating critique that he has already suffered at the hands of both dream-figures, devastating because of its demand that he face aspects of himself that he would rather not see. As Lane Fox has remarked, Hermas' visions are "a printout of Christianity's impact on a sensitive Christian soul."[42] Also, as the author—the ethical double of the character Hermas—later

[38] On this issue see Oscar J. F. Seitz, "Antecedents and Signification of the Term *Dipsychos*," pp. 131–40.

[39] *Vis.* 1.2.2 (trans. Lake, p. 11). Lane Fox has pointed to Hermas' indebtedness to "the imagery of divination and pagan inquiry, in which a man, whether Jew or pagan, could ask the gods and angels for advice. It is this tradition which explains details of his visions of the Church. The chair and ivory bench, their coverlets, the sitting position, the use of a staff, the words of greeting and inquiry: these features can all be matched with the patterns of inquiry which we find in pagan texts of oracular spells and in questions to an attendant divinity" (*Pagans and Christians*, p. 389).

[40] *Vis.* 1.2.2–3.3. Hermas' fright is not surprising. As Artemidorus remarks, "A book [in a dream] indicates the life of the dreamer"—and Hermas has just been worrying precisely about the conduct of his life (Artemidorus, *Onir.* 2.45 [ed. Pack, p. 179; trans. White, p. 125]).

[41] *Vis.* 1.3.3 (trans. Lake, p. 15).

[42] Lane Fox, *Pagans and Christians*, p. 389.

shows by means of the parabolic images of the shepherd, the community of the church is also the object of the old woman's words. In the misuse of financial patronage by its wealthy members, as well as in the community's schismatic quarrels, the Roman church is vulnerable to the charge of heathenish and apostate behavior.[43]

In any case, this is not the only time that Hermas will have trouble with the old woman's words. Yet she leaves him cheerfully, saying "Play the man," as though to suggest that if he will listen to her dream-words he will be a man and no longer the miserable and confused boy that he is at this moment.[44]

About a year later, Hermas is again seized by the spirit and taken to the same oneiric country as before. Again the old woman appears, reading aloud from a little book. She asks Hermas to take this verbal message to his community, but he can't remember it all so she gives the book to Hermas to copy. Hermas comments: "I took it and went away to a certain place in the country, and copied it all, letter by letter, for I could not distinguish the syllables."[45] Hermas is not yet astute enough to understand this dream-writing. The syllables that he cannot distinguish are, of course, part of the total oneiric image, by which he is baffled; yet, by the end of this cycle of dreams, he will be able to read and distinguish those "syllables," the dream-images themselves, very well. Thus part of Hermas' therapy—his initiation into repentance, and so into salvation—is literacy: he must learn to read the images of dream, just as the author's community must read the words of *The Shepherd*. What the text presents as a painful autobiographical journey toward enlightenment is also a practical theological handbook for a community that is in danger of falling under the sway of a corporate angel of wickedness.

A dramatic turning point for Hermas occurs some fifteen days after this exercise in copying. Another dream reveals "the knowledge of the writing"; as it happens, the syllables were descriptive of Hermas himself![46] Furthermore, the teaching about *metanoia* is delivered in no uncertain terms:

> All the sins which [Christians] have formerly committed shall be forgiven them . . . up to this day, if they repent with their whole heart and put aside double-mindedness from their heart. If there be still sin after this day has been fixed, they shall find no salvation; for repentance for the just has an end.[47]

[43] *Sim.* 2.1–10; 9.18–23; see Maier, *The Social Setting of the Ministry,* pp. 64, 66–68.
[44] *Vis.* 1.4.3.
[45] Ibid. 2.1.4 (trans. Lake, p. 19). Taken literally, Hermas' reference is to the continuous script of early manuscripts in which there were no divisions between words; in the present context, his inability to read the oneiric writing has a metaphorical as well as a literal significance.
[46] Ibid. 2.2.1.
[47] Ibid. 2.2.4–5 (trans. Lake, p. 21).

Following this dream, which has unlocked the meaning of images in another dream just as the text of *The Shepherd* unlocks the meaning of Christian ethics, Hermas moves from uncertainty or "double-mindedness" about his dreams to curiosity. Indeed, so curious does he become, pestering the old woman for the meaning of his dreams' every detail, that she becomes exasperated with his continual questioning. Nonetheless, she explains fully the oneiric images of the tower, the stones, the maidens, and so on.[48]

The dreams are teaching Hermas his "letters"; that is, dreams are instructing him in the interpretation of dreams. The dream-text interprets, and the interpretation is the dream-text. Furthermore, Hermas has suffered *metanoia*, the repentance that consists in a change of consciousness. He is now involved hermeneutically with the dreams, which not only teach him *about* salvation but themselves *constitute* his haven of safe return from ignorance, doubt, and self-division.

Leading up to the moment when the shepherd is bestowed on him as a permanent companion, Hermas has a whole series of dreams. I will focus on three of them. In the first, the old woman appears to Hermas; this time, she is the framing dream.[49] She directs Hermas to go into the country, where he finds, surprisingly, an ivory couch sitting in the wilderness. The woman appears in the company of six young men, whom she directs to "go and build." Hermas begs to know about this and thus commences the dream-within-the-dream, the building of the tower. When this inner dream is over, Hermas, back in the outer dream, asks its meaning: "Lady, what does it benefit me to have seen these things, if I do not know what they mean?" She explains that the inner dream about the building of the tower is a parable and that, further, she herself is the tower, which is also the church.[50] Old woman, tower, and church exist in a metamorphic relation to each other; as images, they move in a kinetic swirl of signification that again underscores the reflexive density of this text. For the reader, it becomes difficult to distinguish which dream-image is frame for the other as the signifying ground continues to shift. Inner and outer change place and are multiplied metonymically; this, I suggest, is one of the text's signals that the reader is being led by an oneiric pedagogy into a form of consciousness in which multiple perspectives can be entertained and analyzed.

Having said that dream is parable, the old woman cautions Hermas: "Do not be double-minded as to what you see."[51] In order not to be double-

---

[48] Ibid. 3.2.3–8.11. The phenomenon of dream-images interpreting each other appears again later in the text; the parables that the shepherd dictates to Hermas are often further explications of the earlier visions. See, for example, *Sim.* 9.13, in which Hermas' dream of a tower in *Vis.* 3.2.4–9 is interpreted in detail.

[49] Ibid. 3.1–10.

[50] Ibid. 3.1.1–8 (trans. Lake, p. 29).

[51] Ibid. 3.3.4.

minded—that is, in order not to waver between two simplistic points of view—one must see parabolically; one must not be afraid of multiple meaning, the gift of oneiric consciousness. As the Lady herself says, the double-minded are those who doubt the visions of dream.[52] This is an important moment in Hermas' education into the literacy appropriate to the country of dreams: its visions are mobile, many-faceted, metaphoric, and, like parable, they shatter the kind of literal-minded consciousness that would ask for single meaning. Hermas is being given "eyes to see." The images of dreams, like those syllables that Hermas earlier could not distinguish, are not to be "figured out" so that their potential to signify is ended. Rather, those images are to be read in such a way that they provide contexts for each other; text and context, image and meaning, exist in a continuously fruitful relationship.

When the old woman tells Hermas not to hesitate or waver on the issue of the validity of the dream as a vehicle for the representation of meaning, she is giving a lesson in hermeneutics not only to the character Hermas but also to the community of the authorial Hermas. As a figure not only for oneiric revelation but also for the church, she speaks with the voice of ecclesiastical authority; her validation of dreams is also a validation of Hermas' dream-book, *The Shepherd,* as an authoritative guide for the Christian community. Once again, the self-reflexive strategy of this text is evident. Furthermore, the lesson in hermeneutics also pertains to the condition of double-mindedness, which is frequently raised as a problem by this text. Double-mindedness is not only a negative ethical stance, but also a negative interpretive stance that resists the use of dream and parable as resources for the construction of religious identity and meaning. It is in this context that this text's complicated strategy of self-validation is situated.

One of the striking features of *The Shepherd* is that the double-minded businesspeople of Hermas' community are being invited by the text to evaluate their status as members of the community in terms of dreams and parable. As I have tried to suggest, there is a mimetic appeal operative in the text, whereby the reader is asked to see his or her own condition mirrored in the plight of the main character, Hermas. Because the bulk of Hermas' dream-instructions come in the form of parables, the reader, likewise, is being invited to "read" his or her thoughts and actions with a poetized eye. Indeed, in one of its longest parables, the text presents a vividly imaged, and very beguiling, picture of Hermas frolicking with the dream-maidens who build the tower that is the church:

The maidens said to me: "Today the shepherd is not coming here." "What then," said I, "shall I do?" " Wait for him," said they, "until the evening, and if

[52] Ibid. 3.4.3.

he comes he will speak with you; and if he does not come you shall remain here with us until he does come." . . . "Where shall I stay then?" I said. "You shall sleep with us," they said, "as a brother and not as a husband, for you are our brother and for the future we are going to live with you, for we love you greatly." But I was ashamed to stay with them. And she who seemed to be the first of them began to kiss and embrace me, and the others seeing her embracing me began to kiss me themselves, and to lead me around the tower, and to play with me. I, too, had become young again, and began to play with them myself, for some were dancing, others were leaping, others were singing, and I walked in silence with them around the tower, and was merry with them.[53]

This is a picture of what it is like not to be double-minded. As the shepherd explains later in the parable, the maidens have names: Faith, Continence, Power, Long-Suffering, Simplicity, Innocence, Holiness, Joyfulness, Truth, Understanding, Concord, and Love.[54] They are the virginal powers of the ethical soul, and, in Brown's felicitous phrasing, "they rustled in [Hermas'] capacious mind, light-footed girls, dancing on the green meadows of a Christian Arcadia."[55] Looking in this mirror, the reader receives an education in ethics in which ethical behavior is shown to be a multifaceted undertaking. It is not enough simply to have faith, for example; all twelve virtues must dance in the practice of every individual. From the perspective of parable, ethics is presented as a poetics of self-reflection that demands more individual responsibility than a simplistic preaching of moral law.

The condition of being double-minded in the context of ethical decision-making has been a frequent topic of scholarly commentary on *The Shepherd*. Perusal of that literature might lead one to think that the opposite of double-mindedness is single-mindedness. Because, according to these readings, *dipsūchos* means "double-hearted," "hesitating," "unstable," "having mixed motives," and afflicted with "inner disunity," then its opposite must be singleness of purpose, "whole-hearted," "single-minded."[56] Hermas has been understood to be preaching a rather simplistic morality of devotion and obedience, especially when double-mindedness or the lack thereof is placed in conjunction with repentance and consequent salvation.

However, the text itself does not bear out the standard reading of it that would make a simplistic moral stance the precondition of salvation. As we will see, one of the main problems of the double-minded ones in Hermas' community is that they shuttle back and forth between two literalisms: a simplistic standard of behavior in the secular world, and a simplistic stan-

[53] *Sim.* 9.11.1–5 (trans. Lake, p. 247).
[54] Ibid. 9.15.2.
[55] Brown, *The Body and Society*, p. 72.
[56] See Seitz, "Antecedents and Signification of the Term *Dipsychos*," pp. 211–15; Reiling, *Hermas and Christian Prophecy*, pp. 32–57; Joly, ed. and trans., *Hermas le Pasteur*, p. 91n.5.

dard of behavior in the religious community. This wavering between two literalisms has both ethical and hermeneutical implications. Of course the text strongly urges the reader to choose, and so to end double-minded attitudes and behavior; but the choices that the text advocates lead to what I have called multiple consciousness, a many-faceted view both of ethics and of revelatory authority. Thus the "opposite" of double-mindedness is not single-mindedness but rather a mental and psychic disposition that cultivates a differentiated and nuanced perspective.

The fact that *The Shepherd* offers an expansive rather than a reductionist view of ethics is indicated by the text's use of several parables (ten in all) to convey its hermeneutical lesson about interpreting the moral dispositions of the self by way of image and metaphor. As the parabolic figures shift, the reader is initiated into the flexibility of mind needed both to entertain shifts in perspective and to recognize the relevance of those figures to his or her own life. Many of the parables are directed to the wealthy members of Hermas' religious community. As Maier has observed:

> In Hermas' view there is a direct relationship between undue regard for riches and lack of allegiance to the church. Because of their riches wealthier members do not "cleave to the saints" but involve themselves instead in "heathen" friendships. The result is that the wealthy members, who perhaps rely on their worldly connections for the success of their businesses, find it difficult to separate themselves from their economic interests when it is necessary to show their solidarity with the wider community, as for example in times of persecution, and end in denying their faith.[57]

Thus the rich are charged with impurity, a double-mindedness that takes the form of divided loyalty. Also, they are guilty of "glorying in their wealth," as the oneiric Rhode had remarked; hoarding their money in a display of financial pride, the rich members of the Christian group deprive the poor of the alms needed to sustain them. Further, by their parsimony they deprive themselves of the intercessory prayers that are the spiritual gift of the poor to the wealthy.[58]

The rich, then, are prominent among those who in Hermas' view have damaged the ethical identity of the community by double-minded attitudes and practices, and they are the ones who are subjected to the imagistic jolts to consciousness that the parables provide. The parables offer not only a cure for ethical misbehavior but also a vision of a multifaceted ethical self whose contours are most forcefully delineated by the imagistic language of oneiric revelation. As the parables are narrated by the shepherd, interro-

[57] Maier, *The Social Setting of the Ministry,* pp. 66–67.
[58] *Sim.* 1.8–11; 2.7–11; 5.3.7–8; *Mand.* 2.4–6; see Maier, *The Social Setting of the Ministry,* pp. 60–61.

gated by the character Hermas, and written down by the author, a rich variety of images is offered to the reader to "try on" in terms of his or her own ethical condition. Sterile elm trees and fruitful vines, budding and withered trees, frolicking sheep and sheep caught in thorny ravines, green and dessicated branches of a willow tree, stones of various colors, some rough and some finely hewn: these are a sample of the oneiric images that form *The Shepherd*'s lexicon of ethical self-reflection.[59]

The mirroring function of these parabolic images is indicated by the second series of dreams that come to Hermas prior to the appearance of the shepherd. Here Hermas reveals to the reader that the old woman had actually appeared to him in three forms: first as very old, then as having a youthful face but an aged body, and finally as quite young and beautiful.[60] Hermas asks what these three forms mean, and the old woman sends him a dream in the form of a young man (perhaps a foreshadowing of the shepherd himself).[61] Hermas puts the same question to the young man: "Sir, I only ask you that there may be a complete revelation concerning the three forms of the ancient lady." The dream-figure answers: "How long are you foolish? You are made foolish by your double-mindedness and because your heart is not turned to the Lord."[62] He then reveals that the three forms of the woman are three dimensions of Hermas himself.[63] The woman's transformation is an enactment, in dream-image, of the change in Hermas' own understanding. Showing a movement from spiritual old age, which the dream connects with double-mindedness, to the youthful renewal of the spirit, which the dream connects with seeing the oneiric parables, the triple-formed dream-figure is the text of Hermas' soul as well as a demonstration of how to read texts that are multiple, "three-formed." This is what Hermas is learning to embrace as the salvific way.

That Hermas does indeed learn the letters of dream is shown dramatically in the third of the dreams that I will consider. Again on the road, Hermas asks God for a dream to complete the earlier ones.[64] No longer subject to invasion and seizure by dream, Hermas is now eager for one as the country of dream assumes its full stature as a source of authoritative revelation. Hermas says, "And while I was giving thanks to the Lord an answer came to me as an echo of my voice, 'Do not be double-minded, Hermas.'"[65] The statement that Hermas hears marks a crucial moment in his change of consciousness, for what he hears as an echo of his *own* voice is the message

[59] See *Sim.* 2, 4, 6, 8, and 9.
[60] *Vis.* 3.10.1–6.
[61] Ibid. 3.10.6–7.
[62] Ibid. 3.10.7–10 (trans. Lake, p. 55).
[63] Ibid. 3.11–13.
[64] Ibid. 4.1.3.
[65] Ibid. 4.1.4 (trans. Lake, p. 61).

that the dream-figures had been saying to him all along. Now the dream-voice is *his* voice, an echo of his own deepened perspective.

In the dream itself, Hermas encounters "a great beast like some Leviathan, and fiery locusts were going out of his mouth. . . . And I began to weep and to pray the Lord to rescue me from it, and I remembered the word which I had heard, 'Do not be double-minded.' Thus I took courage and faced the beast. I came near to it, and the Leviathan for all its size stretched itself out on the ground, and put forth nothing except its tongue, and did not move at all until I had passed by."[66] By not being double-minded, Hermas is able to face even the most nightmarish of oneiric images. He has received the courage to dream, and his dreams have given him courage.

Passing by the beast, the ancient lady, now in the guise of a bride, meets Hermas, and interprets the colors of the Leviathan in terms of Hermas' own world—indeed, one of the colors, the gold, reflects Hermas himself.[67] Hermas is now having dreams that interpret each other. He thus presents a very compelling picture of a finely tuned oneiric sensibility, one in which personal voice and dream-voice have been united.[68] This union of personal voice with dream-voice shows how far Hermas has come from his earlier condition of confusion, doubt, and self-deception to his present state of interpretive confidence, and also of moral confidence; as the old woman explains, Hermas' golden color signifies his achievement of a responsible ethical perspective.[69]

Hermas' transformation is graphically depicted in the final dream of *The Shepherd,* in which he receives the shepherd as a permanently indwelling figure.[70] As the "angel of *metanoia,*" the shepherd is the embodiment of Hermas' changed consciousness. He is Hermas' dream-companion, signifier of the parabolic perception that is now Hermas' own. Like the old woman, the shepherd commands Hermas to write down his mandates and parables, which are what we, as readers, are offered by this text. It would appear, interestingly, that the author Hermas was emboldened by the oneiric imagination just as his character was: as Robert Grant has observed, "Hermas is not deterred by the Jewish Ten Commandments from offering twelve more, or by the parables of Jesus from hazarding ten of his own."[71] Hermas is the scribe of the dream-world to which his angelic companion is hermeneut. Or, perhaps it would be better to say that the shepherd is Hermas' own new-found potential as interpreter, and this time he does not

---

66 Ibid. 4.1.6–9 (trans. Lake, pp. 61–63).

67 Ibid. 4.3.1–5.

68 On the phenomenon of dreams interpreting other dreams, see Artemidorus, *Onir.* 4.72; 4.80 (ed. Pack, pp. 293–94, 297; trans. White, pp. 215–16).

69 *Vis.* 4.3.4.

70 Ibid., 5.1–7.

71 Edgar J. Goodspeed and Robert M. Grant, *A History of Early Christian Literature,* p. 31.

fail to "read the syllables." Through dreams, Hermas has undergone a change of consciousness, and that new consciousness is parabolic. Further, parabolic understanding is salvific, as the shepherd says.[72]

Hermas is saved, as the dream-figures eventually tell him that he is. But this salvation is not salvation *from* the world, nor is it *out of* the world; rather, salvation is his experience of being *in* the world, engaged with his context in a more insightful way. He now knows that he is implicated in the salvific process. No longer a passive confessor of sin, he is an active interpreter of his world, which he has learned to read as parable.[73] Oneiric perception, now a permanent dwelling-place, is his haven, a refuge from literalism. Through the lens of his personal struggle with dreams, Hermas the shepherd offered his community a hermeneutic for addressing practical problems in a therapeutic way.

[72] *Vis.* 5.7.

[73] See ibid. 3.1.6; *Mand.* 4.2.1–4, 10.2–3; *Sim.* 5.1.1–5, where the old woman and other dream-figures exhort Hermas to end his passive confessional stance and to take the more active role of pursuit of righteousness.

CHAPTER SIX

Perpetua and Her Diary of Dreams

I saw a bronze ladder, marvelously long, reaching as far as heaven, and narrow too: people could climb it only one at a time. And on the sides of the ladder every kind of iron implement was fixed: there were swords, lances, hooks, cutlasses, javelins, so that if anyone went up carelessly or not looking upwards, she would be torn and her flesh caught on the sharp iron. And beneath the ladder lurked a serpent of wondrous size, who laid ambushes for those mounting, making them terrified of the ascent.[1]

THE YOUNG woman who dreamed this dream was killed on March 7, 203 C.E., in an amphitheater in Carthage.[2] Her name, Vibia Perpetua, may indicate that she came from a family of senatorial rank, but there is no doubt that she was well-born and well-educated.[3] The occasion of her death was "the surreal horror of the *damnatio ad bestias,*" the condemnation of criminals to the ravages of wild beasts that formed part of Roman festival games; this particular "game" of torture was part of the city's celebration of the birthday of the emperor Septimius Severus' younger son Geta.[4]

Some weeks prior to her death, Perpetua and four members of her household had been arrested by provincial authorities on the charge of being Christians. Although there was no imperial legislation designating the profession of Christianity as a criminal offense, local provincial governors could exercise punitive authority against any group deemed to be threatening to civic order.[5] As such a group, Christians were susceptible to

---

[1] *Passio Sanctarum Perpetuae et Felicitatis* 4.3–4 (ed. Van Beek, p. 12). I have used the translation of Perpetua's dream-diary by Dronke, *Women Writers of the Middle Ages,* pp. 2–4. Also useful is the translation of the entire *Passio* by Musurillo, *The Acts of the Christian Martyrs* pp. 107–31.

[2] The precision of this traditional hagiographical dating of Perpetua's martyrdom has been disputed, although it has been shown compellingly that Geta Caesar's birthday, the day of the martyrdom itself, was in early March, and there is no doubt that this text stems from very early third-century African Christianity. See Barnes, *Tertullian,* pp. 263–65.

[3] On the proconsular Vibii as possible ancestors of Perpetua's family, see Barnes, *Tertullian,* p. 70; the *Passio* states that Perpetua was "*honeste nata, liberaliter instituta*": "well-born and well-educated" (*Pass. Perp.* 2.1 [ed. Van Beek, pp. 6–8]).

[4] The quotation is from Brown, *The Body and Society,* p. 75; for references to this event in the text, see *Pass. Perp.* 6.6, 7.9, 16.3, 19.1–21.10 (ed. Van Beek, pp. 18, 22, 40, 44–52).

[5] Barnes, *Tertullian,* pp. 143–61; Lane Fox, *Pagans and Christians,* pp. 421–26.

the charge of atheism because of their refusal, on the basis of their mono-theism, to participate in ritual gestures of honor toward the gods and the emperor; by their refusal, they were seen as flouting the traditional reli-gious and political structures that undergirded the welfare of the society.[6] Because of its apparent blasphemy against cherished canons of "Ro-manity," Christian obstinence presented a particularly troublesome situa-tion to local governors, who, as Lane Fox has observed, were "sensitive to charges of treason or disloyalty, not least because they could be prosecuted in Rome for failing to take them seriously."[7] Further, Christians in a large city like Carthage were vulnerable to the prejudice of the crowd against a group perceived to be subversive. Given the prominence, in Roman civic life, of games and festivals in which gladiatorial contests and the execution of criminals were featured, "Christians, as criminals, could be employed for public entertainment. Prejudice against an alien group could be acti-vated by the desire to enjoy a spectacle."[8]

Perpetua's story conforms to this scenario of localized persecution of Christians. Her father, urging her to recant her faith, accused her of pride: "Don't flaunt your insistence, or you'll destroy us all!"[9] At the judicial hearing, the governor Hilarianus asked Perpetua to have pity on her father by performing the standard act of ritual respect: "Offer the sacrifice for the Emperor's welfare." When she refused and persisted in identifying herself as Christian, Hilarianus sentenced her and her colleagues to a contest with the beasts.[10] They thus furnished at least some of the human material needed to celebrate Geta Caesar's birthday with a spectacle, indicated in part by the fact that Perpetua and her party were dressed in ritual costumes before they entered the amphitheater. Although they refused to undergo their ordeal in this dress, they were sent into the arena nonetheless and attacked by wild animals to the reported delight of the crowd, and were finally killed by soldiers who slashed their throats with swords.[11]

At the time of her arrest, Perpetua was twenty-two years old, married, and nursing an infant. An aristocratic *matrona*, she was also a Christian catechumen, as were one of her brothers and two of the family's slaves. Their religious instructor, a man named Saturus, had not been present when the arrest occurred but later turned himself in to the authorities and joined them in their confinement. At first the group was detained under

---

[6] For discussions of the development of these issues, see W.H.C. Frend, *Martyrdom and Persecution in the Early Church*, pp. 162–253; see also Lane Fox, *Pagans and Christians*, pp. 425–26.

[7] Lane Fox, *Pagans and Christians*, p. 426.

[8] Barnes, *Tertullian*, p. 160.

[9] *Pass. Perp.* 5.4 (ed. Van Beek, p. 16).

[10] Ibid., 6.3–6 (ed. Van Beek, pp. 16–18).

[11] Ibid., 18.4–21.10 (ed. Van Beek, pp. 42–52).

house arrest, and it was during this time that the catechumens were baptized. Some time later, they were transferred to prison.[12] While in prison, Perpetua kept a diary, and Saturus wrote down a long dream. An anonymous author combined these two documents with an account of the gruesome scene in the amphitheater to form a *passio*, an account of martyrdom called the *Passio Sanctarum Perpetuae et Felicitatis*.[13] This *passio* was part of a literary genre in early Christianity in which martyrdom was conceptualized as an illustrious combat followed ineluctably by spiritual victory.[14]

In her diary, Perpetua recorded the agonizing conversations that she had with her father, her worries about her child, the judicial hearing, and her fright at the darkness and intense heat of the prison. Dominating the diary, however, is a series of four dreams. Like other martyrs both before and after her, Perpetua was a dreamer; persecution and oneiric revelation formed a pair as the imminence of death provoked premonitory dreams.[15] Characterized by one interpreter as spontaneously symbolic rather than artificially allegorical, the dreams of martyrs can be said to have proceeded from their physical and psychological condition, assuaging their fears and giving fortitude in the face of expectations of torment.[16] I will argue later in this chapter that Perpetua's dreams were not merely mimetic to her experience as a martyr, as the foregoing perspective suggests. In the perspective that I will develop, the dreams were also, and more importantly, expressive of a creative view of herself and her role as a Christian woman. However, I am going to attend first to the contexts in which Perpetua's dreams have typically been placed by contemporary scholars. Then I will turn to a discussion of the document of her dreams as one that expresses the self-awareness of a specifically *female* dreamer.

Perpetua saw her first dream in response to a suggestion of her brother's: "'My lady, my sister,' he said, 'you are now greatly blessed: so much so that you can ask for a vision [*visionem*], and you will be shown

---

[12] Ibid., 3.1–6 (ed. Van Beek, p. 8).

[13] For discussions of the authenticity of the diary and the dream of Saturus, once (but no longer) thought to be forgeries, see Dodds, *Pagan and Christian in an Age of Anxiety*, pp. 47–52; J. Amat, "L'Authenticité des Songes de la Passion de Perpetué et de Felicité," pp. 177–91; Barnes, *Tertullian*, p. 263; see *Pass. Perp.* 2.3 and 11.1 (ed. Van Beek, pp. 8, 28) for the anonymous author's statements that he is presenting texts written by the martyrs themselves. Perpetua's diary composes sections 3–10 of the *Passio*, and Saturus' dream, sections 11–13; sections 1–2 are the author's preface, and 14–21 recount the martyrs' deaths.

[14] For a discussion of the genre as well as of the *Pass. Perp.* in the context of other martyrdoms, see Amat, *Songes et Visions*, pp. 52–55, 66–86; also Dulaey, *Le Rêve*, pp. 41–46.

[15] Polycarp and Cyprian are notable examples of other martyrs who received premonitory dreams concerning their own deaths; for discussions of these martyr-dreamers, see Dulaey, *Le Rêve*, pp. 42–44 (Cyprian) and Amat, *Songes et Visions*, pp. 62–66 (Polycarp); see also Pierre Courcelle, *Les Confessions de Saint Augustin dans la tradition littéraire*, pp. 127–30.

[16] Amat, *Songes et Visions*, pp. 53, 67–68.

[*ostendatur*] if it is to be suffering unto death or a passing thing.'" "And I," she continues, "who know I was in dialogue with God [*ego quae me sciebam fabulari cum Domino*], whose great benefits I had experienced, promised him faithfully, saying, 'Tomorrow I'll tell you.' And I asked for a vision, and this was shown to me."[17] Characterizing herself as one who could "talk with God" (*fabulari cum Domino*), Perpetua betrays her oneness with her culture, which understood dreams as a form of communication with heavenly figures. Perpetua is one of those whom her contemporary Carthaginian, Tertullian, might have included in his remark that most people get their knowledge of God from dreams.[18] What Perpetua asks to see is first called a *visio*, a technical onirological term designating a prophetic dream; later her oneiric experience, here and elsewhere in the diary, is further specified by verbal forms of the noun *ostensio*, a term that carries a symbolic or figurative sense in late-antique texts. As Amat has observed, "for Perpetua, as for Apuleius, the word [*ostensio*] appears to designate a striking scene, close to prodigious, that manifests divine power completely"; it denotes a type of figurative revelation that explains divine secrets.[19] The figurative quality of Perpetua's vision is also conveyed implicitly by the word she uses to characterize her speaking. *Fabulari*, from *fabulor*, "to converse" or "chat," not only suggests that dreaming is a linguistic event, a kind of discourse; it also suggests that the dream is a *particular* kind of discourse, one associated with imaginative story-telling, with a "fabled" or poeticized perspective.[20] Again like Tertullian, who thought of dreams as parables, Perpetua's language implies an understanding of dreams as imaginal events.

From antiquity to the present, commentary on the dreams has generally located Perpetua's oneiric imagination in the context of her roles as catechumen and martyr. As the following summaries of reflections on her diary will show, the dreams have been construed as texts that mirror theological ideas and cultural praxis; curiously, their function as *oneiric* experiences—that is, as expressions of transformations of self-identity and deepened self-consciousness—has been largely neglected. A notable exception to the dominant interpretive perspective is that of Peter Dronke, who cautions that "Perpetua did not intend to construct spiritual allego-

---

[17] *Pass. Perp.* 4.1–2 (ed. Van Beek, pp. 10–12).

[18] For Tertullian's oneiric theory, see pp. 66–70 above.

[19] Amat, *Songes et Visions*, p. 68; for further uses of *ostensio* to designate oneiric experience, see *Pass. Perp.* 7.3 and 8.1 (ed. Van Beek, pp. 20, 22). The religious intensity of dreaming was underscored by a later *passio* that used the *Pass. Perp.* as its model. In the *Passio Mariani et Iacobi*, the narrator exclaims, "O sleep more intense than all our waking hours!" and remarks about the martyr-dreamers in his text that, while their companions cared for them by day, Christ cared for them by night in dreams (7.5; 6.2, ed. and trans. Musurillo, pp. 205, 201).

[20] See Lewis and Short, *A Latin Dictionary*, s.v. *fabulor, fabula*.

ries for the benefit of later Christians."[21] The tendency of the scholarly tradition has been nonetheless to isolate the various images of Perpetua's dreams and to amplify them in terms of theological materials exterior to the texts of the dreams themselves.

DREAM ONE

In response to her brother's recognition of her visionary ability and his suggestion that she ask for a dream to discern her and her companions' fate, Perpetua had the following dream:

> I saw a bronze ladder, marvellously long, reaching as far as heaven, and narrow too: people could climb it only one at a time. And on the sides of the ladder every kind of iron implement was fixed: there were swords, lances, hooks, cutlasses, javelins, so that if anyone went up carelessly or not looking upwards, she would be torn and her flesh caught on the sharp iron. And beneath the ladder lurked a serpent of wondrous size, who laid ambushes for those mounting, making them terrified of the ascent. But Saturus climbed up first (he was the one who at a later stage gave himself up spontaneously on account of us—he had built up our courage and then, when we were arrested, had been away). And he reached the top of the ladder, and turned and said to me: "Perpetua, I'm waiting for you—but watch out that the serpent doesn't bite you!" And I said: "He won't hurt me, in Christ's name!" And under that ladder, almost, it seemed, afraid of me, the serpent slowly thrust out its head—and, as if I were treading on the first rung, I trod on it, and I climbed. And I saw an immense garden, and in the middle of it a white-haired man sitting in shepherd's garb, vast, milking sheep, with many thousands of people dressed in shining white standing all round. And he raised his head, looked at me, and said: "You are welcome, child." And he called me, and gave me, it seemed, a mouthful of the cheese he was milking; and I accepted it in both my hands together, and ate it, and all those standing around said: "Amen." And at the sound of that word I awoke, still chewing something indefinable and sweet. And at once I told my brother, and we understood that it would be mortal suffering; and we began to have no more hope in the world.[22]

In a general sense, the commentaries on this dream have taken their clue from Perpetua's remark that she and her brother realized that their future would be one of suffering (*intelleximus passionem esse futuram*). The dream has been construed as participant in a martyrological tradition of premoni-

[21] Dronke, *Women Writers of the Middle Ages,* p. 7.
[22] *Pass. Perp.* 4.3–10 (ed. Van Beek, pp. 12–14).

tory dreams, in which the dream serves to prepare the martyr psychologically to withstand the forthcoming ordeal.[23] Dreams like this one of Perpetua's have been compared with the dreams of prisoners in the Nazi concentration camps during the Second World War; in both cases, visions of sumptuous, paradisal scenes serve to protect the dreamer from the horrors of the real world in which he or she is living.[24] From the perspective of Perpetua's role as martyr, this dream has been said to have a double thematic: the image of the dangerous ladder, bedecked with weapons of war, prefigures the martyr's present and future torture, while the image of the shepherd in the garden prefigures the martyr's delivery to another world where peace and blessing prevail.[25]

Ancient commentators also appropriated the dream as a witness to the phenomenon of martyrdom, although they placed it in a theological rather than a psychological context. Augustine, who preached three sermons on the festal days marking the commemoration of the martyrdom of Perpetua and Felicitas, emphasized the dedication to the faith that the martyrs' actions demonstrated and situated their witness theologically with a vocabulary dominated by the categories of virtue and triumph.[26] In comments on this particular dream, he noted its ascensional aspect: the ladder was "that by which the blessed Perpetua went to God."[27]

Augustine, of course, no longer had to worry about governmental persecution of Christians and so was free to use the testimony of Perpetua's diary in a generalized way as an ideal model of Christian ethics and dedication. Earlier in the African Christian tradition, however, Tertullian was not free of such worries, and he focused his theological vision more narrowly on this dream as proof of the privilege enjoyed by martyrs after death. In his *De anima*, Tertullian included a long section on Christian views of hell, and it was in this context that he referred to the dream of Perpetua.[28] According to Tertullian, hell is a vast and deep space in the interior of the earth to which all souls, even those of Christians, descend at death, there to stay imprisoned until released at the second coming of the Christ.

---

[23] Dodds, *Pagan and Christian in an Age of Anxiety,* p. 50; Dronke, *Women Writers of the Middle Ages,* pp. 7–8; Amat, *Songes et Visions,* p. 50; Lane Fox, *Pagans and Christians,* pp. 400–401.

[24] Dulaey, *Le Rêve,* pp. 44–45.

[25] Amat, *Songes et Visions,* p. 67; Dronke, *Women Writers of the Middle Ages,* pp. 7–8.

[26] Augustine, *Sermons* 280–82, collected in Van Beek, ed., *Passio Sanctarum Perpetuae et Felicitatis,* pp. 149*–154* (=*PL* 38.1280–1286). Barnes notes that, in Augustine's era, the *Pass. Perp.* was read in church and regarded by some as canonical (*Tertullian,* p. 79); see Augustine, *De natura et origine animae* 1.10.12, in Van Beek, p. 154* (=*CSEL* 60.312).

[27] Augustine, *Serm.* 280.1 (in Van Beek, p. 150*).

[28] Tertullian, *De an.* 55–58 (ed. Waszink, pp. 73–80); for detailed discussions of Tertullian's views of the afterworld and hell, see Waszink, *Tertulliani De anima,* pp. 553–93; Amat, *Songes et Rêves,* pp. 148–53.

Arguing against Christians who asserted that Christ's descent into hell had relieved them of that underworldly sojourn, Tertullian counters with a reference to Perpetua's dream: if all Christians go immediately to paradise at death, how is it that Perpetua saw only Christian *martyrs* there?[29] Seizing upon the dream's image of "many thousands of people standing around [the shepherd]" (*circumstantes candidati milia multa*), Tertullian apparently took *candidati* to refer to martyrs as "candidates" for paradisal beatitude.[30] Thus he appropriated the dream for a theological program that extended to martyrs alone the privilege of entering paradise immediately after death, a program that may well have been influenced by the high esteem accorded to martyrdom by Montanism, a prophetic movement whose tenets Tertullian eventually embraced wholeheartedly.[31] "The only key to paradise is your own blood," is Tertullian's terse summary of his view of Perpetua's dream.[32]

While contemporary scholarship has noted the martyrological aspects of this dream as well as the other three, it has given more attention to the dreams as representative of Perpetua's status as a catechumen, that is, as one newly converted to and instructed in Christian doctrine. Thus the images of the dreams have been scrutinized for evidence of both Perpetua's recent immersion in Christian belief and writings and her "pagan" past (because the author of the *Passio* described her as *liberaliter instituta*, "well-educated," she can be presumed to have been familiar with polytheist practice and belief). With regard to this first dream, commentators have focused on the images of the ladder and the shepherd.

Dronke's cautionary note deserves to be sounded at the outset. Because "this is a painstakingly truthful record of authentic dreams . . . Perpetua's account must be respected in every detail, not 'smoothed' into more conventional patterns, whether of a Christian or Gnostic or Jungian kind." Although he does not doubt that the images in Perpetua's dreams have associations with what she was experiencing in prison as well as with what she had read and been taught, he argues that equating the ladder of Perpetua's dream with Jacob's ladder, the shepherd with the Good Shepherd, and the cheese with the Eucharist constitutes a forced interpretation of the dream's images that turns the individuality of Perpetua's dream-images into "Christian commonplaces."[33] Many commentators have in-

[29] Tertullian, *De an.* 55.3–4 (ed. Waszink, pp. 73–74).

[30] Tertullian may have conflated the dream of Saturus, which does use the word *martyr* to describe those whom he saw in heaven, with the first dream of Perpetua, which does not refer to martyrs per se. See *Pass. Perp.* 11.9 (ed. Van Beek, p. 30) and the discussion in Waszink, *Tertulliani De anima,* pp. 561–62.

[31] For a thorough discussion of Tertullian's relationship with Montanism, see Barnes, *Tertullian,* pp. 164–86; the role of Montanism in the church will be discussed later in this chapter.

[32] Tertullian, *De an.* 55.5 (ed. Waszink, p. 74).

[33] Dronke, *Women Writers of the Middle Ages,* pp. 6–7.

deed treated the dream's images as though they were transparent reflections of Christian belief and practice; implicitly, at least, the dream has been treated as though it were an allegory reflecting eschatological and theological doctrine (resurrection and the nature of God) and ecclesiastical ritual (the Eucharist). Also characteristic of the standard approach is a construal of the dream's images as a pastiche of references to a variety of scriptural passages.

First, then, the ladder. An entire biblical tradition has been assembled in the scene of the ladder: Jacob's dream of a ladder stretching from earth to heaven in Gen. 28 has been petitioned as a source, as has the appropriation of the image of Jacob's ladder in the Gospel of John 1.51, where the Christ becomes the ladder upon which angels ascend and descend; furthermore, Perpetua's confrontation with the serpent at the foot of the ladder has been seen as a reflection of Gen. 3:15, which envisions an enmity between woman and serpent, whose head will be bruised; and there is also Revelation 12, in which a woman newly with child escapes mortal danger posed by a dragon and is nourished in a wilderness.[34] Theologically, the image of Jacob's ladder appears to have been prominent in African Christian catechesis, where it served as a judgmental warning that some would ascend and some would not.[35] Perpetua's ascent of her ladder has been taken to signify not only in this eschatological context but also as a kind of proto-asceticism in which spiritual ascent and detachment from earthly concerns form a pair.[36] Finally, the serpent at the ladder's foot has been viewed theologically as a cipher for the devil, whom Perpetua, armed with the name of Christ, vanquishes.[37]

The fact that the ladder bristles with weapons has been interpreted psychologically as a reflection of Perpetua's fear of being lacerated, although it has also been seen as an oneiric reference to the actual *catasta*, or platform, upon which martyrs were tortured.[38] From the perspective of the phenomenology of religions, Dronke has suggested that the threaten-

---

[34] Miller, "'A Dubious Twilight': Reflections on Dreams in Patristic Literature," pp. 158–59; Amat, *Songes et Visions*, pp. 70, 74.

[35] See Amat, *Songes et Visions*, p. 70. For Tertullian's use of the image of Jacob's ladder in this way, see p. 103 above; see also the slightly later Carthaginian text, the *Passio Sanctorum Montani et Lucii* 7.6 with its oneiric reference to "the sign of Jacob" (ed. and trans. Musurillo, p. 218).

[36] Dronke, *Women Writers of the Middle Ages*, p. 8; Amat, *Songes et Visions*, p. 71; Marie-Louise Von Franz, *The Passion of Perpetua*, p. 18.

[37] Amat, *Songes et Visions*, p. 73; Von Franz, *The Passion of Perpetua*, pp. 24–25, for a psychological reading of the serpent; Dronke, *Women Writers of the Middle Ages*, pp. 8–9, sees in this scene "the traditional gesture of the victor in ancient combats," and he suggests further that the juxtaposition of the serpent with the ladder of weapons may be a reminiscence from Perpetua's reading of Virgil, *Aeneid* 2.469–75, where the warrior Pyrrhus, who breaks the bronze doors of Priam's palace, is described in terms of weapons and a snake.

[38] Amat, *Songes et Visions*, p. 72 and n. 145.

ing ladder is an instance of a widespread tendency in many religious traditions to use the image of the ladder to evoke "the challenge of crossing into the beyond"; by climbing her ladder successfully, Perpetua achieves symbolically a kind of shamanic initiation into the celestial realm.[39] Amat has also noted the archetypal character of the image of the ladder of immortality and, while maintaining the primacy of the scriptural ladder of Jacob as source for Perpetua's ladder, she suggests possible iconographic influence from the prominence of ladders in the cult of Mithras as well as from the presence of the motif of the ladder on stelae dedicated to the African god Saturnus.[40]

Although the image of the ladder has generally been interpreted in the context of Perpetua's newly found Christianity, this has not been the case with the shepherd. The setting in which the dream places the shepherd, the spacious garden, is said to draw on the convention of the *locus amoenus* or "pleasant spot" characteristic of Latin literature from Virgil and Ovid on.[41] The shepherd who presides over this idyll has been connected with the shepherds in both the *Shepherd* of Hermas and the Hermetic *Poimandres* and has been thereby assimilated to a cultural typology that, cutting across lines of religious affiliation, envisaged cosmic figures of enlightenment and redemption in a pastoral guise.[42] Furthermore, Perpetua's shepherd, described as a man "with the grey hair of the aged" (*hominem canum*), does not match early Christian iconography depicting the Christ as the Good Shepherd, an image familiar from the parable of the good shepherd in the Gospel of Luke as well as from Psalm 22. Catacomb iconography contemporary with Perpetua's era showed the

---

[39] Dronke, *Women Writers of the Middle Ages,* pp. 7–8, suggests a shamanic context for understanding Perpetua's dream after observing the important differences between Perpetua's dream of a ladder and Jacob's. The only feature that the two ladders share is that they stretch from earth to heaven:

> None of the other connotations of Jacob's ladder has any particular bearing on Perpetua's dream. Jacob himself does not mount his ladder—it is angels who go up and down on it . . . Yahweh leans over the top of that ladder, offering Jacob earthly prosperity. Perpetua's ladder, by contrast, is one that she must climb; it is a means of ascent only, not descent. There are no angels on it, for it is too narrow for more than one being to mount at a time. It is a painful way of climbing, encompassed by terrors. . . . (p. 7)

[40] Amat, *Songes et Visions,* pp. 69–70 and "L'Authenticité des Songes," p. 183.

[41] Amat, *Songes et Visions,* p. 119; see also Lane Fox, *Pagans and Christians,* p. 438, for observations on similar visions of the "pleasant spot" in the *Pass. Mariani et Iacobi* 6.12 and 11.9 (ed. and trans. Musurillo, pp. 202, 208). For a discussion of the possible influence of the pastoral visions of the *Shepherd of Hermas* on the *Pass. Perp.,* see Amat, *Songes et Visions,* p. 119. Daniélou, on the other hand, thought that the dream's picture of paradise as an "immense space of garden" came from Judaeo-Christian apocalyptic (in *A History of Early Christian Doctrine Before the Council of Nicaea,* 3:60).

[42] Von Franz, *Passion of Perpetua,* pp. 27–32.

shepherd-Christ to be young and handsome, hardly a match for the figure who appears in the dream.[43]

Despite this testimony, Amat has argued forcefully for the Christian provenance of Perpetua's oneiric shepherd. She concedes that Perpetua's oneiric imagination has modified iconographic representations but suggests that Perpetua's image of a hoary shepherd is a reminiscence of images of God presented in Daniel 7:9 and Revelation 1.14; thus the shepherd, God as the "ancient of days," and the Christ have been transposed in the dream.[44] She finds additional evidence for a Christianized reading of the image in the use of shepherd-imagery by Perpetua's contemporary, the Carthaginian theologian Tertullian (in his *De pudicitia*), as well as in baptismal and catechetical use of Psalm 22, where the one newly cleansed of sin by baptism is a lamb led by the Lord as shepherd.[45]

Interpretive decisions about the character of the shepherd have guided the way in which the shepherd's activity has been interpreted. Milking sheep, he calls Perpetua to him and gives her "a mouthful of the cheese (*caseo*) he was milking." Musurillo mistranslated *caseum* as "milk," perhaps to make this scene more realistic, or, more likely, because he understood the scene as a reminiscence of baptism, as suggested by his reference to Tertullian's *De corona* 3.3, where there is a remark about drinking milk after baptism.[46] Ancient interpreters also made the switch from cheese to milk.[47] Amat, who notes the strangeness of the mouthful of cheese, understands this substance as "lait caillé," curdled milk, at once both food and drink. Placing the scene in both baptismal and eucharistic contexts, she assembles a wide variety of possible contexts for amplifying the shepherd's gift: the biblical evocation of a "land of milk and honey," used in early Christian prebaptismal rituals; references to milk as the drink of eternity in other African martyrologies; the transformative power attributed to cheese in magic; the use of curdled milk as a sign of creative power in Job 10:10 ("Didst thou not pour me out like milk, and curdle me like cheese?") and, finally, the ritual structure of the scene, with its offer of symbolic nourishment accompanied by the formal "Amen!" of the crowd.[48]

Dodds, on the other hand, found "cheese-eating in Heaven" to be "quite

---

[43] Dronke, *Women Writers of the Middle Ages*, p. 9; Amat, *Songes et Visions*, pp. 119–21 and especially the iconographical references on p. 121n. 24.

[44] Amat, *Songes et Visions*, p. 121; Daniélou, *A History of Early Christian Doctrine Before the Council of Nicaea*, 3:60.

[45] Amat, *Songes et Visions*, pp. 119–21.

[46] Musurillo, *Acts of the Christian Martyrs*, p. 113 and n. 8.

[47] See the reference in Quodvultdeus, *Sermo* 5.6 (ed. Van Beek, p. 156* [=*PL* 40.703]) to the lactating Perpetua accepting milk from the fatherly shepherd; see also Pseudo-Augustine, *Sermo* 394 (ed. Van Beek, p. 161* [=*PL* 39.1716]).

[48] Amat, *Songes et Visions*, pp. 75–76.

unorthodox" and dismissed reference to the sect known as the Artotyrites ("bread-and-cheesers") as anachronistic.[49] From his perspective, the scene in which cheese is milked directly from the sheep derives its sense not from Christianity but from Freudian psychology: it shows "the sort of time-compression which is common in dreams" and is thus testimony to the autonomy of the oneiric imagination.[50] Among the non-Christian amplifications of this scene, the most ingenious is that offered by Dronke. He notes that, in other contexts, Perpetua's manner of receiving the cheese, with her hands held together, might well be a ritual sacramental gesture; but, in her case, he imagines that the gesture is a practical one, "to prevent the runny curds from spilling." As he explains, he envisions "a cheese rather like mozzarella, from which some liquid would ooze in the handling. What Perpetua receives is no Christian sacrament, nor any usual paradisal sustenance—nectar and ambrosia, milk and honey—but the food that, in many times and places, has symbolized the embryo and the process of birth."[51] Petitioning the "cheese analogy of conception" found in Aristotle as well as in Graeco-Roman medicine and folk belief, Dronke interprets the cheese as a symbol of the embryo and birth: "What Perpetua is given with her morsel of cheese is her destiny, her celestial birth."[52]

To conclude: although these diverse amplifications of the dream's images appear to fragment the dream by focusing only on its various parts, most interpreters have nonetheless viewed the whole dream as a two-part panorama of Perpetua's future. As a typical, if unusually detailed, member of the prophetic class of ancient onirology, this first dream of Perpetua's provides a forecast of her suffering and its consoling reward.

DREAMS TWO AND THREE

Because these two dreams form a sequence, with the second of the two providing a resolution of the agonized problematic of the first, they will be discussed together. The quotation begins with Perpetua's own explanation of the context in which the first of these dreams occurred:

> A few days later, while we were all praying, suddenly in the middle of my prayer I let slip a word: Dinocrates. And I was amazed, for he had never entered my thoughts except just then. And I grieved, remembering his plight. Then at once

[49] Dodds, *Pagan and Christian in an Age of Anxiety*, p. 51; to the contrary, Amat, *Songes et Visions*, p. 75.
[50] Dodds, *Pagan and Christian in an Age of Anxiety*, p. 51.
[51] Dronke, *Women Writers of the Middle Ages*, p. 9.
[52] Ibid.

I realized that I was entitled to ask for a vision about him,[53] and that I ought to; and I began to pray for him a lot, and plaintively, to God. That very night, this is what I was shown: I saw Dinocrates coming out of a dark place, where there were many people. He was very hot and thirsty, his clothes dirty and his looks pallid—he still had on his face the same wound as when he died. When alive he had been my brother, who at the age of seven died wretchedly, of a cancer of the face, in such a way that everyone saw his death with revulsion. So I prayed for him, and between him and me there was a great gap, such that we could not come near each other. Beside Dinocrates was a pool full of water, with a rim that was higher than he. And Dinocrates stretched up as if to drink. I was full of sorrow that, even though the pool had water, the rim was so high that he could not drink. And I awoke, and realized that my brother was struggling. Yet I was confident that I could help him in his struggle, and I prayed for him every day, till we moved to the military prison—for we were destined to fight in the garrison-games: they were on Emperor Geta's birthday. Day and night I prayed for Dinocrates, groaning and weeping that my prayer be granted.

On a day when we remained in fetters, I was shown this: I saw the place I'd seen before, and there was Dinocrates, clean, well-dressed, refreshed; and where the wound had been I saw a scar; and the pool I'd seen previously had its rim lowered: it was down to the boy's navel. And he was drinking from the pool incessantly. Above the rim was a golden bowl full of water. Dinocrates came near it and began to drink from that, and the bowl never ran dry. And when he had drunk his fill, he began to play with the water, as children do, full of happiness. And I awoke: I realized then that he'd been freed from pain.[54]

Commentary on this dream has centered on determining the status of the dark place in which the hot and thirsty Dinocrates first appears and, in consequence, on deciding which structures of religious praxis best explain Perpetua's intercessory power. Those who see the scene in terms of Perpetua's Christian beliefs place it in the context of the parable of the rich man and Lazarus in Luke 16:19–31, which envisages an uncrossable abyss between the abode of the blessed ("Abraham's bosom") and Hades (presented as a hot place with no water). Tertullian's use of the same parable to reinforce his belief that Hades will not be opened until the second coming of the

---

[53] Musurillo, *Acts of the Christian Martyrs*, p. 115, translates this passage as follows: "At once I realized that I was privileged to pray for him" [*et cognoui me statim dignam esse et pro eo petere debere*]. Dronke's translation, "I realized that I was entitled to ask for a vision about him," distinguishes between *petere*, "to seek or request," and *orationem facere*, "to offer prayers," in the next sentence; Dronke's translation maintains a structural analogy between this scene and Perpetua's request for a vision in Dream One and is, in my view, the more appropriate of the two translations.

[54] *Pass. Perp.* 7.1–8.4 (ed. Van Beek, pp. 18–22).

Christ is petitioned as proof of the authentically Christian quality of the oneiric construct of the first of these two dreams, in which Perpetua and her brother are separated by a great gap (although Tertullian's dismissal of appearances of the dead as demonic fictions seems to me to disqualify his thought as a useful theological context).[55] The second of the two dreams has been constructed as Christian on the basis of Perpetua's apparent reference, when she remarks that Dinocrates now appears "refreshed" (*refrigerantem*), to early Christian belief in an otherworldly *refrigerium* or *locus refrigerii*, a "cooling" or "refreshing" place.[56] Further, the pool from which Dinocrates is at first banned, but in which he later plays, may recall the scriptural image of the healing of the paralytic by the side of the pool at Bethsaida.[57]

There has been some question about whether the dark place in which the suffering Dinocrates is first located represents a prototype of later, more developed ideas about purgatory, a place for the chastisement of Christians who have sinned after baptism.[58] Augustine assimilated the plight of Dinocrates to his theological view that unbaptized children, even babies, were damned. According to his interpretation of these two dreams, Dinocrates must have been baptized (even though evidence from the diary suggests that most members of Perpetua's family were not Christian), or else Perpetua could not have interceded for him successfully; the child was in an other-worldly predicament in the first place because he had sinned after baptism— the wound on his face signifying, so Augustine said, the wound on his soul.[59] Most modern commentators, however, have followed Dölger in interpreting these two dreams as instances of the "pagan" substrate of the newly converted Perpetua's imagination.[60] According to this view, the first dream conforms to the view that the dead are thirsty, and that they appear, as apparitions, with the same physical characteristics they had when they

[55] Musurillo, *Acts of the Christian Martyrs*, p. 115n.10; Amat, *Songes et Visions*, p. 129. See Tertullian, *De an.* 57.1–12 (ed. Waszink, pp. 76–78, and Waszink's commentary on pp. 574–75).

[56] Amat, "L'Authenticité des songes," p. 180; Jacques Le Goff, *The Birth of Purgatory*, pp. 48–50. Dronke, *Women Writers of the Middle Ages*, p. 285n.46, cautions that "it is important to realize that Perpetua also uses *refrigerare* twice with an unequivocally earthy significance" at *Pass. Perp.* 3.7 and 9.1.

[57] Amat, *Songes et Visions*, p. 130.

[58] Le Goff, *The Birth of Purgatory*, pp. 49–50, argues that the *Pass. Perp.* offers a "glimpse" of what will later be a fully developed idea of purgatory: "The importance of the *Passion of Perpetua and Felicitas* in the prehistory of Purgatory should be neither exaggerated nor minimized. It is not Purgatory as such that is being discussed here, and none of the images contained in Perpetua's two visions recur in medieval imagery associated with Purgatory." See also Amat, *Songes et Visions*, pp. 128–29, 131.

[59] Augustine, *De nat. et or. an.* 4.18.27 (ed. Van Beek, p. 155*=CSEL 60. 405.

[60] Franz Joseph Dölger, "Antike Parallelen zum leidenen Dinocrates in der Passio Perpetuae," pp. 1–40.

died.[61] The second dream conforms to the belief in the efficacy of intercessory prayers for those who have died prematurely.[62]

These two dreams have also attracted psychological readings. Both Dodds and Dronke follow Von Franz's suggestion that Dinocrates "embodies a spiritual content in Perpetua herself so that his suffering, as portrayed in the dream, is in some way identical with her painful condition." Thus "this little brother who died in early childhood, together with all the memories which are linked with him, undoubtedly represents a piece of her own past, something child-like, a spirit in herself as yet unbaptised for whom the redeeming truth, symbolized by the water, is literally 'too high.'" The refreshed Dinocrates, in consequence, represents Perpetua's coming to terms with inner conflict that had threatened her resolve.[63] With a lighter psychological touch, Dronke has perceptively observed that this pair of dreams occurs immediately after Perpetua recorded, in her diary, her relief at her discovery that her baby no longer needed her milk, thus enabling her to leave him in her family's care without worry.[64] After the dreams, Dronke remarks, "Perpetua feels for the suffering not of the living but of the dead. She finds she can make her brother well again by praying. Symbolically, it suggests that she can give spiritual help to all her family, and it is this that finally relieves her earthly anxieties over them."[65]

DREAM FOUR

This dream, the longest and most elaborate of the four, is the final entry in Perpetua's diary.

[61] Ibid., p. 29; Amat, *Songes et Visions*, pp. 128–29; Dronke, *Women Writers of the Middle Ages*, p. 11, suggests that Perpetua's reading of Virgil's *Aeneid* might also have influenced her oneiric vision of Dinocrates: "She would have remembered the wails and weeping of dead infant souls that greeted Aeneas when he had been ferried across the Styx; and she would have retained in her fantasy the dark, muddy place, and the haunting images that follow, of those who, like Dido, perished through their wounds and still bore those wounds in Hades" (see *Aeneid* 6.426ff.).

[62] See Dölger, "Antlike Parallelen zum leidenen Dinocrates in der Passio Perpetuae," pp. 13–15, 29–34, who cites as a parallel a passage from the *Acts of Paul and Thecla* 28, in which the dead daughter of a noble woman speaks to her mother in a dream, asking that Thecla pray for her so that she might be transferred to the otherworldly place of the righteous; on the idea of the intercessory "power of the keys" wielded by martyrs, see Frederick C. Klawiter, "The Role of Martyrdom and Persecution in Developing the Priestly Authority of Women in Early Christianity: A Case Study of Montanism," pp. 254–60; on the motif of the *aoroi*, the untimely dead, see J. H. Waszink, "Mors immatura," pp. 107–12.

[63] Von Franz, *The Passion of Perpetua*, p. 36, 37–43; Dodds, *Pagan and Christian in an Age of Anxiety*, p. 51; Dronke, *Women Writers of the Middle Ages*, p. 12.

[64] See *Pass. Perp.* 6.7–8 (ed. Van Beek, p. 18).

[65] Dronke, *Women Writers of the Middle Ages*, p. 11.

The day before our fight, this is what I saw in vision: Pomponius the deacon was coming to the prison gate and knocking urgently. And I went out to him and opened for him. He was wearing a loose, gleaming white tunic, and damasked sandals, and he said: "Perpetua, we are waiting for you: come!" He took my hand and we began to go over rough, winding ways. We had hardly reached the amphitheatre, breathless, when he took me into the middle of the arena, and said: "Don't be afraid; here I am, beside you, sharing your toil." And he vanished. And I saw the immense, astonished crowd. And as I knew I had been condemned to the wild beasts, I was amazed they did not send them out at me. Out against me came an Egyptian, foul of aspect, with his seconds: he was to fight with me. And some handsome young men came up beside me: my own seconds and supporters. And I was stripped naked, and became a man. And my supporters began to rub me with oil, as they do for a wrestling match; and on the other side I saw the Egyptian rolling himself in the dust. And a man of amazing size came out—he towered even over the vault of the amphitheatre. He was wearing the purple, loosely, with two stripes crossing his chest, and patterned sandals made of gold and silver, carrying a baton like a fencing-master and a green bough laden with golden apples. He asked for silence, and said: "This Egyptian, if he defeats her, will kill her with his sword; she, if she defeats him, will receive this bough." And he drew back.

And we joined combat, and fists began to fly. He tried to grab my feet, but I struck him in the face with my heels. And I felt airborne, and began to strike him as if I were not touching ground. But when I saw there was a lull, I locked my hands, clenching my fingers together, and so caught hold of his head; and he fell on his face, and I trod upon his head. The populace began to shout, and my supporters to sing jubilantly. And I went to the fencing-master and received the bough. He kissed me and said: "Daughter, peace be with you!" And triumphantly I began to walk towards the Gate of the Living. And I awoke. And I knew I should have to fight not against wild beasts but against the Fiend; but I knew the victory would be mine.

This is what I have done till the day before the contest; if anyone wants to write of its outcome, let them do so.[66]

This dream has been read as a structural homologue to the first dream in that it is both premonitory of suffering and predictive of consolation and triumph.[67] As the fourth in a sequence of dreams, it is climactic: as the actual confrontation drew nearer, the images of Perpetua's dreams were intensified, both in terms of imaginal forms of terror—from cold-blooded snake to ill child to full-grown Egyptian warrior—and in terms of imaginal forms of spiritual reward—from heavenly cheese to ever-flowing water to golden

[66] *Pass. Perp.* 10.1–15 (ed. Van Beek, pp. 24–28).
[67] Dodds, *Pagan and Christian in an Age of Anxiety,* pp. 50–51; Amat, *Songes et Visions,* p. 76; Dronke, *Women Writers of the Middle Ages,* p. 13.

apples.[68] Again as with the first dream, so also here Perpetua herself offers her own interpretive key to the dream's significance. The wild beasts whose onslaught she will suffer are the material signs of a spiritual struggle with the devil (*et intellexi me non ad bestias, sed contra diabolum esse pugnaturam*), whom she will overcome. The devil himself appears, in his turn, to be a sign both for the familial and cultural opponents of Perpetua's embrace of Christianity because, earlier in the diary, Perpetua recounts her father's anger at hearing the word *Christian* as well as his attempts to shake her resolution. When she remains firm, she reports, "He departed, defeated along with his devilish arguments" (*profectus est victus cum argumentis diaboli*).[69] Father, beast, and Egyptian are thus related metonymically as signs of the forces that "bedevil" Perpetua and that succumb to her religious resolve.[70]

In commentaries on this dream, the indebtedness of the oneiric imagination to elements of the "pagan" culture in which Perpetua was raised and educated has been emphasized. Dodds, arguing that the dream-cycle is authentic and not the product of Christian propaganda, notes that the judge of the combat in the arena is not pictured as Christ but as a trainer of gladiators and that the reward is not the expected martyr's crown but the mythic golden apples of the Hesperides. "This pagan imagery," he argues, "is entirely natural in the dreams of a quite recent convert."[71] Dronke also notes the dream's pagan substrate but underscores the dreamlike qualities of the text as dream—its "sense of phantasmagoria" and its surreal details of flying and gender-transformation.[72]

The most thoroughgoing reading of the dream in terms of its social context is that offered by Louis Robert. In his discussion, there is nothing surreal about the dream, which he reads as a straightforward reflection, in exacting detail, of the ecumenical games held in Carthage in honor of the Pythian Apollo, the *Pythia Carthaginis*.[73] Arguing on the basis of the Greek rather than the Latin text of the diary, he shows that the Latin word used to describe the Judge (*lanista* = "fencing master" or "trainer of gladiators") has misled interpreters to view the scene of combat as a gladiatorial contest. Instead, what Perpetua's dream envisages is a *pancration*, a contest combining boxing and wrestling. The oneiric images of Perpetua's nudity, the oiling of her skin, and her sex-change are all seen as naturalistic details

---

[68] Von Franz, *The Passion of Perpetua*, pp. 52, 71; Dronke, *Women Writers of the Middle Ages*, p. 15.

[69] *Pass. Perp.* 3.3 (ed. Van Beek, p. 8).

[70] See Mary R. Lefkowitz, "The Motivations for St. Perpetua's Martyrdom," p. 418: "We can recognize in Perpetua's resistance to her father and gradual withdrawal from her family the standard behavior pattern of conversion; a wish to break from the past, a need to substitute strong new ties that can replace the old."

[71] Dodds, *Pagan and Christian in an Age of Anxiety*, p. 52.

[72] Dronke, *Women Writers of the Middle Ages*, p. 14.

[73] Louis Robert, "Une Vision de Perpetué martyre à Carthage en 203," p. 232.

necessary to participation in this particular form of *agōn*. The dress of the judge, as well as his baton and branch of apples, are all authentic features as attested particularly by bas-reliefs and coins; by calling the *agonothete* a *lanista*, the Latin text has transposed onto the figure of the judge another official, one who supplied gladiators for games and also trained them.[74]

Following Robert, Amat also recognizes the dream's indebtedness to the iconography of the amphitheater.[75] However, she finds the significance of the dream not in its mirroring of a cultural phenomenon but rather in its representation of the martyr as athlete of Christ, particularly because this theme is present in other martyrological literature as well as in the letters of Paul. The theme of the martyr-athlete is the ground upon which Amat constructs an interpretation of the dream's images in Christian terms. Imaginally linked by the loose tunics that they wear, Pomponius the deacon and the supernaturally large judge are both symbols of Christ, Pomponius because his knocking at the prison gate "prefigures the eschatological 'passage' to Christ," the judge because the bands of purple symbolize the passion and are also found in representations of divine apparitions in catacomb paintings.[76] The judge's baton is reminiscent of the rod used by God to punish transgressions in Ps. 89.32 and foreshadows Perpetua's death by sword.[77] Perpetua's oneiric picture of golden apples, while originally part of the mythic cycle of Heracles' labors, is an example of the way in which her imagination has been guided by images in Christian literature and art: the tree of temptation in Genesis that becomes the tree of life in paradise regained, the tree of life with fiery fruits in apocryphyal apocalypses, and pictorial uses of apples to symbolize the orchard of paradise are all suggested as possible influences on the dream's image.[78] Similarly, the oil rubbed on the oneiric Perpetua's body is a memory of prebaptismal unction, and the image of the devil-as-Egyptian recalls the biblical condemnation of Egypt in the book of Exodus.[79]

Although Dronke for the most part resists this kind of allegorical translation of the dream's images, he contributes to a reading of the dream as a

---

[74] Robert, "Une Vision de Perpetué martyre à Carthage en 203," pp. 255–71.

[75] Amat, *Songes et Visions*, pp. 77–79.

[76] Ibid., pp. 80–81.

[77] Ibid., pp. 78–79. For other symbolic associations of the baton, see Martine Dulaey, "Le Symbole de la baguette dans l'art paléo-chrétien," pp. 3–38.

[78] Amat, *Songes et Visions*, p. 80.

[79] Ibid., pp. 82–83; Robert, on the other hand, sees the presence of the Egyptian in the dream as an accurate reflection of the participation of large numbers of Egyptians in athletic competitions in the imperial era ("Une Vision de Perpetué martyre à Carthage en 203," pp. 272–73); Dronke, referring to Graeco-Roman associations of Egypt with "pagan sacred wisdom," suggests that the Egyptian represented for Perpetua an "Egypt of the mind" which, after her conversion to Christianity, she was struggling to overcome (*Women Writers of the Middle Ages*, p. 14).

product of Perpetua's Christian training by offering a unique exegesis of the opening of the dream as a reminiscence of the fifth chapter of the biblical Song of Songs. Perpetua's dreaming has been influenced by early Christian mystical readings of the scenario of the Song's bride awakened, called, abandoned by her lover-brother, and tormented as "a moment of divine visitation, both summoning and harshly testing the soul that loves God."[80]

Despite the debates over the sociocultural or religious derivation of the individual elements of this dream, commentators agree that the outstanding theme of the dream is the martyr's courageous resolve to remain faithful to her new religious commitment. Facing physical death, Perpetua dreamed of spiritual life.

THE foregoing interpretations of Perpetua's dreams exemplify the way in which the interpreter's choice of perspective and context will to a large extent determine the kind and range of readings that a given text can yield. When the dreams are interpreted from the perspective of martyrdom, the texts yield a reading of Perpetua's psychological condition as well as a view of her historical situation as one at the nexus of a religio-political conflict. On the other hand, when the dreams are interpreted from the perspective of Christian catechetical training, the texts yield a reading of Perpetua's religious consciousness either as one immersed in Christian scripture and cultic practice, or as one that reflects the persistence of "pagan" literary and religious forms in the thought-patterns of the new convert.

In their various ways, these interpretive stances read Perpetua's dreams as mimetic to the culture in which they occurred; this is part of their attempt to reproduce the text's (and Perpetua's) meaning. However, as John Winkler has pointed out, such attempts to reproduce an author's meaning are involved in an important methodological issue: "Should we concede that much authority to the writers we read? If our critical faculties are placed solely in the service of recovering and reanimating an author's meaning, then we have already committed ourselves to the premises and protocols of the past"—a past whose structures of cultural violence, such as the metanarrative of patriarchy that I will explore in the following pages, continue to exert a pernicious influence in the present.[81] Winkler recommends the strategy of "reading against the grain" of conventional interpretive positions as a means to engage such protocols and also as "an occasion to struggle against the tacit, conventional, and violent embrace in which we are held by the past."[82]

The reading of Perpetua's dreams that I will offer is such a "reading

[80] Dronke, *Women Writers of the Middle Ages*, p. 13.
[81] Winkler, *The Contraints of Desire*, p. 126.
[82] Ibid.

against the grain" which views the dreams as expressions of a Christian *woman*, as differentiated from conventional readings of them as expressions of a *Christian* woman. In so doing, I do not mean to displace or deny other readings but rather to add to the range of interpretive possibilities that these texts present. Using, as context, a perspective that dreams are vehicles for the forging of new understandings of self-identity, I will read Perpetua's dream-diary as *both* reflective of *and* resistant to the sexual politics of her community, a community in which there was a power struggle that was engendered in male and female terms. When read as a critique of culture rather than only as a mirror of it, Perpetua's diary offers a powerful articulation of a woman's struggle to establish her own voice in the context of patriarchal devaluations of female witness.

In what follows, the term *patriarchy* will be used to designate a metanarrative. A metanarrative is a system of thought, or a structure of thinking, that suppresses difference in order to legitimate its own vision of reality; because it makes totalizing claims to universal validity, a metanarrative suppresses or devalues discourses that are "other," that are different. As a metanarrative, patriarchy supports the dominance of the paternal metaphor in the establishment of meaning. I am going to argue that Perpetua's diary, written in such a patriarchal context, can be read as an expression of difference, a voice of otherness that questions the dominance of maleness in the construction of meaning. In order to enable this voice of difference to speak from the diary, I will use interpretive strategies taken from French feminist writers. My own strategy in this endeavor is not to do violence to the historical specificity of an ancient text by replacing, and so erasing, its categories with those of a contemporary discourse, but rather to show another integrity in the text that is also consonant with contemporary discourse. The writers whose literary and feminist theory provide the interpretive position of the discussion that follows are Julia Kristeva and Luce Irigaray, both of whom are in the vanguard of an ongoing critique of monological values in Western culture.

In an essay entitled "Word, Dialogue and Novel," Kristeva presents and develops the idea of "carnivalesque discourse" introduced by the Russian theorist Mikhail Bakhtin.[83] In contrast to linguistic practices that are univocal and prohibitive of polysemy, carnivalesque discourse is discourse that achieves a poetic logic: "By adopting a dream logic, it transgresses rules of the linguistic code and social morality as well."[84] In the discourse of the carnival, words are poetic, "polyvalent and multidetermined," and they conform to a "logic exceeding that of codified discourse," coming to expression fully only in the margins of culture.[85]

---

[83] Kristeva, "Word, Dialogue and Novel," pp. 64–91.
[84] Ibid., p. 70.
[85] Ibid., p. 65.

Carnivalesque language is thus language that constitutes an "other" side of the discourse that is dogmatic, determined by what Kristeva calls Law and Definition. In the carnival, authority is challenged because words are freed from presupposed values; carnivalesque discourse is rebellious and subversive insofar as it allows the articulation of marginal, misunderstood, or repressed perspectives to emerge.[86] Transformation of values in language is the experience of the carnival.

The exuberance suggested by the metaphor of the carnival has, however, its sinister aspect. As Kristeva says, "Pathological states of the soul, such as madness, split personalities, daydreams, dreams, and death, become part of the narrative."[87] Such pathological elements—dreams, split personalities, death—are pertinent to carnivalesque discourse because "they destroy man's epic and tragic unity as well as his belief in identity and causality; they indicate that he has lost his totality and no longer coincides with himself."[88] In the carnival, one dreams subversive, irreverent dreams and in the process sees his or her identity split, dead, no longer "total." Further, in the carnival a transformation of identity is taking place, and that transformation is accomplished through the polysemantic discourse of a perspective that has been repressed or marginalized by univocal structures of discourse usually attributed to Law, God, and Father—that is, to the metanarratives of patriarchy.

It has been noted by interpreters of Perpetua's diary that, in the course of discussions with her father and the judge at her trial, Perpetua gives up her name. "*Christiana sum,*" she says: "I am a Christian/I am Christiana."[89] She thus loses—even denies—the identity given her by the dominant culture.[90] Interestingly, in the *Acta minora*, a shorter, somewhat later version of Perpetua's story, the "carnivalesque" quality of Perpetua's change of name is reinforced by the following statement attributed to her. In reply to the judge's question whether she is a Christian, she says, "I am a Christian, and I follow the authority of my name, that I may be perpetual" (*Christiana sum, et nominis mei sequor auctoritatem, ut sim perpetua*).[91] Her embrace of the

---

[86] Ibid., pp. 70, 78–80.

[87] Ibid., p. 83.

[88] Ibid., p. 83.

[89] *Pass. Perp.* 3.2; 6.4 (ed. Van Beek, pp. 8, 18).

[90] On the status of the name Christian, Peter Brown observes about the martyrs that "friendship with God raised the Christians above the identity that they shared with their fellows. The *nomen Christianum* they flaunted was a 'non-name.' It excluded the current names of kin and township. . . ." (*The Making of Late Antiquity*, p. 56). See also Dronke, *Women Writers of the Middle Ages*, p. 5, for his characterization of Perpetua's insistence on her new name as a kind of "grammatical Platonism" for which "names are not arbitrary; there is a primordial, divinely ordained harmony between names and things."

[91] *Acta minora* 5.9: "Proconsul ad Perpetuam dixit: 'Quid dicis, Perpetua? Sacrificas?' Perpetua respondit: 'Christiana sum, et nominis mei sequor auctoritatem, ut sim perpetua" (ed. Van Beek, p. 66).

Christian "non-name," which is itself a "new" name, at the same time reveals another dimension of her "old" name.[92]

Curiously, to follow the authority of the name is to flout authority. Perpetua's new name sets her free from paternal and social definition. In Kristeva's terms, this name is a word from the carnival, because in the carnival words are freed from presupposed values and so are subversive of the master narratives of established authority. Luce Irigaray might agree, but she would describe this scene differently, arguing not from literary theory but rather from a feminist perspective. The purpose for bringing these two theorists, Kristeva and Irigaray, together is to show that there is a feminist dimension of carnivalesque discourse—or better, to suggest the ways in which the language of the carnival is particularly pertinent to female discourse and, more basically, to female presence in language.

In her book *This Sex Which Is Not One*, Irigaray argues that, because of male dominance in language and culture, the female has been reduced to a kind of "shadow" of the male. She quotes the psychiatrist-philosopher Jacques Lacan to this effect: "'There is no woman who is not excluded by the nature of things, which is the nature of words. . . . '"[93] This means that "*the feminine occurs only within models and laws devised by male subjects.*"[94] Women, then, are "objects" deprived of an authoritative discourse of their own.

Irigaray does not resolve the problem of feminine silence at the hands of masculine definition, but she does provide gestures toward possibilities of the expression of the feminine in language; these are the points at which her theory makes contact with Kristeva's notion of the carnivalesque. Irigaray writes that if there were to be such a thing as "feminine syntax" in language—that is, an "order" of discourse not organized by conceptual, representational thinking—"there would no longer be either subject or object, 'oneness' would no longer be privileged, there would no longer be proper meanings, proper names, 'proper' attributes. . . . It would preclude any distinction of identities, any establishment of ownership, thus any form of appropriation."[95] Surely this is what Kristeva describes as carnivalesque discourse, which precisely splits identity and subverts totality. As with Perpetua, "proper" names break apart and reveal dimensions not authorized by Father or Law. Indeed, when Perpetua declares *Christiana sum*, her father rushes at her as though to pluck out her eyes, and the judge condemns her to the beasts.[96] Her discourse, however, declares that she will not be owned by masculine definitions of what it means to be "Perpetua."

For Irigaray, the issue in the "issue" of a feminine presence in discourse is

[92] Brown, *The Making of Late Antiquity*, p. 56.
[93] Luce Irigaray, *This Sex Which Is Not One*, p. 87.
[94] Ibid., p. 86 (italics in original).
[95] Ibid., p. 134.
[96] *Pass. Perp.* 3.3; 6.5–6 (ed. Van Beek, pp. 8, 18).

not the elaboration of a "new theory of which woman would be the *subject* or the *object*, but of jamming the theoretical machinery itself, of suspending its pretension to the production of a truth and of a meaning that are excessively univocal."[97] The idea of "jamming" discursive practices that depend upon such distinctions between subject and object will be pertinent to my analysis of Perpetua's oneiric discourse as one in which subject and object, author and text, are confabulated as "author" becomes "character" in her own narrative, which, as dream, is not univocal but polyvalent.[98]

If there were to be such a thing as "her language," what would it be? For Irigaray, it would be "somewhat mad from the standpoint of reason, inaudible for whoever listens to [it] with ready-made grids, with a fully elaborated code in hand."[99] Further, "one would have to listen with another ear, as if hearing an 'other meaning,' always in the process of weaving itself, of embracing itself with words. . . . "[100] The "other ear" hears a whisper of an "other" that lies waiting within fixed, congealed perspectives: the laughter of the carnival, but also its discourse of dream and death.

According to Irigaray, women are outside the system. On the one hand, this means that "woman does not have access to language, except through recourse to 'masculine' systems of representation which disappropriate her from her relation to herself. . . . "[101] On the other hand, being outside the system gives her critical leverage on it—even if her only means of expressing something different from the system is the dream-speech of the carnival.

Perpetua wrote her diary in a time and place in which the masters of discourse were men and maleness was the determinant of meaning. In order to understand how feminist theory can be useful in eliciting a reading of Perpetua's diary that allows her voice to be heard as a woman's voice, some attention to the patriarchal narratives that dominated the sexual politics of her social and religious world is necessary.

Foremost among the representatives of the patriarchal perspective in Perpetua's own community in Carthage was Tertullian, arguably the most prominent Latin Christian theologian of his day. In his writings, the patriarchal contours of the context in which Perpetua professed her faith can be clearly discerned. Tertullian's most basic dictum on woman is his characterization of her nature in theological terms. The truth of woman's condition, he says, should be enacted bodily: she must avoid elegant dress and wear rags, thus presenting herself as a mourning and repentant Eve.[102] Tertullian

[97] Irigaray, *This Sex Which Is Not One*, p. 78.
[98] This is where Perpetua's characterization of her dream-speech with the verb *fabulor* assumes its importance as a perspective on oneiric constructions; see p. 151 above.
[99] Irigaray, *This Sex Which Is Not One*, p. 29.
[100] Ibid.
[101] Ibid., p. 85.
[102] Tertullian, *De cultu feminarum* 1.1.1 (CCL 1.343).

thought that woman's outer appearance should match her inner nature, indelibly tainted by "the disgrace of the first transgression and the odium of the ruin of humankind."[103] Everywoman is Eve, and she lives under the judgment of God. In a famous piece of rhetoric, Tertullian says: "You are the devil's gateway; you are she who unsealed that tree; you are the first deserter of divine law; you are the one who persuaded him whom the devil was not able to bribe; you easily destroyed the image of God, the man Adam."[104] This is a blunt articulation of the univocal discourse of representation in which a masculine "subject" judges a feminine "object," depriving her of access, except through male discourse, to relations with God, herself, and (as we shall see) to speech as well. In Irigaray's terms, Tertullian's construction of woman exemplifies the sexual logic that privileges the paternal metanarrative.[105]

Theologically, woman is defined sexually, and her sexuality is negative; it is something to be repressed, subjected to submission, plainness, and lack of show. These qualities are the proper character of women's dress that most appropriately signify her inner condition.[106] Tertullian presents his definition of woman as though it had the character of theological law. How could a woman like Perpetua come to terms with such a definition? How could a female martyr acknowledge the value of a Law that stigmatized her as "the devil's gateway"?

There is a striking passage in Perpetua's diary that might speak to these questions. Perpetua reported that, following her baptism while under arrest, "the spirit enjoined me not to seek from that water any favor except physical endurance" (*sufferentiam carnis*).[107] Her inspiration pertained to endurance, perseverance, suffering of the flesh. The meaning of such a statement in the context of her captivity seems clear: she wanted the strength to live in order to testify. In the context that I propose, however, her statement speaks on another plane of signification altogether. What might suffering the flesh connote for a woman whose "flesh" had been so degraded theologically? What might physical endurance mean in a condition of captivity to a discourse for which a female witness must surely have been a paradox, if not a contradiction in terms? One of the most compelling of Irigaray's arguments revolves around what she calls "sexual indifference": if

103 Ibid.

104 Ibid. 1.1.2 (*CCL* 1.343).

105 Irigaray, *This Sex Which Is Not One,* p. 90.

106 This is Tertullian's argument throughout *De cultu fem.* See, for example, his concluding chapter, in which he states that it is not enough for Christians to be modest; they must also present a modest appearance. "[Christian modesty] must be complete to such an extent that it emanates from the soul to the clothing and bursts out from the conscience to the outer appearance" (*De cultu fem.* 2.13.3 [*CCL* 1.369]).

107 *Pass. Perp.* 3.5 (ed. Van Beek, p. 8).

the female exists only insofar as she is defined by the male, then there is actually only one sex.[108] This phenomenon showed itself, for example, in Augustine's sermons, where the "virile" quality of Perpetua's acts as martyr is constantly underscored. This is an interpretive move that effectively reduces, if it does not deny altogether, the possibility of conceptualizing spiritual courage as female. Indeed, Augustine went so far as to say that Perpetua's virtuous mentality had made her "sexuality according to the flesh" "invisible" and that, in her oneiric fight in the arena, the devil had felt himself in the presence of a woman who acted like a man.[109] Given this kind of assimilation of the female to the male, Perpetua's petition for "endurance of the flesh" can be read as a petition for, and a spirited affirmation of, the perseverance of her very body—her female being—as a fitting testament to a system that would not, theologically, allow such a testament.

In Kristeva's terms, Perpetua's statement is a "poetic word," because it "adheres to a logic exceeding that of codified discourse," the theological discourse of her own church.[110] Perhaps such multi-determined words were the only kind available to her, given Tertullian's pronouncement on female speech. Commenting on various practices of heretics, Tertullian explodes:

> These heretical women—what impudence! They dare to teach, to engage in argument, to perform exorcisms, to promise healings, and perhaps even to baptize.[111]

Elsewhere, Tertullian shows that it is not only heretical women who, by virtue of speaking, are immodest. In fact, the real heresy is that women should speak at all. In one treatise, he attacked a woman who taught and led one of the North African congregations, calling her a "viper," and in another he petitioned "the precepts of ecclesiastical discipline concerning women":

> It is not permissible for a woman to speak in church, nor is it permitted for her to teach, to baptize, or to offer [the Eucharist], nor can she claim a share for herself in any masculine office, not to speak of any priestly duty.[112]

If, as Tertullian makes so clear, woman was cut off from the discourse as well as the sacramental offices of the institution, what role did she play in the church? For she did have a role to play. In the following quotation, it is

---

[108] Irigaray, *This Sex Which Is Not One*, p. 69.

[109] Augustine, *Serm.* 280.1 (in Van Beek, p. 150*); *Serm.* 281.2 (in Van Beek, p. 152*); *De nat. et or. an.* 4.18.26 (in Van Beek, p. 155*); see also *Serm.* 282.3 (in Van Beek, pp. 153*–54*).

[110] Kristeva, "Word, Dialogue and Novel," p. 65.

[111] *De praescriptione haereticorum* 41.5 (*CCL* 1.220).

[112] On the "viper," see *De baptismo* 1.2–3 (*CCL* 1.277); on the denial of official ecclesiastical duties to women, see *De virginibus velandis* 9.1 (*CCL* 2.1218–19).

evident once again that sexual logic dominated Tertullian's description of (apparently permissible) female Christian activities. This passage comes from a lengthy letter to his wife, in which Tertullian raises the specter of the scenario that might occur should a Christian woman marry a pagan man.

> Who would allow his wife, for the sake of visiting the brethren, to go around from street to street to other men's meager huts? Who will willingly tolerate her being snatched from his side by nocturnal assemblies? Who will bear without anxiety [her attendance] all night long at the Paschal rites? Who will, without his own suspicion, send her forth to attend the Lord's Supper, which they defame? Who will suffer her to creep into prison for the purpose of kissing a martyr's fetters or, indeed, to exchange the kiss with some one of the brothers?[113]

As outlined here by Tertullian, women's duties as Christians are erotic—or at least potentially so from the male perspective. Deprived of speech, woman is the one who creeps into jail to kiss the chains of martyrs, and who can tell what might transpire during the ritual of the kiss of peace? Thus, even when she is serving the discourse of the Law, woman is erotically suspect, tainted by her sex.[114]

As a context for understanding Perpetua's historical situation, Tertullian's unremittingly patriarchal construction of woman in theological terms may not tell the whole story. There is a possibility that Perpetua had been a participant in a revivalist movement within Christianity, the "New Prophecy" of Montanus, that held out tantalizingly "liberationist" promise for women. Montanism, as the movement was later called after the name of its founder, originated in Phrygia in Asia Minor in the late 150s or early 160s, when Montanus began to fall into ecstatic trances, claiming that his prophetic utterance was the voice of the Holy Spirit speaking through him.[115] He was joined by two female prophets, Priscilla and Maximilla. Central to the message of this movement was the conviction that the Spirit could still speak directly to the Christian community through inspired individuals, whether male or female. Envisaging the imminent end of the world and the

---

[113] *Ad uxorem* 4.2–3 (*CCL* 1.389).

[114] Lefkowitz, "Motivations for St. Perpetua's Martyrdom," has pointed out that the church fathers praised Perpetua and Felicitas for "acting uncharacteristically for women, in overcoming the inherent weakness and sinfulness of their flesh." She goes on to note "the consistent failure of male scholars to acknowledge the positive significance of femininity in the performance of certain heroic acts" (p. 421 and n.13). In a similar vein, Stevan Davies has discussed the roles of women in early Christian *Acta*, showing that women were often categorized (negatively) according to conventional values and that they were denied "apostolic" roles, even when they had shown themselves to be as chaste, as pious, and as devoted as their male companions. See *The Revolt of the Widows: The Social World of the Apocryphal Acts,* passim.

[115] Montanism's date of origin is disputed; for discussion, see Robert M. Grant, *Augustus to Constantine,* pp. 132–33.

descent of the heavenly Jerusalem, the New Prophecy urged its followers to testify publicly on behalf of their faith, thus appearing to encourage martyrdom.[116]

This movement was notable for the leadership roles that it accorded to women, as its opponents did not fail to perceive.[117] According to the fourth-century heresiologist Epiphanius, Montanists viewed Eve as the source of knowledge and also admired the prophetic sister of Moses.[118] In this movement, even divine sources of revelation could be feminized, as the following oracle attributed to Priscilla suggests: "Appearing as a woman clothed in a shining robe, Christ came to me [in sleep]; he put wisdom into me and revealed to me that this place is sacred and that here Jerusalem will come down from heaven."[119] Most important to a view of the New Prophecy as a movement that offered expanded opportunities to women was its apparent claim that confessor-martyrs, once released from prison, had ministerial status, at least in Asia Minor. Central to this claim was the view that martyrs could exercise "the priestly power of the keys," that is, the power to forgive sinners and so restore them to the faith. As Frederick Klawiter has explained:

> By exercising this power to forgive, the martyr was able to restore a lapsed person back into communion with Christ and his church. Since the power of the keys had been traditionally in the hands of the bishop-presbyter, anyone who exercised such power was thereby demonstrating a ministerial power. Strict logic would lead one to conclude than an imprisoned confessor could have the status of a minister.[120]

Thus both in its individualistic view of prophecy and in its attribution of priestly power to martyrs, Montanism posed a political threat to the stable hierarchy of the church as an institution and it challenged its construction of ecclesiastical authority as male.[121]

Despite the condemnation of Montanus and his followers by Asian bishops and eventually by the bishop of Rome as well, the New Prophecy

[116] Klawiter, "The Role of Martyrdom and Persecution in Developing the Priestly Authority of Women in Early Christianity," p. 253; Grant, *Augustus to Constantine*, pp. 133–35; Barnes, *Tertullian*, p. 131.

[117] See Lane Fox, *Pagans and Christians*, p. 407, for the insistence of Montanism's opponents on viewing prophets as male. Evidence for the persistence of such misogyny is his quotation of a lexical article on Montanism in the *Dictionary of Christian Biography*, published in 1882: "If Montanus had triumphed, Christian doctrine would have been developed not under the superintendence of the Christian teachers most esteemed for wisdom, but of wild and excitable women" (p. 409).

[118] Epiphanius, *Panarion* 49.2 (*PG* 41.882A).

[119] Ibid., 49.1 (*PG* 41.880C), translated by R. M. Grant, *Second-Century Christianity: A Collection of Fragments*, p. 96.

[120] Klawiter, "Role of Martyrdom and Persecution," p. 254.

[121] For a discussion of these issues, see Ross Shepard Kraemer, *Her Share of the Blessings*, pp. 165–66, 170, 177–81.

spread westward rapidly, taking hold especially in Carthage.[122] The two main witnesses to the strength of Montanism in the Cathaginian church are Tertullian, who became a full-fledged adherent of the movement, and the *Passion of Perpetua and Felicitas*.[123] The anonymous author who wrote this *passio* incorporated the writings of Perpetua and Satyrus in a frame that is clearly Montanist in perspective, offering the visions of these two martyrs as proof that the Holy Spirit continues to speak and emphasizing the "grace" of martyrdom.[124] A Montanist-inspired respect for women may be indicated by the title of the work, which names the female martyrs even though the stories of their male companions are also part of the document, as well as by the lengthier narrative attention given to describing the deaths of the two women.[125]

Was Perpetua herself an adherent of the New Prophecy, and if so, was she attracted to this movement within Christianity because of its empowerment of women? The evidence is suggestive. Her firm espousal of martyrdom as well as her oneiric visionary abilities are consonant with the beliefs and practices of the New Prophecy.[126] Furthermore, her understanding of her dream of her brother Dinocrates as evidence of her ability to release him from punishment may stem from the role played by "the power of the keys" in the New Prophecy's view of the status of martyrs.[127] Also, the author of the *passio* twice calls attention to Perpetua's role as leader of the group of martyrs in prison.[128]

While this evidence is suggestive, it is not definitive. If Perpetua *was* a Montanist, this dimension of her profession of Christianity was ignored or suppressed by later interpreters like Augustine, who used her witness as exemplary of orthodox Christian courage and faith and, as we have seen, understood her fortitude as male.[129] Also, even the author of the *passio*, who appears to highlight the importance of the female martyrs, has framed Perpetua's diary in a theological context that directs attention away from the specificity of her testimony as a woman by using it to polemicize on behalf of the New Prophecy's spiritualist revivalism. There are even paternalistic touches in this author's commentary: he calls Perpetua "a wife of Christ,"

[122] Grant, *Augustus to Constantine*, pp. 135–38; Barnes, *Tertullian*, p. 131.

[123] See Barnes, *Tertullian*, pp. 130–42, for a full account of Tertullian's Montanist views.

[124] *Pass. Perp.* 1.1–6 (ed. Van Beek, pp. 4–6); see Barnes, *Tertullian*, p. 77; Kraemer, *Her Share of the Blessings*, p. 161; Klawiter, "The Role of Martyrdom and Persecution in Developing the Priestly Authority of Women in Early Christianity," p. 257.

[125] Kraemer, *Her Share of the Blessings*, p. 161.

[126] See Epiphanius, *Panarion* 49.1–2 (*PG* 41.880–82), for evidence that Montanists practiced dream-incubation.

[127] Klawiter, "The Role of Martyrdom and Persecution in Developing the Priestly Authority of Women in Early Christianity," pp. 256–60; Barnes, *Tertullian*, pp. 77–78.

[128] *Pass. Perp.* 16.2–4; 18.4–6 (ed. Van Beek, pp. 38–40, 42–44).

[129] On the later use of Perpetua as an exemplary figure, see Dronke, *Women Writers of the Middle Ages*, pp. 16–17.

and his description of Perpetua in the arena, tidying her hair and covering her thighs after having been tossed by a heifer, coheres more with Tertullian's view of female modesty than it does with the Perpetua of the diary.[130] As Dronke remarks, such a woman "will hardly have gone to her death in a fit of prudery."[131] Finally, Tertullian's view of women, particularly his refusal to accord them any kind of institutional authority, shows that, at least in Carthage, being Montanist did not necessarily entail an acceptance of expanded roles for women in the church. Thus while Perpetua may have perceived the liberationist elements that the New Prophecy held out for women, the institution to which she belonged did not choose to incorporate those elements into its theology or its praxis.[132]

As opposed to these various strategies that deflect a reading of Perpetua's diary as a *woman's* testimony, I suggest that, when it is so read, it expresses the plight of a woman caught in the cross-currents of a theological debate in which sexual politics played a prominent role. Although the evidence is not conclusive, it is certainly strong enough to indicate that there was a debate about the status of women's leadership and authority in the Carthaginian church. It appears that in Perpetua's religious context femaleness was affirmed by the views and practices of a revivalist movement, but finally subjected to the dictates of the patriarchal metanarrative of the larger institution.

Given such a context, it is not surprising that all of the figures in Perpetua's dreams, her own presence excepted, are male. Maleness is the fundamental trope of her oneiric language. From the perspective of dream, male figures are constitutive of her martyred condition, and it is these that are being acknowledged—but they are also being subverted because, as Kristeva indicates, oneiric language is a discourse of the carnival. Significantly, the male figures of Perpetua's dreams are not single but double, both positive and negative, perhaps reflecting the division in her community regarding women but also indicating an unhinging of the masculine from its univocal moorings in authority.[133]

---

[130] *Pass. Perp.* 18.2; 20.3–5 (ed. Van Beek, pp. 42, 46–48).

[131] Dronke, *Women Writers of the Middle Ages*, p. 15.

[132] Klawiter's conclusion is worth quoting:

In the catholic church woman was 'liberated' to become a minister as long as she participated in the suffering of Christ. The moment she was set free from the suffering of prison, she was placed back into the 'imprisoning' role of female subordinate to male. In the New Prophecy, liberation also came by participating in the suffering of prison on account of the name, but a release from such suffering did not mean a retreat to the former role of subordinate female prior to prison experience. ("The Role of Martyrdom and Persecution in Developing the Priestly Authority of Women in the Early Church," p. 261).

[133] See Dronke, *Women Writers of the Middle Ages*, pp. 5–6 for a discussion of the juxtaposition of positive and negative male figures in Perpetua's diary.

The masculine image in the first dream, the shepherd, has uniformly been viewed as a kind, fatherly figure, and the discussion of Dream One above has shown how commentaries have domesticated the meaning of this dream, including the image of the shepherd, in service to a theological metanarrative by placing it in the context of catechetical and martyrological teaching and scriptural references.[134] From a carnivalesque perspective, however, this dream speaks differently. The gray-haired shepherd does seem to be kindly and paternal; indeed, he is a paternal figure shown in a maternal stance, milking sheep and thus connected with female sexual fluids. However, he is, as the dream says, "huge" or "vast" (*grandem*). What looms large here is the male; the female, in the form of Perpetua, is suppliant, obviously subordinate to this Father in his immense garden. Further, the shepherd is linked by the ladder to the serpent, a signifier whose exaggerated phallicism is clearly a threatening trope of male domination. The ladder that links these two may indeed be an image of otherworldly initiation, as some have argued.[135] But its function as something that establishes a *connection* between the figures of shepherd and serpent has not to my knowledge been noticed. Laden as it is with sharp, pointed weapons (metallic repetitions of the phallic serpent), and described as flesh-rending and mangling, the ladder suggests that "beneath" the paternal position lurks a phallic figure of destruction. In the carnival of Perpetua's first dream, kindly shepherd and destructive serpent belong together. This is indeed an "other" world.

A further issue in this dream is the stance of Perpetua as oneiric figure. Again the serpent is important. As the factor that tries to prevent Perpetua from stepping on the ladder, the serpent is that which might undermine her stance or standpoint. Perpetua, however, is unafraid of phallic terrorization and treads on its head, thus taking a first step toward that transformation of identity characteristic of the carnivalesque discourse of dream. Just as male identity is split open (like the split personality of the carnival) and subverted by the connection between shepherd and serpent, so female lowliness is here countered with an assertion of power. We will meet again this "repeated metaphor of trampling," because there is in Perpetua's dreams "a curiously consistent association of feet with power."[136]

A final perspective on this first dream is provided by the frame of the dream, the narrative portion of the diary. At several points, Perpetua describes the agonized relationship she had with her father.[137] He was opposed to her insistence on following the martyr's path and tried to dissuade

134 See pp. 152–58 above.

135 There are extended discussions of the ladder as symbolic of an initiate's journey to a higher or heavenly consciousness in Dronke, *Women Writers of the Middle Ages,* pp. 7–8, and Von Franz, *The Passion of Perpetua,* pp. 16–20.

136 Lefkowitz, "The Motivations for St. Perpetua's Martyrdom," p. 419.

137 *Pass. Perp.* 3.1–3; 5.1–6; 6.2–5 (ed. Van Beek, pp. 8, 14–18).

her. Two of his attempts at dissuasion involved force, one when he rushed at her as though to pluck out her eyes, and the other during her trial, when he pulled her off the step of the tribunal (just as the serpent tried to keep her from the rung of the ladder).[138] In the longest scene between them, Perpetua's father appealed to her sense of duty as daughter and mother and characterized her commitment to her faith as pride. In so doing, he framed her within the sexual dictates of patriarchal law: her being is filial and maternal only, and her courage is reduced to a moral vice. He ends this interview by throwing himself at her feet, while Perpetua remains unmoved.

Perpetua's standpoint, signified by her feet, is unshaken by the Father's emotional appeal in the face of the breakdown of its own authority. The paradox here is that the "real" Perpetua lived out literally a masochistic fantasy, at least when her death is viewed as support for a theology that denied the value of her being, while the oneiric Perpetua of the diary engaged in a discourse that mocked the very structures that mediated the "real" woman's death. As an imaginal space, the dream was a vehicle for articulating a view of female worth that revised cultural norms.

Death was much on Perpetua's mind, not only in the immediate circumstance of her forthcoming contest in the arena, but in her dreams as well. Subsequent to the emotional interview with her father, Perpetua saw the two dreams of her brother Dinocrates. The first of these dreams presents an extremely pathologized image: it shows Dinocrates in a dark, dirty place with the cancerous facial wound that would kill him still festering. As one commentator has suggested, "The dream-figure Dinocrates is suffering from a cancer: that is to say, he is subjected to a state of inner decay which cannot be arrested."[139] Furthermore, his wound is on his *face*; what is cancerous, from the perspective of the dream, is this male persona that is "brother" to Perpetua. This persona is placed by the dream in heat, dirt, and darkness.

Once again, maleness is the problematic that is being troped by the dream. It is striking that, in the narrative portion of the diary that introduces this dream, Perpetua described the presentation of the word *Dinocrates* to her conscious awareness as a slip: "I was amazed," she wrote, "for he had never entered my thoughts except just then." A word from the carnival intruded itself, and this was followed by the fully developed carnivalesque picture of the dream, a picture that suggests that it was precisely what she had embraced as "brother" that was cancerous. If one reads these dreams as constitutive of Perpetua's conflicted situation, then the testimony offered in this dream is especially strong. As a trope of maleness, the brother is afflicted with a deadly wound—yet he is alive in the carnival of the dream as a dimen-

---

138 Dronke, *Women Writers of the Middle Ages,* p. 6.
139 Von Franz, *The Passion of Perpetua,* p. 37.

sion of Perpetua herself because, in dream, author becomes character in her own narrative. Other readers of this dream have also noted that in some way Dinocrates' suffering is an image of Perpetua's painful condition.[140]

Whatever one might say about the painful situation of the "actual" Perpetua, existing within a system that would allow her no discourse other than that of the dominant male grid, the oneiric Perpetua *does* articulate her suffering. In this dream, suffering is presented as a state of decay in the persona of the brother. Suffering is also presented as a great abyss that separates Perpetua and her brother; it is a separation so profound that no approach is possible. What the female and the male both appear to be lacking is the possibility of approach, that is, the possibility of relationship, each allowing the other to be. In this context, the separation between the two figures can be read as a sign that sexual difference—as opposed to sexual *in*difference—is a possibility; yet no approach to a situation in which the female is granted independent value is possible as long as she is tormented by the cancerous aspect of the male.

Certainly the theological discourse of Perpetua's time did not valorize male and female equally, and it was to the institution that authorized this discourse that Perpetua had committed her faith; she was, after all, preparing to die for it. Yet, in the polysemantic language of her dreams, it appears that, paradoxically, what she was dying for was itself dying, yielding to a logic that exceeded that of the conventional code.

There is a further scene of suffering in this dream. Dinocrates, hot and thirsty, stands by a pool whose rim is too high to allow him to drink. Separated, with no approach open to his sister, the brother has no access to the water of life.[141] Surely the conventional code would have reversed this scene because, according to one of its representatives, Tertullian, God's image was man's prerogative, ruined by woman. Should not she be parched, rather than he? A transformation has occurred in this dream, a transformation that becomes more evident in the dream that followed this one.

Upon awakening from the dream of Dinocrates and realizing his suffering, Perpetua began to pray for him, confident that she could help. Her subsequent oneiric image of Dinocrates showed him clean, healed, drinking water and even playing in it. The precondition for this dream was an assertion of power by Perpetua; she knew that she could help that ailing male so separate from her, yet so near. Once inside the dream, there is immediately a change of face, that is, a change in the way in which the male trope is "faced" or presented. Now it is healed, no longer dark and dirty. When the female is empowered, the male is no longer in a state of inner decay; the badly faced

---

[140] Ibid., p. 36; Dronke, *Women Writers of the Middle Ages*, p. 12.

[141] On the water of immortality, see M. Meslin, "Vase sacrés et boissons d'éternité," pp. 127–36.

aspects of maleness have been faced and released into play. As Dronke has suggested, Perpetua "transforms the Dinocrates element in herself from something anguished into something liberated."[142]

This release has something to do with water, the dream's major metaphor. There is an abundance of water, both in the pool and in the golden bowl. The bowl is said specifically to be a container that does not contain, in that it never runs out of water, while the rim of the pool, whose containing sides were earlier formidably high, has now been lowered; its barrier is down. Such containers of fluid substances are feminized images, particularly of breasts, suppliers of the milky water of life.[143] In the first dream of Dinocrates, where the male is so cancerous that no approach by the female is possible, such containers are inaccessible; the univocal world of patriarchal discourse prevents the flow of life's substance. When that discourse is "split" by contact with the empowered female, however, healing occurs, and the brother is released into play. Just as, in Perpetua's first dream, the shepherd as male trope has been feminized by its contact with the maternal sheep, so here maleness is "refreshed" when it approaches or makes room for the female. In these dreams, the discourse of a marginalized perspective is coming to expression, just as the discourse of mastery is being exposed and split apart.

When she awakened from this dream of the healed brother, Perpetua wrote, "I realized that he'd been freed from pain" (*intellexi translatum eum esse de poena*). Literally, Dinocrates has been "translated" from torment. The term *translatum* is derived from *transfero*, which means not only "to carry or bring over," but also "to translate into another language," "to use figuratively or tropically." *Translatio* means "trope" or "metaphor."[144] In the present context, this language suggests that in the carnivalesque discourse of dreams there is a translation taking place, a troping of suffering, and, for Perpetua, a release into a language different from the paternal metanarrative.

Prior to her fourth and final dream, Perpetua had a final interview with her father. She writes in the diary that "wasted and worn, he began to tear out the hair of his beard and fling it on the ground, and he hurled himself headlong and cursed his life, and said such things as would move every living creature. I ached for his unhappy old age."[145] Dronke's observations on Perpetua's reaction to her father in this scene are compelling. "While she depicts him more impassioned and desperate than ever," he notes, "a tone almost of detachment enters her description, as if her father's behaviour had

---

[142] Dronke, *Women Writers of the Middle Ages*, p. 285n.51.

[143] For a discussion of such female symbols, see Page duBois, *Sowing the Body*, pp. 47–49, 107–9, 110–29. See also Nor Hall, *The Moon and the Virgin*, pp. 53–58.

[144] Lewis and Short, *A Latin Dictionary*, s.v. *transfero* and *translatio*.

[145] *Pass. Perp.* 9.2–3 (ed. Van Beek, p. 24).

become more like a histrionic performance, which she was watching sadly but without any impulse to participation. The last phrase—'I ached for his unhappy old age'—while voicing compassion, comes so abruptly after his extremes of pleading that it has a strangely dry effect. She has made herself deaf to him."[146] Although I do not want to deny the father's real grief, I would extend Dronke's observations by adding that Perpetua had "made herself deaf" to her father as patriarch who had once tried to confine his daughter within the dictates of a male economy of power; that patriarch is now powerless, prostrate, his face in the dust. This scene from the diary provides an appropriate context for Perpetua's final dream, which repeats and intensifies the "doubled male" as well as the female desire of earlier dreams.

In this dream, maleness is again the major trope, so much so that Perpetua herself becomes male. In comparison with the other dreams, a striking transformation in the dream's masculine images has occurred. In the dream of shepherd, ladder, and serpent, the two male images were equally huge; the sinister serpentine figure, signifier of phallic mastery, was equal in size, and so in importance, to the kindly paternal shepherd. In this last dream, however, the bestial opponent, the Egyptian, while still male, is reduced in size. This dimension of mastery, associated with the phallic sword as instrument of death, is now seen by Perpetua "rolling himself in the dust." This figure is decisively defeated as Perpetua, flying, knocks him down on his face and steps on his head, just as she had done before with the serpent. Further, the Egyptian, like both her father and the serpent, is unable to threaten her stance, even though he tries to do so by grabbing at her feet. The transformative message is that, when the female is in the ascendant, elevated above the foul figure of repressive structures, that foul figure succumbs to the liberating rebellion of what it had marginalized.

The Egyptian's oneiric double is Pomponius, equal in size to the Egyptian but opposite him in the dream's valorization. Pictured by the dream as the caring deacon who called Perpetua out from prison, Pomponius takes her to the scene of the contest, assures her of his presence, and disappears. Immediately following his disappearance, the Egyptian appears; in the dynamic of the dream, both aspects of maleness have been quickly juxtaposed. It is significant that Pomponius and the Egyptian are not related to each other as the images of the shepherd and the serpent were in the first dream. There is no link between them, because Pomponius vanishes before the Egyptian enters the scene. It would seem that, in the oneiric imagination, the destructive aspects of paternal kindliness have been erased. In the figure of Pomponius, the ecclesiastical "prison" has opened itself to a recognition of the value of the female.

[146] Dronke, *Women Writers of the Middle Ages*, p. 13.

The male trope that dominates this dream both literally and figuratively is the fencing-master. Surprisingly, what the dream emphasizes in its description of this figure is not his symbol of authority, the baton, which may have been understood in antiquity as a personification of the *agon*.[147] De-emphasizing the sign that would link this figure with male contestation, the dream associates him with exquisitely ornate sandals, and with a branch laden with golden apples, whose importance is underscored by being mentioned three times. The sandals are made of silver and gold; unlike the metal attached to the ladder of the first dream, which was shaped into weapons that inflict pain, these metals are precious, and they "contain" the stance or standpoint of a male trope no longer undermined by a sinister figure as large as itself. Further, this is the standpoint that emerges immediately following Perpetua's transformation into a man. How is this juxtaposition to be understood?

Commentators both ancient and modern have remarked that Perpetua's transformation into a man signifies her recognition that she would need "male" qualities in order to brave the ordeal that she was facing. According to this view, Perpetua realized that she must shed all that was "womanish" in her—in this case, her female body, and so also her sexual identity—in order properly to testify.[148] This kind of reading views the dream as a mirror of the conditions of Perpetua's social situation, which denied the value of female witness. In order to be valuable, her witness must be male. In this interpretation, the dream would merely replicate the conventional code of patriarchal denial of power to women.

From the perspective developed in this chapter, however, the oneiric imagination is transformative and not only mimetic. For although the dreams do present a picture of Perpetua's painful situation within the paternal order, they also present a vision of a new, empowered sense of self-identity that is "other" to the constructs of the social order. Thus the dream is an irruption into the master narrative of paternal logic, which it subverts and rebels against, offering as it does a competing vision of the female.

Perpetua's dream does not mean that she somehow "became male." Such a perspective undermines her sexual being, her worth as a woman. It is important to emphasize that it was *in the carnival* that Perpetua became

[147] Robert, "Une Vision de Perpetué Martyre à Carthage en 203," p. 261.

[148] Brown, *The Body and Society*, p. 75, understands her transformation as "a triumph of Perpetua's will"; Dronke, *Women Writers of the Middle Ages*, p. 14, remarks that the change in gender is "not so much a sexual fantasy as a willed identification, in her dream, with the heroine's end to which she aspires. . . . Perpetua wants to strip herself of all that is weak, or womanish, in her nature." See also p. 163 above. Amat, *Songes et Visions*, p. 83, says that the change of sex "materialized the masculine aspects of the young woman's personality and qualities of audacity," although she admits that the mutation is "not exempt from some misogyny" (p. 84).

male; the transformation took place in oneiric image, not spiritual or physical fact. This moment in the dream suggests that what was formerly signified by male images no longer pertains. Sinister shepherd, cancerous brother: these tropes of a totalizing discourse of mastery and domination have been emptied of their power. Now the masculine trope can be embraced; it has become the site for an expression of otherness. How this is accomplished in the poeticized logic of the dream will take the discussion back to the fencing-master's bough of apples.

Throughout antiquity, the apple was thought to be an erotic, female fruit.[149] Frequently used as a symbol for women's breasts, the apple was above all the fruit of Aphrodite and so was seen as an embodiment of *eros* and of female desire in particular.[150] As a figure of love, the apple played a role in courtship and marriage, processes of erotic binding. Literary renditions of this role show, for example, the lovers Daphnis and Chloe throwing apples at each other; Philostratus portrays *Erōtes* kissing an apple that they throw back and forth; and "Lucian adds the refinement of biting a piece out of an apple to cast into the bosom of the girl."[151] In the social realm, brides were to munch an apple of Cydon before crossing the threshold of the bridal chamber by order of the Solonic code. According to Plutarch, apple-eating would give the bride sweet words![152] Medicinally, the apple was thought to be an antidote to poison; as a poisoner of poison, it was the fruit of life and death, as in the tale of Callimachus and Chrysorrhoe, in which an apple both kills the hero and brings him back to life. Finally, apples were the only fruit, or so the lore had it, that would give relief to a woman in labor.[153]

In Perpetua's dream, the fencing-master holds a bough of apples. Thus connected with an object with Aphroditic associations, this male trope has been intensely feminized or radically eroticized in the direction of female desire. The fencing-master appears in the dream just after Perpetua has become a man: just at the moment when she fully embraces the male, that trope is itself troped by the appearance of an image of sexual identity that is female and not inscribed within the code of patriarchal definition. When Perpetua embraces the male, what appears is an image of maleness whose highly valued stance is a recognition of female identity. The "sweet words"

[149] For an extensive collection of literary references, see A. R. Littlewood, "The Symbolism of the Apple in Greek and Roman Literature," pp. 147–81. For mythological and social functions of the apple, see Marcel Detienne, *Dionysos Slain*, pp. 40–44.

[150] Littlewood, "The Symbolism of the Apple in Greek and Roman Literature," pp. 159–60; Detienne, *Dionysos Slain*, pp. 40–44.

[151] Littlewood, "The Symbolism of the Apple in Greek and Roman Literature," pp. 153–55 and n.15.

[152] Detienne, *Dionysos Slain*, p. 43, referring to Plutarch, *Moralia* 2 (*Conjugal Precepts*): 138D.

[153] Littlewood, "The Symbolism of the Apple in Greek and Roman Literature," pp. 167n.40, 174–75, 159n.25.

that these apples offer is the possibility of a female discourse or, as Irigaray says, a "feminine syntax" that would "preclude any distinction of identities, any establishment of ownership, and thus any form of appropriation."[154] In the image of the fencing-master, the masculine is released from the destructive code of univocal discourse by virtue of its recognition of female value. Such recognition is, indeed, the defining quality of this dream-image. To use Kristeva's formulation, the male "has lost his totality and no longer coincides with himself."[155] The "irreverent" dream of this carnival releases the male as well as the female from the prison of sexual indifference.

In her dream, Perpetua wins the golden apples for herself and is kissed by the fencing-master, who wishes her peace. She then walks alone toward the Gate of Life in triumph. The oneiric Perpetua was, one might say, a woman in labor for whom the apples were a prize signifying both life and death. What dies in her dream-discourse is the master narrative of theological doctrine that so devalued female identity. In this sense, the dreams unlock theological prejudice by exposing it to the polyvalent discourse of the oneiric imagination. Similarly, what comes to life in the dreams' poetic logic is a series of gestures toward the expression of female desire. The *eros* of Perpetua's dream-diary is its articulation of the value of difference, and its imaginal empowering of a woman's voice.

[154] Irigaray, *This Sex Which Is Not One*, p. 134.
[155] Kristeva, "Word, Dialogue and Novel," p. 83.

CHAPTER SEVEN

Aelius Aristides and *The Sacred Tales*

[Asclepius] commanded that I go down to the river, which flows before the city, and bathe. . . . It was the middle of winter and the north wind was stormy and it was icy cold, and the pebbles were fixed to one another by the frost so that they seemed like a continuous sheet of ice, and the water was such as is likely in such weather. When the divine manifestation was announced, friends escorted us and various doctors, some of them acquaintances, and others who came out of concern or even for the purposes of investigation. . . . When we reached the river, there was no need for anyone to encourage us. But being still full of warmth from the vision of the god, I cast off my clothes, and not wanting a massage, flung myself where the river was deepest. Then as in a pool of very gentle and tempered water, I passed my time swimming all about and splashing myself all over. When I came out, all my skin had a rosy hue and there was a lightness throughout my body. There was also much shouting from those present and those coming up, shouting that celebrated phrase, "Great is Asclepius."[1]

By January of 149 c.e., the date of this dream-induced plunge into a river in Smyrna, Aelius Aristides had already had three and a half years' experience of what he called "wintry, divine, and very strange baths."[2] These baths were part of the god Asclepius' response to Aristides' physical complaints: "I had catarrhs and difficulty with my palate, and everything was full of frost and fire, and among many other various difficulties, my stomach trouble was at its peak."[3] Following the particular bath just described, Aristides reported that his body had achieved a state of peaceful equilibrium matched by a contented frame of mind:

During the rest of the day and night till bed time, I preserved the condition which I had after the bath, nor did I feel any part of my body to be drier or moister. None of the warmth abated, none was added, nor again was the warmth such as one would have from a human contrivance, but it was a certain continuous body heat, producing the same effect throughout the whole of my body and during the whole time. My mental state was also nearly the same. For there was neither, as it were, conspicuous pleasure, nor

---

[1] Aelius Aristides, *Sacred Tales* 2.18–21 (trans. Behr, *Complete Works*, 2:295–96).
[2] Ibid. 2.24 (trans. Behr, *Complete Works*, 2:296).
[3] Ibid. 2.46 (trans. Behr, *Complete Works*, 2:300).

would you say that it was like a human joy. But there was a certain inexplicable contentment. . . . Thus I was wholly with the god.[4]

Having come through the dream and the river, Aristides' painful physical sensation of frost and fire had been transformed into a rosy hue; a warm sense of well-being that was emotional as well as physical had replaced the feverish shivers of ill health.

What is one to make of this "pink professor," as Peter Brown has dubbed the post-bath Aristides?[5] It is difficult to decide whether the conditions of Aristides' life provoked his prolific dreaming, or whether his dreams "produced" his life. Perhaps it is a case of oscillation between both. What is undeniable, however, is that Aristides' long-term oneiric association with the healing god Asclepius made a dramatic impact on his body. Aristides' body, indeed, provided the "ground" upon which his oneiric experiences were constructed. This chapter will explore one late-antique person's involvement with Asclepian therapy, a form of oneiric healing which focused on the human body.[6] I will argue that, in this particular case, the body was a medium for the expression of self-identity, and, as such, it was both the raw material and the trope of the "I." As a metaphorical substance, Aristides' body, hedged about by dreams, was both metaphor and substance of his sense of himself.

As one whose aspirations toward a renewed physical self had implications for perceptions of the inner self as well, Aristides was not unique in his culture. Under the rubric of "the care of the self," Michel Foucault has identified one of the ways in which the raw material of bodily symptoms came to be used as icons of personal identity. He traces the development, in the first centuries of the Graeco-Roman era, of what he calls "the cultivation of the self wherein relations of oneself to oneself were intensified and valorized."[7] One type of self-cultivation was the following of a medical regimen, and simultaneously, the production of narratives of illness. There were, in Foucault's words, "inducements to acknowledge oneself as being ill or threatened by illness," in part because the increased concern for the self's well-being was correlated with medical thought: "everyone must discover that he is in a state of need."[8] Physical symptoms and bodily dysfunctions took on the huge importance that they did because, in a culture that was theoretically soul-oriented, such bodily symptoms functioned as signs of threats to the soul, that is, threats to the integrity of one's self-identity.[9]

[4] Ibid. 2.23 (trans. Behr, *Complete Works*, 2:296).
[5] Brown, *The Making of Late Antiquity*, p. 54.
[6] See pp. 109–17 above for a discussion of oneiric healing in the cult of Asclepius.
[7] Michel Foucault, *The History of Sexuality*, 3:43.
[8] Ibid., pp. 54, 57.
[9] Michel Foucault, *Technologies of the Self: A Seminar with Michel Foucault*, p. 29.

Bodies, then, could function as psychic texts, with their "petty miseries," as Foucault calls them, operating as concretizations of the self's hopes and fears.[10] It is in this context that the case of Aelius Aristides belongs. An orator who was frequently ill, Aristides was proud of having delivered speeches from his sickbed.[11] He regarded his physical ailments not as "petty miseries" but as virtual tempests, yet he stated in writing more than once that his disease was profitable.[12] Indeed, he quoted a fellow orator as having said of him "that I had become ill through some divine good fortune."[13] The questions that need asking about such a statement are these: how could a tempestuously sick body be a sign of divine good fortune? what kind of desire found concrete expression in Aristides' body?

Aelius Aristides was born in late November of 117 C.E. on the family estate in northern Mysia in the Roman province of Asia.[14] The family had been granted Roman citizenship by the emperor Hadrian, and its members were also citizens of Smyrna, the preeminent city of coastal Asia Minor.[15] As the son of a family of wealth and status, Aristides was well-educated and studied in Smyrna, Pergamum, and Athens with some of the most famous sophists of the era, among them Polemo and Claudius Herodes.[16] Unfortunately, the promising oratorical career of this young man of privilege and talent was blighted by illness. First striken while on a tour of Egypt in 142, Aristides was to struggle with physical afflictions for the rest of his life.

Perhaps the most poignant of these early bouts with disease came on the eve of his departure for Rome in December of 143. Ill with a cold, he left for the imperial city anyway; no doubt the prospect of dazzling the court with his oratorical powers and so establishing his reputation in circles of political and social influence overpowered bodily discomfort.[17] "I set out for Rome in the middle of winter," he reports, "although I was sick right at the start . . . [but] I paid no heed to my present ailments, but trusted to the training of my body and to my general good luck."[18] His training and his luck did not hold. Instead, he felt that his teeth were about to fall out, his throat was so constricted that his breathing was blocked, and he choked on his food.[19] Such dysfunctions, centered around the mouth and

[10] Foucault, *The History of Sexuality* 3:57.
[11] *Sacred Tales* 1.64 (trans. Behr, *Complete Works*, 2:289).
[12] Ibid. 1.3; *Or.* 23.16 (trans. Behr, *Complete Works*, 2:278, 29); see Behr, *Aelius Aristides and the Sacred Tales*, p. 46.
[13] *Sacred Tales* 4.27 (trans. Behr, *Complete Works*, 2:323).
[14] See Behr, *Complete Works*, 2:438n.105.
[15] Behr, *Aelius Aristides and the Sacred Tales*, pp. 1–5.
[16] Ibid., pp. 9–13.
[17] Ibid., pp. 23–25.
[18] *Sacred Tales* 2.60 (trans. Behr, *Complete Works*, 2:303).
[19] Ibid., 2.62–64 (trans. Behr, *Complete Works*, 2:303–4).

the throat, made declamation impossible, and they suggest that his speech-ifying ambition and his body were strongly at odds with each other. Tellingly (as will be seen), his body was beginning to function as the signifying ground of a troubled psyche. "Rome, the stage of his ambitions, became the cemetery of his hopes," as his biographer Charles Behr has remarked.[20] Aristides returned home.

Homecoming did not bring relief. Aristides wrote that "the hardest and most difficult thing of all was that my breathing was blocked. With much effort and disbelief, scarcely would I draw a rasping and shallow breath, and a constant constriction in my throat followed and I had fits of shivering."[21] He went to the warm springs just outside Smyrna, but neither their warmth nor the ministrations of doctors proved helpful. It was during his stay at the springs that Aristides received the first of his oneiric revelations from the god Asclepius.[22] The dream prescribed a mild form of shock therapy—walking barefoot outside—yet on the basis of this and subsequent dream-remedies, Aristides wrote that he decided "to submit to the god, truly as to a doctor, and to do in silence whatever he wishes."[23] In the summer of 145, he felt himself called to the temple of Asclepius at Pergamum; here he spent the next two years, a period of his life that he referred to as the *Cathedra*.[24]

When Aristides remarked that he had resolved "to do in silence whatever [Asclepius] wished," he surely intended the word *silence* to be understood metaphorically as a gesture of submission and obedience to the god, for he did not remain literally without words. The god commanded him to write down his dreams.[25] He recorded them in large parchment books, and he used the memory of what he had written in them when, years later, he wrote *The Sacred Tales*. This document is a remarkable autobiographical experiment in which oratory, Asclepius and dreams, and Aristides' body are so thoroughly fused that it is difficult to extricate one from the others. On the face of it, *The Sacred Tales* are a record of Aristides' illnesses and the therapeutic dreams that gave him relief; but there is much more as well. From the vantage point of his later years, during which time *The Sacred Tales* were written, Aristides saw that his body and his career were both gifts of the healing god, produced through the medium of dreams. Even

---

[20] Behr, *Aelius Aristides and the Sacred Tales*, p. 24.

[21] *Sacred Tales* 2.6 (trans. Behr, *Complete Works*, 2:293).

[22] Ibid., 2.7 (trans. Behr, *Complete Works*, 2:293); for a discussion of Aristides' sometime contempt for human doctors when compared with Asclepius, see Behr, *Aelius Aristides and the Sacred Tales*, pp. 168–70, and Temkin, *Hippocrates in a World of Pagans and Christians*, pp. 184–87.

[23] *Sacred Tales* 1.4 (trans. Behr, *Complete Works*, 2:278).

[24] Ibid., 2.70, 3.44 (trans. Behr, *Complete Works*, 2:305, 315); see Behr, *Aelius Aristides and the Sacred Tales*, pp. 26, 41–60, for a discussion of this period of Aristides' life.

[25] *Sacred Tales* 2.2–3 (trans. Behr, *Complete Works*, 2:292); see Behr, *Aelius Aristides and the Sacred Tales*, pp. 116–30, for a chronological account of the composition of the *Sacred Tales*.

the title of this narrative came from Asclepius, who had said in a dream-appearance to Aristides' foster father that Aristides' speeches were "sacred tales."[26] Just as Aristides wrote oratorical speeches, so he also "wrote" his body by recording its miseries and its recoveries in his Asclepian memoirs. Both kinds of writing were associated and in collusion with the oneiric god of health.

Another such association of oratory, dream, and body, less direct but perhaps more telling, comes from the period of the Cathedra in the Asclepieium in Pergamum. Dreaming and aching in a seemingly endless cycle, Aristides composed one of his lengthiest orations. It was an oration in defense of oratory.[27] During a time when he was choking, vomiting, unable to breath, with his jaws locked together, and suffering fiery pains in his head and pressure in his temples, Aristides wrote an oration in which he tells a myth about the divine origins of oratory. Ironically, it is a narrative that constructs oratory as the protector of the human body!

According to this myth, in the beginning, when animals and humans were first on the earth, there was disaster for human beings because of the inadequacy of their bodies; not only were they inferior to the large beasts, but "in the fitting out of their body they were inferior not only to sheep but also to snails, since none of them was self-sufficient."[28] Observing that the human race was dying out, Prometheus appealed to Zeus on its behalf, and Zeus ordered Hermes "to go to mankind with the art of oratory"—but only to those with the "strongest and noblest" natures.[29] Thus, according to Aristides, "when oratory had come in this way from the gods to mankind, men were able to escape their harsh life with the beasts, and all men everywhere stopped being the enemies of one another, and they discovered the beginning of community" and learned from this gift about the existence of the gods.[30] In this elevated view, oratory is the matrix of civilized life: religion, community, and the human body exist in its salvific embrace.

In his discussion of oratory as the founding gesture of civilization, Aristides treats the conjunction of the saved human body with the saving words of oratory in an abstract, impersonal way, even though we, as readers, know from *The Sacred Tales* that his body was anything but an abstraction as he wrote the myth of oratory. Years later, close to the end of his life, Aristides wrote an oration in honor of Asclepius in which he placed *his own* body in an aboriginal context. The connection between the myth of oratory just described and this later text is the figure of Prome-

---

[26] *Sacred Tales* 2.9 (trans. Behr, *Complete Works,* 2:293).
[27] *Oration* 2: "To Plato: In Defense of Oratory" (trans. Behr, *Complete Works,* 1:78–150).
[28] *Or.* 2.396 (trans. Behr, *Complete Works,* 1:141).
[29] Ibid. 2.396–97 (trans. Behr, *Complete Works,* 1:141).
[30] Ibid. 2.398 (trans. Behr, *Complete Works,* 1:141–42).

theus; taken together, these two orations repeat in stunning fashion the confabulation of body, oratory, and Asclepian dreaming that characterizes *The Sacred Tales*.

The later oration, entitled "An Address Regarding Asclepius," was delivered, probably in January of 177, during a festival at the temple of Zeus Asclepius in Pergamum.[31] It is a short treatise that praises the healing act of the god. Aristides notes that many men and women "even attribute to the providence of the god the existence of the limbs of their body, when their natural limbs had been destroyed."[32] But for his part, Aristides says, "it is not only a part of the body, but it is the whole body which [Asclepius] has formed and put together and given as a gift, just as Prometheus of old is said to have fashioned man."[33] Through the medium of Asclepius, Aristides traces *his* body back to the Promethean creation of *the* body. Thus, like oratory, Aristides' body is aboriginal, and both oratory and his body are gifts of the gods.

There is in Aristides' writing an insistent thematic move whereby oratorical writing and the symptomatic "writing" of the body function as signs of each other, all under the aegis of Asclepian oneiric practice. Even a gesture seemingly so innocent as Aristides' choice of the name *Cathedra* to characterize his two-year stay at the Asclepieium in Pergamum falls under the spell of this associative movement. For, while *kathedra* certainly means "idleness" or "inactivity," it also denotes the chair of a teacher, the seat from which one professes.[34] This choice of name suggests that Aristides found his profession—his professing voice—not in spite of the illness that had brought him to Asclepius, but *in* it.

Was his sense of identity an effect of the conflation of his body with oratory and the healing god? It seems clear at the very least that he viewed his body as a site of knowledge and as a medium of thought. In *The Sacred Tales,* he praised the oneiric presence of Asclepius as having simultaneously raised up his body, strengthened his soul, and increased the glory of his oratorical career.[35] Yet, in this triad of body, soul, and oratory, the body is the primary signifying ground, because its symptoms were what originally constituted, and continued to sustain, the divine Asclepian persona that Aristides so cherished.

Contemporary interpreters have connected Aristides' physical condition with oratory and Asclepian dreaming in a number of ways. Most have been variations on an explanatory strategy that intertwines social and

[31] For the date of this oration, see Behr, *Complete Works*, 2:416n.1.

[32] *Or.* 42.7 (trans. Behr, *Complete Works*, 2:248); see pp. 112–13 above for other examples of renewal of the body in an Asclepian context.

[33] *Or.* 42.7 (trans. Behr, *Complete Works*, 2:248).

[34] Liddell, Scott, Jones, *A Greek-English Lexicon*, s.v. *kathedra*.

[35] *Sacred Tales* 5.36 (trans. Behr, *Complete Works*, 2:346).

religious data with psychological observations. Aristides is so forcefully present in *The Sacred Tales* as a distinctive personality that it has been hard to resist bringing him into the clinic for analysis.[36]

In his study of the "Second Sophistic," the philological designation of an oratorical movement that coincided with the Antonine age, G. W. Bowersock emphasized the "intensified general interest in the human body and its diseases" that characterized these second-century sophists, Aristides among them.[37] The revival of sophistry was part of a wider intellectual renaissance in which medicine, philosophy, and rhetoric were entertained together with equal enthusiasm; particularly notable was the emergence of a close association between medicine, the cult of Asclepius, and oratory.[38]

In this era, Asclepian religion and medicine could be seen as complementary rather than as competing practices. The eminent physician Galen, whom Bowersock takes to be representative of the second century's "renaissance men," reported that he did not, like others, scorn dreams but had in fact performed surgical operations based on oneiric instructions.[39] Nor were philosophy and religion opposed: witness the group of litterati with whom Aristides shared both incubation and dreams, as well as philosophical shoptalk, during his stays in the temple compounds of Asclepius.[40] According to Bowersock, Aristides was a typical, if exaggerated, example of the period's "hypersensitivity" to bodily care, a hypersensitivity that extended to literature and Asclepian religion as well. Giving this intellectual movement a psychological twist, Bowersock concludes that there is "abundant and often disagreeable evidence for an inordinate obsession with bodily ailments which has to be denominated hypochondria."[41]

While Bowersock has situated Aristides within the context of the most important literary movement of his age, Peter Brown arrives at his understanding of the man in terms of the Antonine age, the period's political and social designation. As Brown notes, scholarly estimations of this age have tended to be extravagant and negative. It has been called an "age of indolence and "impenitent extroversion" in which "an excess of public life" caused "emotional deprivation."[42] It has been described as a "pathologically traditionalist" society "whose energies were wasted on externals: by trivial-

---

[36] With regard to the character of Aristides' illness, Brown cautions against relying on a "cheap triumph of modern clinical knowingness at the expense of the dead" (*The Making of Late Antiquity*, p. 45).

[37] Bowersock, *Greek Sophists in the Roman Empire*, p. 69.

[38] Ibid.

[39] See the discussion of Galen by Bowersock, *Greek Sophists in the Roman Empire*, pp. 68–74.

[40] See Behr, *Aelius Aristides and the Sacred Tales*, pp. 42, 47–49; and André-Jean Festugière, *Personal Religion among the Greeks*, pp. 86–87.

[41] Bowersock, *Greek Sophists in the Roman Empire*, p. 72.

[42] Brown, *The Making of Late Antiquity*, p. 27.

ization, by pedantry, by showmanship. . . ."[43] Disagreeing with these evaluations, Brown replaces them with the following characterization: the Antonine age was an age of "delicate equipoise" between the competitive
ambitions of individuals and the collective life of towns and cities.[44]

In contrast to negative estimations of this period, Brown offers a func-
tionalist model for understanding the cultural milieu of people like
Aristides:

> Features that have struck the historian as oppressively backward-looking or as
> dangerously superficial take on a different meaning if seen as devices for main-
> taining an equilibrium. Civic munificence, the studied revival of traditional
> collective cults and their accompanying ceremonies, emphasis on the common-
> places of classical culture—these were the governors of an engine that was in
> constant danger of overheating.[45]

Thus Brown discerns among the ambitious elite the presence of a "model of
parity" that kept overly strenuous assertions of individual power and superiority in check.[46]

Into this context of an almost-overheated engine, Brown introduces Aelius Aristides, "a hypochondriacal gentleman of indomitable will."[47] He is
particularly interested in Aristides' relationship with Asclepius as one with a
"stable ideal figure" who provided Aristides with an inner resource for the
public expression of a superiority that was not threatening to his peers
because it did not entail undue assumptions of actual political and social
power.[48] Hence the oneiric visitations that Aristides received that portrayed
him as having equal stature with such figures as Socrates, Sophocles, Demosthenes, Alexander the Great, and others allowed him to nourish and
express his ambition without overstepping the bounds of parity so carefully
guarded by his social and political equals.[49] Furthermore, Aristides'
"heat"—the boiling up of his internal "engine"—was kept under control in
a literally physical way by the numerous oneiric directions that prescribed
lustral uses of water, most strikingly the wintry plunges in rivers of which
Aristides was very proud.[50]

Brown concludes that Aristides was "caught on a knife-edge by the de-

[43] Ibid.
[44] Ibid., pp. 30–31.
[45] Ibid., p. 30.
[46] Ibid., p. 35.
[47] Ibid., p. 41.
[48] Ibid., p. 42.
[49] See, for example, *Sacred Tales* 4.15; 4.60; 5.49 (trans. Behr, *Complete Works*, 2:320, 330, 348–49).
[50] Brown, *The Making of Late Antiquity*, p. 43; for Aristides' baths in rivers, see *Sacred Tales* 2.21, 48, 53, 78–79; 4.11; 5.49–55 (trans. Behr, *Complete Works*, 2:295, 300, 301, 306, 319, 348–50).

mands of a model of parity" and asks the following question: "Did the rising within [Aristides] of a threatening sense of superiority backed by considerable energy and aggression unconsciously help bring on the illnesses and the murderous cures that tied his energy down to a battle with his body, so that Aristides' overweening ambition was safely locked away in a world of grandiose dreams and visions?"[51] Brown's estimation that this was indeed the case carries an implicit suggestion that Aristides' diseased body was the stage upon which specific religious and sociopsychological scenarios were enacted.

The implications of the view of Aristides' body as a stage that provided space for the dramas of a troubled psyche are made explicit in the two discussions of Aristides that emphasize a psychological approach for interpreting the man and his *Sacred Tales*. A.-J. Festugière portrayed the case of Aristides as one of a psychological addiction to illness that had religious ramifications. His formulation follows:

> Let us imagine a sick man who places all his confidence not in a doctor, but in a god. The god appears before him at night, gives him directions, usually paradoxical, which amount to a series of ordeals. That he may be closer to the god, the sick man takes up residence in the sanctuary itself. . . . The sick man obeys all orders blindly; and, since the imagination plays a large part in certain chronic illnesses, particularly when the patient is of a nervous temperament, the orders actually do him good, bodily and especially mentally. They help him; but he is not cured. Better say: they help him, and therefore he is not cured, because fundamentally he does not want to be cured. To be cured would mean no longer to enjoy the presence and companionship of the god; and precisely what the patient needs most is the companionship of the god. . . . Thus he comes to be no longer able to do without the god, and by the same token to be no longer able to do without his sickness.[52]

In his discussion of the intertwining of illness and religion in the case of Aristides, Festugière is not interested so much in the psychological pathology of this double addiction as he is in cultural inducements to intimate relationships with divine figures. For him, Aristides stands as a paradigmatic instance of Graeco-Roman cultivation of "personal religion."[53]

E. R. Dodds agrees that the intensity and duration of Aristides' relationship with Asclepius is properly interpreted as a "curious symbiosis between man and God."[54] However, his understanding of Aristides is thoroughly psychological and unfolds out of his use of Freudian theory to elucidate the self-hatred that he found to have been endemic to the age. Comparing

[51] Brown, *The Making of Late Antiquity*, p. 43.
[52] Festugière, *Personal Religion among the Greeks*, p. 86.
[53] Ibid., p. 98.
[54] Dodds, *Pagan and Christian in an Age of Anxiety*, p. 44.

Aristides' unswerving obedience to the often cruel dream-prescriptions of Asclepius with the "self-inflicted torments" of Christian ascetics, Dodds argues that "for these people the price of health, physical or spiritual, is the unending expiation of an unconscious guilt."[55] In Dodds's view, this guilt stemmed from an introjection of hostile feelings toward the outer world: "resentment against the world becomes, or carries with it, resentment against the ego" and is expressed either by "the purely mental torment inflicted by a too tender conscience" or by "physical acts of self-punishment."[56]

Aristides' physically punishing regimen of fasting and vomiting and the icy walks and baths certainly fit Dodds's description of an unconscious need for self-torment, as do the anxiety dreams of being poisoned and attacked by forces both human and bestial.[57] Asclepian practice would seem in this case to be a necessary illusion for psychic survival whereby feelings of self-hatred were simultaneously expressed, in the form of dreams—and effaced, by giving them divine sanction. Like Festugière, Dodds argues that Asclepius' function as the companion of Aristides was crucial to the latter's emotional well-being, because it released him from the prison of "the dreadful loneliness of the neurotic."[58] Particularly significant for Dodds are the oneiric revelations of unity between Aristides and his divine healer, and he concludes his discussion of Aristides by suggesting that the vision of unity is a symbol of "the reconstruction of a broken personality which has found peace through self-identification with the image of an ideal Father."[59]

Brokenness runs like a leitmotif through all of these discussions of Aristides. Related to the theme of brokenness is the sense that Aristides' attachment to Asclepius was a sign of his need for a stabilizing figure that might serve as an interior anchor. Yet although these interpreters agree that there is brokenness in Aristides' story, they differ concerning the cause of that brokenness. Was Aristides' fragile body a sign of a fragile soul in need of a strong father-figure, as both Dodds and Festugière suggest? Or was his physical misery a means for displacing an inner self that was too strong, as Brown argues? Or, finally, was his hypersensitive attentiveness to his body simply a reflection of a cultural obsession, as Bowersock would have it?

Despite their differing explanations of the etiology of Aristides' brokenness, these interpreters are united in their dislike of the man. "Brainsick in a not very pleasant way"; grandiose and ambitious; "incredibly vain, profoundly egotistical": all of these remarks imply that Aristides' personality

[55] Ibid., p. 42.
[56] Ibid., pp. 27–28.
[57] *Sacred Tales* 1.9, 13, 22, 54; 5.8 (trans. Behr, *Complete Works,* 2:279, 280, 281, 287, 341).
[58] Dodds, *Pagan and Christian in an Age of Anxiety,* p. 44.
[59] Ibid., p. 45.

has been conceived in terms of psychological ego-inflation. I agree that Aristides presents the interpreter with a scenario of brokenness, but I think that his disease, or perhaps better, his dis-ease, was a sign of a disturbance of identity that was more profound than an exaggerated sense of self-importance. I also would like to position Aristides as a barometer of his culture, but I will argue that, as such, his case reflects *both* an acceptance of his culture's values *and* a rejection of them. Aristides configured his body, his career, and his god in ways that suggest both rebellion against and acceptance of the culture in which he lived.

In that culture, it was not unusual to view the body as a concretization of desire, that is, as a material expression of inner drives. Irenaeus, a contemporary of Aristides, could even use this idea sarcastically when he described the Gnostic view of the creation of the world as a materialization of the passions of Wisdom, mythologically conceived as the feminine Sophia.[60] In the medical literature of the time, care of the body was one of the practices of concern for the self, as Foucault has shown.[61] Doctors offered detailed regimens for eating, sexual intercourse, and exercise, all aimed at balancing the humours and so ensuring tranquility of the spirit. Moderation and self-control were key ingredients in the manner in which Aristides' culture "produced" the body. As Brown has observed, "we are dealing with men whose gait must be measured, whose gestures were controlled, and who were advised by Plutarch in his *Advice on Keeping Well* to maintain their health by reading aloud from harmoniously composed declamations, and to avoid 'passionate and convulsive vociferations' of any kind."[62]

Yet as detailed as were these practices that circumscribed the body for its own, and its psyche's, good, it was nonetheless the case that undue attentiveness to the body was not commended.[63] In this context of restrained body and modulated desire, Aristides' affirmation of his sick, out-of-balance body as providential, his flamboyant attentiveness to his body's every woe, and his conviction that that very body was the constant object of his divine oneiric patron's concern, all stand out in sharp relief. Aristides' gaze at his own body appears to be an aggressive expression of self-identity when viewed against the backdrop of a culture recommending moderation.

If Aristides' narrative production of his body in his dreams and in *The Sacred Tales* that record them is read as a countercultural gesture, it presents the oddity of an identity being forged in the midst of its own destruction. The symptomatic speech of Aristides' body displays an identity that is dying and being born at once. As an icon of a self in the midst of reformulation, no one of Aristides' symptoms speaks more clearly, and more abjectly, than does

[60] Irenaeus, *Haer.* 1.4.2 (*ANF* 1:321).
[61] Foucault, *The History of Sexuality*, 3:57.
[62] Brown, *The Body and Society*, p. 18.
[63] Ibid., p. 27.

his vomiting. In *The Sacred Tales,* Aristides presents his vomiting both as a sign of his illness and as a practice of his cure. Particularly telling is his understanding of the need to expel as a token of Asclepius' oneiric care.[64] As his body was emptied, so his sense of himself was expelled and refashioned. Dreams provided both the visualization and the technique for activating a change in self-understanding.

In the section of *The Sacred Tales* in which the practice of vomiting is most prominent, Aristides recorded two dreams that attest to the inner struggle to which his body was giving expression. In the first, he dreams that he is in the temple of Asclepius. "I examined [in this temple] a statue of me. At one time I saw it as if it were of me, and again it seemed to be a great and fair statue of Asclepius. Then I recounted to Zeno himself these things which appeared in my dream. And the part about the statue seemed to be very honorable."[65] In this straightforward fantasy of identification, Aristides sees himself and the god as interchangeable figures. Such a vision of the merging of the human with the divine certainly lends itself to the psychology of ego-inflation that has so often been applied to Aristides, but another view is possible as well. I suggest that Aristides' ego, his "I", is not inflated in this dream; it is replaced. The "I" marks in the dream the place where the other speaks. Significantly, this "other" is a figure of healing, and it is also a figure of intimacy, manifesting its presence in the condition of the dreamer's own body. This dream of identity with the god—and it is not the only one—suggests that Aristides no longer construed his identity in terms of a public persona.[66] Furthermore, his culture's view of the well-tuned body as a nexus of social relations and as a literal embodiment of civic order was also expelled as Aristides' sick body took him literally and figuratively inside the temple, where his body was an oneiric gift of the god, and out of the public arena.[67]

These two statements are true—but not quite. For Aristides' story is suggestive of a struggle between conflicting cultural tendencies—one in the direction of the private, the introspective, and the ascetic, and the other in the direction of the public and of the duties and rewards of civic life. The fact is that the temple, while competing with the forum, had not yet replaced it

---

[64] See *Sacred Tales* 1.9, 15, 21, 28, 32, 40, 50, 53, 55, 59, 65; 3.24; 4.6 (trans. Behr, *Complete Works,* 2:279, 280, 281, 282, 283, 284, 286, 287, 288, 289, 312, 319).

[65] *Sacred Tales* 1.17 (trans. Behr, *Complete Works,* 2:280); the identity of Aristides' friend Zeno is unknown.

[66] See *Sacred Tales* 4.52 (trans. Behr, *Complete Works,* 2:328), where Aristides reports the following oneiric statement by Asclepius: "He said that it was fitting that my mind be changed from its present condition, and having been changed, associate with god, and by its association be superior to man's estate, and that neither was remarkable, either by associating with god, to be superior, or being superior, to associate with god."

[67] See Veyne, *History of Private Life,* pp. 241–42, on the relation between the body and the social order.

in Aristides' view of himself. Evidence for the continuing appeal of public visibility for Aristides' sense of himself can be found in the second of the two dreams that have significance in the context of Aristides' physical condition of vomiting. Only eleven days following the dream of identity with the god, Aristides saw this dream: "As if my birthday were approaching, I sent servants to the Temple [of Asclepius] conveying certain offerings, and I also wrote down inscriptions on that which they conveyed. And I used artifice for the sake of a good omen, so that I might succeed in all that is needed in speaking."[68] This dream, which calls attention to itself as a metaphor for the dawn of new possibilities (*as though* it were my *birthday*), shows that Aristides had not abandoned his hope for success in oratory, his chosen field and certainly one of the most public of late-antique professions. Yet it appears that those very hopes were making him sick. If, nonetheless, Aristides hoped for the rebirth of his career out of the ruins of his body, it was to be a new creation under the auspices of Asclepius. The temple had not replaced the forum, but it had redefined it, and Aristides began to view his speeches as virtual dictations of the god. As he says in his oration to Asclepius, "I say that I am the actor of your compositions. For you yourself have exhorted me to oratory and have guided my training."[69]

In the oration in defense of oratory that Aristides composed during his first stay in a temple of Asclepius, oratory was presented as that which had both saved the human body from destruction and brought knowledge of the gods to human consciousness. In *The Sacred Tales*, written after long years of oneiric experience, oratory is no longer the originary term; it is Asclepius. Now the god gives both body and speech. This shift in allegiance is a sign of the deep disturbance of Aristides' identity, and it is also an emblem of the cultural dis-ease that I think Aristides was suffering. To understand this shift, a further exploration of the practice of oratory, and Aristides' relation to it, is necessary.

In a study of the role of physiognomy in constructing paradigms of masculinity in the second century C.E., Maud Gleason has shown the keen attention that upper-class males paid to details of physical appearance and deportment.[70] The glitter, color, and movement of the eyes; the shape of the neck; the tone of the voice; the gait; the gestures of the arms—all of these features of the surface of the body were used to make judgments about a man's character. According to Gleason, the physiognomical handbooks that

---

[68] *Sacred Tales* 1.31 (trans. Behr, *Complete Works*, 2:283).

[69] *Or.* 42.12 (trans. Behr, *Complete Works*, 249–50); *Sacred Tales* 4.38 (trans. Behr, *Complete Works*, 2:325) is one of the many passages in which Aristides remembers dreams in which Asclepius commanded him to compose speeches, poetry, and hymns.

[70] Maud Gleason, "The Semiotics of Gender: Physiognomy and Self-Fashioning in the Second Century C.E.," pp. 389–415.

provided guides for making such "inferences from human surfaces to human depths" provide evidence for "a technology of suspicion that evolved inside what we lightly call today the 'face-to-face society' of the ancient Mediterranean city. To enter this face-to-face society is in fact to enter a forest of eyes—a world in which the scrutiny of one's fellow man was not an idle pastime but an essential survival skill."[71] This intense scrutiny to which men were subjected, making them vulnerable to the pressure of the public gaze, was especially evident in the field of oratory. Deviations from the cultural norm of the "impeccably poised gentleman" could have real consequences for the social and political aspirations of orators: if one did not "walk like a lion," could he declaim before emperors and win their friendship and patronage?[72]

As Amy Richlin has shown, "the wholesale manufacture of scurrilous propaganda was a favorite Roman political activity," and some of this political gossip took its cue from sharp-eyed observations about a man's physical presence in determining whether he measured up to proper standards of the manly man.[73] In Aristides' era, masculinity was an achieved state; it was a "system of signs" that constituted a "language that anatomical males were taught to speak with their bodies."[74] Rhetorical training was heavily involved with teaching this body language. As Gleason explains:

> The process of forging masculine deportment that could begin as early as infancy continued during literary education, when the linguistic mastery that was the exclusive prerogative of upper-class males was attained under pain of physical punishment at the hands of the *grammaticus* and under pain of social humiliation in the school of the *rhetor*. At this stage of their education young men learned, while declaiming, to maintain decorum under conditions of competitive stress. Their instructors also performed publicly in a kind of ritualized cockfighting that mesmerized the leisured elite. From these confrontations emerged the infamous professional quarrels of the sophists, in which their pupils took sides.[75]

Gleason concludes that "competing paradigms of masculinity" were forged in the midst of these rhetorical competitions.[76]

Aristides was not a stranger to these practices of constructing one's masculinity on the proving ground of rhetoric. Polemo, Smyrna's most famous orator, was one of his teachers; this man wrote physiognomical handbooks

---

[71] Gleason, "The Semiotics of Gender," p. 389; Brown, *The Body and Society,* p. 11.
[72] Gleason, "The Semiotics of Gender," p. 393.
[73] Amy Richlin, *The Garden of Priapus,* pp. 92–94.
[74] Gleason, "The Semiotics of Gender," p. 402.
[75] Ibid., p. 404.
[76] Ibid.

in which the language of the body speaks pointedly about the moral and virile fiber of a man.[77] In his *Lives of the Sophists,* Philostratus recorded a memorable debate in which this elder contemporary of Aristides participated.

> When a quarrel arose between Timocrates and Scopelian, because the latter had become addicted to the use of pitch-plasters and professional hair-removers, the youths who were then residing in Smyrna took different sides, but Polemo, who was the pupil of both men, became one of the faction of Timocrates.[78]

In choosing Timocrates over the hair-free Scopelian, Polemo was following in the train of a cultural bias that "read" practices like depilation as signs of passive homosexuality, a much-derided practice so damaging to one's masculinity that such men were often described as though they were women.[79] Polemo favored Timocrates also because of his "headlong style of oratory," for when he declaimed, "the hair on his head stood up like a lion's when it springs to the attack."[80] As Gleason aptly remarks, "In this contest between hirsute philosophy and depilated rhetoric . . . Polemo chose his paradigm according to physiognomical principles," because in his own handbook the lion is the theriomorphic sign of dominant masculinity.[81]

Evidence in Aristides' orations suggests that he had learned well his teacher's physiognomical code for deciphering properly masculine behavior, particularly regarding the practice of oratory. In an oration written during the period of the *Cathedra,* Aristides describes the inspired speaker as one whose hair stands on end, thus using a leonine metaphor that matches the image approved by Polemo.[82] He writes in favor of bold and spontaneous speech and pictures the orator as one "from whose very head the goddess [Athena] emits fire."[83] The good orator, Aristides continues, does not posture either with words or gestures to astound his audience, a view that coheres with the physiognomical code of masculine self-possession.[84]

Aristides wrote this oration in self-defense. He had been accused of immoderate pride when, in the course of an earlier speech, he had remarked extemporaneously on the excellence of the speech that he had just delivered.[85] The images in his lengthy response to this critique are, thus, self-

---

[77] For a good discussion of Polemo's *Physiognomonica,* see Elizabeth Cornelia Evans, "The Study of Physiognomy in the 2nd century A.D.," pp. 96–108.

[78] Philostratus, *Vitae sophistarum* 536 (text and trans. in Wright, pp. 116–19).

[79] Richlin, *Garden of Priapus,* pp. 41, 93, 137, 168, 188–89.

[80] Philostratus, *Vit. soph.* 536 (text and trans. in Wright, pp. 116–17).

[81] Gleason, "The Semiotics of Gender," pp. 404–5.

[82] *Or.* 28.114 (trans. Behr, *Complete Works,* 2:131).

[83] Ibid. 28.103, 110 (trans. Behr, *Complete Works,* 2:128, 130).

[84] Ibid. 28.11, 128–129 (trans. Behr, *Complete Works,* 2:109, 133–34).

[85] Ibid. 28.21 (trans. Behr, *Complete Works,* 2:111).

referential; he was constructing his own masculinity as he wrote. Drawing on the theriomorphic lexicon of physiognomy, he compares himself to an eagle, while his opponent is merely a garrulous crow; he is a lion in the face of his critic, a brazen fox.[86] Turning from animal metaphors of the manly man to human models, Aristides offers a whole catalogue of military and sports heroes as examples of those who justly praise their own abilities, thus linking himself with their masculine prowess.[87]

While Aristides constructed a picture of himself using a code of masculinity, he portrayed his opponents by using a code of femininity. If masculinity was an achieved state, it was achieved at the expense of femininity, which was viewed by the physiognomists and many others as unrelievedly negative. To portray a man as "womanish" was to condemn him. Indeed, the sharpness of the physiognomical gaze in the public "forest of eyes" was honed precisely on detecting such backsliding toward the feminine.[88] Thus when Aristides describes those who criticize him as jewelry lovers and addicts of the baths, and when he describes his opponents in oratorical contests as men who are "anointed with oil, who carry about palm-leaf fans," he is drawing on a well-established stock of slurs pointing to the womanish softness of his male competitors.[89] Aristides reserved his most scathing characterizations for certain unnamed orators who had thrilled their audiences by accompanying their speeches with song and dance. Dancing was considered effeminate in men, and Aristides did not miss his chance to lampoon the competition by pointing out their sophistic pandering to audiences, comparing their performances to "indecent comic dance."[90] Drawing explicitly on gender-based jibes, Aristides describes the behavior of such rhetors as like that of hermaphrodites and eunuchs; worse, they are whores and female entertainers, having changed from men into women.[91]

Gleason has observed that "norms of masculine behavior were enforced largely through threat of censure and ridicule," demonstrating that "physiognomical scrutiny belongs to a large-scale coercive social process."[92] The comments of Aristides noted above show how biting such censure and ridicule could be, and they also show his eagerness to conform to the masculine norm, not only by constructing himself as possessed of truly masculine prowess but also by constructing his opponents with the damning lexicon of feminine physiognomical traits.

[86] Ibid. 28.55–56 (trans. Behr, *Complete Works*, 2:118–19).

[87] Ibid. 28.25–104 (trans. Behr, *Complete Works*, 2:112–29).

[88] Brown, *The Body and Society*, pp. 10–11; Gleason, "The Semiotics of Gender," pp. 394–402; Foucault, *The History of Sexuality*, 2:19.

[89] *Or.* 33.25, 27 (trans. Behr, *Complete Works*, 2:170–71).

[90] Ibid. 34.47 (trans. Behr, *Complete Works*, 2:181); on dancing as a sign of effeminacy, see Richlin, *The Garden of Priapus*, pp. 92, 98, 101.

[91] *Or.* 34.48, 56, 61 (trans. Behr, *Complete Works*, 2:181, 183, 184).

[92] Gleason, "The Semiotics of Gender," p. 406.

Aristides' aspiration toward embodying male virtue in the specific arena of his profession, oratory, also expressed itself in his dreams. In one dream, he speaks to the Athenians as though he were Demosthenes, and in another he hears the emperors thank god to have known such a fine orator as he.[93] Particularly revealing of the competitiveness within whose purview the norms of conformity assumed their significance is the dream in which Aristides talks to Sophocles: "When we appeared to be at the front door, one of the very distinguished sophists of our time slipped and lay to the left a little apart from the door." In oneiric revery, the competition lies fallen, while Aristides alone remains to converse with the "handsome old man" Sophocles.[94] It was only in dreams, however, that Aristides towered over his rhetorical colleagues, and, as readers of *The Sacred Tales*, we know that Aristides' desire to comply with the cultural code was realized most fully only in dreams as well. Outside the oneiric realm, his body rejected the demand to conform that was dictated by the coercive social process in which he was enmeshed by virtue of his profession. His body registered nausea. If we take seriously his culture's view of the body as a psychic text that could both register and reflect threats to self-identity, Aristides' physical ailments present a text of desire that opposes the desire to conform.

Aristides' most persistent physical afflictions were a constricted throat, blocked breathing, choking, and vomiting, all of which made the practice of his profession—public speaking—difficult, and sometimes impossible. His body, and then his dreams, and then an inseparable combination of them both removed him from the forest of eyes, from the relentless scrutiny of the public gaze. As a text, Aristides' body is inscribed with the symptoms of a rebellion against his culture's construction of masculinity; taken together, these symptoms articulate a desire for the intimacy and privacy that cultural codes denied to men of his standing and profession.

One of the signs of Aristides' refusal of the public persona required of an orator was his understanding of oratory as a religion. In *The Sacred Tales*, Aristides prefaces his account of the dream in which he takes on the persona of his rhetorical forebear Demosthenes with the following dream: "I dreamed that I had the clothes of a priest and that I saw the priest himself present. I also dreamed that when I saw one of my friends limping from the region of his seat, I said to him that rest would cure this."[95] In quick succession, Aristides' oneiric visualization of his identity moves from that of an Asclepian priest who dispenses healing advice to that of a legendary orator. Aristides does not elevate either of these oneiric identities over the other in terms of value; both seem satisfying as mirrors of self-understanding.

[93] *Sacred Tales* 1.16, 49 (trans. Behr, *Complete Works*, 2:280, 286).

[94] Ibid. 4.60–61 (trans. Behr, *Complete Works*, 2:330).

[95] Ibid. 1.15 (trans. Behr, *Complete Works*, 2:280).

This juxtaposition of priestly and rhetorical personae in the *Sacred Tales* is amplified in Aristides' orations. He gave a speech in which he represented oratory as a mystery religion, pure and sacred. The orator, he wrote, is a *mystes*, an initiate.[96] In another oration, the sacral character of the orator is heightened even more: "he preserves a divine trace in himself."[97] This view of the orator is quite different from the leonine figure of the masculine code to which Aristides also testified. It is an orator whose calling is not to the public forum but to the private cult. Significantly, Aristides also conceived of the cult of Asclepius as a mystery religion. In the following passage, his embrace of the private over the public is clear:

Neither membership in a chorus, nor the companionship of a voyage, nor having the same teachers, is so great a circumstance, as the gain and profit in having been fellow pilgrims at the Temple of Asclepius and having been initiated in the highest of the rites under the fairest and most perfect Torch-bearer and Mystagogue, and under him to whom every law of necessity yields.[98]

Aristides concludes this oration by observing that, under the protection of Asclepius, he won approval, an approbation "in place of which I would not choose all the so-called felicity of mankind."[99] Under the rubric of "mystery religion," oratory and Asclepian practice are assimilated to each other, although it is the sign of the protecting god that prevails over the limelight of public acclaim.

If the sense of self that was dying on the battleground of Aristides' body was the self of public visibility, the self that was being born on that body was a self of introspective feeling. What Aristides wanted was warmth. Again and again, he recorded in the *Sacred Tales* that the dreams of the god and the therapeutic acts prescribed by him gave him warmth, mental contentment, harmony, spiritual strength, and comfort.[100] Not surprisingly, the inner feelings of well-being were also inscribed on his body, in the form of a rosy hue, as we have seen.[101] In fact, the oneiric regimens made his body feel light.[102] This sense of physical euphoria, of feeling "light," was induced not only by dreaming but also by oratory. In the oration in which Aristides defended himself against attack by aligning himself with the physiogno-

---

[96] *Or.* 34: "Against Those Who Burlesque the Mysteries (Of Oratory)" (trans. Behr, *Complete Works*, 2:173–84; 398n.1); see also Behr, *Aelius Aristides and the Sacred Tales*, pp. 45, 106–7.

[97] Ibid. 28.122 (trans. Behr, *Complete Works*, 2:132).

[98] Ibid. 23.16 (trans. Behr, *Complete Works*, 2:29).

[99] Ibid.

[100] See, for example, *Sacred Tales* 2.21, 28, 53, 73; 3.13; 4.1–2, 7, 38, 62; 5.3 (trans. Behr, *Complete Works*, 2:296, 297, 301, 305, 310, 318, 319, 325, 330, 340, 305).

[101] For another reference to redness as a sign of physical well-being, see *Sacred Tales* 2.53 (trans. Behr, *Complete Works*, 2:301).

[102] Ibid. 2.21 (trans. Behr, *Complete Works*, 2:295–96).

mists' code of the masculine orator, he wrote that oratory instilled warmth and made his body become light; he describes the inspirational effects of oratory on the body with a series of dazzling metaphors that are part of a "secret tale in a religious myth," thus underscoring once again Aristides' tendency to construct oratory in terms of religion, Asclepian religion in particular.[103] Pathetically, these remarks on oratory and bodily buoyancy were written during the *Cathedra*, Aristides' first Asclepian sojourn, which was a period of intense physical disability when Aristides' body was in fact heavy with pain, not soaring like an eagle with wings spread.[104] The lightness given by oratory was a culturally encoded desideratum, not a bodily fact. Unfortunately, the physical and emotional warmth that he desired kept flaring up in the form of bodily fevers and in the form of the hot pursuit of critical competitors in the oratorical forum.

The gap between the cultural ideal of the orator's vigorous masculine body and the reality of Aristides' convulsively sick body was bridged by dreams, which offered visions of a new kind of self-understanding that was untouched by the oppressive gaze of the public eye. Aristides' *Sacred Tales* give vivid testimony to the way in which dreams could function as vehicles for the "care of the self" in which a person's self-image was radically transformed. Re-reading his experience and his culture through his dreams, Aristides reached for a more satisfying context within which to construe his sense of himself. One of the most climactic of these oneiric alterations of identity came early on in his relationship with Asclepius; and by his own testimony years later when he recorded this dream in *The Sacred Tales*, it had given him the courage to live. In August of 147, Aristides dreamed that he was in a temple of Asclepius:

> First the cult statue [of Asclepius] appeared to have three heads and to shine about with fire, except for the heads. Next we worshippers stood by it, just as when the paean is sung, I almost among the first. At this point the god, in the posture in which he is represented in his statues, signaled our departure. All the others were going out, and I was turning to go out, and the god, with his hand, indicated for me to stay. And I was delighted by the honor and the extent to which I was preferred to the others, and I shouted out, "The One," meaning the god. But he said, "It is you."[105]

Part of the interest of this dream lies in the henotheistic acclamation of Asclepius as "The One," a form of address in Graeco-Roman religion that denoted strong personal devotion to a particular god.[106] However, Asclepius' comment to the oneiric Aristides, "'It is you,'" is even more remark-

---

[103] *Or.* 28.113–15 (trans. Behr, *Complete Works*, 2:130–31).

[104] Ibid. 28.115 (trans. Behr, *Complete Works*, 2:131).

[105] *Sacred Tales* 4.50 (trans. Behr, *Complete Works*, 2:328); for a discussion of the appearance of the gods in dreams in the form of statues, see pp. 28–35 above.

[106] See H. S. Versnel, *Inconsistencies in Greek and Roman Religion*, 1:35, 92.

able for its explicit statement of identity between the god and his worshiper. If the acclamation "The One" can be applied both to Asclepius and to Aristides, they are then mirror images of each other.

Aristides followed the recording of this dream in *The Sacred Tales* with narratives of two more dreams that indicate an altered sense of self-identity.

[Asclepius] said that it was fitting that my mind be changed from its present condition, and having been changed, associate with god, and by its association be superior to man's estate, and that neither was remarkable, either by associating with god, to be superior, or being superior, to associate with god.[107]

With his mind thus oneirically "changed from its present condition," Aristides next dreamed that the god had given him a new name, Theodorus, which means "gift of the god."[108] These dreams are blatant demonstrations of the dreamer's desire for change, a change of "association" with the gaining of a new conversation partner, and a change of persona with the bestowal of a new name. Yet "outside" the dreams, Aristides' repeated attempts to renew his oratorical career, and so to return to his "old" associations and persona, show that the dreams did not accomplish their transformative goal.[109]

The dissonance between Aristides' conflicting aspirations continued to sound a jarring note in his life. Aristides' story is that of a man torn between desires that he could not reconcile. I suggest that his struggle was symptomatic of a shift in cultural values, a "crisis of the subject" that would not appear as a crisis of major cultural importance until a century later.[110] More specifi-

[107] *Sacred Tales* 4.52 (trans. Behr, *Complete Works*, 2:328).

[108] Ibid. 4.53–54 (trans. Behr, *Complete Works*, 2:329).

[109] For an account of Aristides' return to his oratorical career, see Behr, *Aelius Aristides and the Sacred Tales*, pp. 91–102.

[110] For discussion of the cultural upheavals in the third century, see Brown, *Making of Late Antiquity*, pp. 58–80. John Gager has observed that

the case of the second-century rhetor Aelius Aristides . . . is at once atypical of normal aristocratic religiosity and indicative of new currents in his day. For it was in the second century that the emperors Hadrian and Marcus Aurelius became initiates of the Eleusinian mysteries, that Antoninus Pius legalized the enthusiastic Phrygian cult of Cybele, and that senatorial participation in non-Roman (Mithras, Dionysus) or Greco-Roman (Isis-Diana, Serapis-Jupiter) cults increased markedly. (*Kingdom and Community*, pp. 98–99)

In "Misery and Mystery: Aelius Aristides," Smith has added to this view the following remarks that are pertinent to the perspective within which I understand Aristides' self-division: "The second century was a time when rapid changes in world view and new social developments were inevitably being incorporated into the perceptive human viewpoint. Yet not all persons saw the changes that were taking place before their eyes. Old views were not quickly abandoned but were losing their ability to compel assent. Deep rifts were growing between inherited beliefs and perceived reality" (30). Aristides was an early witness to the "spiritual revolution" that was in the making (31). For a discussion of the phrase "crisis of the subject," see Foucault, *The History of Sexuality*, 3:95.

cally, it was a crisis of a male subject becoming increasingly unable to bear the persona whereby he was publicly constructed and so recognized as properly male. I would reintroduce at this point a thesis that I think Brown dismisses too quickly, the view that the Antonine age witnessed an excess of public life that caused emotional deprivation.[111] Certainly Aristides' case presents a compelling portrayal of the need for intimacy and the drastic effects of its absence. The tensions created by the demand to live in the forest of eyes were inscribed on Aristides' body as sickness—a sickness, I think, that indicated a need for a change in the way in which male identity was culturally encoded.

Despite his dreams, Aristides never surmounted the conflicting currents that pulled him toward *both* the public forum *and* the private cult. Alternately retreating to and emerging from his dreamy Asclepian world, he failed to live up to the promise of either "Aristides" or "Theodorus," and his body continued to register the tensions of that conflict. Later men did surmount the conflict. They retreated first into chastity, and then to the desert, abandoning the civic codes of masculine identity that had proved to be at once too large and too small. I read Aristides' story, finally, as an early harbinger of the ascetic movement that released men from the confines of a definition of masculinity that was psychologically cramping. The sick body of Aristides, only fitfully cured by his visions of other possibilities of self-construction, stands as a telling counterpoint to the body of the ascetic St. Antony; as his biographer Athanasius reported, *his* body was perfect.[112]

---

[111] Brown, *Making of Late Antiquity*, p. 27. It should be noted that the demands on wealthy aristocratic landowners like Aristides to live public lives, particularly by holding public office, were immense. Aristides was elected against his will to the office of tax collector in Smyrna, and appointed, also against his will, as police commissioner of his district. In both cases he protested and after lengthy lawsuits was granted immunity from holding public office. See Behr, *Aelius Aristides*, pp. 77–86. Interestingly, despite his obvious desire to excel as a public speaker, Aristides did not have a natural flair for extempore speaking. As Philostratus reports, Aristides compensated for this failing by striving for accuracy and perfection of style, and by reading past masters of rhetoric. Nonetheless, "he so greatly admired extempore eloquence that he used to shut himself up in a room and practise it in private. And he used to work it out by evolving it clause by clause and thought by thought. But this process we must regard as chewing rather than eating, for extempore eloquence is the crowning achievement of a fluent and facile tongue" (*Vitae sophistarum* 582–83 [text and trans. in Wright, pp. 214–19]). Philostratus' rather withering conclusion reinforces the pathetic picture of a man who would have preferred to sit in his room and read, yet who felt compelled to compete in a public arena for which he had little taste or talent, at least of the "crowning" sort.

[112] Athanasius, *Vita Antonii* 14 (*PG.* 26.864C): after twenty years of ascetic practice, Anthony's body, like his soul, was without blemish.

CHAPTER EIGHT

Jerome and His Dreams

When I was living in the desert, in that vast solitude . . . , inflamed by the burning heat of the sun, how many times did I imagine myself amid the delights of Rome! . . . Although in my fear of hell I had condemned myself to this prison, with scorpions and wild beasts as my only companions, I was often surrounded by troops of dancing girls. My skin was pale with fasting but, though my frame was chilled, my mind was burning with desire, and the fires of lust bubbled up while my flesh was barely alive.[1]

As THIS passage attests, the man who wrote it was possessed of a lively imagination, enhanced in no small part by a considerable rhetorical flair: he was Jerome, the eminent Biblical translator and commentator of the late fourth century. Jerome included this steamy memory in a letter to a young Christian woman named Eustochium, a letter whose aim was, in part, to warn her about the dangers of sexual desire. When he wrote this letter in 384 C.E., Jerome was no longer living with scorpions in the desert but rather in Rome, well-connected both to the Pope and to circles of aristocratic Christians eager to learn from this erudite teacher.[2] Yet, despite his change in circumstance, the memory of his unfortunate visionary experience in the desert, a memory by this time some ten years old, was still strongly charged with feeling.[3] Dismissive of the passing of time, the images of Jerome's tormenting fantasies continued to operate in the inner space of his mind.

Jerome knew that dreams were phenomena of the psyche, expressive of mental rather than literal seeing. His comment on the biblical prophet Daniel—that his visions were properly said by Scripture to be "in his head" rather than in his eyes—might well have been applied to his own inner seeing as well.[4] This, however, was the only similarity between Jerome and Daniel for, by and large, Jerome was an unhappy dreamer. His visions—of dancing girls and other urban delights—were not prophetic but rather reflective of the struggle of the ascetic with persistent sexual desire.

Jerome did not call his desert fantasies dreams; yet, if his experience is

---

[1] Jerome, *Ep.* 22.7.1–3 (*CSEL* 54.152–53).

[2] See J.N.D. Kelly, *Jerome*, pp. 80–103.

[3] For the date of Jerome's retreat to the desert, see Kelly, *Jerome*, p. 46.

[4] *In Dan.* 1.28 (*CCL* 75A.791); see also Dulaey, *Le Rêve*, p. 62.

placed in the context of the well-documented problematic of the monastic struggle with obsessive sexual imaginings, it may well have been an oneiric experience. Living chaste lives in the desert, monks who were attempting to tame their bodies saw erotic visions and dreams, often in the form of seductive women.[5] Most were not as lucky as Abba Elias, whose dream of being castrated by angels relieved him of his desire.[6] Rather, as Aline Rousselle has observed, "By day the conscious mind found that when it wanted to concentrate on prayer it was besieged by thoughts and visions of women. At night, dreams would wake the hermits." As she goes on to say, distinguishing between waking dreams and dreams that occur in sleep is difficult in this context—I would say, probably impossible.[7] Seen in this light, Jerome's fantasies, too, can be construed as oneiric phenomena. In any case, whether their status was that of waking visions or nocturnal dreams, these imaginal experiences were important to Jerome. He did not doubt that such ephemeral images were scaringly alive as accurate indicators of psychic struggle—a struggle, as we shall see, in which Jerome was reaching toward an altered sense of self-identity.

Although he did not write on dreams or oneiric theory in a sustained way as his contemporaries in the Greek East, Gregory of Nyssa and Synesius of Cyrene, were to do, Jerome was familiar with his culture's differentiated views on oneiric phenomena. Remarks scattered throughout his works reveal his knowledge of the classification of dreams into the two broad categories of truth-telling dreams, especially of the premonitory and predictive type, and dreams that are either insignificant or false.[8]

Concerning the category of insignificant and false dreams, Jerome quotes a passage from Tertullian's *De anima* in which the emotive affect of dreams is dismissed as an aspect of illusory movements of the soul during sleep. Such emotion-packed images, says Jerome, are not to be taken seriously: if one person attempts to incriminate another on the basis of a dream, he should heed prophetic teaching against belief in dreams, "for to dream of adultery does not lead me to hell, nor does dreaming of a martyr's crown elevate me to heaven."[9] Using his own nocturnal adventures as proof, Jerome remarks, "How often have I seen myself dead and placed in a tomb! How often have I flown over the earth, carried over mountains and seas as if swimming in the air! One might therefore compel me not to live or to have wings on my back, because my mind has often been

---

[5] Rousselle, *Porneia,* pp. 150–51; Brown, *The Body and Society,* pp. 230–34.

[6] See p. 108–9 above.

[7] Rouselle, *Porneia,* p. 151. On the difficulty of distinguishing between dream and vision, see also John Hanson, "Dreams and Visions in the Graeco-Roman World and Early Christianity," pp. 1407–8.

[8] See Dulaey, *Le Rêve,* pp. 61–63, and Amat, *Songes et Visions,* pp. 217–19.

[9] Tertullian, *De an.* 45.4 (ed. Waszink, p. 62); Jerome, *C. Ruf.* 1.31 (*PL* 23.423C).

deluded by such vain imaginings."[10] Jerome goes on to give further stock examples of these "vain imaginings" (*vanis imaginibus*): the beggar who dreams of riches, the thirsty people who dream of drinking water. These non-significative dreams are what Artemidorus called *enúpnia*, dreams that simply reproduce the conscious preoccupations of the dreamer.[11]

Jerome also knew the psychobiological theory of dreaming, which connected dreams with the digestive process and so dismissed them as vehicles of significant meaning.[12] In the same letter in which he recounts his visions in the desert, he refers sarcastically to the religious pretensions of some Christian widows whose chaste life-style was more apparent than real: "After a rich meal," he remarks, "they go to sleep and dream of the apostles."[13] Even the dreams of these women are a sham; they are simply the psychic by-product of overeating. Finally, Jerome also knew the Christian view pertaining to the demonic inspiration of dreams. In his *Life of Hilarion,* he pictures the monk at night, fending off the mocking and frightening visions sent by evil spirits with the sign of the cross, and, most notably, suffering the demons' oneiric tricks of appearing to the sleeping monk in the form of naked women.[14]

With regard to meaningful dreams, Jerome was familiar with theories of divine inspiration as well as theories about their predictive value, whether as moral warnings or as symbolic bridges between the present and the future.[15] Like Tertullian, he read scriptural stories like those in the book of Daniel about Nebuchadnezzar's dreams as affirmations of the view that pagans and sinners as well as morally upright people can receive true dreams, although understanding them is the province of saints.[16] Further, his critique of some who think that every dream they receive is divinely inspired reveals his view that some dreams are indeed authentically revelatory and god-sent.[17]

This latter kind of dream is, in fact, the type for which Jerome supplies examples. In his *Life of Paul the Hermit,* Jerome recounts how the monk Anthony was inspired by a divine dream to seek out the eremite Paul, his venerable predecessor in the desert.[18] In a letter to his good friend Marcella, one of the ascetic women in Jerome's circle of aristocratic friends,

---

[10] *C. Ruf.* 1.31 (*PL* 23.423C).

[11] See pp. 80–81 above.

[12] See pp. 42–51 above.

[13] *Ep.* 22.16.3 (*CSEL* 54.164). See also *In Hierem.* 23.25 (*CCL* 74.225), where Jerome criticizes those who think that all dreams are spiritually revelatory.

[14] *Vita Hilarionis* 6–7 (*PL* 23.38); on the relation between dreams and demons, see pp. 63–65 above.

[15] For theories pertaining to meaningful dreams, see pp. 81–83 above.

[16] *In Dan.* 1.29 (*CCL* 75A.792); see Tertullian, *De an.* 47.2 (ed. Waszink, p. 65).

[17] *In Hierem.* 23.25 (*CCL* 74.225).

[18] *Vita Pauli* 7 (*PL* 23.22B).

Jerome wrote about the dream of the father of another of these women, Asella.[19] Before Asella was born, Jerome writes, her father dreamed of a brilliant crystal bowl, purer than any mirror. The dream was a prefigura-tion of Asella's future; she would adopt a virgin life-style and thus become an unspotted mirror of divine blessing.[20] Here Jerome draws on a long cultural tradition of premonitory dreams that reveal a person's future voca-tion,[21] and he also shows his knowledge of the semiotic register of dream-speech wherein oneiric signs demand interpretation, for the metaphoric resonance between a sparkling crystal bowl and the ascetic profession of an unborn baby is not immediately clear. In the case of this dream, Jerome's method of interpretation is strikingly like that of Artemidorus; perhaps with the aid of Asella herself, he has read the sign of the dream "backward" from its known outcome and has then presented the sign as an allegory of the future.[22]

It would seem that the dreams in which Jerome was most interested were those, like the dream of Asella's father, that were connected in some way with virginity and monastic or ascetic life-styles. A striking example of Jerome's fascination with ascetically oriented dreams, as well as his view of dreams as premonitions, is the dream he tells in yet another letter to an aristocratic woman. Laeta was the daughter-in-law of Jerome's dear friend Paula (mother of the young woman named Eustochium to whom Jerome had written about his visions in the desert).[23] Laeta had written to Jerome for advice about how to bring up her young daughter in the properly ascetic way, and in the section of his response in which he warns Laeta not to adorn her daughter with jewels, fine clothes, and cosmetic refinements, Jerome tells Laeta the following cautionary tale about how inner purity should be mirrored in outward appearance. There was once, writes Je-rome, a noblewoman named Praetextata, who was married to the uncle of Eustochium, the young virgin mentioned above. Praetextata "changed Eustochium's dress and appearance" by having her hair waved, "desiring to conquer the virgin's resolution and her mother's wishes."[24] In the evening of that very day, Jerome continues, an angel with a terrible face appeared to Praetextata in her dreams. Threatening her with punishment, the angel said, "'Have you dared to touch the head of a virgin with sacrilegious hands? This very hour, those hands will wither, and, feeling tormenting pain, you will recognize what you have done, and at the end of the fifth

---

[19] For discussions of Jerome's friendships with Marcella and Asella, see Kelly, *Jerome*, pp. 92–96, and Elizabeth A. Clark, *Jerome, Chrysostom, and Friends*, pp. 44–45, 76–77.

[20] *Ep.* 24.2 (*CSEL* 54.215).

[21] Amat, *Songes et Visions*, p. 218.

[22] See pp. 83–91 above for Artemidorus' interpretive techniques.

[23] Kelly, *Jerome*, pp. 273–75.

[24] *Ep.* 107.5.2 (*CSEL* 55.296).

month you will be led to hell.'" "All these things were fulfilled in turn" is Jerome's triumphant conclusion to the story.[25]

Unlike the enigmatic dream of Asella's father, this dream belongs to the theorematic category of dreams in which dream-image and event correspond exactly.[26] Although Jerome does not call attention to the taxonomic status of this dream, he is clearly aware of the phenomenon and does not doubt the possibility of this kind of literal interchange between oneiric image and historical fact. What Jerome appears to value most about this dream is its theological affirmation of asceticism and especially female virginity. Like Tertullian before him, he drew on the witness of punitive dream-angels for moral support in his campaign to reshape the body along rigorous ascetic lines.[27]

Adhering to a perspective similar to that of Artemidorus, Jerome emphasized the material conditions of the symbolic process of dreaming. The dreams that he chose to present have a strikingly physical quality, and they alert the dreamer to his or her condition in quite concrete ways. Even in those cases in which dreams are said to be non-significative or demonically inspired, like the widows' dreams and the monk Hilarion's visions, they are used by Jerome to make a point about the dreamer's life. The point is typically conveyed by reference to the person's body, particularly insofar as the body is related to the ascetic life-style and its attendant dangers. The "true" dream-images, like the crystalline "body" of the virgin Asella and the withered hands of Praetextata, both idealize the virginal state and warn against sullying it.

Unlike Artemidorus, however, Jerome did not draw on a large vocabulary of oneiric images. Instead, it was the body that provided the central signifying ground in the dreams that interested him. Especially intriguing is Jerome's tendency to use images of the body that he thought were negative—the withered hands, the naked women and dancing girls—to argue positively for a remaking of the body in ascetic terms. Jerome used this method of interpreting such "negative" images of the body positively on his own dreams as well as on those of others. Indeed, Jerome's use of such oneiric images was part of his program of revisioning the body ascetically. This may explain why he did not present his own visions in the desert as demonic dramas, as he did in the case of Hilarion. Those visions, as oneirically constructed signs of the body's treachery, were for Jerome too important to dismiss because they functioned for him as vehicles for self-reflection. They allowed him to berate himself, thus negatively reinforcing the positive ascetic ideal of release from physical desire.

[25] Ibid.
[26] See p. 82 above on theorematic dreams.
[27] See pp. 66–70 above for Tertullian's use of dreams.

Jerome recorded what is now his most famous dream in the same letter to the virgin Eustochium in which he had narrated his tormenting visions in the desert. Jerome recounts his dream to Eustochium in the course of advising her not to be overly stylish either in her pronunciation of words or in her choice of reading material. Such affectations, whether of speech or literature, are not becoming to an ascetic; indeed, Jerome calls them an "adultery of the tongue," using a sexual metaphor that extends the arena of sexuality considerably beyond the body.[28] Like the body, language too can be an instrument of desire. Jerome follows this statement linking language to desire with a paraphrase of Tertullian: "What has Horace to do with the psalter, Virgil with the gospels, Cicero with the Apostle?"[29]

As though in direct answer to those questions, Jerome then narrates his dream. He prefaces the narrative of the dream with a brief account of the beginning of his ascetic practice: unable to give up his beloved library, he would fast—only to be able afterward to read Cicero as a reward for his labors. So too with Plautus and, by implication, the rest of the secular corpus that he so admired. Sadly, he remembers, the style of the Scriptures seemed rude and repellent by comparison.[30] It was while Jerome was in this vacillating state of mind that he fell ill, and in the midst of this illness he dreamed the following dream:

> Suddenly I was caught up in the spirit and dragged up to the tribunal of a judge. . . . Asked about my identity, I replied, "I am a Christian." And he who sat [behind the tribunal] said, "You are lying; you are a Ciceronian, not a Christian; for where your treasure is, there is where your heart is also." Immediately I became mute, and, amid the floggings—for he had ordered that I be beaten—I was tortured more strongly by the fire of conscience, pondering within myself that verse, "In hell who shall acknowledge you?" Nevertheless I began to cry out and woefully to say: "Have mercy on me, Lord, have mercy on me." Amid the lashings this sound rang out. Finally those who were standing around, falling down on their knees before the one who was presiding, begged that he have mercy on my youth and give me the opportunity for penitence. There would be more torture at a later point if I were ever again to read pagan literary books. . . . I began to make an oath and, calling on his name as witness, I said "Lord, if at any time [in the future] I possess pagan writings or read them, I will have denied you." Dismissed after this oath, I returned to the upper world. . . . This was not an idle

[28] Ep. 22.29.6 (CSEL 54.188).
[29] Ibid. 22.29.7 (CSEL 54.189); for Tertullian's famous exclamation, "What has Athens to do with Jerusalem, or what has the Academy in common with the church?," see his Praescr. haer. 7 (CSEL 70.10).
[30] Ep. 22.30.2 (CSEL 54.189).

dream. . . . My shoulders were black and blue, and I felt the bruises after I awoke from sleeping. Thenceforth I read the divine books with much more eagerness than I had read the books of human beings.[31]

It is likely that Jerome was presented with this dream during the Lenten season of 374 C.E., about a year before he retreated to the Syrian desert near Chalcis.[32] Some interpreters have seen the dream as a second conversion that settled Jerome's crisis of conscience concerning what being an ascetic Christian entailed.[33] From this perspective, the dream both reflected and resolved the conflict between what Kelly has described as Jerome's "enthusiastic world-renouncing aspirations on the one hand, and his wholehearted delight in the classical, humanist culture, to which everything he wrote at the time bears witness, on the other."[34] Other interpreters, however, have downplayed the significance of the dream, either by dismissing it as a product of the delirium that accompanies illness or by doubting its authenticity, seeing it merely as a rhetorical contrivance for proselytizing on behalf of ascetic practice.[35]

It is true that Jerome did not keep the promise he made in his dream regarding the reading of secular literature, because later in his life he devised a theory for the judicious use of such literature by Christians.[36] It is also true that the letter in which the dream is narrated, indeed even the account of the dream itself, is studded with allusions to the very classical texts that he had supposedly foresworn.[37] Nonetheless, I agree with Kelly that the dream was an authentic and moving experience for Jerome.[38] In the first place, in the letter to Eustochium the dream is formally parallel to his account of his visionary experience in the desert. Jerome remembers himself as caught between two irreconcilable attachments in both cases. Just prior to his retreat to the desert, the dream presented Jerome to himself as the locus of a clash between two cultures, one secular and one religious; once he was in the desert, his visions of women's bodies showed Jerome that he was caught between an ascetic view of the body and an obsessive eroticism. The structural similarity between these two oneiric

---

[31] Ibid. 22.30.3–5 (*CSEL* 54.190–91).

[32] Kelly, *Jerome*, p. 41; for the date of the dream, see J. J. Thierry, "The Date of the Dream of Jerome," 28–40.

[33] Kelly, *Jerome*, p. 41; Amat, *Songes et Visions*, p. 222.

[34] Kelly, *Jerome*, p. 43.

[35] For the view that Jerome's dream was due to delirium induced by illness, see Paul Antin, "Autour du songe de Saint Jérome," pp. 354, 364–65; on the dream as a rhetorical device, see Dulaey, *Le Rêve*, p. 62, and Pierre de Labriolle, "Le Songe de St Jérome," pp. 227–35.

[36] *Ep.* 70 (*CSEL* 54.700–708); see Kelly, *Jerome*, pp. 43–44.

[37] David S. Wiesen, *St. Jerome as a Satirist*, pp. 119–27; see also Kelly, *Jerome*, p. 43.

[38] Kelly, *Jerome*, p. 43.

sequences suggests that both are authentic reflections of Jerome's divided state of mind at that time in his life. He was suffering the return of what he was trying to repress: Cicero and the dancing girls would not give way to Scripture and chastity.

In the second place, there is the important fact that Jerome never denied the authenticity of the dream. In the letter to Eustochium, he insists that his experience was not a *vana somnia*, an "idle dream."[39] It is true that, some sixteen years later, Jerome appears to have reversed himself, using his own dreams of flying, dying, and so on as proof that dreams are *vanae imagines*, "vain imaginings."[40] However, Jerome wrote this remark in an apologetic treatise in which he was defending himself against an attack by his old friend, now turned enemy, Rufinus. Rufinus knew how Jerome had used his dream in the letter to Eustochium and had accused him of subsequently breaking his oneiric oath never to read secular literature again.[41] In response, Jerome objects to being taunted with a "mere dream"; but he also says that the promise made in the dream pertained to the future and that, if he still quotes secular literature, it is from memory, which he can't erase, and not from his post-oneiric reading practices.[42] Thus, in this defensive context, Jerome tried to occupy both sides of the issue and ended in the curious position of slighting dreams as airy fantasies while at the same time affirming, even heightening, the importance of the impact of one particular dream on his life.

Jerome viewed his dream as divinely inspired, like the dream of Praetextata. Also like hers, Jerome's dream was premonitory, and frighteningly so, because the avenging figure in his dream is not simply an angel but a figure of the Christ as judge.[43] Further, both of these dreams are good examples of the way in which dreams were viewed in Graeco-Roman culture as semiotic constructs that functioned as a means for articulating inchoate thoughts and emotions. Dreams provided a language for interpreting life's experiences while one was in the midst of living them; it was a language that allowed for reflection on the meaning of one's actions.[44] Thus Praetextata was, by Jerome's account, shocked into a recognition of the error of her actions, while Jerome himself was presented with a forcefully articulate picture of his own situation of vacillation, a situation that the dream both reflects and reformulates. As a "detective of his heart's secret," the dream

---

[39] *Ep.* 22.30.6 (*CSEL* 54.191).

[40] *C. Ruf.* 1.31 (*PL* 23.423C); see above, pp. 206–7.

[41] Rufinus, *Apol.* 2.6–8 (*CCL* 20.87–90).

[42] *C. Ruf.* 1.30–31 (*PL* 23.421B–424A).

[43] Antin, "Autour du songe de Saint Jérome," p. 352, points out that the picture of Christ as judge stems from Rom. 14.10 and 2 Cor. 5.10.

[44] See pp. 54–63 above for a discussion of the reflective qualities of oneiric language.

made Jerome fully conscious, at last, of his schizoid swing between denial and gratification.[45]

By his own testimony in his apologetic treatise against Rufinus, Jerome was a prolific dreamer. However, he chose to emphasize only two of his oneiric experiences, those that he recorded in his letter to Eustochium, and both are used as a vehicle for warning Eustochium about the difficulties of the ascetic life. In the form of his oneiric memories, Jerome presents himself as a counter-example of the image to which he hopes Eustochium will conform. Furthermore, from his repertory of dream-images he chose those that focused on the body, on *his* body, which he offers as a negative sign of his attempt to reimagine the body along the lines of an ascetic ideal that he viewed as a positive one. Particularly telling in this regard is Jerome's account of the movement of his flagellated body from oneiric into conscious reality. Bruised and battered, his body functions as a sign of a dramatic change of consciousness. In this oneiric image, which Jerome sets forth for Eustochium to "view" in the text of his letter, the negative and positive values of the body-as-sign coalesce. For Jerome, the physical body is also a psychic "body," and both can carry positive and negative charges in the ascetic context in which they have meaning for him. Thus his black-and-blue body points to his abject condition, felt both literally and spiritually, as well as to his change in perspective, which again is not only spiritual but literal, involving a different practice of reading.

As his narrative construction of both of his oneiric experiences makes clear, Jerome directed his program of ascetic reimagining not only at the body but also at the psychic makeup of the self. In his dream of flagellation, for example, it is clear that he conceived of the oneiric body as the signifying ground upon which a new, ascetic version of the whole person could be explored and constructed. Similarly, the visions in the desert point as much toward psychic desire as they do toward bodily needs. Despite all of his talk about the taming of the physical body in order to harness it to the ascetic cause, however, that body remained a problem to Jerome, as his presentation of his own body to Eustochium makes clear. This may be due to one of the central problematics of the role of the body in asceticism, in which the body is both an object of disgust as well as a potential instrument of personal transformation. As Geoffrey Harpham has observed, the ascetic's attempt to escape the desirable world and to deny gratification to the body's senses actually "pitched the ascetic into the world of desire," in which the ascetic was flooded with images that held forth the very pleasures that he was trying to renounce.[46] Materiality was hard to banish. As Harpham goes on to say,

[45] For the view of dreams as detectives of the heart's secrets, see p. 59 above.
[46] Geoffrey Galt Harpham, *The Ascetic Imperative in Culture and Criticism* p. 55.

"The desert does not even provide a true refuge from the material world. Sartre speaks of the 'enchanted' world of desire as 'a destructured world in which things have lost their meaning and jut out like fragments of pure matter.' Objects emerging under the 'enchantment' of desire acquire not an ideality but a refined materiality."[47]

As I will argue, the theory of sexuality that Jerome sets forth in his letter to Eustochium can be conceptualized as a theory that attempts to transform the body precisely into "refined matter." Gross physicality is rejected as contaminating, but this rejection makes the body available for use at the level of figuration. It is in this context that Jerome's use of dreams in the letter is significant. He had ready-to-hand a transformative figurative language in which his theory of ascetic sexuality was both represented and formulated. As Jerome's understanding of the bodies in his dreams as "negatively positive" signs has already shown, Jerome accomplished the body's transformation by constructing it in such a way as to distance himself from it; yet the body is retained in the form of bodily *metaphors* that signify the condition of the inner self. For the ascetic Jerome, the body is useful mainly as a sign of psychic terrain. Again, as Harpham has argued, the ascetic "manages" the material world, which includes especially the human body, by using a discourse composed of "rhetorical and figural substitute[s] for the gratifications of the senses that the ascetic denies himself." Further, "in such rhetoric, the excluded world makes a triumphantly innocent appearance through a figurality that condemns it only to recover it, essentialize it, and wash it clean of its worldliness. . . . In figurality ascetic writers discovered an element in language that enabled them to recover and, in a sense, control the world they had renounced."[48]

In the letter to Eustochium, which will be the focus of the rest of this discussion, Jerome used two linguistic forms that function as complementary strategies for washing the body clean of its worldliness, a dynamic in which the negated physical body is more present than ever by means of its figural substitutes. Those two forms—the oneiric writing of his own body and the metaphorizing of Eustochium's body by means of scriptural images—all serve Jerome's ascetic program by providing mediating discourses in which the self can be transformed and its "matter" refined. Although the letter is addressed to Eustochium, I suggest that it can also be read as a form of self-address in which Jerome, attempting to surmount his own, very problematic, physicality, shifts the apprehension of meaning from the physical to the rhetorical, from the literal to the imaginal, from the profane to the scriptural. Through all of these shifts, the ascetic paradox of the absent-present body structures Jerome's writing and infuses the letter

[47] Ibid.
[48] Ibid., pp. 70–71.

with that sense of unfulfilled—indeed, unfulfillable—desire that Harpham argues is at the heart of asceticism.[49]

By his own admission, Jerome was a lover of words. Late in his life, he reports that he still dreamed of himself as a youth, "curly-headed, dressed in my toga, declaiming a controversial thesis in front of the rhetorician."[50] It is thus not surprising that he turned to language as the medium for exploring the conundrums of the ascetic life and particularly for transferring passion from the physical to a spiritual register. In his letter, there is a net of relationships in which the body, desire, and language are intertwined; the forms in which this intertwining occurs will be the focus of what follows. I am going to explore each of these mediating discourses in turn, with a view toward demonstrating how Jerome's use of narrative accounts of his own dreams in this letter was crucial to his strategy of reimagining the self in ascetic terms. I will begin with Jerome's remaking of the body of Eustochium by translating it from the physical to a spiritual register by means of scriptural images.

JEROME wrote his letter to Eustochium in 384 C.E. during his second sojourn in Rome.[51] These were heady days: consultant to Pope Damasus, spiritual advisor to a circle of talented and wealthy Christian women, Jerome was riding high on the crest of rigorous ascetic doctrine that he was urging on the Roman church.[52] This letter is generally considered to be the finest expression of his ascetic doctrine, a "systematic theory of sexuality."[53] Eustochium was an adolescent girl who had already dedicated her life to ascetic practice, and to perpetual virginity in particular.[54] To her Jerome wrote a very long letter characterized by one interpreter as "the greatest slander of women since Juvenal's sixth satire."[55] Eustochium, it should be noted, was not the one so slandered in the letter; on the contrary, she is highly praised, and Jerome's estimation of her worth is focused on her status as a virgin. Jerome describes Eustochium almost entirely in terms of her body and her sexuality, which are repeatedly pictured by images drawn from the bridal imagery in the biblical Song of Songs.[56] Jerome is especially

[49] Ibid., pp. 45–66.

[50] *C. Ruf.* 1.30 (*PL* 23.422B).

[51] For the dating of Jerome's letters, I have followed the chronology of Kelly, *Jerome,* passim (for the date of the letter to Eustochium [*Ep.* 22], see ibid., p. 100).

[52] Ibid., pp. 100–101; see also F. Cavallera, *Saint Jerome,* 1:104–13; Wiesen, *St. Jerome,* pp. 68–74.

[53] Kelly, *Jerome,* p. 102.

[54] For detailed discussions of Jerome's circle of women friends in Rome, see Clark, *Jerome, Chrysostom, and Friends,* pp. 44–79; Kelly, *Jerome,* pp. 91–103; Philip Rousseau, *Ascetics, Authority, and the Church in the Age of Jerome and Cassian,* pp. 108–13.

[55] Wiesen, *St. Jerome,* p. 164.

[56] *Ep.* 22.1.2–5, 2.1, 6.2, 17.4, 24.1–25.1, 26.2, 35.3 (*CSEL* 54.144–46, 150–52, 166, 176–79, 181, 198).

interested in her closed virginal body as a signifier of a soul already "laden with gold," yet he insists that the object of his letter is not praise of virginity. Rather, his goal is that Eustochium should understand that she is "fleeing from Sodom and should be fearful of the example of Lot's wife."[57]

Commentators have noted the oddity of Jerome's warm friendships with women in the face of his advice to other men to avoid women's lascivious, contaminating company.[58] In the case of this letter, there is the further incongruity of sending to a woman a portrait of women that is filled with biting ridicule. There is, however, no doubt that Jerome intended his critique to be religiously instructive. As Elizabeth Clark has pointed out, "[Jerome's] letters to women are in fact educational devices for Scriptural instruction," and the letter to Eustochium is no exception with its hundreds of references to biblical texts.[59]

Jerome's stated intention as author was to warn Eustochium about the dangers to spirituality that were posed by the body, and, on its surface, the letter presents itself as an expression of pastoral care for the moral well-being of its recipient. The explicit intentions of an author, however, cannot always control or limit the meanings that arise from associative movements and configurations of his or her text's tropes and metaphors. Texts can articulate perspectives and bear significations that are quite different from the announced goals of the author.[60] Thus in exploring the relationships among body, language, and desire in Jerome's letter, I am going to follow the metaphorical figurations of the text rather than Jerome's explicit intention of offering avuncular advice to the daughter of his friend. When the letter is read by attending to the figural languages—oneiric and scriptural—that are used to (re)construct the body, such metaphors as the "flight from Sodom" take on a life of their own apart from Jerome's vitriolic cautionary tale.

The first mediating form I will consider, across which Jerome transforms the body, pertains to Eustochium. Here the metaphor of the flight from Sodom assumes its full significance. There is a double movement in Jerome's letter which can be described as a "flight" *from* the literal female body as well as a "flight" *toward* a metaphorical female body that is a creation of language, a textual body that is the object of Jerome's desire.

In the letter to Eustochium, Jerome describes the body in general as "fragile"; it is bestial, it is voracious, but most of all it is sexual.[61] The

---

[57] Ibid. 22.2.1, 3.1 (*CSEL* 54.146).

[58] Wiesen, *St. Jerome,* p. 164; Clark, *Jerome, Chrysostom, and Friends,* p. 45.

[59] Clark, *Jerome, Chrysostom, and Friends,* pp. 47, 75–76.

[60] For discussions of the issues of authorial and textual intentionality, see Foucault, "What is an Author?" pp. 141–60; Barthes, "The Death of the Author," pp. 142–48.

[61] *Ep.* 22.4.1 (*CSEL* 54.148) and throughout the letter. See the discussion by Brown, *The Body and Society,* pp. 376–77, who remarks that, for Jerome, "the human body remained a darkened forest, filled with the roaring of wild beasts, that could be controlled only by rigid codes of diet and by the strict avoidance of occasions for sexual attraction. . . . Men and women were irreducibly sexual beings" (376).

"Sodom" of the body is its *libido*, its desire, which "titillates the senses"; even more, "the seductive fire of sensual pleasure floods us with its sweet heat."[62] According to Jerome, the body's major tendency is to be on fire. Speaking against the drinking of wine, he asks, "Why do we throw oil on the flame? Why do we supply kindling-wood to a little body that is already burning with fire?"[63]

This blazing body is burning with the signifiers of desire. For Jerome, the fiery flesh is not only a physical fact; it is also a psychic landscape or, perhaps better, it is a physical alphabet of the inner person's most basic drives.[64] Already it is clear that, in the very act of talking about the body, Jerome is transforming it into a signifier of something else—in this case, the psyche's erotic impulses. In the letter to Eustochium, it is the physical bodies of women with which Jerome is seemingly most concerned. The sensuality and lewdness of women is described in terms of their bodies: what they wear, what they eat and drink, the color of their skin, their gestures, their pronunciation of words are all paraded before the reader's eyes.[65] From the pompous display of a rich widow distributing alms, to the women who disfigure their faces and lower their voices to a whisper to simulate fasting, women's physicality is presented as both disturbing and disgusting.[66]

Dismayed by the pornographic bodies of women, which he interprets as though they were texts to be inspected for clues to psychic flaws, Jerome proceeds to transform those bodies by reimagining them linguistically, using Eustochium as his model for what Harpham called "refined materiality." The female body, fearful for "its power to articulate itself,"[67] is re-articulated by Jerome. This re-articulation is based on what Jerome presents in his letter as criticism of the public behavior of Roman Christian women, whom he had observed firsthand. However, it has been shown convincingly

---

[62] *Ep.* 22.6.4 (*CSEL* 54.151).

[63] Ibid. 22.8.2–3 (*CSEL* 54.154–55). On the medical view of the body as a "little fiery universe," see Brown, *The Body and Society,* pp. 17–20; on Jerome's reliance on medical advice concerning avoidance of foods, including wine, that might increase the body's heat, see Rousselle, *Porneia,* p. 174. Doctors recommended a dietary regimen of cool and dry food for reducing sexual desire (Rousselle, *Porneia,* p. 19).

[64] Brown, *The Body and Society,* pp. 223–37, and Rousselle, *Porneia,* pp. 141–59, for ascetics' use of the body to articulate the desires of the soul.

[65] *Ep.* 22.8 (*CSEL* 54.154–56), wine and food; *Ep.* 22.10–11 (*CSEL* 54.157–59), gluttony, luxury, dainty food; *Ep.* 22.13–14 (*CSEL* 54.160–62), false virgins with swelling wombs, clothing; *Ep.* 22.16 (*CSEL* 54.163–64), clothes as signifiers of inner dispositions; *Ep.* 22.17 (*CSEL* 54.164–66), skin color; *Ep.* 22.27 (*CSEL* 54.182–84), physical gestures of false humility; *Ep.* 22.29 (*CSEL* 54.186–89), affectations of speech. See Wiesen, *St. Jerome,* pp. 119–65.

[66] *Ep.* 22.32 (*CSEL* 54.193–95), the rich widow; *Ep.* 22.27 (*CSEL* 54.184), simulation of fasting.

[67] This phrase is from Susan Gubar, "'The Blank Page' and the Issues of Female Creativity," p. 76. Gubar traces the history, in Western culture, of woman's body as a "blank page" written on by men, with an emphasis on the nineteenth and twentieth centuries.

that Jerome's "observations" are not straightforward descriptions but caricatures. He based his portraits on the rhetorical conventions of Roman
satire and mimicry.[68] The conceit of this aspect of the letter is a critique of
religious pretension, which disguises the rhetorical indebtedness of the text
to a literary technique. But the satirical rhetoric of the text disguises another
of the text's figurations, which is Jerome's re-articulation of the too-open
body of woman as the closed body of the virgin.

Women's bodies were disturbingly open for Jerome not only because they
were obviously open to sexual penetration. Rather, encoded in that open-
ness was the dangerous strength and persistence of that fiery desire that
Jerome came to identify with the flesh, where "flesh," as a signifier of one
aspect of the body, is already a metaphorical substitute for the body as a
whole, although it can also signify the sexual condition of the literal body.[69]
Writing, for example, about good and bad virgins, Jerome argues that
virginity is not only a condition of the body, but also of the inner self.
Virginity may be lost even by a libidinous thought: such are "evil virgins,
virgins in the flesh, not in the spirit."[70] Jerome goes on to argue in this
passage that physical virginity in itself is not salvific; indeed, the non-
virginal mind shows that the literal body's virginity is a sham. Jerome appears to be caught in an interpretive dilemma: on the one hand, the literal
bodies of women are blatant signifiers of psychic *libido* and other moral
flaws; but on the other hand, as in the case of the evil virgin, the literal body
can lie, presenting a false mirror of the soul.

Because of the semiotic problems presented by the female body, I suggest,
Jerome moved away from the literal physicality of women altogether, and he
did so by shifting to a figurative mode of interpretation in which the psyche
is described with bodily *metaphors*. To return to the evil virgins: following
his statement that their virginal flesh does not reflect a virginal spirit, Jerome
then characterizes loss of virginity in the inner self with bodily metaphors
drawn from Scripture. Such women will be found with their skirts over their
faces, opening their legs to all who pass by.[71] Using images of prostitution
from the biblical prophets Jeremiah and Ezekiel, who had themselves appropriated the female body metaphorically as a sign of spiritual debasement,
Jerome moves from the semiotically unstable physical body to a textual
body that does not lie.[72]

[68] See Wiesen, *St. Jerome,* pp. 7–15, 119–28 on the satirical elements in *Ep.* 22.

[69] Brown, *The Body and Society,* pp. 376–77, discussed Jerome's "definitive sexualization of
Paul's notion of *the flesh*" (emphasis in original).

[70] *Ep.* 22.5.3 (*CSEL* 54.150).

[71] Ibid. 22.6.2–3 (*CSEL* 54.150–51).

[72] Ibid. (*CSEL* 54.151). The biblical quotations are from Jer. 13.26 ("I myself will lift up
your skirts over your face, and your shame will be seen.") and Ezek. 16.25 ("At the head of
every street you built your lofty place and prostituted your beauty, offering yourself to any
passerby, and multiplying your harlotry.") (RSV).

In his discussion, Jerome has shifted his focus from the actual physicality of women (whose grossness is apparent even, or especially, in his caricatures) to bodily metaphors used to describe psychic states. It is at the level of physical metaphor that Jerome's rewriting of the female body takes place, and it is there that he will construct an erotics of asceticism. As Jerome distances himself from the libidinal contagion of literal female bodies, the "blaze" of the body burns more brightly in the metaphorical constructions of his text. With regard to Eustochium, whose body will be a sign of Jerome's own desire, it is the transmutation of the physical body into a textual—specifically, a scriptural—body that is most striking, and that engages Jerome's interpretive energy.

Jerome begins by giving Eustochium the usual ascetic advice, encouraging her in the course of action that she had already undertaken. Counseling avoidance of wine and delicate food, he pictures Eustochium's body reductively as "a rumbling stomach and fevered lungs," both of which are images that he has drawn rather arbitrarily from scriptural passages.[73] Eustochium's body is not only reduced to three of its organs, it cannot even be understood apart from textual references. The body's physical needs, like eating and drinking, can corrupt the soul; in order for a soul to flee from its own Sodom, it must have a newly inscribed body, rewritten in scriptural metaphors. Much of Jerome's practical advice to Eustochium repeats this movement from the physical to the metaphorical. Paradoxically, the virginal body is achieved at the expense of the actual physical body; biological femaleness is not overcome or erased but *transformed* by being absorbed into scriptural texts.[74] Once safely textualized, its materiality refined by a figural whitewashing, that body was ready for use as a signifier of theological desire.

It is when Jerome writes Eustochium's virginity as such, as differentiated from advice on how to avoid losing it, that the displacement of the physical by the metaphorical is most stark and also most voluptuous. The virginal body breaks the biblical curse: "Death came through Eve, but life through Mary. For that reason, the gift of virginity comes forth more richly in women because it began from a woman."[75] The virginal body is most essentially a female body, yet it becomes the site for Jerome's drive toward signifying his ascetic ideal, applicable to men as well as to women. Although physical woman, as Jerome so satirically shows, is "nothing," her textual body is really "something," and it provides the space for a stunning theological articulation of desire.[76]

[73] *Ep.* 22.11.1 (*CSEL* 54.158). Jerome supports this image with a concatenation of verses from Job, Ps., Gen., Ex., Matt., Lk., and Ezek.

[74] For a discussion of other ways in which Jerome attempted to transform the femaleness of his friends, see Clark, *Jerome, Chrysostom, and Friends*, pp. 48–59.

[75] *Ep.* 22.21.7 (*CSEL* 54.173).

[76] I owe this play on the words *something* and *nothing* to David L. Miller, "Why Men Are Mad! Nothing-Envy and the Fascration Complex," pp. 71–79.

Jerome accomplishes the transformation of Eustochium's physical body into a metaphorical body by way of tropes from the Song of Songs. From the many images offered by this biblical poem, Jerome draws almost exclusively on two kinds: images of closure and images of seductive sexual foreplay. Eustochium is, as Jerome often says, God's bride, and as such she lives in a "paradise of virginity." Textually speaking, paradise is found in a scriptural love poem, where Eustochium is the Shulamite, the bride, the black but comely one who, in Jerome's words, has been "washed white" (*dealbata*).[77] The coarse and disturbing physicality of her body, characteristic of all women's bodies, has been whitewashed in the course of its transformation into a poetic body of Jerome's construction. It is an imaginal body that becomes a signifier of desire precisely because of its closure.

Again practically speaking, Jerome advises Eustochium to stay inside her house.[78] Thus domestically sequestered, she is doubly enclosed, and the physical space of her enclosure underscores the psychic significance of her virginity. Jerome's imaginal articulation of her enclosed body places her, however, in the king's chamber of the Song of Songs.[79] This is no ordinary room, but a bridal chamber, a space of sexual love. Eustochium's refined body is for Jerome "a garden enclosed, a fountain sealed,"[80] but this closing of the body does not end erotic desire. It intensifies it.

Jerome's choice of the king's bridal chamber and the enclosed garden as images that articulate Eustochium's body leads directly to the other set of images from the Song of Songs to which he appeals. The king desires his bride and will lead her into his chamber with his own hand; he will kiss her, and she will seek him by night; he will put his hand through the opening and her inner body will be moved for him.[81] As Jerome remarks, "Desire is

[77] *Ep.* 22.2.1, 6.2, 8.1, 16.1, 20.2, 25.1–26.4 (*CSEL* 54.145, 151, 154, 163, 170–71, 178–82), "God's bride"; *Ep.* 22.18.2 (*CSEL* 54.167), "paradise of virginity"; *Ep.* 22.1.5 (*CSEL* 54.145), "washed white."

[78] Ibid. 22.17.1, 25.2 (*CSEL* 54.164–65, 179).

[79] Ibid. 22.1.5, 6.2, 25.1 (*CSEL* 54.145, 151, 178–79).

[80] Ibid. 22.25.1–5 (*CSEL* 54.178–80); this is the most extended passage in the letter in which Jerome eroticizes Eustochium's body with imagery from the Song of Songs.

[81] Ibid. 22.25.1 (*CSEL* 54.179). Song of Songs 5.4 is translated by the RSV as "My beloved put his hand to the latch, and my *heart* was thrilled within me" (emphasis added). Translations of Jerome's *Ep.* 22.25.1 render Jerome's quotations of this verse as follows: "He will come and put his hand through the hole of the door, and your *heart* shall be moved for him" (*NPNF* 6:32, emphasis added); "He 'will put his hand through the opening and will touch your *body*'" (*ACW* 33,1:152, emphasis added). My own translation ("He will put his hand through the opening and your *inner body* will be moved for him") attempts to be more faithful to Jerome's use of the Latin *venter* to translate the word *koilia* in Greek and *ma'im* in Hebrew. The Hebrew *ma'im* does not mean either "heart" or "body," as the translations above would have it. Rather, it means "internal organs," "inward parts," "belly," "womb" (see Brown, Driver, and Briggs, *Hebrew and English Lexicon of the Old Testament*, s.v. *mah*). Similarly, the Greek *koilia*, used by the Septuagint to translate the Hebrew *ma'im*, means

quenched by desire": the imaginal body is an erotic body of the highest degree; it is the text of inner desire.[82] Thus, across the mediating discourse of scriptural images, Jerome can "safely" contemplate the female body as he could not do in the desert; as a metaphor of spiritual desire, that body has been distanced from its own physical reality and appropriated for the ascetic cause.

Interpreters have noted how peculiar it is to find such sensuous language in a text that argues for rigorous asceticism. In his biography of Jerome, J.N.D. Kelly, for example, observes that "it is ironical to reflect that, in urging a young girl like Eustochium to crush the physical yearnings of her nature in the effort to surrender herself the more completely to Christ, he should feed her fantasy with such exciting images."[83] Similarly, Geoffrey Harpham makes the following comment on Jerome's use of the scriptural scene of sexual foreplay: "The difference between the pleasures of the figural bridegroom and those of any literal one is not altogether clear; one cannot say with complete confidence that ascetic 'sport' is altogether non-erotic."[84] To Kelly's sense of the irony of Jerome's use of the Song of Songs in an ascetic context and Harpham's sense of the blurring of boundaries between the literal and the figural, I would add Julia Kristeva's understanding of the Song of Songs, which will help to show the appropriateness of Jerome's use of this love poem in his rewriting of the female body.

Kristeva notices that union is not achieved in the Song of Songs. There is no sexual intercourse. "Conjugal, exclusive, sensuous, jealous—love in the Song of Songs is indeed all of that at the same time, with in addition the unnameable of carnal union."[85] Love in the Song of Songs is "sensuous and deferred"; never fulfilled, the erotic sensibility in this poem is "indissolubly linked with the dominant theme of absence, yearning to merge," such that the poem is "a legitimation of the impossible, an impossibility set up as amatory law."[86] The Song of Songs constructs erotic love in such a way that its climax is always deferred, never quite reached, yet it holds out union as the end toward which the lovers strive. Desire is continuously kindled but never satisfied.

For Jerome, too, union was the ideal. It was his "amatory law." As he says in the letter to Eustochium, "Flesh desires to be what God is" (*cum caro cupit*

"cavity of the body," especially the intestines, bowels, and womb (Liddell, Scott, Jones, *A Greek-English Lexicon*, s.v. *koilia*). The word *venter* carries the same meanings (Lewis and Short, *A Latin Dictionary*, s.v. *venter*). My translation of this term as "inner body" attempts to be more faithful both to etymology and to the erotic suggestiveness of the verse.

82 *Ep.* 22.17.4 (*CSEL* 54.166).
83 Kelly, *Jerome*, p. 103.
84 Harpham, *The Ascetic Imperative in Culture and Criticism*, p. 46.
85 Julia Kristeva, *Tales of Love*, p. 97.
86 Ibid., pp. 96, 94, 97.

esse, quod deus est).[87] Like the "unnameable" of the carnal union of the bride
and the bridegroom in the Song of Songs, however, the union of flesh with
God is perpetually deferred but also tantalizingly seductive in its ongoing
appeal. As Harpham has suggested, "Asceticism is essentially a meditation
on, even an enactment of, desire. . . . While asceticism recognizes that desire stands between human life and perfection, it also understands that
desire is the only means of achieving perfection, and that the movement
towards ideality is necessarily a movement of desire."[88]

Jerome chose to move toward ideality by reconfiguring the female body
as a text that could mediate between the flesh and God. Eustochium's
virginal body, which closes the fearful articulation of women's physical
bodies, becomes a poetic text, but the paradox is that her *imaginal* body is
still articulate, but now its message is one of theological desire. Interestingly,
the overtly erotic body with which Jerome endows the ascetic Eustochium
carries a strong positive charge, while the erotic dancing girls of his dreams
in the desert were negative signifiers. It is as though Jerome's dreams
showed him the need to re-evaluate the eroticism that his culture associated
with women. From this perspective, his dreams formed the foundation
upon which his imaginal version of Eustochium's body was constructed.

Jerome accomplished his movement from the bodies of the dancing girls
to Eustochium's body without relinquishing sexual metaphors. His persistence is using such language is understandable when placed in the context
of a series of remarks by the Italian novelist Italo Calvino. In one of his
literary-critical essays, Calvino wrote that "the language of sexuality makes
sense only if it is placed at the top of a scale of semantic values. When the
musical score needs the highest and lowest notes, when the canvas requires
the most vivid colors: this is when the sign of sex comes into operation. . . .
The positive or negative connotation that accompanies the signs of sex in
every single literary production determines how values are assigned within
the text."[89] Asceticism was Jerome's musical score, and he used the language
of sexuality to hit the highest and lowest notes—Eustochium and the dancing girls respectively. This helps to explain how the figuration of women's
bodies in Jerome's letters signifies more than social critique or satiric exercise in misogyny. Their bodies were important as figurations, both negative
and positive, of life lived ascetically. While the dancing girls hit the low note
of the temptations that asceticism fosters, the paradisal body of Eustochium
hits the high note by providing a space for an expression of the erotic desire
that asceticism only seemingly denies.[90]

[87] *Ep.* 22.40.5 (*CSEL* 54.209).
[88] Harpham, *The Ascetic Imperative in Culture and Criticism*, p. 45.
[89] Italo Calvino, *The Uses of Literature*, pp. 67–68.
[90] See the remarks of Harpham, *The Ascetic Imperative in Culture and Criticism*, pp. 70–71:

We may recall how Jerome's formula, "Desire is quenched by desire," offers a rhetorical
and figural substitute for the gratifications of the senses that the ascetic denies himself.

Why did Jerome choose the female body for the articulation of his erotics of asceticism? It has already been noted that Jerome wrote to Eustochium that virginity, as the gift of Mary, was in a sense engendered as female. Thus the female body is the more appropriate one for ascetic signification. Accordingly, in the letter Jerome develops a theory of ascetic sexuality whose positive metaphors are female, but the theory applies to men as well as to women—and, given the letter's self-referentiality, it applies particularly to himself. Woman's erotic body has become a text to be read by women *and* men. The erotic ideal of a theological union that is never consummated— that is to say, the constant desire for God, for what is other-than-oneself— has been encoded as female.[91] What is other to the self, which constitutes the goal of the self's desirous yearning, is figured as woman, for whom Eustochium stands as a sign.

Just as his dreams provided Jerome with a set of images that he used to engage reflectively with the emotional difficulties of ascetic practice, so his discourse about Eustochium provided the opportunity to articulate a theory of sexuality that redirected those very emotions, harnessing them for rather than against the ascetic vision of reality. Jerome's statement that "desire is quenched by desire" needs to be taken seriously as an indication of his awareness that the remedy for *eros* is not denial but displacement.[92] In the context of the letter, Eustochium functions as a figural substitute that defuses the unbridled eroticism of Jerome's visions in the desert while at the same time allowing *eros* a role to play in asceticism. In a sense, the metaphorizing discourse about Eustochium's body worked for Jerome as the magical spells of attraction worked for those who sent them: both strategies provided therapeutic means for dealing with strong erotic impulses by projecting them on a visual screen of an "other" who is a mirror of the self and its desires.[93]

It should be noted that eroticism is here understood, as it was in the case of the oneiric love spells of magic, as a desire for what is other to the self. As Anne Carson has explained, "*eros* denotes 'want,' 'lack,' 'desire for that which is missing.' The lover wants what he does not have."[94] Construing desire as "want" catches nicely the ambiguity inherent in the concept, a simultaneous feeling of yearning and recognition of absence. Desire fulfilled would no

---

Such a strategy permits the entry of desire, even of lust and wantonness, into the arena of denial that constitutes the official program of asceticism. . . . In figurality ascetic writers discovered an element in language that enabled them to recover and, in a sense, control the world they had renounced.

[91] See Alice A. Jardine, *Gynesis*, p. 25 and *passim*, for a statement in terms of modern literature of a phenomenon that also occurred in antiquity, namely, that what is other to the self is "coded as *feminine*, as *woman*" (italics in original).

[92] *Ep.* 22.17.4 (CSEL 54.166).

[93] See the discussion on pp. 121–23 above.

[94] Carson, *Eros the Bittersweet*, p. 10.

longer be desire. This is as true of theological as it is of carnal desire, a fact
that makes Jerome's use of the Song of Song's dynamic of unfulfilled and so
continuously present desire so fitting as a trope of ascetic desire.

It should also be remembered, however, that in Graeco-Roman antiquity
intense desire was thought to be a "diseased state affecting the soul and the
body" in which *eros* was "described in a pathology of physical and mental
disturbance."[95] While Jerome presented the imaginal body of Eustochium
as a sign of the cure of erotic disease, his presentation of his own body
remained pathological rather than curative. He did try to shift the grounds
for determining his own ascetic identity from the physical to the imaginal
plane, and he did so by narrating his dreams, thus making his oneiric body
into a written text, useful for reflection. However, the visual representations
of his body in the text of the dreams show that body to be a battleground
and *not* a serenely closed vehicle for theological desire like Eustochium's
body. Perhaps Jerome found that it was easier to shift the sexuality of
another person from the literal body to the medium of language than it was
to shift his own.

Jerome's ascetic project of providing figural substitutes for the body in
order to find a safe space for the expression of *eros* was problematic when
that body was his own because of the *type* of figuration that he had found to
be most appropriate for achieving real distance from physicality and its
untamed eroticism. As we have seen, Jerome does accomplish the transformation of Eustochium's body into language, the true medium of ascetic
sexuality, as Harpham has argued.[96] However, she does not assume the
character of language in general, but of a specific language, the language of
Scripture as found in the Song of Songs. This was not a language that was
available to Jerome for the erotic textualization of his own body because, as
Peter Brown has observed, "the language of the Song of Songs . . . came, in
the course of the fourth century, to settle heavily, almost exclusively, on the
body of the virgin woman."[97] Jerome did not have access to the kind of
scriptural metaphor of desire that he used to construct Eustochium's body
as an ascetic text.

Interestingly, Jerome made one attempt in the letter to textualize his own
body by using a female metaphor drawn from Scripture. Describing to
Eustochium his struggles with the "bubbling fires of lust" in the desert,

---

[95] Winkler, *The Constraints of Desire,* pp. 82, 84.

[96] Harpham, *The Ascetic Imperative in Culture and Criticism,* p. 132; Harpham further
describes asceticism as "an attempt by human beings to stand 'outside the world' by assuming
the character of language." Also, "asceticism is an application to the self of certain insights
into language: to be ascetic is to make oneself representable" (27).

[97] Brown, *The Body and Society,* p. 274; see also Elizabeth A. Clark, "The Uses of the Song
of Songs: Origen and the later Latin Fathers," pp. 386–427, an essay that shows in detail
how Latin authors, especially Jerome, appropriated the Song of Songs for ascetic purposes.

Jerome casts himself in the role of the sinful woman of Luke 7.37–50, who had washed the feet of Jesus with her tears and dried them with her hair. "Helpless," Jerome wrote, "I threw myself at the feet of Jesus, watered them with tears, dried them with my hair, and I subdued my resistant body with weeks of fasting."[98] Sadly, this attempt at encoding his body with a scriptural metaphor was not theologically satisfying for Jerome. Unlike his troping of Eustochium's body with an erotic metaphor of virginity, Jerome troped his own body with an image of prostitution, and it served only to remind him of his own lost virginity: "I do not blush with shame [in the face of] my wretchedness, rather I lament aloud that I am not now what I used to be."[99] This failed attempt at textualizing his body with a scriptural metaphor suggests the difficulty that the encoding of virginity as female presented for Jerome, because the literal male body is not easily metaphorized with images of closure and intactness. This may explain Jerome's fascination with Eustochium's body as the most appropriate field for the cultivation of ascetic virtue: as a paradigm, her body functioned as an erotic allure that fired his ascetic longings as well as his attempts to conceive his own body in an imaginal way.

It appears that Jerome was doubly bound by his physical maleness and loss of virginity and by his inability to find a scriptural metaphor that would, by textualizing his body, safely remove him from the fiery *libido* of the flesh. Nonetheless, he experimented with a language to use for articulating his desire, and that language was one of oneiric memory. This experiment, I suggest, can be seen as a step in Jerome's journey toward the paradigmatic goal that he so forcefully expressed under the sign of "Eustochium."

The space of Jerome's letter to Eustochium consists of oddly juxtaposed passages in which the presentation of Eustochium's idealized body gives way to Jerome's presentation of his own body. These shifts of focus are accompanied by shifts in language, for while the language of Scripture applies most successfully to Eustochium, the language of remembered dreams applies to Jerome. There is a passage in Aristotle's *Rhetoric* that can provide a helpful interpretive framework for understanding Jerome's presentation of his body in this way. Aristotle defined desire as "a reaching out for the sweet"; in her discussion of this passage, Carson explains that he goes on to say that "the man who is reaching for some delight, whether in the future as hope or in the past as memory, does so by means of an act of imagination (*phantasia*)."[100] Desire is encoded imaginally, that is, in lan-

---

[98] *Ep.* 22.7.3 (*CSEL* 54.153); my thanks are due to Elizabeth A. Clark for calling this passage to my attention.

[99] Ibid. 22.7.3 (*CSEL* 54.153); for discussion of the identity of the Lukan woman as a prostitute, see Elizabeth Schüssler Fiorenza, *In Memory of Her*, pp. 127–29; on Jerome's reference to his loss of virginity in *Ep.* 49.20.2 (*CSEL* 54.385), see Kelly, *Jerome*, p. 21.

[100] Aristotle, *Rhet.* 1.1370a6, quoted and translated by Carson, *Eros the Bittersweet*, p. 63.

guages of figural perception. While Jerome did not have the imaginative code of the Song of Songs to use in constructing his erotic body, he did have the language of dream-memories, a language that deals, in Aristotle's terms, with both the past and the future. It was this language that Jerome used to "reach for delight" as he investigated the possibilities for articulating an imaginal body for himself.

There are two places in the letter to Eustochium where Jerome's body is figurally present. The first is his memory of his visionary experiences in the desert, in which he composes an image of his remembered body with metaphors of *libido*. In this written version of his memory, Jerome presents himself as a lustful bag of bones, tormented body and soul by physical and psychic heat.[101] The second is his nightmare, a brutal projection of his future should he continue in his Ciceronian reading habits and, implicitly, a hopeful forecast of a literary life wholly devoted to Scripture.[102] These two references to his person accord well with Aristotle's sense that desire, the reaching out for delight, is configured imaginatively either in terms of the future or the past. However much a nightmare experience of the future and a memory of tormenting visions may not seem to partake of delight, both oneiric memories are exercises of *phantasia* and both are grounded in *eros*.[103]

The language of oneiric memory is erotic because it participates in lack— and here I petition the "wanting" and "lacking"dimensions of *eros,* discussed above, that give the term *erotic* a meaning that is more encompassing than "mere" delight. In oneiric memory, the imagination constructs as present objects that are literally absent. "Eros is lack," and, as Freud and many others both ancient and modern have shown, "that which is known, attained, possessed, cannot be an object of desire."[104] What Jerome did not possess was his body, that is, the metaphoric body that would make union with God, the goal of his desire, possible. In written memories of dreams, then, Jerome constructed an imaginal body, a move that paradoxically both displaced his literal body and underscored its problems all the more forcefully.

The other of the self that Jerome desired was the ideal face of his soul's divinity, the union of his flesh with God.[105] Such unachievable perfection was tauntingly seductive, and I suggest that it was with a sense of the impossibility of what was nonetheless an "amatory law" that Jerome dreamed and remembered his body. What he found there, however, was lack

[101] *Ep.* 22.7.1–4 (*CSEL* 54.152–54).

[102] Ibid 22.30.3–6 (*CSEL* 54.190–91).

[103] For discussions by Jerome's contemporaries on these issues, see Augustine, *Conf.* 10, where memory is discussed as a storehouse of images, and Synesius of Cyrene, *De ins.* 3–5, on the connection between dreams and imagination.

[104] Carson, *Eros the Bittersweet,* p. 65.

[105] *Ep.* 22.40.5 (*CSEL* 54.209).

and an uncomfortable feeling that something was missing, that his body was too "open" and not yet virginally "closed." Carson has written in this regard that, "reaching for an object that proves to be outside and beyond himself, the lover is provoked to notice that self and its limits. From a new vantage point, which we might call self-consciousness, he looks back and sees a hole. . . . Desire for an object *that he never knew he lacked* is defined, by a shift of distance, as desire for a necessary part of himself."[106] Having constructed his paradigm in his figural translation of Eustochium's body, Jerome then used dreams to explore his own body as part of his journey to a closed "female" body of his own.

Just prior to the account of his visions in the desert with which this chapter opened, Jerome had been telling Eustochium about the inner heat that attacks the senses: "lust [*libido*] titillates the senses" and "the seductive fire of sensual pleasure floods us with its sweet heat."[107] Such inner heat, for Jerome a phenomenon both physical and psychological, apparently reminded Jerome of the literal heat of the desert sun; it was a libidinal theory of the body that triggered his memory. He closes the narrative about the visions of dancing girls by saying, "I feared my cell as though it knew my thoughts."[108] As with Eustochium, Jerome pictures himself as enclosed, he in a cell, she in a garden. Her garden, however, is sealed, while his cell opens on a torrid landscape of psychic fever.

Peter Brown has described this narrative as an "artistically brilliant contraposto of the sweltering body of the monk and the untamed sexual drives of his mind."[109] However, apart from the opening reference to the burning desert sun, Jerome describes his body as literally icy cold, his flesh as good as dead. The literal pallor and chill of a body ravaged by ascetic fasting was not matched by a cooling of desire; indeed, Jerome's libidinal imagination was producing very erotic visions. As with the evil virgin described earlier, Jerome's literal body was not a trustworthy mirror of the condition of his psyche. I suggest that Jerome's picture of himself as *exusta solis ardoribus,* "inflamed by the burning heat of the sun," is a portrayal of his *imaginal,* not his literal, body. *Exusta,* from *exuro,* can carry the metaphorical sense of "inflamed" as well as the literal sense of "burned" or "dried up."[110] Whatever one might say about his actual body, it was the "body" of his imagination that was on fire.

It was this kind of passage that led an older generation of scholars to view

---

106 Carson, *Eros the Bittersweet,* pp. 32–33 (italics in original).

107 *Ep.* 22.6.4 (*CSEL* 54.151); Jerome again discusses the topic of "innate heat" in *Ep.* 54.9 (*CSEL* 54.475), appealing for authority to the Greek physician Galen. For the evidence from ancient medical writings on this and related topics, see Rouselle, *Porneia,* pp. 5–23.

108 *Ep.* 22.7.1–4 (*CSEL* 54.152–54).

109 Brown, *The Body and Society,* p. 376.

110 Lewis and Short, *A Latin Dictionary,* s.v. *exuro.*

the basis of asceticism as a dualistic split between body and soul; hatred and therefore punishment of the body were the complement of spiritual devotion.[111] A newer generation of scholars has almost completely reversed this view. In the words of Brown, "Seldom, in ancient thought, had the body been seen as more deeply implicated in the transformation of the soul; and never was it made to bear so heavy a burden. . . . In the desert tradition, the body was allowed to become the discreet mentor of the proud soul."[112] I agree with this perspective as an overview, but in Jerome's case I think it needs to be qualified. Given his flight from the actual body and his attempts to construct a paradigm of an ideal body whose "matter" is refined, the question that presents itself is, *Which* body served as mentor to the soul? It would appear that only the oneiric body, the body-as-metaphor, could serve Jerome as psychic tutor.

In his narrative presentation of himself in this memory-space of desire, Jerome has taken the steps he took when writing about women's bodies: he has noted his own gross physicality, and he has then shifted his vision to a bodily metaphor—the chorus of girls—to signal his psychic condition. What he has not yet attained, however, is a safe figural substitute that would allow him to express his erotic drives in a register other than the carnal. The one scriptural image that he does find and that he quotes just after his narrative of his visions, the Lukan image of the penitent prostitute, only underscores his dilemma. Lacking, then, a transformative scriptural body, Jerome remained too open to the fearful articulations of his *libido*. Only by assuming the character of language in the mode of the chaste eroticism of the Eustochium-paradigm could Jerome unite his physical and psychic bodies in that "third" body where erotic expression could be given free rein.

Harpham has written that the man who went to the desert had placed himself "under a virtual obligation to reinvent himself."[113] The self of the ascetic in the desert was an unfinished work of art for whom "the personal is the trivial; it is that which must be sacrificed in the interests of form."[114] This was exactly Jerome's situation in the desert—at least, this was Jerome's situation in his written account of his experience in the desert. In this textualization of his memory, he was struggling to banish the personal and, like his view of Eustochium, to become the form of his own imaginal body. That he took a step toward the final chiseling of himself in the desert is not part of his narrative to Eustochium, but we know from elsewhere that he did take that step, and he did it in and by language.

---

[111] Emblematic of this generation is Dodds, *Pagan and Christian in an Age of Anxiety,* pp. 29–36, who wrote that "contempt for the human condition and hatred of the body was a disease endemic in the entire culture of the period" (35). See Brown, *The Body and Society,* p. 235nn. 103–4, for further examples.

[112] Brown, *The Body and Society,* pp. 235, 237.

[113] Harpham, *The Ascetic Imperative in Culture and Criticism,* p. 24.

[114] Ibid., p. 25.

Given the specific scriptural images that Jerome used to rearticulate Eustochium's body, it is interesting that, while he was in the desert, he asked Rufinus to send him a copy of a then-popular commentary on the Song of Songs.[115] It would seem that, burning with oneiric "heat" as he was at that time, he needed textual images of eroticism to gratify his desire. The language of the Song of Songs was not, however, the language that provoked a turn in Jerome's relation with carnality; rather, that language was Hebrew.

In a letter written some thirty years after his stay in the desert, Jerome wrote:

> When I was a young man walled in by the solitude of the desert, I was unable to resist the allurements of vice and the hot passions of my nature. Although I tried to crush them with repeated fastings, my mind was in a turmoil with sinful thoughts. To bring it under control, I made myself the pupil of a Christian convert from Judaism. After the subtlety of Quintillian, the flowing eloquence of Cicero, the dignified prose of Fronto, the smooth grace of Pliny, I set myself to learn an alphabet and strove to pronounce the hissing, breath-demanding words.[116]

Language—in this case, the scriptural language of Hebrew—provided Jerome with a refuge from his body. But it also proved itself to be an erotic outlet, with its "hissing words" that made him literally "pant" for breath.[117] Only by submerging his desire in a language that took his breath away could he begin to experience the closure for which he longed. Jerome had discovered that his fasting could not satisfy the voracious hunger of his inner self. Contrary to his ascetic expectations, a hungry body did not make for a chaste psyche.[118] Like the haiku poet who said,

> I can't eat all this
> lust

Jerome found another way in which to engage his desires.[119]

Jerome's goal was to cure his body through language. The idea that language might be a therapy of the body is not unique, it would appear, to contemporary psychoanalysis; it was already at work in Jerome's quest for

[115] *Ep.* 5.2.2 (*CSEL* 54.22); see Kelly, *Jerome,* p. 48.

[116] *Ep.* 125.12 (*CSEL* 56.131), trans. by Kelly, *Jerome,* p. 50.

[117] See Kelly, *Jerome,* p. 50n17: "The participle 'anhelantia' (lit. 'panting') refers to the drawing of breath required for pronouncing certain aspirate or guttural sounds in Hebrew." Such forceful drawing-in of the breath would require a correlatively forceful exhalation."

[118] On the relation between food and sexuality in ascetic thinking, see Rousselle, *Porneia,* pp. 160–78. Both doctors and ascetics subscribed to the idea that a severely restricted diet would reduce sexual urges, and Jerome was no exception (see n. 63 above); in his case, however, the diet didn't work.

[119] This haiku is by Morimoto Norio and is quoted in Hiroaki Sato, *One Hundred Frogs,* p. 143.

healing.[120] In the account of his famous dream of flagellation induced by secular literary tastes, there is explicit evidence of a conviction that a new language, the language of Scripture, could bring Jerome closer to the refined self of his desire. This dream presented to Jerome the "other" of his Ciceronian self, which was a healed self no longer torn between competing languages. Yet, given the Graeco-Roman convention, and Jerome's own recognition, regarding the future-oriented nature of dreams, this dream presented to Jerome a picture of a self that did not yet exist. The dream was a text of desire, founded on lack. Further, because the source of dreams was located in otherness—in God—the dream presents the dreamer to himself as "written" by what is other to himself. The "I" of the dreamer is estranged from its conventionally constituted self, decentered, and reformulated.

Harpham notes that St. Anthony urged his followers to write down their dreams, thus "moving textuality into the undisclosed regions of the self."[121] From this perspective, Jerome's dream is doubly textual and also doubly disclosive. Written in the letter to Eustochium, the dream is a text that is about text, and it reveals not only an undisclosed region of Jerome's self but also an unknown aspect of his body. For Jerome, writing down his dream issued in a textualization of the unknown self that he desired, that is, the self that could express desire theologically rather than carnally. This was so because language, as Jerome knew, was itself a medium of sexuality that could be either adulterous, as he remarked to Eustochium, or chastely erotic, as in the virginal images of the Song of Songs. Thus the dream's demand that Jerome move from Cicero to Scripture was a demand that redirected Jerome's desire as well as his reading material. As I remarked earlier, in the oneiric experiences that Jerome reports in the letter, Cicero and the dancing girls are structurally parallel; they belong together as images that mirror both each other as well as that untamed *libido* from which the ascetic needs to escape.

Just as Jerome shifted the apprehension of meaning from Eustochium's literal body to a figural, scriptural one, so his dream shifted the grounds of his own self-awareness. Like a specter, his black-and-blue body floated before his eyes as a signifier of his ascetic desire. Encoded in those oneiric bruises was Jerome's longing to reinvent himself in terms of scriptural images. More so than his memory of the visions in the desert, this dream encapsulates and brings to expression the intricate relationships among body, desire, and language that fuel the letter's exploration of ascetic desire. Furthermore, the dream—an imaginal form of apprehension, as Jerome

---

[120] For a good contemporary discussion of Freud's "talking cure" and its therapeutic effects on the body, especially on the bodies of hysterics, see Dianne Hunter, "Hysteria, Psychoanalysis, and Feminism: The Case of Anna O.," pp. 89–115.

[121] Harpham, *The Ascetic Imperative in Culture and Criticism,* p. 14.

knew—was a fitting vehicle for his ascetic drive to shift the grounds of self-identity from the physical to the spiritual arena.[122]

In fact, Jerome used the discourse of dreams in his revisioning of Eustochium's identity as well. The most heavily eroticized passage in Jerome's letter to Eustochium, in which her body is aroused by the sexual foreplay of the bridegroom, is presented by Jerome as a dream! Here are his words: "The secrets of your bedchamber always guard you; your bridegroom always sports with you on the inside. Do you pray?: you speak to the bridegroom. Do you read?: he speaks to you. And, when sleep comes upon you, he will come behind the wall and put his hand through the opening and touch your inner body, and trembling you will rise up and say, 'I am wounded by love.'"[123] In this passage, the two discourses that mediate Jerome's theory of ascetic sexuality come together: at its most erotic pitch, Eustochium's metaphorized body is oneiric. As imaginal forms capable of representing the self's desire for what it is not, dreams served Jerome well as vehicles for the ideal ascetic self, wholly external to its own carnality but voluptuous nonetheless, ephemeral in its figural composition yet tangible as a textual "magnet for erotic interest."[124]

A written dream is a curious combination of the ephemeral (the dream) and the permanent (the text). Thus the dream-as-text is a paradoxical construction that matches perfectly the paradox of chaste eroticism that formed the basis of Jerome's ascetic theory. Jerome could not, finally, do without his dreams, for they reflected both the substance and the form of his revisioning of the identity of the self.

[122] See p. 205 above. Jerome's use of the term *imago*, even when valenced negatively, shows that he placed the phenomenon of dreams in the province of imagination, much as did his contemporary Synesius of Cyrene, whose theory of oneiric imagination is discussed on pp. 70–73 above.

[123] *Ep.* 22.25.1 (*CSEL* 54.178–79).

[124] This phrase is taken from Harpham, *The Ascetic Imperative in Culture and Criticism*, p. 51.

CHAPTER NINE

The Two Gregorys and Ascetic Dreaming

Then shall I see Caesarius himself, no longer in exile, but brilliant, glorious, heavenly, such as in my dreams I have often beheld you, pictured thus by my desire, if not by the very truth.[1]

It seemed [in the dream] that I was holding in my hands the relics of martyrs, and there flowed from them such a bright beam of light, like that from a spotless mirror placed facing the sun, that my eyes were blinded by its brilliance.[2]

THESE TWO dreamers, Gregory Nazianzen and Gregory of Nyssa, were prominent Christian theologians whose lives spanned the greater part of the fourth century C.E. Although both were bishops and participated publicly in ecclesiastical affairs, both preferred the contemplative quiet of their country estates in their native Cappadocia.[3] The two Gregorys are notable for their contributions to Christian ascetic theory and to the development of a Platonized theology whose goal was the mystical union of the soul with God.[4] But they were also dreamers, and it is to their dreams that this chapter will look as clues to the ways these two men understood themselves in the context of their ascetic theological perspectives.

In the cultural and religious milieu in which these Cappadocians lived, described by Peter Brown as "a stern, ceremonious Christianity, firmly rooted in the continued life of great households," the ascetic embrace of sexual renunciation was a dramatic gesture that threatened noble, land-owning families such as the Gregorys belonged to with social extinction.[5] This "drift toward a social void,"[6] which thoroughly altered the defining characteristics of the human person as a social being, was matched by a

---

[1] Gregory Nazianzen, *Or.* 7.21 (*PG* 35.784B), trans. in *NPNF* 7:237.

[2] Gregory of Nyssa, *Vita Sanctae Macrinae* 15.15–19 (*PG* 46.976B), ed. and trans. Maraval, p. 193.

[3] For biographical information on Gregory Nazianzen, see Donald F. Winslow *The Dynamics of Salvation*, pp. 1–21, and Denis Molaise Meehan, trans., *Saint Gregory of Nazianzus: Three Poems*, pp. 1–21; on Gregory of Nyssa, see Jean Daniélou, "Le Mariage de Grégoire de Nysse et la chronologie de sa vie," pp. 71–78.

[4] The classic study of Gregory of Nyssa's mystical theology is by Jean Daniélou, *Platonisme et théologie mystique: Doctrine spirituelle de Saint Grégoire de Nysse;* for Gregory Nazianzen, see Winslow, *Dynamics of Salvation*, pp. 73–87, 179–99, and Brooks Otis, "The Throne and the Mountain," pp. 146–65.

[5] Brown, *The Body and Society,* p. 285.

[6] Ibid., p. 293.

similar drift, in the Gregorys' theology, toward a kind of metaphysical "void," in which the heretofore defining characteristics of an individual's sense of self-identity were altered theologically by the goal of "emptying" the self in a beatific vision of, or union with, God.[7]

Thus both asceticism and theology contributed to a destabilizing of the identity of the person, whose constitution became a problematic in the thought of both Gregorys. For both, "the present constitution of the human person represented a nadir of uncertainty";[8] as Gregory of Nyssa observed, "the life of man is at present subjected to abnormal conditions."[9] Brown has explained that, in the view of the Cappadocians, "Men and women were poised between an original, lost prototype of human nature, created by God *in His own image,* and revealed to the visible world in the shimmering 'angelic' majesty of Adam, and a fullness of humanity that would come about, through the restoration of Adam's first state, at the Resurrection."[10] Part of the dilemma implied by this condition of being poised between two paradigmatic states of human being at its fullest lay in finding a language appropriate to the expression of the human that was not tainted by the fallen condition in which human life is lived. It is in the context of this dilemma that the dreams of the two Gregorys assume their importance.

WE MEET our first dreamer in the midst of one of life's most poignant experiences, the moment when one struggles to come to terms with the death of a beloved person. The dreamer is Gregory Nazianzen, who wrote a funeral oration for his younger brother Caesarius after his death in 369 C.E.[11] It was in this oration that Gregory recorded the passage above in which he reveals that he had dreamed of his brother following his death. Gregory places the oneiric visions of his brother in the eschatological context of his own death, when he too will be in that beatific state signified by paradise. By his own report, his dreams of his brother appear to have mirrored the paradisal existence that he believes his dead brother now to be enjoying, and that he too longs for. The oneiric picture of the brilliant Caesarius is a construction of the human person that Gregory wishes to appropriate for himself; thus the dreams of his brother are as much about Gregory as they are about his brother.

---

[7] For Gregory Nazianzen's idea of *theiosis,* union with God, see the detailed discussion by Winslow, *Dynamics of Salvation,* pp. 179–99; for Gregory of Nyssa's idea of *theōria,* mystical vision or contemplation, see Daniélou, *Platonisme et théologie mystique de Saint Grégoire de Nysse,* pp. 134–35, 148–63, 175–77, 197–200.

[8] Brown, *The Body and Society,* p. 293.

[9] *Or. Catechetica* 5.45 (*PG* 45.24B), trans. in Brown, *The Body and Society,* p. 293.

[10] Brown, *The Body and Society,* pp. 293–94.

[11] On Caesarius, see Gregory Nazianzen, *De rebus suis* 2.1.1.165–229 (*PG* 37.982A–987A).

There is an oddity about Gregory's conviction that these dreams reflected the resurrected body in all its glory. Earlier in the funeral oration
for Caesarius, he described human life, the life of the living, as a "day of
mirrors and enigmas" in which it is possible to see only a "slender rivulet"
of the light that streams from God.[12] In one of his poems, he welcomes
death as a release from the earthbound condition of human knowing, in
which truth is apprehended "as if in a mirror reflected on the water's
surface."[13] Because the human mind cannot contain the "lightning flash"
of direct knowing, it must unhappily make do with a kind of impression-
istic knowledge that is itself composed of images that easily slip away.[14]
Given this view of the mediated state of human consciousness, how can
Gregory's view of his dreams of his brother's shining form be understood?
Were these dreams among those slender rivulets of light that somehow
shine through the enigmatic mirroring of ordinary human knowing, or
were they, too, only faint impressions of a truth that can never be fully
disclosed to a living person?

Gregory attributed the epistemological dilemma in which he found
himself in large part to the sheer physicality of the human condition. The
"thick covering of the flesh" is an obstacle to the full disclosure of divine
truth.[15] His goal was to press toward the life above, "deserting the earth
while we are still upon the earth," but the body formed a constant road-
block on that upward path.[16] So strong was the theologically induced
prejudice against physical being-in-the-world under which Gregory la-
bored that, in one of his long autobiographical poems, he characterized
the body and physical life with bestial metaphors. Life in the world is life
lived in "the mighty maw of the dragon," where one's spirit is "the prey of
Belial."[17] Bitter serpents biting, jackals swarming and snarling, wild animals with tusks, the sepia fish with its poisonous black vomit, herds of
swine, lions, bears, the entrails of Jonah's monster: all these describe what
it is like to live in a body.[18] The body impairs our gaze upon the holy. In a
striking story, now using vegetative rather than bestial images, Gregory
tells of an incident in his life when he was idly toying with a twig: "I drove
a thorn into my eyeball and made it all bloody."[19] The bloodied eye quickly

---

[12] *Or.* 7.17 (*PG* 35.776C), trans. *NPNF* 7:235.

[13] *Niobuli filii ad patrem* 2.2.4.85 (*PG* 37.1512A), trans. Winslow, *Dynamics of Salvation*, p. 170.

[14] *Or.* 45.3 (*PG* 36.625C–628B).

[15] Ibid. 28.4 (*PG* 36.32A), trans. *NPNF* 7:290.

[16] Ibid. 7.20 (*PG* 35.780BC), trans. *NPNF* 7:236.

[17] *De rebus suis* 2.1.1.344–45 (*PG* 37.996), trans. Meehan, p. 36.

[18] Ibid., lines 4 (lion), 5 (Jonah's monster), 21 (wild beasts), 183 (jackals), 191–92 (tusked animal), 235 and 619 (serpents), 498 (sepia fish), 585 (swine), 617 (bear) (*PG* 37.969–70, 971, 984, 987–88, 1007, 1013, 1016, trans. Meehan, pp. 25, 31, 33, 41, 44, 45).

[19] Ibid., lines 330–32 (*PG* 37.995), trans. Meehan, pp. 35–36.

becomes for Gregory a metaphor for the bloodied vision of human life, where insight is damaged by physicality.

One of the reasons that the body damages insight is that the sign of the flesh is differentiation; embodied life is a life in which difference reigns in such divisions as male and female, slave and free, and so on.[20] Original unity has been fragmented, and thus shows itself in language as well. As Gregory laments, "It is difficult to conceive God, but to define him in words is an impossibility."[21] As a tool of life in the flesh, words can be just as misleading, for seeming to say something "real," as the body, which seems real in its own tangible way. Yet it is all an illusion. Using dream as a negative metaphor, Gregory Nazianzen wrote in one oration that "we are unsubstantial dreams, impalpable visions, like the flight of a passing bird . . . a flower that quickly blooms and quickly fades."[22] And, in another discourse, he observed that, apart from sin and paradise, all else is a "dream-vision, making sport of realities, and a series of phantasms which lead the soul astray."[23]

Given Gregory's view of the embodied condition of human life as, on the one hand, illusory, and, on the other, all-too-bestially physical, his report of his dreams of his brother Caesarius is intriguing. Gregory reports that he has seen a brilliant and heavenly Caesarius in his dreams, a figure "pictured thus by my desire, if not by the very truth." Yet, what Gregory "saw" in dreams was not the real body of his dead brother but a phantasmal body, an oneiric body constructed by desire. However, this body of oneiric fantasy was a picture of Caesarius "no longer in exile"; this was a paradisal body. The dream-body was, somehow, no longer the alien body of earthly exile but a body in truth, a heavenly body. On the other hand, Gregory's phrase, "pictured thus *by my desire,* if not by the very truth," suggests that the dream-body is a fabrication of the dreamer's own desire, a picture that fills a lack in his life. Yet this reading is tempered by the phrase that follows, "pictured by my desire, *if not by the very truth,*" a phrase that suggests that the dreams may well image that paradigmatic "other" world of Adamic existence.

Still, Gregory's phrasing leaves his understanding of the status of these dreams undecidable. Did his dreams of Caesarius show the very truth, or were they constructions of his desire that only approximated the truth? The dreams were visions of a brilliant body signifying paradisal existence —but they can also be seen as examples of the ascetic paradox of the return of the rejected body as sign.[24] From Gregory's perspective, when his

---

[20] *Or.* 7.23 (*PG* 35.785C), trans. *NPNF* 7:237.

[21] Ibid. 28.4 (*PG* 36.29C), trans. *NPNF* 7:289.

[22] Ibid. 7.19 (*PG* 35.777C–D), trans. *NPNF* 7:235.

[23] Ibid. 18.42 (*PG* 35.1041B), trans. *NPNF* 7:268.

[24] For a discussion of the theme of ascetic use of the body as signifier in the writings of Jerome, a contemporary of the two Gregorys, see Chapter 8 above.

brother was alive in his physical body, he was in exile, and the mark of exile was precisely the body. In the dreams, the body returns, but now it speaks a paradisal language of that perfected heavenly "otherness" that aided the reformulation of the identity of the dreamer. I emphasize the dreams' role in reformulating the identity of the *dreamer*, because these dreams were not about Caesarius; they were about what *Gregory* does and shall see. They picture in imaginal terms what Gregory is *not* but deeply desires to be: no longer in exile.

Leaving Gregory Nazianzen in exile for the moment, I will turn to the other Gregory, Gregory of Nyssa, whose dream of the dead body of his sister Macrina also participates in the ascetic paradox of the signifying return of the body.

The time was 379 or 380 C.E., some ten years after Gregory Nazianzen had dreamed of his brother.[25] Gregory of Nyssa was on the road with the intent of visiting his sister at the community of celibate women that she had established on the family estate at Annesi. He had not seen Macrina for many years, and when he was only one day's travel away from her convent, he had a worrisome dream. In his biography of his sister, he wrote, "I saw in dream a vision that made me apprehensive for the future. It seemed that I was holding in my hands the relics of martyrs, and there flowed from them such a bright beam of light, like that from a spotless mirror placed facing the sun, that my eyes were blinded by its brilliance. This vision occurred three times during that night, and although I was not able to interpret clearly the enigma of the dream, I nonetheless sensed some sorrow for my soul. . . ."[26] While traveling the next day, Gregory learned that Macrina was seriously ill; in fact, when he arrived, she was laid out on the ground, dying.[27]

Despite the severity of her physical condition, which Gregory compares with the disease-ravaged body of Job, Macrina "refreshed her body as though with dew" and conversed with Gregory about the destiny of the soul.[28] Finally she suggested that her brother get some rest to recover from his long journey; Gregory, however, could not sleep. He wrote, "What I had seen seemed to unravel the enigma of the dream. The sight set before me was in truth the remains of a holy martyr, the remains of one who had been dead to sin, but shining with the presence of the Holy Spirit."[29] In his dream, Gregory had seen himself holding relics of martyrs, fragments of dead bodies that gleam brilliantly, charged with the power of the religious devotion that had once animated them. Upon beholding his dying

[25] For a discussion of the date of Gregory's visit with his sister, see Pierre Maraval, trans. and ed., *Grégoire de Nysse: Vie de Sainte Macrine*, pp. 57–67.

[26] *Vita S. Macrinae* 15.14–21 (*PG* 46.976A–B), ed. and trans. Maraval, p. 193.

[27] Ibid., 15.23–17.3 (*PG* 46.976B–D), ed. Maraval, pp. 193–97.

[28] Ibid., 17.9–18.22 (*PG* 46.977B–C), ed. and trans. Maraval, pp. 197–201.

[29] Ibid., 19.11–15 (*PG* 46.980A), ed. and trans. Maraval, p. 203.

sister, he understood that the dream referred to her: the relics were her glowing bones. Thus the dream not only predicted her death but also showed her translation to heavenly status in a transformed body, fragmentary though it was. The spell of this dream also influenced the way in which Gregory saw his sister after her death. After her body was prepared for burial, it was covered by a dark cloak; yet, Gregory reports, "she shone even in that dark clothing, no doubt because the divine power added such grace to her body that, just as in the vision in my dream, beams of light seemed to shine out from her beauty."[30] Like Gregory Nazianzen's dreams of his brother, Gregory of Nyssa's dream of his sister allowed him to see through a dead body to a body that was lively in another register.

Gregory knew that there was something special about his older sister. In his biography of her, he reports that his mother, Emmelia, had had a dream about Macrina when her labor pains began. In the dream, repeated, like Gregory's, three times, an angelic figure addressed the child as Thecla; upon awakening, Emmelia knew that the dream prefigured the reality in which her child would live, and Thecla became Macrina's "secret name."[31] Thecla, a legendary figure whose cult was widespread in Asia Minor by the fourth century, was a patron saint of the ascetic life, especially among women.[32] Thus Emmelia's dream was a mirror of the ascetic vocation of her daughter, herself a mirror of the great Thecla, just as Gregory's dream mirrored the beatific result of that vocation.

Brown has remarked that, for Gregory, Macrina's body was "the untarnished mirror of a soul that had caught, at last, the blinding light of the *katharotés*, the radiant purity, of God."[33] Yet despite all of his metaphors of light, Gregory seems reluctant to let Macrina's body disappear in a blaze of glory. He insists that her dead body was a sign of that paradigmatic radiance that marks the true identity of the human, but the body is still there as a sign. About Macrina while she was alive, he wrote that "it was as if an angel had providentially taken human form, an angel with no attachment to or affinity for life in the flesh"; Macrina had not become ensnared by "the passions of the flesh."[34] He further describes her life as one poised on the boundary between "human life and bodiless nature."[35] In Gregory's view, so close had Macrina come to that drastic transformation of identity

[30] Ibid., 32.8–12 (*PG* 46.992C–D), ed. and trans. Maraval, p. 247.

[31] Ibid., 2.21–34 (*PG* 46.961B), ed. and trans. Maraval, pp. 145–49; such annunciatory dreams were common in late antiquity; see above, p. 208 and, for a list of parallels of dreams sent to pregnant women, see Maraval, *Vie de Sainte Macrine,* p. 146n1.

[32] On the cult of St. Thecla in Asia Minor, see Dagron, *Vie et Miracles de Sainte Thècle,* pp. 55–79; Maraval, *Vie de Sainte Macrine,* p. 146n.2; see the discussion above, p. 117.

[33] Brown, *The Body and Society,* p. 300.

[34] *Vita S. Macrinae* 22.27–31 (*PG* 46.981D–984A), ed. and trans. Maraval, p. 215.

[35] Ibid., 11.34–35 (*PG* 46.972A), ed. and trans. Maraval, p. 179. On Gregory's idea of the *methorios,* the boundary, see Jean Daniélou, "*Methorios:* La Notion de confins chez Grégoire de Nysse," pp. 161–87.

from the human to the angelic that she appears to have achieved what Gregory Nazianzen described as deserting the earth while still on it. As a shimmering object that mediated the gap between the paradigmatic worlds of Adam and the resurrection, Macrina's body provided a glimpse of the transformation that all might hope for. Her body was thus a formal analogue to Gregory's dream, itself a mediatorial vehicle that initiated Gregory, briefly, into a form of consciousness in which fleshly eyesight is "blinded" by beatific vision. Indeed, Macrina's body and Gregory's dream can hardly be separated, because it was the dream that had given him "eyes to see" the truth of his sister's body.

When he was not dreaming, however, Gregory's view of bodies was not usually so generous. In his essay *On the Making of the Human Being*, Gregory tries to envision the human person as a harmonious blend of spiritual and physical parts. Using the metaphor of a musician playing a lyre, he explains that as long as the lyre, the body, is ruled by the mind, the musician, the body can be viewed positively; it is only when the mind debases itself in following physical desires that the notion of "flesh" assumes a negative connotation.[36] Nonetheless, our bodies are not like the body of the archetypal Adam before the fall, a body untouched by the brutish physicality that characterizes the bodies of the human beings now.[37] For Gregory, it was difficult to maintain the distinction between thoughts of the flesh and the flesh itself because the tug of the senses was capable of dragging the mind down to bodily concerns so easily. In his treatise *On Virginity*, the distinction tends to collapse as he describes human physicality as "earthly wretchedness" and, like Gregory Nazianzen, he uses a metaphor of injured eyesight to depict the sense of estrangement that the body inflicts on us.[38] Where Gregory Nazianzen had used bestial images, however, Gregory of Nyssa uses images of dirt: the "filth of the flesh" now covers what was once a divine image, Adam, who in his original state "looked freely upon the face of God" and mirrored that brilliance.[39]

Yet, despite this rather alarming view of human physicality, Gregory's real despair centered not on the literal body but on the fall of human beings into time. As Brown has persuasively argued, Gregory thought that for the archetypal Adam, time had been infinitely open-ended, whereas now it was measured by a person's lifetime, with death marking the end.[40] Whereas Adam could have lived clear-sightedly into a "future" with no

---

[36] *De hom. op.* 8.4–12.14 (PG 44.144D–164D). See also Gregory's *De virg.* 13 (PG 46.376D–381B), where it is the thought of the flesh rather than the body itself that is problematic.

[37] See *De hom. op.* 16.7, 9 (PG 44.181A–C) and 12.9 (PG 44.161C).

[38] *De virg.* 12.4 (PG 46.369D–372A); see Brown, *The Body and Society*, pp. 300–301.

[39] Ibid. 11–12 (PG 46.363B–375C), trans. Callahan, pp. 41–46.

[40] Brown, *The Body and Society*, p. 297.

end, human beings after Adam were condemned to a lifetime of anxieties regarding the future. To stave off those anxieties, especially anxieties about death, human beings placed their hopes—and also their sense of identity—on their bodies, in the form of marriage and children: "the most distinctive trait of a humanity caught in 'tainted' time," Brown writes, was "the obsession with physical continuity."[41] This kind of continuity was not satisfying, because it implied that a person's sense of self was rooted in the particulars of concrete history, producing a materialistic model of self-perception rather than a spiritual one.[42]

The glowing body of his virginal sister was so important to Gregory because it was a sign that a momentous shift in the constitution of the human person with respect to time was possible. Time understood as a series of lurching movements from one sensuous gratification to the next could be voided by taking off the "torn garment" of the historically constituted self.[43] What kind of "person" emerged from this divestment? Gregory's picture of Macrina offers some clues. Both in the *Life of Macrina* and in the essay *On the Soul and Resurrection*, which is structured as the dialogue that occurred between Gregory and Macrina as she lay dying, Macrina is presented as one for whom the grounds for the apprehension of meaning have shifted so dramatically away from tangible and personal concerns that she has become a living abstraction, her earthy being absorbed almost completely into theological ideas about the soul.[44] At the very moment of her painful dying, she is pictured as conversing theologically in a manner appropriate to Gregory's construction of her as a near-angel. For some, this would be a scene of terrible poignancy, but not for Gregory; this represents his view of the person at its finest. In Gregory's presentation of his sister, it is hard to recognize her as a "self" with an "identity" in any conventional sense of the word, for, as Stephen Crites has remarked, "angels do not have biographies."[45]

Were it not for his dream of Macrina, Gregory's construction of her as an image of the human person whose "self" has become a kind of "no-self" would be uncompromising in its austerity. Gregory's ascetic theology tended toward the production of a view of the person that was radically ahistorical. However, in the dream, she still has a body, and even though it is a body distilled to its structural form, its bones, it nonetheless functions as a signifying vestige of Macrina's identity as a recognizable human indi-

[41] Ibid., p. 298.

[42] See *De virg.* 20 (*PG* 46.397B–400D) and *De an. et res.* (*PG* 46. 12A–B), trans. Callahan, pp. 198–99.

[43] *De an. et res.* (*PG* 46.158B), trans. Callahan, p. 266.

[44] *Vita S. Macrinae* 17.21–30, 18.1–22, 22.1–40 (*PG* 46.977A–B, 981A–985A), ed. Maraval, pp. 199–201, 213–17.

[45] Stephen Crites, "Angels We Have Heard," p. 41.

vidual, a person with a name, because, when Gregory actually sees his dying sister, he knows that the glowing relics were images of her, and not someone else.

Gregory seems to have been consistent in his attempt to view martyrs' relics as sites for the conjunction of personal and impersonal images of human identity. In his *Encomium on St. Theodore,* he wrote about relics that "those who behold them embrace, as it were, the living body in full flower, they bring eye, mouth, ear, all the senses into play, and there, shedding tears of reverence and passion, they address the martyr their prayers of intercession as though he were present."[46] Bones, clearly, can be just as sensuous as a real body, but the difference between the two is that relics are signifiers of a person who is both absent and present at once, or perhaps one should say, a person who is neither absent nor present. It was in this mediatorial gap between absence and presence, the gap expressed by Gregory's phrase "*as though* he were present," that the body continued to function as a magnet for expressing views of identity in an ascetic context.

It is significant that Gregory chose to reveal the relic-like state of his sister by narrating his dream. Like relics, and like the almost-angelic identity of the accomplished ascetic, dreams are neither ploddingly historical nor transparently spiritual; rather, they mediate that sense of "time that is no-time" by using images. In fact, such an oneiric image had set Gregory himself on that path out of conventional historical time on which Macrina had traveled so far. In a panegyric to the Forty Martyrs, a group of soldiers who were killed during the Roman persecution of Christians in the early fourth century, Gregory recalls attending a festal occasion in their honor. Instead of keeping watch during the vigil, Gregory fell asleep. He dreamed that the forty martyrs rushed at him threateningly, shaking switches at him and admonishing him for his inattention to his religious duty.[47] For Gregory, this dream was a turning point; he set himself to follow the contemplative life unswervingly. It appears that this dream enabled Gregory to forge a new sense of his own identity, an identity in which the qualifying words "his own" would slowly, he hoped, drop away.

It is curious that Gregory placed so much emphasis on the significations of his dreams, because in his theory of dreaming he is ambivalent about their epistemological value. When viewed as products of physiological processes, they are "fantastic nonsense," but when the mind is allowed a role in their production, their enigmatic images can be trusted to yield a glimmer of the timeless truth of human desire.[48] Perhaps this recourse to dreams is not surprising, because Gregory of Nyssa, like Gregory Nazianzen, had difficulty finding a language appropriate to the expression

[46] *Encomium in Sanctum Theodorum* (PG 46.740B), trans. Brown, *Society and the Holy in Late Antiquity,* p. 7.
[47] *In quadraginta martyres* (PG 46.785A–B).
[48] For a discussion of Gregory's oneiric theory, see above, pp. 47–51.

of the ascetic vision of the self that was not tainted by the illusory world of history and time.

In the context of the autobiography of an ascetic life, dreaming became an important language for the articulation of an "other" sense of the self. Gregory of Nyssa's mystical theology, too, appears to have fallen under the spell of the dream. In the kind of theological language that attempts to express the linguistic analogue to the glowing bones of Macrina, the oxymoron predominates as the privileged vehicle of meaning. Such oxymorons as "sober drunkenness" and "luminous darkness" appear frequently in his mystical writings, but Gregory also created a new oxymoron, "waking sleep," which has been considered among the most important of his expressions of the mystical life.[49] Just as dreams contributed to the emptying out of the conventionally understood self, so paradoxical linguistic constructions use words against themselves to express a view of the human being in those ecstatic moments of contemplative seeing in which temporality gives way to the timeless expanses of eternity. As Jean Daniélou has observed, the oxymoron "waking sleep" contains a negative element,[50] but it is one that is nonetheless revelatory of a transformed sense of human identity.

Having rejected any kind of literal grounds for constructing a view of human identity, Gregory turned to paradox and dream, both imaginal discourses that enabled the literal to return as sign. There was still a self to signify, even if that self was recognizable not in conventional biographical terms but in oneiric image and linguistic paradox. In his willingness to allow such images to function as mirrors of identity, Gregory was unlike his ascetic colleague Evagrius, for whom images, and especially the images of dreams, were usually signs of a soul whose mirror was spotted with passionate involvements.[51] Envisioning the true human being as one who had divested the inner self of such attachments to history, Evagrius appears to have

[49] See the discussion by Daniélou, *Platonisme et théologie mystique*, pp. 274–84.

[50] Ibid., p. 281.

[51] For a thorough discussion of Evagrius' views of dreams, see F. Refoulé, "Rêves et vie spirituelle d'après Évagre le Pontique," pp. 470–516, esp. pp. 488–97; see also Evagrius' *Praktikos* 55 (*PG* 40.1247A):

Natural processes which occur in sleep without accompanying images of a stimulating nature are, to a certain measure, indications of a healthy soul. But images that are distinctly formed are a clear indication of sickness. You may be certain that the faces one sees in dreams are, when they occur as ill-defined images, symbols of former affective experiences. Those which are seen clearly, on the other hand, indicate wounds that are still fresh;

see also 64 (*PG* 40.1231A [#36 in *PG*]): "The proof of *apatheia* is had when the spirit begins to see its own light, when it remains in a state of tranquility in the presence of the images it has during sleep. . . ." and 65 (*PG* 40.1231B [#37 in *PG*]): "The spirit that possesses health is the one which has no images of the things of this world at the time of prayer" (trans. Bamberger, pp. 31, 33–34).

242 PART II: DREAMERS

rejected any autobiographical impulse whatsoever. He had crossed the boundary on which Gregory was poised into a radical emptying of the self into a vast but peaceful nothing that is very different from the glowing bones of Macrina's angelic transformation.[52]

Like Gregory of Nyssa, Gregory Nazianzen was more willing than Evagrius to imagine that dreams had a useful role to play in the transformation of the person. In fact, Gregory Nazianzen was an enthusiastic dreamer. Despite his occasional literary use of dream as a negative metaphor denoting the illusory qualities of embodied life,[53] Gregory often looked to actual dreams as vehicles of meaning and as windows through which one might look for images of authentic senses of human identity. By Gregory's report, he was the child of dreamers—perhaps it was from his mother and father that he derived his own trust in dreams.

Gregory's father had not been a Christian when he married, a situation that caused increasing distress for his wife, who was a committed member of the church.[54] With prayers and reproaches, she urged him to convert. In his funeral oration for his father, Gregory records the following dream:

> My father's salvation was aided jointly by his reason, which gradually accepted the healing remedy, and jointly by the vision of dreams, a benefit which God often bestows on a soul worthy of salvation. What was the vision? He thought that he was singing, what he had never done before, although his wife often prayed and made supplication, these words from the psalms of David: "I rejoiced at the things that were said to me, we shall go into the house of the Lord" [Ps. 121.1]. The psalm was strange and with its singing came desire. When his wife heard it, having now gained her prayer, she seized the opportunity, interpreting the vision most happily and truthfully.[55]

Thus was Gregory's father convinced to become a catechumen. It is interesting that this converting dream is viewed by Gregory as the climactic moment that brought a gradual process of reasoning to fruition. In this passage, dreams are constructed as divine gifts that enable a person to see the nature of his true identity.

Gregory's mother was not only skilled in the interpretation of dreams, as the above passage suggests; she was a great dreamer herself. The dreams that Gregory attributes to her all concern himself. Like Macrina's mother Emmelia, Gregory Nazianzen's mother Nonna had an oneiric premonition about her son-to-be. As Gregory explains, Nonna was anxious to provide the family with a son and prayed that her wish might be fulfilled. His

---

[52] See *Praktikos* 33–39 (*PG* 40.1231A–C) on *apatheia*.
[53] See p. 235 above.
[54] *Or.* 18.11 (*PG* 35.997B–D).
[55] Ibid. 18.12 (*PG* 35.1000A–B), trans. McCauley, p. 128.

account of this dream, which forms part of one of his autobiographical poems, continues:

> God granted the favor, and in her great desire, failing not in loving prayer, she actually anticipated it. There came to her a gracious foretaste, a vision containing the shadow of her request. My likeness and my name appeared clearly to her, the work of a dream by night. Then I was born to them, the gift of God the giver if worthy of the prayer: if not, it was because of my own shortcomings.[56]

This dream of himself as a divinely promised child seems to have been important to Gregory's understanding of himself, for he repeats it, using different terminology, in another autobiographical poem.

> When I was delivered from my mother's womb, she offered me to you [God]. Ever since the day she had yearned to nurse a manchild on her knee, she imitated the cry of the holy Anna. "O King Christ, that I might have a boy for you to keep within your fold. May a son be the flourishing fruit of my birth pangs." And you, O God, granted her prayer. There followed the holy dream which gave her the name. In due time you gave a son. She dedicated me as a new Samuel (if I were worthy of the name) in the temple.[57]

Described as shadows that nevertheless speak clearly, these dreams are holy events in Gregory's view. They give a sense of his mother's character, but more especially they give a sense of Gregory's view of himself. He derives not only his name but his very being from dreams, in which he is constructed religiously as possessed of a prophetic scriptural persona ("a new Samuel"). While he constantly gives voice to doubts about whether his life has conformed to that oneiric picture of himself, the dreams of his mother seem to function as images of reassurance. They are the nodal points upon which his autobiographical identity is constructed. The ascetic Gregory, dedicated from birth to the priesthood, did not shrink from autobiographical writing. Yet the poetic form in which he cast his autobiographical reminiscences, as well as the dreams recorded there that express the essence of his identity, match each other in their construction of the human person by means of images, images that mediate the gap between literal history and spiritual desire. Again, the ascetic self finds its anchor in allusive poetic forms that provide a mediating ground for understanding that self.

For Gregory, the salvific function of dreams was one of their most notable characteristics. Like generations of dreamers and dream-theorists before him, he accepted without question the cultural construction of dreams that emphasized their predictive and healing value. In a section of the funeral oration for his father in which he narrates miraculous occurrences in the

---

[56] *De vita sua* 2.1.11.70–81 (*PG* 37.1034–35), trans. Meehan, p. 79.
[57] *De rebus suis* 2.1.1.425–32 (*PG* 37.1001–2), trans. Meehan, p. 39.

lives of both his parents in which he was himself involved, Gregory recorded several dreams that adhere to the Graeco-Roman view of this role of dreams. Gregory remembers a time when he was sailing from Alexandria, Egypt, to Greece. The ship, caught in a storm, was in danger of capsizing, and all aboard were fearful for their lives. Gregory was fearful not only for life literally but also spiritually, because he had not yet been baptized. His parents, he continues, suffered with him, because they had seen his predicament in a dream: "They brought help from land, calming the waves by prayer, as afterwards we learned upon reckoning the time when I returned home. This was also revealed to me in a salutary sleep which I at length experienced when the storm abated a little."[58] As if the double dream of his parents and his own reciprocal dream were not enough, Gregory reveals that this event had yielded a third dream:

> Another of my fellow voyagers, a boy very well disposed and dear to me and deeply concerned for me, under the circumstances, thought he saw my mother walk upon the sea and seize the ship and with no great effort draw it to land. And this vision was believed, for the sea began to grow calm, and we quickly arrived at Rhodes, without experiencing any great distress in the meantime.[59]

Here Gregory's mother assumes the form of an autonomous dream-figure, familiar from writers as disparate in time and temperament as Homer and Augustine,[60] who saves her son in dream just as she had oneirically conceived him. Once again, Gregory feels himself to have been saved by dreams for his religious vocation, because he concludes this story by noting that "we promised ourselves to God if we were saved, and, on being saved, we gave ourselves to him."[61]

In the same section of this oration, Gregory records a final dream of his mother in which he himself plays the salvific role. Telling of a time when Nonna was seriously ill, Gregory says that God healed her by sending the following dream:

> She thought she saw me, her darling—for not even in dreams did she prefer any other of us—come up to her suddenly in the night with a basket of purest white bread, and after blessing and signing it with the cross according to my custom, feed and comfort her, and that she then recovered her strength.[62]

Recovering the next day, Nonna thought that her son had actually administered the Eucharistic food to her during the night. Gregory, however, equates the dream with reality—"this vision of the night was a thing of

---

[58] *Or.* 18.31 (*PG* 35.1024B–1025A), trans. McCauley, pp. 144–45.
[59] Ibid. 18.31 (*PG* 35.1025A), trans. McCauley, p. 145.
[60] See above, pp. 17–19, 41–42.
[61] *Or.* 18.31 (*PG* 35.1025A), trans. McCauley, p. 145.
[62] Ibid. 18.30 (*PG* 35.1023A), trans. McCauley, p. 144.

reality."[63] For him, it was the *oneiric* act that had healed, not a literal one. Having once spent time in a monastery on the grounds of the incubatory cultic center of St. Thecla in Seleucia, Gregory would probably have been familiar with the Christian appropriation of Asclepian oneiric therapy.[64] It is certain, at the very least, that he viewed his own oneiric persona as having had a healing effect on his mother's body.

It is significant that, even with regard to the dreams that drew on conventional cultural associations of dreams with prediction and healing, Gregory was most interested in their images as mirrors of spiritual identity. He looked to the imaginal language of dreams as an autobiographical resource. Oneiric discourse was useful, especially in the context of Gregory's asceticism, because it was a discourse in which an "other" self was projected on the screen of consciousness. Dreams could reflect an autobiographical "I" that was distanced from the "I" of messy historical entanglements. In his own life, Gregory located the mess of history not only in the fact of having a body, but also in his entanglements in ecclesiastical affairs, most notably the bitter battles with Arian Christians during his brief tenure as bishop of Constantinople in 379–381 C.E.[65] Perhaps it is no wonder that Gregory dreamed of a time when he would be like his brother Caesarius, glowingly free of the turmoil of this life.

There is one more autobiographical dream of Gregory's that I wish to present. A return to his ascetic understanding of the body as sign will provide a context for what was undoubtedly the most spectacular of all his dreams. In the passage of his funeral oration for Caesarius that concludes with his dreams of his brother, Gregory engaged in theological speculation about the resurrected body. He wrote that at death the soul is released from the body, a "darkening element" that had functioned as a "hard prison," binding the "wing of the intellect" with fetters.[66] Once aloft, the soul "enters into the possession of the blessedness reserved for it such as it has already conceived in imagination"—including especially the oneiric imagination with which this section concludes.[67] Gregory continues:

> Shortly afterwards, [the soul] takes up its own related flesh, united with which it meditated on heavenly topics, from the earth which both gave it and was

[63] Ibid.

[64] Gregory retreated to the center of St. Thecla in order to avoid being ordained bishop of the small church at Sasima to which his friend Basil of Caesarea had appointed him. See *De vita sua* 2.1.11, lines 547–49 (*PG* 37.1067A), trans. Meehan, p. 92. On the connection between Asclepian oneiric therapy and St. Thecla, see above, p. 117.

[65] See Gregory's *De se ipso et de episcopis* 2.1.12 (*PG* 37.1166–1227), trans. Meehan, pp. 49–74, and *De vita sua* 2.1.11.562–1871 (*PG* 37.1068–1160), trans. Meehan, pp. 93–128.

[66] *Or.* 7.21 (*PG* 35.781B–C), trans. McCauley, p. 22.

[67] Ibid. 7.21 (*PG* 35.781C).

entrusted with it, and, in a way which God knows who bound them together and separated them, [the flesh] is joint heir with [the soul] of supernal glory.

And just as such a soul shared its sufferings because of its natural union with its flesh, so also it shares its own joys with it, having assumed [the flesh] wholly into itself and having become with it one spirit and mind and good, life having absorbed the mortal and transitory element.[68]

Gregory, whose theology was geared toward the recovery by the human being of its divine image,[69] condemned one kind of body, the imprisoning body of earth, only to petition heavenly pleasure through the sign of that very body, now transformed, now "related." But his only access in the present to that imagined theological body of bliss was through the imagistic discourse of the bodies of his dreams.

Frequently in his writing, Gregory indicated his longing for access to the language of God, the proper language of human beings from which they have been separated.[70] Again and again, the sign of that separation is the body, which makes human life so weak and ponderously earthbound.[71] Gregory described his rejection of life in the world as bishop of Constantinople and his subsequent return to ascetic seclusion as follows: "I was running to reach God; thus I climbed the mountain and penetrated the cloud, going inside away from matter and material things, concentrating on my inner self as much as possible; but when I looked, I caught a view only of God's back, and that scarcely."[72] Giving a negative turn to the biblical scene in which Moses is permitted to see God's back (Ex. 33.20–22), Gregory felt this sight to be a mark of deprivation, not blessing as in Moses' case. This knowledge, he says, exists like a shadow in water—yet his description of this moment of mystical approach shows the strength of his desire to be other, to be remade and allowed expression in another form of identity.

"I am connected with the world below, and likewise with God; I am connected with the flesh, and likewise with the spirit."[73] When he was not dreaming, Gregory felt himself to be split between two discourses, and it made him feel estranged from his own true idiom. The following passage

---

[68] Ibid. 7.21 (*PG* 35.781C–784A).

[69] The following observation by Winslow, *Dynamics of Salvation,* p. 88, is a good indicator of Gregory's position: "The *theiosis* of Christ's human nature is not the disappearance of his humanity or the total absorption of the lower into the higher . . . rather, it is the participation of the human nature in the divine, a participation so complete, so intimate and interpenetrating, that to call the 'deified' human nature 'God' is not a semantic trick but a description of reality."

[70] See pp. 234–35 above.

[71] See *Or.* 28.3 (*PG* 36.29A–C), trans. *NPNF* 7:289.

[72] Ibid. 28.3 (*PG* 36.29A), trans.*NPNF* 7:289.

[73] Ibid. 7.23 (*PG* 35.785B), trans. McCauley, p. 24.

from one of his long autobiographical poems makes this feeling of estrangement clear:

> So came I then into this life below
> Molded of mire—ah me—of that low synthesis
> That dominates us or barely yields to our control.
> But still I take it as a pledge of what is best—
> My very birth!
> No right have I to carp.
> But at my birth, I immediately became an alien
> In alienation best.
> For unto God I'm given as some lamb, some sacrificial calf,
> Offering noble and adorned with mind.[74]

Picturing himself as molded of mire and of mind, Gregory feels that he was an alien at birth. Intriguing in the light of Gregory's description of himself is a statement by the contemporary philosopher and psychologist Jacques Lacan: "A certificate tells me that I was born. I repudiate this certificate: I am not a poet, but a poem. A poem that is being written, even if it looks like a subject."[75] Lacan's denial of the subject—that is, his repudiation of a substantially constituted self—along with his view of the self as a poem in the making, sounds very like Gregory's poetically phrased autobiographical desire, expressed from within the depths of his alienation, to be rewritten in terms of the other.

Indeed, following his most significant dream in terms of his ascetic desire, Gregory reported that he had sensed the death of himself as a subject: "I died to the world and the world to me, and I am become a living corpse as devoid of strength as a dreamer. Since that day my life is elsewhere."[76] The dream that follows is the dream that led Gregory to reconceive his identity in ascetic terms. It forms part of one of his autobiographical poems:

> Two women appeared to me, brilliant in clothing shining with light, virgins, and they came close to me. Both were beautiful but neglectful of the usual adornments of women—no jewelry, no cosmetics, no silk, nothing of those things invented by men for the appearance of women in order to excite passion. Veils shrouded their heads in shadows; their eyes were lowered to the ground, their cheeks colored with the rosy tint of modesty; they were like dewy rosebuds, their lips silent. It was a great joy to contemplate them, since I was sure they were more-than-human. Because I had charmed them, they gave me kisses

---

[74] *De vita sua* 2.1.11.82–90 (*PG* 37.1035–36), trans. by Otis, "The Throne and the Mountain," p. 150.

[75] Jacques Lacan, *The Four Fundamental Concepts of Psycho-Analysis*, viii. I thank Professor David L. Miller of Syracuse University for bringing this quotation to my attention.

[76] *De rebus suis* 2.1.1.202–4 (*PG* 37.985), trans. Meehan, pp. 31–32.

with their lips, as though I were a beloved child. I asked who they were, and they replied, Chastity and Wisdom, who lead humans close to Christ, rejoicing in the celestial beauty reserved for virgins. "Come child," they said, "unite your spirit to ours and bring your flaming torch to join ours so that we can take you across the sky and place you in the splendor of the Trinity." With these words they raised themselves into the sky and I watched as they flew.[77]

Along with his mother's dream about his birth, this dream was a foundational sign of Gregory's sense of himself. He remarks in his "Epitaph for Himself" that "a fervent aspiration for purity was in me aroused by a vision of the night; of all these things Christ was the author."[78] The dream showed Gregory that his life was a poetic text being written, not by himself, but by that divine "other" in whose image he desired to be remade.

This, then, was the dream that placed Gregory's life elsewhere. In the autobiographical poem in which this dream is recorded, Gregory commented on his experience of the dream that his heart was ravished by the beauty of its radiant virginity.[79] From the vantage point of his later years, he looked back and saw that this dream had been the beginning of his profession of asceticism.[80] Into the midst of what he characterized as a hostile life came a dream of the soul's desire, tantalizing in its call to transformation. The oneiric images of Chastity and Wisdom are analogues of the oneiric image of his brother Caesarius as mirrors of the self-identity that Gregory thought was appropriate for an ascetic. Like the oneiric Caesarius, they are recognizably human—they have bodies and names—yet they are also more-than-human in their mirroring of an altered sense of what constitutes human being.

Unlike the image of Caesarius, however, the two female images of this dream, with their flaming torches and dewy lips, carry a strong erotic charge that makes their use as ascetic signifiers rather ironic. Gregory's association of these two images with rosebuds is a key to their erotic construction, because the rose was preeminently the flower of Aphrodite, patron of sensuous physical love.[81] Thus this dream, with its erotic female images that are taken to signify the ascetic self, would seem to be the return, with a vengeance, of the rejected body as sign. However, as Geoffrey Harpham has observed, "asceticism is essentially a meditation on, even an enactment of,

[77] *De animae suae calamitatibus carmen lugubre* 2.1.45.229–66 (*PG* 37.1369–72), here adapted from a translation by Carmen-Marie Szymusiak-Affholder, "Psychologie et histoire dans la rêve initial de Grégoire la théologien," pp. 302–3.
[78] *Epitaphium sui ipsius* 2.1.92.5–6 (*PG* 37.1447–1448), trans. by Winslow, *Dynamics of Salvation*, p. 14.
[79] *De animae suae calamitatibus carmen lugubre* 2.1.45.265–66 (*PG* 37.1372).
[80] Ibid. 2.1.45.230 (*PG* 37.1369). See the discussion by Szymusiak-Affholder, "Psychologie et histoire," p. 309.
[81] See Charles Joret, *La Rose dans l'Antiquité et au Moyen Age*, pp. 47–50.

desire. . . . While asceticism recognizes that desire stands between human life and perfection, it also understands that desire is the only means of achieving perfection, and that the movement toward ideality is necessarily a movement of desire."[82] Thus the erotic images of Gregory's dream can be understood as signs that articulate the ascetic desire for the movement toward ideality to which Harpham refers. Further, the rose was often used by Christians as a symbol both of martyrdom and of virginity.[83] And the magically transformative quality of the rose is well attested in Apuleius' *Metamorphoses*, in which the hero Lucius regains his humanity from his descent into bestial nature by eating a rose.[84] Like the fictional Lucius, the human Gregory also hoped for transformation, and the rosy-figured images of his dream fueled his ascetic desire for release from the bestial body of his temporal self. These oneiric images, with their erotically chaste character, are appropriate vehicles for the paradoxical sense of self that developed in the thought of ascetics like Gregory.

Gregory patterned the rest of his life on the basis of this dream. Yet he was not healed. In the dream, the women flew away, leaving him ravished by the appeal of their message. His conventionally constituted identity had been shattered by the dream but, although the poetic form of his autobiographical writings suggests that he did come to see himself as a poem being written by that desired "other," he remained distant from the self of his desire— except in his dreams.

It is no wonder that the two Gregorys dreamed. In dreams, those oneiric spaces on the border between the physical and the spiritual, they found a language that made expressions of ascetic self-identity possible. Like the mythic Narcissus, wondering at the watery depths of his own reflection, the Gregorys were grappling with a fundamental human question, "Who am I?" Dreams were a medium for their reflections on this question, and they used them to explore that most difficult of identities, the ascetic self. What they found in their explorations was not a unitary, epistemologically certifiable self, but something more unsettling that only the allusive images of dreams could articulate.

[82] Harpham, *The Ascetic Imperative in Culture and Criticism*, p. 45.

[83] See Suzanne Poque, "Des Roses du Printemps à la rose d'automne," pp. 155–69, on martyrdom; Dulaey, *La Rêve*, pp. 222–23, on virginity.

[84] Apuleius, *Metamorphoses* 11.13 (text and trans. in Griffiths, p. 85).

Conclusion

IN A RECENT set of lectures on critical theory delivered at the University of California in Irvine, Hélène Cixous has lamented the loss of oneiric resources in the contemporary world. She writes:

> There are few dreams in books. It's as if they have a bad reputation. There are
> fewer and fewer of them. Dreams used to occur in all the great books—in the
> Bible, in epic poems, in Greek literature, in the Babylonian epic poems, in
> Shakespeare—in an archaic mode, then they became more remote. I associate
> this increasing remoteness, this dessication, with the diminishment of other
> signs. In the same way we find:
>
> > less and less poetry
> > less and less angels
> > less and less birds
> > less and less women
> > less and less courage.
> > Jacob wakes up, he gets up. What becomes of the ladder?
> > You have to take a rock, put it under your head, and let
> > the dream ladder grow. It grows down—toward the depths.[1]

In sharp contrast to the late-twentieth-century culture of Cixous's construction, the culture of Graeco-Roman antiquity knew, as Clement of Alexandria had remarked, that rocky pillows make for superhuman visions.[2] The sign-world of late antiquity did not lack for dreams, or ladders, or angels. On the contrary, this was a culture in which theories and practices of dreaming actively engaged the intellectual and personal interests of a wide spectrum of people irrespective of social, economic, religious, or philosophical differences. Far from being a sign of "dessication," to use Cixous's term, late-antique dreaming provided fertile ground for fostering insight in surprisingly varied contexts—from the cosmic speculations of philosophers like Macrobius to the erotic obsessions of lovers in the magical papyri. It should be clear from the preceding pages that late-antique "dream ladders" not only grew down to the depths of the world of individual concerns but also reached up to the world of gods and other spiritual

---

[1] Hélène Cixous, *Three Steps on the Ladder of Writing*, pp. 107–8.
[2] Clement of Alexandria, *Paed.* 2.9.78 (ed. and trans. Mondésert, p. 157).

powers, linking both worlds with a distinctive discourse of imagination that had both hermeneutical and therapeutic qualities.

The types of interpretation in which dreams functioned as nodal points for reflection were many, and in all of them dreams provided a rich resource for apprehending matters both theoretical and personal in a concrete, visual way. Constituting an imaginal, rather than a solely empirical, or a solely conceptual, discourse, dreams were useful as vehicles for the discovery of complex insights about human life. Providing *both* the impulse to interpret *and* the matter for interpretation, dreams found a signifying home in the allegorical imagination of thinkers like Macrobius and Augustine; in the taxonomic imagination of Artemidorus, Tertullian, and other classifiers; in the psycho-dramatic imagination of the dream-senders of magic, as well as in the tormented psyches of people like Jerome and Perpetua; in the socio-ethical imagination of Hermas and Apuleius; in the philosophical imagination of Plutarch and the theological imagination of virtually everyone; and in the healing imagination, where healing can be construed in emotional terms, as in Gregory of Nazianzus and Gregory of Nyssa's coming to terms with the deaths of loved ones by means of dreams, and in physical terms, as in the oneiric therapies provided by the Asclepius cult. Dreaming was indeed an interpretive "language" with many "dialects," as this study has argued throughout.

Equally as diverse as the interpretive constructs within which dreams were situated were the ways in which dreamers interacted with and characterized their dreams. Perpetua and Aristides, for example, asked for dreams and, although their petitionary techniques were different—prayer and incubation, respectively—both actively sought the consolation offered by oneiric visions. Hermas and Jerome, on the other hand, felt invaded by the dreams that forced them to confront crises of conscience and behavior. Metaphors for dreams also carried positive and negative feeling tones: the arboreal bats of Virgil and the demon-dreams of the Christian apologists carry a sense of brooding or haunting that stands in contrast with the oneiric angels of Origen and the Asclepian dream-statues of Aristides. Likewise, Plutarch's placement of dreams in a cosmic mixing bowl conveys a sense of dreaming that is quite different from Ovid's placement of them in an underworld of cobwebs and shape-shifting counterfeits.

What units this disparate material is the way in which late-antique dreamers used dreams to find meaning and order in their worlds. The flexibility of dreams as hermeneutical devices is particularly evident when the variety of those "worlds" is considered. From dramatic contexts of life-and-death choices such as Perpetua faced, through literary contexts involving textual exegesis such as rabbinic interpreters were engaged in, to practical contexts of social and economic anxiety such as Artemidorus' catalogues give testimony to, dreams functioned as occasions for formulating coherent understandings as well as for giving articulate expression to perceptions of self and world.

As the foregoing studies of individual dreamers' relations to their dreams give witness, ancient dreams were not usually experienced as simple mirrors held up to the thoughts and concerns of everyday life. Such dreams, indeed, were relegated to the trashbin of psychic trivia by Artemidorus in his taxonomy of dreams. Instead of being seen as mimetic to reality, dreams were valued by Graeco-Roman dreamers for their ability to shift the grounds of perception by bringing into sharp focus those ideas and emotions that would otherwise have remained inchoate and by making clear the potential consequences for the future of thoughts and behaviors in the present.

Much of the time, the images offered in dreams were enigmatic, and it was precisely that riddling quality which demanded the kind of reflective engagement that produced new insight. For example, the allegorical personifications of virtues and vices in Hermas' dreams, while at first baffling to him, eventually led him to reassess the moral character of his own and his religious community's lives. Likewise, the haunting character of the glowing bones of Gregory of Nyssa's dream led him to understand something about the quality of his sister's life and also served to console him following her death. The imagistic constructions of Perpetua's dreams of heavenly ascent and gladiatorial combat not only reconciled her to the certain outcome of the course of action that she had chosen but also allowed her to frame her actions as a woman in terms that were not theologically debasing.

Even when oneiric images seemed clear, that is, transparent to the meaning conveyed, they functioned to bring submerged thoughts and fears to conscious awareness and provoked the dreamer to new forms of interaction with the world. Jerome's reaction to his dream of being tried and convicted for his non-scriptural reading habits is a good example of the way in which a more acute form of self-awareness could both force its way into consciousness by the agency of dreams and instigate decisive action. Gregory of Nyssa's dream of being beaten by the Forty Martyrs and Gregory of Nazianzus' dream of beguilingly chaste women, both of which prompted these men not only to reflection about the ascetic life but also to the adoption of its practices, similarly demonstrate the manner in which dreams were understood as barometers of inner dispositions and as roadmaps for negotiating the intersection of personal conscience and public action.

A demonstration of the significance of dreams in the personal and cultural construction of meaning in late antiquity has been the aim of this study. Even though the use of dreams to discern orderly structures in the world and to provoke reorientations in self-understanding may seem strange to us in the late twentieth century, particularly if we inhabit the poetically diminished world of Cixous's lament, it is nonetheless the case that for many people in late antiquity, dreaming provided a way for imagining the world well. For them, the sometimes terrifying, sometimes consoling "angels" of dreams gave them a more secure, because more thoughtful, context in which to live.

Bibliography

Ancient Sources

Achilles Tatius. *Leucippe and Clitophon.* Trans. by John J. Winkler. In *Collected Ancient Greek Novels.* Ed. B. P. Reardon. Berkeley: University of California Press, 1989, 170–284.

Acta minora. In *Passio Sanctarum Perpetuae et Felicitatis,* 59–73. Ed. C.I.M.I. Van Beek. Nijmegen: Dekker and Van de Vegt, 1936.

Aelius Aristides. *Orations.* Tr. Charles A. Behr. In *P. Aelius Aristides: The Complete Works.* 2 vols. Leiden: E. J. Brill, 1981.

———. *The Sacred Tales.* Tr. Charles A. Behr. In *P. Aelius Aristides: The Complete Works,* vol. 2:278–353. Leiden: E. J. Brill, 1981.

Aeschylus. *The Libation-Bearers.* Tr. Richmond Lattimore. In *The Complete Greek Tragedies,* vol. 1. Ed. David Grene and Richmond Lattimore. Chicago: University of Chicago Press, 1959.

———. *The Persians.* Tr. Seth Benardete. In *The Complete Greek Tragedies,* vol. 1. Ed. David Grene and Richmond Lattimore. Chicago: University of Chicago Press, 1959.

Ambrose. *On Belief in the Resurrection.* Ed. Philip Schaff and Henry Wace. In *Nicene and Post-Nicene Fathers,* 2nd ser., vol. 10. New York: The Christian Literature Company, 1896.

Apuleius. *De deo Socratis.* Ed., tr. Jean Beaujeu. *Apulée: Opuscules Philosophiques et Fragments.* Paris: Société d' Edition "Les Belles Lettres," 1973.

———. *Metamorphoses.* Text and tr. of Book 11 in J. Gwyn Griffiths, *Apuleius of Madauros: The Isis-Book ("Metamorphoses," Book XI).* Leiden: E. J. Brill, 1975.

Aristotle. *De divinatione per somnum.* Tr. David Gallop, *q.v.*

———. *De insomniis.* Tr. David Gallop, *q.v.*

———. *De somno.* Tr. David Gallop, *q.v.*

Artemidorus. *Oneirocritica.* Ed. Roger Pack. Leipzig: B. G. Teubner, 1963. English translation: *Artemidorus: The Interpretation of Dreams.* Tr. Robert J. White. Park Ridge, New Jersey: Noyes Press, 1975.

Arthanasius. *Contra Gentes.* Ed., tr. Robert W. Thomson. Oxford: Oxford University Press, 1971.

———. *De vita Antonii.* PG 26.837–976.

Athenagoras. *Legatio.* Tr. Cyril Richardson. In *Library of Christian Classics,* vol. 1: *Early Christian Fathers.* Philadelphia: Westminster Press, 1953.

Augustine. *De civitate Dei.* Tr. M. Dods. In *Basic Writings of Saint Augustine,* vol. 2. Ed. Whitney J. Oates. New York: Random House, 1948.

———. *De civitate Dei.* Tr. Henry Bettenson. Baltimore: Penguin Books, 1972.

———. *De cura pro mortuis gerenda.* Ed. J. Zycha. *CSEL* 41:619–660.

———. *De genesi ad litteram.* Ed. J. Zycha. *CSEL* 28 (1894). English translation: *St. Augustine: The Literal Meaning of Genesis.* 2 vols. Tr. John Hammond Taylor. Ancient Christian Writers 41, 42. New York: Newman Press, 1982.

———. *De natura et origine animae*. Ed. C. Urba and J. Zycha. *CSEL* 60 (1913):303–419.

———. *Sermones. PL* 38.

Berakoth. Tr. Maurice Simon. In *The Babylonian Talmud*, vol. 1. London: Soncino Press, 1948.

Callistratus. *Ekphraseis*. Tr. Arthur Fairbanks. In *Philostratus: Imagines and Callistratus: Descriptions*. London: William Heinemann, 1931.

Cicero. *De divinatione*. 2 vols. in one. Ed. A. S. Pease. In *M. Tulli Ciceronis De Divinatione*. New York: Arno Press, repr. 1979.

Clement of Alexandria. *Paedagogus*. 2 vols. Ed., tr. Claude Mondésert. In *Clément d'Alexandrie: Le Pédagogue*. Sources Chrétiennes 108. Paris: Les Editions du Cerf, 1965.

———. *Protrepticus*. Ed., tr. Claude Mondésert. In *Clément d'Alexandrie: Le Protreptique*. Sources Chrétiennes 2. Paris: Les Editions du Cerf, 2nd ed., 1949.

Corpus Hermeticum. 4 vols. Ed. A. D. Nock. Tr. A.-J. Festugière. Paris: Société d'Editions "Les Belles Lettres," 1945–54.

Cyprian. *Ad Quirinum*. Ed. G. Hartel. *CCL* 3.

1 Enoch. 2 vols. Ed., tr. Michael A. Knibb. In *The Ethiopic Book of Enoch*. Oxford: The Clarendon Press, 1978.

Epiphanius. *Panarion. PG* 41.174–1200.

Euripides. *Hecuba*. Text in *Euripides I*. Ed. and tr. Arthur S. Way. Cambridge: Cambridge University Press, 1966. English translation: *The Complete Greek Tragedies*, vol. 3. Ed. David Grene and Richmond Lattimore. Tr. William Arrowsmith. Chicago: University of Chicago Press, 1959.

———. *Iphigeneia in Taurus*. Text in *Euripides II*. Ed. and tr. Arthur S. Way. Cambridge: Harvard University Press, 1965. English translation: *The Complete Greek Tragedies*, vol. 3. Ed. David Grene and Richmond Lattimore. Tr. Witter Bynner. Chicago: University of Chicago Press, 1959.

Eusebius. *Historia ecclesiastica*. English translation: *Eusebius: The Ecclesiastical History*, vol. 1. Tr. Kirsopp Lake. Cambridge: Harvard University Press, 1965.

Evagrius of Ponticus. *Praktikos. PG* 40.1220–1252. English translation: *Evagrius Ponticus: The Praktikos and Chapters on Prayer*. Tr. John Eudes Bamberger. Kalamazoo: Cistercian Publications, 1981.

Galen. *De usu partium*. 2 vols. Ed. G. Helmreich. Leipzig: B. G. Teubner, 1909.

———. *Commentarii in Hippocratis de humoribus*. In *Claudii Galeni Opera Omnia*, vol. 16. Ed. C. G. Kühn. Hildesheim: Georg Olms Verlagbuchhandlung, 1965.

Gregory Nazianzen. *De animae suae calamitatibus carmen lugubre. PG* 37.1353–1378.

———. *De rebus suis. PG* 37.969–1017. English translation in *Saint Gregory of Nazianzus: Three Poems*. Tr. Denis Molaise Meehan. The Fathers of the Church 75. Washington, D.C.: The Catholic University of America Press, 1987.

———. *De se ipso et de episcopis. PG* 37.1166–1227. English translation in *Saint Gregory of Nazianzus: Three Poems*. Tr. Denis Molaise Meehan. The Fathers of the Church 75. Washington, D.C.: The Catholic University of America Press, 1987.

———. *De vita sua. PG* 37.1029–1166. English translation in *Saint Gregory of Nazianzus: Three Poems*. Tr. Denis Molaise Meehan. The Fathers of the Church 75. Washington, D.C.: The Catholic University of America Press, 1987.

———. *Epitaphium sui ipsius*. PG 37.1447–1448.

———. *Orationes*. PG 35–36. English translations of selected orations: 1. *Nicene and Post-Nicene Fathers*, vol. 7. Ed. Philip Schaff and Henry Wace. New York: The Christian Literature Company, 1894; 2. *Funeral Orations by Saint Gregory Nazianzen and Saint Ambrose*. Tr. Leo P. McCauley. The Fathers of the Church 22. New York: Fathers of the Church, Inc., 1953. (*Or.*)

———. *Poemata quae spectant ad alios*, sec. 4: *Nicobuli filii ad patrem*. PG 37.1505–1521.

Gregory of Nyssa. *De anima et resurrectione*. PG 46.12–160. English translation: *Saint Gregory of Nyssa: Ascetical Works*. Tr. Virginia Woods Callahan. The Fathers of the Church 58. Washington, D.C.: The Catholic University of America Press, 1967.

———. *De hominis opificio*. PG 44.123–256.

———. *De virginitate*. PG 46.317–416. English translation: *Saint Gregory of Nyssa: Ascetical Works*. Tr. Virginia Woods Callahan. The Fathers of the Church 58. Washington, D.C.: The Catholic University of America Press, 1967.

———. *Encomium in Sanctum Theodorum*. PG 46.736–748.

———. *In quadraginta martyres*. PG 46.749–788.

———. *Oratio catechetica*. PG 45.9–105.

———. *Vita Sanctae Macrinae*. PG 46.960–1000. French translation: *Grégoire de Nysse: Vie de Sainte Macrine*. Ed., tr. Pierre Maraval. Sources Chrétiennes 178. Paris: Les Editions du Cerf, 1971.

Heraclitus. *Fragments*. Ed., tr. M. Marcovich. Merida, Venezuela: Los Andes University Press, 1967. English translation in *The Presocratics*. Tr. Philip Wheelwright. Indianapolis: Bobbs-Merrill, 1960.

Hermas. *The Shephered of Hermas*. Ed., tr. Robert Joly. *Hermas le Pasteur*. Sources Chrétiennes 53. Paris: Les Editions du Cerf, 1958. English translations: 1. In *The Apostolic Fathers*, vol. 2. Tr. Kirsopp Lake. London: William Heinemann, 1913; 2. In *The Apostolic Fathers*. Tr. Joseph M.-F. Marique. The Fathers of the Church I. New York: CIMA Publishing Co., 1947.

Hesiod. *Theogony*. Tr. Norman O. Brown. Indianapolis: Bobbs-Merrill, 1953.

Hippolytus. *On the Passover*. Ed., tr. Pierre Nautin. *Hippolyte: Sur la Pâque*. Sources Chrétiennes 27. Paris: Les Editions du Cerf, 1950.

———. *Refutation of All Heresies*. Ed. Philip Schaff and Henry Wace. *Ante-Nicene Fathers*, vol. 5. Grand Rapids: Eerdmans, 1978.

Homer. *Iliad*. 3 vols. in 1. Ed. Thomas W. Allen. New York: Arno Press, Repr. 1979. English translation: *The Iliad of Homer*. Tr. Richmond Lattimore. Chicago: University of Chicago Press, 1951.

———. *Odyssey*. 2 vols. Ed. W. B. Stanford. London: MacMillan, 2nd ed., 1965. English translation: *Homer: The Odyssey*. Tr. Robert Fitzgerald. New York: Doubleday, 1963.

Irenaeus. *Against Heresies*. Ed. Philip Schaff and Henry Wace. In *Ante-Nicene Fathers*, vol. 1. Grand Rapids: Eerdmans, 1979.

———. *Demonstratio*. Ed., tr. L. M. Fridevaux. *Irenée: Démonstration*. Sources Chrétiennes 62. Paris: Les Editions du Cerf, 1959.

Jerome. *Apologia contra Rufinum*. PL 23.415–514. (C. Ruf.).

———. *Commentarius in Danielem*. Ed. F. Glorie. CCL 75A (1964).

———. *De vita Hilarionis*. PL 23.29–54.

——. *De vita Pauli. PL* 23.17–30.

——. *Epistulae.* Ed. I. Hilberg. *CSEL* 54–56 (1910, 1912). English translations of *Ep.* 22: 1. *Nicene and Post-Nicene Fathers,* 2nd series, vol. 6. Ed. Philip Schaff and Henry Wace. New York: The Christian Literature Company, 1893; 2. *The Letters of Jerome.* Vol. 1: *Letters 1–22.* Tr. Charles Christopher Mierow. Ancient Christian Writers 33. Westminster, Maryland: The Newman Press, 1963.

——. *In Hieremiam Prophetam.* Ed. S. Reiter, *CCL* 74 (1960).

Justin Martyr. *Apologia 1.* Tr. Cyril Richardson. In *Library of Christian Classics,* vol. 1: *Early Christian Fathers.* Philadelphia: Westminster Press, 1953.

——. *Dialogue with Trypho.* 2 vols. Ed., tr. G. Archambault. *Justin: Dialogue avec Tryphon.* Paris, 1909.

Lucian of Samosata. *A True Story.* Tr. Lionel Casson In *Selected Satires of Lucian.* New York: W. W. Norton, 1962.

——. *Zeus the Opera Star.* Tr. Lionel Casson In *Selected Satires of Lucian.* New York: W. W. Norton, 1962.

Macrobius. *Commentarii in somnium Scipionis.* Ed. Jacob Willis. Leipzig: B. G. Teubner, 1970. English translation: *Macrobius: Commentary on the Dream of Scipio.* Tr. William Harris Stahl. New York: Columbia University Press, 1952.

Marcus Aurelius. *Meditations.* Tr. Maxwell Staniforth. Baltimore: Penguin Books, 1964.

Midrash Rabbah. Ed., tr. H. Freedman and Maurice Simon. *The Midrash Rabbah,* vol. 1. London: Soncino Press, 1961.

Origen. *Commentarium in Canticum Canticorum.* Ed. W. A. Baehrens. In *GCS, Origenes Werke* 8 (1925). English translation: *Origen: The Song of Songs, Commentary and Homilies.* Tr. R. P. Lawson. Ancient Christian Writers 26. New York: Newman Press, 1956.

——. *Contra Celsum.* 4 vols. Ed., tr. Marcel Borret. *Origène: Contra Celse.* Sources Chrétiennes 132, 136, 147, 150. Paris: Les Editions du Cerf, 1967–69.

——. *De principiis.* Tr. G. W. Butterworth. *Origen: On First Principles.* New York: Harper and Row, 1966.

——. *Epistula ad Julium Africanum.* Ed., tr. Nicholas De Lange. *Origène: La Lettre à Africanus, Sur l'historie de Suzanne.* Sources Chrétiennes 302. Paris: Les Editions du Cerf, 1983.

——. *Homiliae in Exodum.* Tr. Ronald Heine. *Origen: Homilies on Genesis and Exodus.* Fathers of the Church 71. Washington, D.C.: Catholic University of America Press, 1982.

——. *Homiliae in Genesim.* Ed., tr. Louis Doutreleau. *Origène: Homélies sur la Genèse.* Sources Chrétiennes 7 bis. Paris: Les Editions du Cerf, 1976. English translation: *Origen: Homilies on Genesis and Exodus.* Tr. Ronald Heine. Fathers of the Church 71. Washington, D.C.: Catholic University of America Press, 1982.

——. *Homiliae in Ieremiam.* 2 vols. Ed., tr. Pierre Nautin and Pierre Husson. *Origène: Homélies sur Jérémie.* Sources Chrétiennes 232, 238. Paris: Les Editions du Cerf, 1976–77.

Ovid. *Metamorphoses.* Text in *Ovid,* vol. 4: *Metamorphoses.* Tr. Frank Justus Miller. Cambridge: Harvard University Press, 2nd ed., 1984. Other English translations: 1. *Ovid's Metamorphoses.* Tr. Charles Boer. Dallas: Spring Publications,

1989; 2. *Ovid: Metamorphoses*. Tr. Rolphe Humphries. Bloomington: Indiana University Press, 1955.

Palladius. *Lausiac History*. Tr. Robert T. Meyer. Ancient Christian Writers 34. Westminster, Maryland: The Newman Press, 1965.

Papyri Graecae Magicae. 2 vols. Ed. Karl Preisendanz. Rev. ed. by Albert Hinrichs. Stuttgart: B. G. Teubner, 1973–74. English translation: *The Greek Magical Papyri in Translation*. Ed. Hans Dieter Betz. Chicago: University of Chicago Press, 1986.

Passio Sanctarum Perpetuae et Felicitatis. Ed. C.I.M.I. Van Beek. Nijmegen: Dekker and Van de Vegt, 1936. English translation: Peter Dronke, *Women Writers of the Middle Ages: A Critical Study of Texts from Perpetua to Marguerite Porete*. Cambridge: Cambridge University Press, 1984.

Passio Sanctorum Mariani et Jacobi. In *The Acts of the Christian Martyrs*. Ed., tr. Herbert Musurillo. Oxford: The Clarendon Press, 1972.

Passio Sanctorum Montani et Lucii. In *The Acts of the Christian Martyrs*. Ed., tr. Herbert Musurillo., Oxford: The Clarendon Press, 1972. ˙

Pausanias. *Guide to Greece*. 2 vols. Tr. Peter Levi. New York: Penguin Books, 1971.

Philo, *De Iosepho*. Tr. F. H. Colson. In *Philo*, vol. 6. London: William Heineman, 1935.

———, *De somniis*. Tr. F. H. Colson and G. H. Whitaker. In *Philo*, vol. 5. London: William Heineman, 1934.

Philostratus. *Vitae sophistarum*. Ed., tr. Wilmer Cave Wright. In *Philostratus and Eunapius: The Lives of the Sophists*. Cambridge: Harvard University Press, 1968.

Plato. *Phaedrus*. Tr. R. Hackforth. In *Plato: The Collected Dialogues*. Ed. Edith Hamilton and Huntington Cairns. Princeton: Princeton University Press, 1961.

———. *Symposium*. Tr. Michael Joyce. In *Plato: The Collected Dialogues*. Ed. Edith Hamilton and Huntington Cairns. Princeton: Princeton University Press, 1961.

———. *Theaetetus*. Tr. F. M. Cornford. In *Plato: The Collected Dialogues*. Ed. Edith Hamilton and Huntington Cairns. Princeton: Princeton University Press, 1961.

———. *Timaeus*. Tr. R. G. Bury. In *Plato*, vol. 9. Cambridge: Harvard University Press, 1929.

Pliny. *Naturalis historia*. 3 vols. Tr. H. Rackham. Cambridge: Harvard University Press, 1938–40.

Plotinus. *Enneads*. 7 vols. Tr. A. H. Armstrong. Cambridge: Harvard University Press, 1966–88; see also *Enneads*, tr. Stephen MacKenna. 2nd rev. ed. by B. S. Page. (New York: Pantheon Books, 1957).

Plutarch. *De defectu oraculorum*. Tr. Frank Cole Babbitt. In *Plutarch's Moralia*, vol. 5. Cambridge: Harvard University Press, 1936.

———. *De genio Socratis*. Tr. Philip H. De Lacy and Benedict Einarson. In *Plutarch's Moralia*, vol. 7. Cambridge: Harvard University Press, 1959.

———. *De invidia et odio*. Tr. Philip H. De Lacy and Benedict Einarson. In *Plutarch's Moralia*, vol. 7. Cambridge: Harvard University Press, 1959.

———. *De Pythiae oraculis*. Tr. Frank Cole Babbitt. In *Plutarch's Moralia*, vol. 5. Cambridge: Harvard University Press, 1936.

Porphyry. *Contra Christianos*. Ed. Adolf von Harnack. *Abhandlungen der preussichen Akademie der Wissenschafter zu Berlin*. Philosophisch-historisches Klasse, 1916, no. 1.

——. *De antro nympharum.* Ed. A. Nauck. In *Porphyrii philosophi platonici opuscula selecta.* Leipzig: B. G. Teúbner, 1886. English translation: *Porphyry on the Cave of the Nymphs.* Tr. Robert Lamberton. Barrytown, New York: Station Hill Press, 1983.

Pseudo-Augustine. *Sermo. PL* 39.1715–1716.

Pseudo-Callisthenes. *The Alexander Romance.* Tr. Ken Dowden. In *Collected Ancient Greek Novels.* Ed. B. P. Reardon. Berkeley: University of California Press, 1989.

Pseudo-Clement. *Homilies.* Ed. B. Rehm. *GCS* 42 (1953): 236–40.

Ptolemy. *Tetrabiblos.* Ed. and tr. F. E. Robbins. Cambridge: Harvard University Press, 1940.

Quodvultdeus. *Sermo [De tempore barbarico].* PL 40.699–708.

Rufinus. *Apologia contra Hieronymum.* Ed. M. Simonetti. *CCL* 20 (1961).

Sepher Ha-Razim. Tr. Michael A. Morgan. *Sepher Ha-Razim: The Book of Mysteries.* Chico, California: Scholars Press, 1983.

Synesius. *De insomniis. PG* 66.1281–1320. English translation: *The Essays and Hymns of Synesius of Cyrene.* Tr. Augustine Fitzgerald. Oxford: Oxford University Press, 1930.

Tertullian. *Ad uxorem.* Ed. A. Kroymann. *CCL* 1.

——. *Adversus Marcionem.* Ed. A. Kroymann. *CCL* 1.

——. *De anima.* Ed. J. H. Waszink. Amsterdam: J. M. Meulenhoff, 1947.

——. *De baptismo.* Ed. J. G. Ph. Borleffs. *CCL* 1.

——. *De cultu feminarum.* Ed. A. Kroymann. *CCL* 1.

——. *De fuga in persecutione.* Ed. J. J. Thierry. *CCL* 2.

——. *De praescriptione haereticorum.* Ed. R. F. Refoulé. *CCL* 1; also in A. Kroymann, ed. *CSEL* 70 (1942).

——. *De virginibus velandis.* Ed. E. Dekkers. *CCL* 2.

Testament of Levi. In *The Testaments of the Twelve Patriarchs, A Commentary,* 132–55. Ed., tr. H. W. Hollander and M. De Jonge. Leiden: E. J. Brill, 1985.

Virgil. *Aeneid.* In *Opera,* vols. 1–4. Ed. Otto Ribbeck. Hildesheim: Georg Olms, 1966. English translation: *The Aeneid of Virgil.* Tr. C. Day Lewis. New York: Doubleday, 1953.

The Vision of Dorotheus. Ed., tr. A.H.M. Kessels and P. W. Van Der Horst. "The Vision of Dorotheus (Pap. Bodmer 29):" *Vigiliae Christianae* 41 (1987):313–59.

Modern Sources

Ahl, Frederick. *Metaformations: Soundplay and Wordplay in Ovid and Other Classical Poets.* Ithaca: Cornell University Press, 1985.

Amat, Jacqueline. "L'Authenticité des songes de la Passion de Perpetué de Felicité." *Augustinianum* 29 (1989):177–91.

——. *Songes et Visions: L'Au-dela dans la littérature latine tardive.* Paris: Etudes Augustiniennes, 1985.

Amory, Anne. "The Gates of Horn and Ivory." In *Yale Classical Studies* 20: *Homeric Studies,* 3–57. Ed. G. S. Kirk and Adam Parry. New Haven: Yale University Press, 1966.

Antin, Paul. "Autour du songe de Saint Jérome." *Revue des Etudes Latines* 41 (1963):350–77.

Bachelard, Gaston. *La Flamme d'une chandelle*. Paris: Presses Universitaires de France, 1961.

———. *L'Eau et les rêves: Essai sur l'imagination de la matière*. Paris: Librairie José Corti, 1942.

———. *L'Air et les songes: Essai sur l'imagination du mouvement*. Paris: Librairie José Corti, 1943.

Barnes, Timothy David. "Porphyry against the Christians: Date and Attribution of the Fragments." *Journal of Theological Studies*, n.s., 24 (1973):424–42.

———. *Tertullian: A Historical and Literary Study*. Oxford: The Clarendon Press, 1971.

Barthes, Roland. "The Death of the Author." In *Image, Music, Text*. Tr. Stephen Heath. New York: Hill and Wang, 1977, 142–48.

Behr, C. A. *Aelius Aristides and The Sacred Tales*. Amsterdam: Adolf M. Hakkert, 1968.

Benko, Stephen. *Pagan Rome and the Early Christians*. Bloomington: Indiana University Press, 1984.

Berchman, Robert M. *From Philo to Origen: Middle Platonism in Transition*. Brown Judaic Studies 69. Chico, California: Scholars Press, 1984.

Berry, Wendell. "The Meeting." In his *A Part*. San Francisco: North Point Press, 1980.

Betz, Hans Dieter, ed. *The Greek Magical Papyri in Translation*. Chicago: University of Chicago Press, 1986.

Bloom, Harold. "The Breaking of Form." In Harold Bloom et al., *Deconstruction and Criticism*, 1–37. New York: Seabury Press, 1979.

Bowersock, G. W. *Greek Sophists in the Roman Empire*. Oxford: The Clarendon Press, 1969.

Bregman, Jay. *Synesius of Cyrene: Philosopher-Bishop*. Berkeley: University of California Press, 1982.

Brelich, Angelo. "The Place of Dreams in the Religious World Concept of the Greeks." In *The Dream and Human Societies*, 293–301. Ed. G. E. Von Grunebaum and Roger Caillois. Berkeley: University of California Press, 1966.

Brenk, Frederick E. "In the Light of the Moon: Demonology in the Early Imperial Period." In *Aufstieg und Niedergang der Römischen Welt*, II: *Principat*, 16,3, pp. 2068–2145. Ed. Wolfgang Haase. Berlin: Walter De Gruyter, 1986.

Brown, Francis, S. R. Driver, and C. A. Briggs. *A Hebrew and English Lexicon of the Old Testament*. Oxford: The Clarendon Press, 1968.

Brown, Peter. *Augustine of Hippo, A Biography*. Berkeley: University of California Press, 1969.

———. *The Making of Late Antiquity*. Cambridge: Harvard University Press, 1978.

———. *The Cult of the Saints*. Chicago: University of Chicago Press, 1981.

———. *Society and the Holy in Late Antiquity*. Berkeley: University of California Press, 1982.

———. *The Body and Society: Men, Women, and Sexual Renunciation in Early Christianity*. New York: Columbia University Press, 1988.

Burkert, Walter. *Greek Religion*. Tr. John Raffan. Cambridge: Harvard University Press, 1985.

Calvino, Italo. *The Uses of Literature*. Trans. Patrick Creagh. San Diego: Harcourt Brace Jovanovich, 1986.

————. *Six Memos for the Next Millennium*. Tr. Patrick Creagh. Cambridge: Harvard University Press, 1988.

Carson, Anne. *Eros the Bittersweet*. Princeton: Princeton University Press, 1986.

Cavallera, F. *Saint Jérome: Sa Vie et Son Oeuvre*. 2 vols. Louvain: Spicilegium Sacrum Lovaniense Bureaux, 1922.

Chuvin, Pierre. *A Chronicle of the Last Pagans*. Tr. B. A. Archer. Cambridge: Harvard University Press, 1990.

Cixous, Hélène. *Three Steps on the Ladder of Writing*. Tr. Sarah Cornell and Susan Sellers. The Wellek Library Lectures at the University of California, Irvine. New York: Columbia University Press, 1993.

Clark, Elizabeth A. *Jerome, Chrysostom, and Friends*. Studies in Women and Religion 1. New York: Edwin Mellen Press, 1979.

————. "The Uses of the Song of Songs: Origen and the Later Latin Fathers." In *Ascetic Piety and Women's Faith: Essays on Late Ancient Christianity*. Lewiston, New York: Edwin Mellen Press, 1986, 386–427.

Countryman, L. William. *The Rich Christian in the Church of the Early Empire: Contradictions and Accommodations*. New York: Edwin Mellen Press, 1980.

Courcelle, Pierre. *Les Confessions de Saint Augustin dans la tradition littéraire*. Paris: Etudes Augustiniennes, 1963.

Cox, Patricia. "'Adam Ate from the Animal Tree': A Bestial Poetry of Soul." *Dionysius* 5 (1981):165–80.

————. "Origen and the Bestial Soul: A Poetics of Nature." *Vigiliae Christianae* 36 (1982):115–40.

————. *Biography in Late Antiquity: A Quest for the Holy Man*. Berkeley: University of California Press, 1983.

————. "Origen and the Witch of Endor: Toward an Iconoclastic Typology." *Anglican Theological Review* 66 (1984):137–47.

Crites, Stephen. "Angels We Have Heard." In *Religion as Story*. Ed. James B. Wiggins. New York: Harper and Row, 1975, 23–63.

Crouzel, Henri. "La Distinction de la 'typologie' et de l'allégorie.'" *Bulletin de Littérature Ecclésiastique* 65 (1964):161–74.

Culler, Jonathan. *Structuralist Poetics*. Ithaca: Cornell University Press, 1975.

Dagron, Gilbert, ed., tr. *Vie et miracles de Sainte Thècle*. Brussels: Société des Bollandistes, 1978.

Daniélou, Jean. *Platonisme et théologie mystique: Doctrine spirituelle de Saint Grégoire de Nysse*. Paris: Aubier, 1944.

————. *Origène*. Paris: La Table Ronde, 1948.

————. "Le Mariage de Grégoire de Nysse et la chronologie de sa vie." *Revue des Etudes Augustiniennes* 2 (1956):71–78.

————. "*Methorios*: La Notion de confins chez Grégoire de Nysse." *Recherches des Sciences Religieuses* 49 (1961):161–87.

————. *L'Etre et le Temps chez Grégoire de Nysse*. Leiden: E. J. Brill, 1970.

————. "La Notion de personne chez les Pères grecs." In *Problèmes de la personne*. Ed. I. Meyerson. Paris: Mouton, 1973, 113–21.

————. *Gospel Message and Hellenistic Culture.* Tr. John Austin Baker. London: Darton, Longman and Todd, 1973.

————. *A History of Early Christian Doctrine Before the Council of Nicaea.* Vol. 3: *The Origins of Latin Christianity.* Tr. David Smith and John Austin Baker. London: Darton, Longman and Todd, 1977.

Daraki, Maria. "La Naissance du sujet singulier dans les Confessions de Saint Augustin." *Esprit* 2 (1981):95–115.

Davies, Stevan. *The Revolt of the Widows: The Social World of the Apocryphal Acts.* Carbondale, Illinois: Southern Illinois University Press, 1980.

De Certeau, Michel. *Heterologies: Discourse on the Other.* Tr. Brian Massumi. Minneapolis: University of Minnesota Press, 1986.

De Labriolle, Pierre. "Le Songe de St. Jérome." In *Miscellanea Geronimiana.* Rome: Tipografia Poliglotta Vaticana, 1920, 227–35.

Del Corno, D., ed. *Graecorum de re onirocritica reliquiae.* Testi e documenti per lo studio dell'antichita 26. Milan, 1969.

DeLubac, Henri. "Typologie et allégorisme." *Recherches des Sciences Religieuses* 34 (1947):180–226.

Derrida, Jacques. *The Ear of the Other.* Tr. Peggy Kamuf. Lincoln: University of Nebraska Press, 1985.

Detienne, Marcel. *Dionysus Slain.* Tr. Mireille Muellner and Leonard Muellner. Baltimore: The Johns Hopkins University Press, 1979.

Detienne, Marcel, and Jean-Pierre Vernant. *Cunning Intelligence in Greek Culture and Society.* Tr. Janet Lloyd. Sussex: The Harvester Press, 1978.

Dillon, John. *The Middle Platonists.* Ithaca: Cornell University Press, 1977.

Dilthey, Wilhelm. *Gesammelte Schriften.* Vol. 7: *Der Aufbau der geschichtlichen Welt in den Geisteswissenschaften.* Ed. Bernhard Groethuysen. Stuttgart: B. G. Teubner, 1968.

Dodds, E. R. *Proclus: The Elements of Theology.* Oxford: The Clarendon Press, 2nd ed., 1963.

————. *The Greeks and the Irrational.* Berkeley: University of California Press, 1966.

————. *Pagan and Christian in an Age of Anxiety.* New York: W. W. Norton, 1970.

Dölger, Franz Joseph. "Antike Parallelen zum leidenen Dinocrates in der Passio Perpetuae." *Antike und Christentum* 2:1–40. Munich: Verlag Aschendorff, 1974.

Doty, William. "Hermes' Heteronymous Appellations." In *Facing the Gods.* Ed. James Hillman. Irving, Texas: Spring Publications, 1980, 115–33.

Dronke, Peter. *Women Writers of the Middle Ages: A Critical Study of Texts from Perpetua to Marguerite Porete.* Cambridge: Cambridge University Press, 1984.

duBois, Page. *Sowing the Body: Psychoanalysis and Ancient Representations of Women.* Chicago: University of Chicago Press, 1988.

Dulaey, Martine. *Le Rêve dans la vie et la pensée de Saint Augustin.* Paris: Etudes Augustiniennes, 1973.

————. "Le Symbole de la baguette dans l'art paléo-chrétien." *Recherches Augustiniennes* 19 (1973):3–38.

Edelstein, Emma J., and Ludwig Edelstein. *Asclepius: A Collection and Interpretation of the Testimonies.* 2 vols. in 1. Baltimore: The Johns Hopkins University Press, 1945. Repr. 1975 by Arno Press.

Eitrem, Samuel. "Dreams and Divination in Magical Ritual." In *Magika Hiera.* Ed.

Christopher A. Faraone and Dirk Obbink. New York: Oxford University Press, 1991, 175–87.

Epstein, William H. *Recognizing Biography.* Philadelphia: University of Pennsylvania Press, 1987.

Evans, Elizabeth Cornelia. "The Study of Physiognomy in the 2nd century A.D." *Transactions and Proceedings of the American Philological Association* 72 (1941):96–108.

Festugière, André-Jean. *La Révélation d'Hermès Trismégiste.* Vol. 1: *L'Astrologie et les Sciences Occultes.* Paris: Librairie Lecoffre, 1944.

––––––. *Personal Religion among the Greeks.* Berkeley: University of California Press, 1960.

Flamant, Jacques. *Macrobe et le Néo-Platonisme Latin, à la fin du IVᵉ-Siècle* Leiden: E. J. Brill, 1977.

Foucault, Michel. "What Is an Author?" In *Textual Strategies: Perspectives in Post-Structuralist Criticism.* Ed. Josué V. Harari. Ithaca: Cornell University Press, 1979, 141–60.

––––––. *Technologies of the Self: A Seminar with Michel Foucault.* Ed. Luther H. Martin, Huck Gutman, and Patrick H. Hutton. Amherst: University of Massachusetts Press, 1988.

––––––. *The History of Sexuality.* 3 vols. Tr. Robert Hurley. New York: Vintage Books, 1988.

Frend, W.H.C. *Martyrdom and Persecution in the Early Church.* Garden City, New York: Doubleday and Company, 1967.

Gager, John. *Kingdom and Community: The Social World of Early Christianity.* Englewood Cliffs, New Jersey: Prentice-Hall, 1975.

Gallagher, Eugene. *Divine Man or Magician? Celsus and Origen on Jesus.* SBL Dissertation Series 64. Chico, California: Scholars Press, 1982.

Gallop, David. "Dreaming and Waking in Plato." In *Essays in Ancient Greek Philosophy.* Ed. John P. Anton and George L. Kustas. Albany: State University of New York Press, 1971, 187–94.

––––––. *Aristotle on Sleep and Dreams: A Text and Translation with Introduction, Notes and Glossary.* Peterborough, Ontario: Broadview Press, 1990.

Gaudin, Collette, tr. *On Poetic Imagination and Reverie: Selections from the Works of Gaston Bachelard.* Indianapolis: Bobbs-Merrill, 1971.

Getty, Robert J. "Insomnia in the Lexica." *American Journal of Philology* 53 (1933):1–28.

Gleason, Maud. "The Semiotics of Gender: Physiognomy and Self-Fashioning in the Second Century C.E." In *Before Sexuality: The Construction of Erotic Experience in the Ancient Greek World.* Ed. David M. Halperin, John J. Winkler, and Froma I. Zeitlin. Princeton: Princeton University Press, 1990, 389–415.

Goodenough, Erwin R. *Jewish Symbols in the Greco-Roman Period,* vol. 8, 2. New York: The Bollingen Foundation, 1958.

Goodspeed, Edgar J., and Robert M. Grant. *A History of Early Christian Literature.* Chicago: University of Chicago Press, 1966.

Grant, Frederick C. *Hellenistic Religions.* Indianapolis: Bobbs-Merrill, 1953.

––––––. ed. *Ancient Roman Religion.* New York: Liberal Arts Press, 1957.

Grant, Robert M. *Second-Century Christianity: A Collection of Fragments.* London: S.P.C.K., 1957.

———. *Gnosticism and Early Christianity.* New York: Harper and Row, 1959.

———. *Augustus to Constantine: The Thrust of the Christian Movement into the Roman World.* New York: Harper and Row, 1970.

———. *Eusebius as Church Historian.* Oxford: The Clarendon Press, 1980.

Griffiths, J. Gwyn. *Apuleius of Madauros: The Isis-Book (Metamorphoses, Book XI).* Leiden: E. J. Brill, 1975.

Gubar, Susan. "'The Blank Page' and the Issues of Female Creativity." In *Writing and Sexual Difference.* Ed. Elizabeth Abel. Chicago: University of Chicago Press, 1982, 73–93.

Hall, Nor. *The Moon and the Virgin.* New York: Harper and Row, 1980.

Halliday, W. R. *Greek Divination: A Study of Its Methods and Principles.* London: MacMillan, 1913.

Hanson, John S. "Dreams and Visions in the Graeco-Roman World and Early Christianity." In *Aufstieg und Niedergang der Römischen Welt,* II: *Principat,* 23,2, pp. 1395–1427. Ed. Wolfgang Haase. Berlin: Walter de Gruyter, 1980.

Hanson, R.P.C. *Allegory and Event.* London: John Knox Press, 1959.

Harpham, Geoffrey Galt. *The Ascetic Imperative in Culture and Criticism.* Chicago: University of Chicago Press, 1987.

Highbarger, E. L. *The Gates of Dreams: An Archaeological Examination of Vergil, Aeneid VI.893-9.* Baltimore: The Johns Hopkins University Press, 1940.

———. "Summary of Research." *Proceedings of the American Philological Association* 76 (1945):xxxiii.

Hunter, Diane. "Hysteria, Psychoanalysis, and Feminism: The Case of Anna O." In *The (M)other Tongue: Essays in Feminist Psychoanalytic Interpretation.* Ed. Shirley Nelson Garner, Claire Kahane, and Madelon Sprengnether. Ithaca: Cornell University Press, 1985, 89–115.

Irigaray, Luce. *This Sex Which Is Not One.* Tr. Catherine Porter with Carolyn Burke. Ithaca: Cornell University Press, 1985.

Jackson Knight, W. F. *Elysion: On Ancient Greek and Roman Beliefs Concerning a Life after Death.* London: Rider, 1970.

Jameson, Fredric. "Foreword." In Jean-François Lyotard, *The Post-Modern Condition: A Report on Knowledge.* Tr. Geoff Bennington and Brian Massumi. Minneapolis: University of Minnesota Press, 1984.

Jardine, Alice. *Gynesis: Configurations of Woman and Modernity.* Ithaca: Cornell University Press, 1985.

Joret, Charles. *La Rose dans l'antiquité et au Moyen Age.* Paris: Emile Bouillon, 1892.

Kee, Howard C. "Self-Definition in the Asclepius Cult." In *Jewish and Christian Self-Definition,* vol. 3: *Self-Definition in the Graeco-Roman World.* Ed. Ben F. Meyer and E. P. Sanders. Philadelphia: Fortress Press, 1982, 118–36.

Kelly, J.N.D. *Jerome: His Life, Writings, and Controversies.* New York: Harper and Row, 1975.

Kessels, A.H.M. "Ancient Systems of Dream-Classification." *Mnemosyne* 22 (1969): 389–424.

———. *Studies on the Dream in Greek Literature.* Utrecht: HES Publishers, 1978.

Klawiter, Frederick C. "The Role of Martyrdom and Persecution in Developing the Priestly Authority of Women in Early Christianity: A Case Study of Montanism." *Church History* 49 (1980):251–61.

Kraemer, Ross Shepard. *Her Share of the Blessings: Women's Religions Among Pagans, Jews, and Christians in the Greco-Roman World*. New York: Oxford University Press, 1992.

Kristeva, Julia. "Word, Dialogue, and Novel." In *Desire in Language: A Semiotic Approach to Literature and Art*. Ed. Leon S. Roudiez. Tr. Thomas Gora, Alice Jardine, and Leon S. Roudiez. New York: Columbia University Press, 1980, 64–91.

———. *Tales of Love*. Tr. Leon S. Roudiez. New York: Columbia University Press, 1987.

Kundera, Milan. *The Unbearable Lightness of Being*. Tr. Michael Henry Heim. New York: Harper and Row, 1984.

Lacan, Jacques. *Four Fundamental Concepts of Psycho-Analysis*. Ed. Jacques-Alain Miller. Tr. Alan Sheridan. New York: W. W. Norton, 1978.

Lamberton, Robert. *Homer the Theologian: Neoplatonist Allegorical Reading and the Growth of the Epic Tradition*. Berkeley: University of California Press, 1986.

Lane Fox, Robin. *Pagans and Christians*. New York: Alfred A. Knopf, 1987.

Lefkowitz, Mary R. "The Motivations for St. Perpetua's Martyrdom." *Journal of the American Academy of Religion* 44 (1976):417–21.

Le Goff, Jacques. *The Birth of Purgatory*. Tr. Arthur Goldhammer. Chicago: University of Chicago Press, 1984.

Leitch, Vincent. *Deconstructive Criticism*. New York: Columbia University Press, 1983.

Lewis, Charlton T., and Charles Short, ed. *A Latin Dictionary*. Oxford: The Clarendon Press, rev. ed., 1969.

Lewis, Naphtali. *The Interpretation of Dreams and Portents*. Toronto: Hakkert, 1976.

Liddell, Henry George, Robert Scott, and Henry Stuart Jones. *A Greek-English Lexicon*. 9th ed. Oxford: The Clarendon Press, 1968.

LiDonnici, Lynn R. *Tale and Dream: The Text and Compositional History of the Corpus of Epidaurian Miracle Cures*. Ph.D. dissertation: University of Pennsylvania, 1989.

Littlewood, A. R. "The Symbolism of the Apple in Greek and Roman Literature." *Harvard Studies in Classical Philology* 72 (1967):147–81.

Luck, Georg. *Arcana Mundi: Magic and the Occult in the Greek and Roman Worlds*. Baltimore: The Johns Hopkins University Press, 1985.

MacMullen, Ramsay. *Paganism in the Roman Empire*. New Haven: Yale University Press, 1981.

Maier, Harry O. *The Social Setting of the Ministry as Reflected in the Writings of Hermas, Clement, and Ignatius*. Dissertations SR 1. Waterloo: Wilfrid Laurier Press, 1991.

Maraval, Pierre, ed., tr. *Grégoire de Nysse: Vie de Sainte Macrine*. Sources Chrétiennes 178. Paris: Les Editions du Cerf, 1971.

Martin, Luther. *Hellenistic Religions: An Introduction*. New York: Oxford University Press, 1987.

———. "Artemidorus: Dream Theory in Late Antiquity." *The Second Century* 8 (1991):97–108.

Meehan, Denis Molaise, tr. *Saint Gregory of Nazianzus: Three Poems*. The Fathers of the Church 75. Washington, D.C.: The Catholic University of America Press, 1987.

Meltzer, Françoise. *Salome and the Dance of Writing: Portraits of Mimesis in Literature.* Chicago: University of Chicago Press, 1987.

Meslin, M. "Vases sacrés et boissons d'éternité." In *Epektasis: Mélanges patristiques offerts au Cardinal Jean Daniélou.* Ed. Jacques Fontaine and Charles Kannengiesser. Paris: Editions Beauchesne, 1972, 127–36.

Meyer, Ben F., and E. P. Sanders. *Jewish and Christian Self-Definition.* Vol. 3: *Self-Definition in the Greco-Roman World.* Philadelphia: Fortress Press, 1982.

Miller, David L. *Christs: Meditations on Archetypal Images in Christian Theology.* New York: Seabury Press, 1981.

———. "Theologia Imaginalis." In *The Archaeology of the Imagination.* Ed. Charles E. Winquist. *JAAR Thematic Studies* 48 (1981):1–18.

———. "Why Men Are Mad! Nothing-Envy and the Fascration Complex." *Spring* 51 (1991):71–79.

Miller, J. Hillis. "The Critic as Host." In Harold Bloom et al., *Deconstruction and Criticism.* New York: Seabury Press, 1979, 217–53.

———. *Fiction and Repetition.* Cambridge: Harvard University Press, 1982.

Miller, Patricia Cox. "'A Dubious Twilight': Reflections on Dreams in Patristic Literature." *Church History* 55 (1986):153–64.

———. "'All The Words Were Frightful': Salvation by Dreams in the Shepherd of Hermas." *Vigiliae Christianae* 42(1988):327–38.

———. "Poetic Words, Abysmal Words: Reflections on Origen's Hermeneutics." In *Origen of Alexandria: His World and His Legacy.* Ed. Charles Kannengiesser and William L. Petersen. Notre Dame: University of Notre Dame Press, 1988, 165–78.

———. "Re-imagining the Self in Dreams." *Continuum* 1 (1991):35–53.

Misch, Georg. *A History of Autobiography in Antiquity.* 2 vols. Tr. E. W. Dickes in collaboration with the author. Cambridge: Harvard University Press, 1951.

Mitchell, W.J.T. *Iconology: Image, Text, Ideology.* Chicago: University of Chicago Press, 1986.

Momigliano, Arnaldo. *The Development of Greek Biography.* Cambridge: Harvard University Press, 1971.

———. "Marcel Mauss and the Quest for the Person in Greek Biography and Autobiography." In *The Category of the Person.* Ed. Michael Carrithers, Steven Collins, and Steven Lukes. Cambridge: Cambridge University Press, 1985, 83–92.

Moore, Marianne. "Poetry." In *A College Book of Modern Verse.* Ed. James K. Robinson and Walter B. Rideout. New York: Harper and Row, 1958.

Musurillo, Herbert, ed. and trans. *The Acts of the Christian Martyrs.* Oxford: The Clarendon Press, 1972.

Nilsson, Martin. *Geschichte der griechischen Religion.* Vol. 2: *Die Hellenistische und Römische Zeit.* Munich: C. H. Beck'sche Verlagsbuchhandlung, 1950.

———. *Greek Piety.* Tr. Herbert Rose. New York: W. W. Norton, 1969.

Nock, Arthur Darby. "A Vision of Mandulis Aion." *Harvard Theological Review* 27 (1934):53–104.

———. Review of E. J. and L. Edelstein, *Asclepius* (1943). *Classical Philology* 45 (1950):45–50.

———. "Greek Magical Papyri." In *Essays on Religion and the Ancient World,* vol. 1. Ed. Zeph Stewart. Cambridge: Harvard University Press, 1972, 176–94.

O'Flaherty, Wendy Doniger. *Dreams, Illusion, and Other Realities*. Chicago: University of Chicago Press, 1984.

Osiek, Carolyn. *Rich and Poor in the Shepherd of Hermas*. Washington, D.C.: Catholic Biblical Association, 1983.

Otis, Brooks. "The Throne and the Mountain: An Essay on St. Gregory Nazianzus." *Classical Journal* 56 (1961):146–65.

Oxford Classical Dictionary. Ed. N.G.L. Hammond and H. H. Scullard. Oxford: The Clarendon Press, 2nd ed., 1970.

Pack, Roger. "Artemidorus and His Waking World." *Transactions and Proceedings of the American Philological Association* 86 (1955):280–90.

Pépin, Jean. *Mythe et Allégorie: Les Origines grecques et les contestations judéochrétiennes*. Paris: Etudes Augustiniennes, 1976.

————. *La Tradition de l'allégorie de Philo d'Alexandrie à Dante*. Paris: Etudes Augustiniennes, 1987.

Pétrement, Simone. *A Separate God: The Christian Origins of Gnosticism*. Tr. Carol Harrison. San Francisco: Harper and Row, 1990.

Poque, Suzanne. "Des Roses du printemps à la rose d'automne." *Revue des Etudes Augustiniennes* 17 (1971):155–69.

Price, S.R.F. "The Future of Dreams: From Freud to Artemidorus." *Past & Present* 113 (1986):3–37.

Quilligan, Maureen. *The Language of Allegory: Defining the Genre*. Ithaca: Cornell University Press, 1979.

Refoulé, François. "Rêves et vie spirituelle d'après Evagre le Pontique." *La Vie Spirituelle* 14 (1961):470–516.

Reiling, J. *Hermas and Christian Prophecy*. Leiden: E. J. Brill, 1973.

Richlin, Amy. *The Garden of Priapus: Sexuality and Aggression in Roman Humor*. New York: Oxford University Press, rev. ed., 1992.

Riginos, Alice Swift. *Platonica: The Anecdotes Concerning the Life and Writings of Plato*. Leiden: E. J. Brill, 1976.

Robert, Louis. "Une Vision de Perpetué martyre à Carthage en 203." *Académie des Inscriptions et Belles Lettres, Comptes rendus des séances de l'année 1982*. Paris: Auguste Picard, 1982, 228–76.

Rousseau, Philip. *Ascetics, Authority, and the Church in the Age of Jerome and Cassian*. Oxford: Oxford University Press, 1978.

Rousselle, Aline. *Porneia: On Desire and the Body in Antiquity*. Tr. Felicia Pheasant. Oxford: Basil Blackwell, 1988.

Russell, D. S. *The Method and Message of Jewish Apocalyptic*. London: SCM Press, 1964.

Sato, Hiroaki. *One Hundred Frogs: Fron Renga to Haiku in English*. New York: Weatherhill, 1983.

Schraeder, F. M. "The Self in Ancient Religious Experience." In *Classical Mediterranean Spirituality*. Ed. A. H. Armstrong. New York: Crossroad, 1986, 337–59.

Schüssler Fiorenza, Elisabeth. *In Memory of Her: A Feminist Theological Reconstruction of Christian Origins*. New York: Crossroad, 1983.

Segal, Alan. *Two Powers in Heaven: Early Rabbinic Reports About Christianity and Gnosticism*. Leiden: E. J. Brill, 1977.

————. "Hellenistic Magic: Some Questions of Definition." In *Studies in Gnosticism and Hellenistic Religions*. Ed. R. Van Den Broek and M. J. Vermaseren. Leiden: E. J. Brill, 1981, 349–75.

Seitz, Oscar J. F. "Antecedents and Signification of the Term *Dipsychos.*" *Journal of Biblical Literature* 66 (1947):211–19.

Smith, Jonathan Z. "Towards Interpreting Demonic Powers in Hellenistic and Roman Antiquity." In *Aufstieg und Niedergang der Römischen Welt*, II: *Principat*, 16,1. Ed. Wolfgang Haase. Berlin: Walter de Gruyter, 1978, 425–39.

————. *Imagining Religion: From Babylon to Jonestown*. Chicago: University of Chicago Press, 1982.

Smith, M. F. "Diogenes of Oenoanda: New Fragments 115–121." *Prometheus* 8 (1982):193–212.

Smith, Morton. *Jesus the Magician*. New York: Harper and Row, 1978.

Smith, Robert C. "Misery and Mystery: Aelius Aristides." In *Pagan and Christian Anxiety: A Response to E. R. Dodds*. Ed. Robert C. Smith and John Lounibos. Lanham, Maryland: University Press of America, 1984, 29–52.

Sprinker, M. "Fictions of the Self: The End of Autobiography." In *Autobiography: Essays Theoretical and Critical*. Ed. James Olney. Princeton: Princeton University Press, 1980, 321–42.

Stahl, William Harris, tr. *Macrobius: Commentary on the Dream of Scipio*. New York: Columbia University Press, 1952.

Steiner, George. "The Historicity of Dreams (Two Questions to Freud)." *Salmagundi* 61 (1983):6–21.

Stevens, Wallace. *The Collected Poems of Wallace Stevens*. New York: Alfred A. Knopf, 1977.

————. *Opus Posthumous*. Ed. Samuel French Morse. New York: Alfred A. Knopf, 1977.

Stroumsa, Gedaliahu. "*Caro Salutis Cardo:* Shaping the Person in Early Christian Thought." *History of Religions* 30 (1990):25–50.

Szymusiak-Affholder, Carmen-Marie. "Psychologie et histoire dans le rêve initial de Grégoire le théologien." *Philologus* 15 (1971):302–10.

Tabor, James D. *Things Unutterable: Paul's Ascent to Paradise in Its Greco-Roman, Judaic, and Early Christian Contexts*. Lanham, Maryland: University Press of America, 1986.

Temkin, Owsei. *Hippocrates in a World of Pagans and Christians*. Baltimore: The Johns Hopkins University Press, 1991.

Theological Dictionary of the New Testament. 10 vols. Ed. Gerhard Friedrich. Tr. Geoffrey W. Bromiley. Grand Rapids: Eerdmans, 1964–76.

Thierry, J. J. "The Date of the Dream of Jerome." *Vigiliae Christianae* 17 (1963):28–40.

Tigner, Steven S. "Plato's Philosophical Uses of the Dream Metaphor." *American Journal of Philology* 91 (1970):204–12.

Tinh, Tran tam. "Sarapis and Isis." In *Jewish and Christian Self-Definition*. Vol. 3: *Self-Definition in the Greco-Roman World*. Ed. Ben F. Meyer and E. P. Sanders. Philadelphia: Fortress Press, 1982, 101–17.

Torgovnick, Marianna. *Gone Primitive: Savage Intellects, Modern Lives*. Chicago: University of Chicago Press, 1990.

Vernant, Jean-Pierre. *Mortals and Immortals: Collected Essays*. Ed. Froma I. Zeitlin. Princeton: Princeton University Press, 1991.

Versnell, H. S. *Inconsistencies in Greek and Roman Religion*. Vol. 1: *Ter Unus: Isis, Dionysus, Hermes, Three Studies in Henotheism*. Studies in Greek and Roman Religion 6. Leiden: E. J. Brill, 1990.

Veyne, Paul, ed. *A History of Private Life*. Vol. 1: *From Pagan Rome to Byzantium*. Tr. Arthur Goldhammer. Cambridge: Harvard University Press, 1987.

Von Franz, Marie-Louise. *The Passion of Perpetua*. Tr. Elizabeth Welsh. Irving, Texas: Spring Publications, 1979.

Walsh, P. G. "Apuleius and Plutarch." In *Neoplatonism and Early Christian Thought. Essays in Honor of A. H. Armstrong*. Ed. H. J. Blumenthal and R. A. Markus. London: Variorum Publications, 1981.

Waszink, J. H., ed. *Tertulliani De Anima*. Amsterdam: J. M. Meulenhoff, 1947.

———. "Mors immatura." *Vigiliae Christianae* 3 (1949):107–12.

White, Hayden. *Metahistory: The Historical Imagination in Nineteenth Century Europe*. Baltimore: The Johns Hopkins University Press, 1973.

———. *Tropics of Discourse: Essays in Cultural Criticism*. Baltimore: The Johns Hopkins University Press, 1978.

Wiesen, David S. *St. Jerome as a Satirist*. Cornell Studies in Classical Philology 34. Ithaca: Cornell University Press, 1964.

Winkler, John J. *The Constraints of Desire: The Anthropology of Sex and Gender in Ancient Greece*. New York: Routledge, 1990.

Winslow, Donald F. *The Dynamics of Salvation: A Study in Gregory of Nazianzus*. Patristic Monograph Series 7. Cambridge: The Philadelphia Patristic Foundation, 1979.

Index

Achilles, 19–20, 35

Achilles Tatius, 11

Aelius Aristides, 66, 128, 132, 134; on Asclepius cult, 110–11, 114–16, 201; and codes of masculinity, 196–200; composition of *The Sacred Tales*, 187–88, 194; dreams of Asclepius as statue, 34–35, 195, 202; illnesses of, 184–87, 192, 194–95, 200, 204; in modern scholarship, 190–94; and oneiric therapy, 184–85, 191–93, 195, 201; and oratory, 186, 188–89, 196, 198–202

Aeschylus, 21

aesthetics, 30–33

Alexander Romance, 7

allegory, 91–105

Ambrose, 101, 103n.122

angels, 51, 103, 109, 237, 250; in magical dream theory, 59–60; in Origen, 94–95; in Philo, 61–62; punitive, in dreams, 66–67, 208–9; in *Shepherd of Hermas*, 131–32, 134, 146

Aphrodite, 182, 248

apocalypses, dreams in, 62–63

Apuleius, 28n.73, 31, 55, 57–59, 117, 131, 151, 249

Aristotle, 42–44, 47, 82n.32, 158, 225

Artemidorus, 29–31, 33, 47, 75, 96, 127, 207, 208–9; and classification of dreams, 77–91

asceticism: and Aelius Aristides, 193, 195, 204; and dreams, 205–13, 226–27, 230–31, 232; and Gregory Nazianzen, 232–35, 245–49; and Gregory of Nyssa, 232–33, 237–41; Jerome's theory of, 214–31; and Perpetua, 155; and sexuality, 213–15; and *Shepherd of Hermas*, 137

Asclepius, 66, 245; in Aelius Aristides' dreams, 184–85, 187, 195–96, 201–3; cult of, 106–8, 109–17, 187, 190, 201; as oneiric statue, 111, 195, 202; statues of, 109–10

Athenagoras, 64

Athenasius, 40, 66, 204

Augustine, 75, 91, 129–30, 244; and cult of St. Stephen, 107; on dreams and allegory, 92–95; on Perpetua, 153, 160, 171, 174; and personal phantom, 41–42, 130

Berakoth, 63–64, 74, 84n.44, 87n.55, 88n.58

Besas, 120

binarism, 10–12, 127

Callistratus, 31–32

Christ, 156–57, 163–64, 173–74, 212, 248

Chthon, 20–21, 25

Cicero, 44–46, 52–53, 95–99, 210

classification of dreams, 26, 29; by Artemidorus, 77–91; by Jerome, 205–8; by Macrobius, 96–97

Clement of Alexandria, 64, 102, 250

Corpus Hermeticum, 31–32, 135, 156

daemons, 51, 55–59

Daniel, as dreamer, 49, 94

demons, 63–65, 68, 207

divination: and allegory, 98; and Cicero, 44–46; concerns addressed in, 8; definition of, 7; and emotional stability, 11; as epistemology, 10; as irrational, 9–10; and poetizing, 32; and prediction, 7; as semiotics, 7; Stoic dream-theory and, 52–55; and *sympatheia*, 50. *See also* fate; foreknowledge; future

diviners: consulted by Artemidorus, 78; criticized by Cicero, 45–46

eidolon, 17, 19–20, 71

enupnion, 47, 80–81, 207

Epiphanius, 173

Eros, 60, 121–22

eros, 122, 182–83, 223–24, 226, 248–49

Euripides, 20–21

Eusebius, 117

Eustathius, 16–17

Evagrius of Ponticus, 241–42

Perpetua: as catechumen, 149–50, 154;
and Dinocrates, 35, 128, 158–61, 174,
177–79; and dream of ladder, 152–56,
176–77, 180; and dream of gladiatorial
contest, 161–65, 175, 180–83; as martyr, 148–50, 153–54, 162–64, 174,
176; and Montanism, 172–75; and oneiric apples, 162–64, 182–83; and oneiric serpent, 155, 162, 176–77, 180;
and oneiric shepherd, 153–54, 156–57,
176–77, 180; and paradisal cheese, 4,
152, 157–58, 162; and patriarchy, 165–
73, 176–78, 180, 182–83; and petitionary dreaming, 134, 150–51; sex
change, dream of, 162–63, 171, 181–
82
phantasmata, 43–44
phantom, 24, 40–42
Philo, 72, 75, 91; on Jacob's dream, 100,
102–4; on oneiric angels, 61–62; on
oneiric images, 92
Philostratus, 77, 113, 182, 198
physiognomy, 196–99
Plato, 3, 4–5, 39–40, 41
Pliny (the Elder), 42
Plotinus, 31–32, 48, 72
Plutarch, 55–57, 72, 131, 182, 194
Polemo, 113, 197–98
Porphyry, 32, 36–38, 73
Proclus, 36–37
psychobiological theory, 42–51
Ptolemy, 11, 78

Sarapis, 110
Scipio, dream of, 95–99

Selene, 59–60, 119–20. *See also* moon
semiotics, 32, 70, 80, 85–91, 95, 97, 128,
218
Simon the Magician, 64–65
sleep, 18–19, 42–43, 47–48, 58, 67–68,
71, 81, 133, 231, 241
Socrates, 3, 4, 5, 10, 127
soul: in Artemidorus' dream-theory, 81–
82; in Augustine's dream-theory, 92;
and daemonic dreams, 56–57; as dream,
37–38; and dream interpretation, 94–
95; in Philo's dream-theory, 61–62; in
psychobiological dream-theory, 42–44,
47–51; in Stoic dream-theory, 52–55;
and theological dream-theory, 39–40,
66–72
statues, oneiric, 28–35. *See also* Aelius
Aristides; Asclepius
Stoics: dream-theory of, 52–55; influence
on Tertullian, 67, 70; on *sympatheia*, 50
Synesius, 70–73, 76

Tertullian: attacks cult of Asclepius, 117;
dream-theory of, 66–70, 206–7; on
Jacob's ladder, 103; as Montanist, 174–
75; patriarchal constructions of women,
159–60, 169–72, 175; on Perpetua's
dream of ladder, 153–54; and punitive
oneiric angels, 66–67, 209; shepherd
imagery in, 157
Thecla, St., 117, 237, 245

Virgil, 24–26, 81, 156, 210
visio, 93, 133, 151

MYTHOS: The Princeton/Bollingen Series in World Mythology

J. J. Bachofen / MYTH, RELIGION, AND MOTHER RIGHT

George Boas, trans. / THE HIEROGLYPHICS OF HORAPOLLO

Anthony Bonner, ed. / DOCTOR ILLUMINATUS: A RAMON LLULL READER

Jan Bremmer / THE EARLY GREEK CONCEPT OF THE SOUL

Martin Buber / THE LEGEND OF THE BAAL-SHEM

Kenelm Burridge / MAMBU: A MELANESIAN MILLENNIUM

Joseph Campbell / THE HERO WITH A THOUSAND FACES

Ananda K. Coomaraswamy (Rama P. Coomaraswamy, ed.) / THE DOOR IN THE SKY: COOMARASWAMY ON MYTH AND MEANING

Henry Corbin / AVICENNA AND THE VISIONARY RECITAL

Henry Corbin / ALONE WITH THE ALONE: CREATIVE IMAGINATION IN THE ṢŪFISM OF IBN 'ARABĪ

F. M. Cornford / FROM RELIGION TO PHILOSOPHY

Marcel Detienne / THE GARDENS OF ADONIS: SPICES IN GREEK MYTHOLOGY

Mircea Eliade / IMAGES AND SYMBOLS

Mircea Eliade / THE MYTH OF THE ETERNAL RETURN

Mircea Eliade / SHAMANISM: ARCHAIC TECHNIQUES OF ECSTASY

Mircea Eliade / YOGA: IMMORTALITY AND FREEDOM

Garth Fowden / THE EGYPTIAN HERMES

Erwin R. Goodenough (Jacob Neusner, ed.) / JEWISH SYMBOLS IN THE GRECO-ROMAN PERIOD

W.K.C. Guthrie / ORPHEUS AND GREEK RELIGION

Jane Ellen Harrison / PROLEGOMENA TO THE STUDY OF GREEK RELIGION

Joseph Henderson & Maud Oakes / THE WISDOM OF THE SERPENT

Erik Iversen / THE MYTH OF EGYPT AND ITS HIEROGLYPHS IN EUROPEAN TRADITION

Jolande Jacobi, ed. / PARACELSUS: SELECTED WRITINGS

C. G. Jung & Carl Kerényi / ESSAYS ON A SCIENCE OF MYTHOLOGY

Carl Kerényi / DIONYSOS: ARCHETYPAL IMAGE OF INDESTRUCTIBLE LIFE

Carl Kerényi / ELEUSIS: ARCHETYPAL IMAGE OF MOTHER AND DAUGHTER

Carl Kerényi / PROMETHEUS: ARCHETYPAL IMAGE OF HUMAN EXISTENCE

Stella Kramrisch / THE PRESENCE OF ŚIVA